Brother Keepers:
New Perspectives on Jewish Masculinity

EDITED BY

HARRY BROD
RABBI SHAWN ISRAEL ZEVIT

Dearest Randall,
To a true mensch among men
And holy brother
You are a gift in the world
[illegible]
[illegible]
[illegible]

MEN'S STUDIES PRESS
HARRIMAN, TENNESSEE
2010

Brother Keepers: New Perspectives on Jewish Masculinity
Edited by Harry Brod and Shawn Israel Zevit

Published by Men's Studies Press, LLC, Harriman, Tennessee 37749

James A. Doyle, Acquisitions editor
Jerry Tracy, Cover design
Diederik Janssen, Interior design and production editor

First Edition
ISBN-13: 978-1-931342-25-4 (paperback)
ISBN-13: 978-1-931342-26-1 (cloth)
ISBN-13: 978-1-931342-27-8 (e-book)

Library of Congress Cataloging-in-Publication Data

Brother keepers : new perspectives on Jewish masculinity / edited by Harry Brod, Shawn Israel Zevit.
p. cm.
Includes bibliographical references and index.
ISBN 978-1-931342-25-4 (pbk. : alk. paper) -- ISBN 978-1-931342-26-1 (cloth : alk. paper) -- ISBN 978-1-931342-27-8 (e-book : alk. paper)
1. Masculinity--Religious aspects--Judaism. 2. Jewish men--Religious life. 3. Jewish men--Conduct of life. 4. Sex role--Religious aspects--Judaism. 5. Homosexuality--Religious aspects--Judaism. I. Brod, Harry, 1951- II. Zevit, Shawn Israel.
BM725.B76 2010
296.7081--dc22

2010020502

TABLE OF CONTENTS

Dedication

A Man of Valor
Rabbi Shawn Israel Zevit

A man of valor
He has been found.
His compassionate heart
Shines like the sun.
His passion is embodied, shared,
More than words,
He lives out the search
For a balanced life
In a loving commitment
To self,
To family,
To community,
And the welfare of the planet.
His love includes and transcends
Those his soul touches.
His courage to explore
New paths
To holy and ethical action
Is not limited by a theological particular
Yet he grasps his place in a cosmos
Of incredible beauty and suffering.
He knows the testament to his leadership
Lies not in how many followers he has
But how many leaders he raises up.
His friendship
Is like the heaviest steel
Unbreakable, yet flexible
In the cauldron of life.
His *neshama*
Radiates the gift
Of acceptance.
He embraces life's lessons.
In his heart there is a longing
To fill the empty spaces
And connect beneath the faces
To touch to feel the intimate.
Through the lessons of his losses
Feel the grief and empty darkness
Fill with deep love and the promise
Of a healing.
A man of valor
A man of God.

We dedicate this book to all the men of valor, and the men and women who supported and challenged them to become the role models, inspirations, and teachers who have enabled us to reach this moment.

Shawn specifically names the following men who have contributed to his understanding of masculinity and Jewish life: Great Zaida Ben Zion Zwet (Zevit), Great Zaida Saul Jacobson, Zaida Aaron Zevit, Zaida Maurice "Jake" Jacobson, his father Lester Zevit, Uncle Bob Paul, Reb Zalman Schachter-Shalomi, Rabbi Arthur Waskow, Jinen Jason Schulman, Rabbi Shalom Schachter, Rabbi Jeff Eisenstat, Rabbi Mordechai Liebling, Robert Bly, stepson Elia Malka, stepson Noah Leavitt, godson Raffi Stein Klotz, Harry Brod, Yosaif August, Allen Spivack and the JMR men, and his Jewish brothers from men's groups over the years in Toronto, Philadelphia, and Cleveland.

Harry specifically names the following who have contributed to his understanding and living of life:

To Artemis and Alexi,
The sweet fruits of the vine,
And to Karen,
My nurturing new roots in diasporic soil.

Introduction: Why Now?

Harry Brod

A rabbi, a professor, and an HIV/AIDS activist walk into a publisher's office....

The result is this book.

Sorry I don't have a better punch line, but this is a true story. (Well, we actually e-mailed rather than walked into the publisher's office, but the line just doesn't work that way.)

This book was originally to have had three coeditors; in addition to Shawn and myself, there was Kevin Eisenstadt, an editor for the World Health Organization in Cairo, Egypt, who had previously worked on HIV-related and Jewish lesbian and gay issues in London, England, the latter also a focus of his work in Cape Town, South Africa.

Some years ago I'd been contacted by Kevin because he wanted to solicit from me an essay for a book on representations of Jewish masculinity that he was putting together for a publisher in the United Kingdom. Originally Sylvia Paskin, now a contributor to this volume, was to have been the coeditor of that book, but she withdrew from the project as time passed. After Kevin had collected essays for the volume, it turned out that the publisher he had lined up was not going to publish the volume after all. (Although this is really another story, the essay I wrote for him has now grown into another book to be published in the near future, *Superman Is Jewish?: How Comic Book Superheroes Came to Serve Truth, Justice, and the Jewish-American Way*). When I got the news from Kevin that the book was not going to be published, I told him not to give up quite yet, that I had an idea that might yet save the day. Enter the other source of this present volume.

For years, Shawn and I had been tossing around the idea of joining to coedit a sequel to an edited book I published in 1988, *A Mensch Among Men: Explorations in Jewish Masculinity*. Through our mutual interest in Jewish men's issues, Shawn and I had gotten to know each other when I lived in Philadelphia in the late 1990s. My idea now was to combine the essays Kevin had in hand with the project Shawn and I had envisioned. We modified what had been the earlier conception of a 20th anniversary edition of *A Mensch Among Men* into a proposal for a new book, with the three of us as coeditors, and went looking for a publisher. The result is this book. Kevin unfortunately had to withdraw from the project for personal reasons, but he remains an important formative influence on the volume.

This book bears the imprints of its three editorial progenitors, who travel in different but overlapping circles. Kevin's project had been focused on representations of Jewish masculinity, so most of the essays dealing with media images of Jewish masculinity, especially though not entirely in our second section on embodiment, are by contributors who originally wrote for that volume and then graciously agreed to endure the additional wait to see their work in print while we prepared this book. They also give the book its international flavor, with contributors and topics from Israel and the United Kingdom. As a rabbi, Shawn is by both temperament and training concerned with matters of the spirit, hence the contributions in our Section IV on "Hearts and Souls" came to us through his connections. The work of friends and colleagues who I came to know through my work in masculinity studies, Jewish studies, and the profeminist men's movement complete the collection.

Our title of *Brother Keepers* is of course intended to provide an affirmative answer to the question posed by Cain, "Am I my brother's keeper?" It is also indebted to the term *brotherkeeper*, originated in the early 1990s by Yosaif August, coauthor of the essay on the Jewish Men's Retreat in this volume. He defined a brotherkeeper as "a man who challenges and supports other men to be and do their best" and used it to create a brotherkeeper button that he continues to see as a catalyst for men to reach out and support each other's growth. Hundreds of these buttons have been utilized as part of the closing ceremonies of the Jewish Men's Retreat over the past 18 years, where each new attendee is given three buttons: one for himself and two to give out to men in his life who either embody the qualities of a brotherkeeper or whom he wants to inspire to move in that direction. This book shares such inspirational aspirations.

This volume is intentionally eclectic. We take as our model of Jewish education the Passover Haggadah, developed over the generations to pass on core Jewish consciousness and identity through the generations. The text is famously structured to respond to questions about the meaning of it all from four kinds of persons: the wise, the foolish, the wicked, and the one who does not even know enough to pose a question. We are instructed to address each according to their nature, in an appropriate form so that they too may reach understanding. We too include here many different forms of discourse, so that each may take and learn from that which they find that addresses them. Herein, one will find scholarly essays, in which some will probably find their academic jargon and abstract ruminations challenging, side by side with personal essays that some may find challenging in their frankness and plain spokenness. We include work by rabbis, artists, activists, writers, academics, and other professionals, producing in different genres: essays, poetry, and ritual. The contributors are diverse: male and female, observant and secular, younger and older. And in the dialogue between a Jew and a non-Jew that constitutes one of the essays, one will even find a debate about whether one of its putative interlocutors should actually be considered to be real or not.

This book is intended to be a contribution to ongoing conversations about Jewish masculinities that were not yet taking place when *A Mensch Among Men* was published more than 20 years ago. These conversations take place among men and women alike in academic books, journals, and conferences, in congregational study and discussion circles, and in popular culture and common conversations. In the proposal we wrote to present this project to our publisher, we said that we couldn't think of a better Bar Mitzvah present. As self-promotional as that line is, we hope readers will come to agree.

This is a particularly good time for this book to appear. As I sit here in December 2009 putting the finishing touches on this introduction, my eye catches several items on my desk. Most prominent is the current issue of *Lilith* magazine (fall 2009, *34*:3), whose masthead announces it is "Independent, Jewish & frankly feminist." In large white letters on a shining red background, its cover proclaims "boys are the new girls," and, following the large asterisk after those words to the bottom of the page, I find smaller letters informing me that inside the magazine I will find "a special section on Jewish men." This includes two articles by rabbis—one writing as "a gay Orthodox feminist" and one on King David and his son Absalom (now there's an archetypically troubled father-son relationship if there ever was one, as William Faulkner recognized in using David's biblical anguished father's cry as the title of one of his novels: *Absalom, Absalom!*)—other analytical and autobiographical reflections, and an article on an initiative for which both the editors and some of the authors of this volume have served as consultants, Moving Traditions' attempt to follow up its innovative programs for girls with a new "Campaign for Jewish Boys." The dynamics behind this and allied efforts to bring more Jewish males back into Jewish ritual and organizational life are discussed in Doug Barden's essay in this volume.

Also on my desk is an announcement of the next conference of the American Men's Studies Association (its 18th annual conference, a "Jewishly" auspicious number), which will for the first time feature a "Panel of Men's College Presidents." Yes, there are indeed a few men's colleges still around. One of them is Saint John's University in Minnesota, from whom I learned during a sabbatical semester I spent there a nice way of distinguishing between a men's college and a college for men: a men's college is one simply by virtue of having no women students, but a college for men (like Saint John's) goes on to use that fact to educate about masculinity or masculinities. In that sense, this is a book for men but not a men's book. That is to say, we include women, but it is about masculinities. I hasten to add that it is a book not just for men, nor is it a book only for Jews, because we believe there is much here from which anyone can learn and benefit.

But our current generation of college students does not have to attend a men's college or a college for men to be presented with new, more progressive models of masculinities on our campuses. Another sign of changes afoot in our national conversation about men, which makes this a good time for this book to enter that conversation, is that just last month there was a conference for which I was privileged to have served as one of the organizers—the First National Conference for Campus-Based Men's Gender Equality and Anti-Violence Groups. This was described by *Ms. Magazine* online as a "historic feminist conference" at which "more than 200 men—and women—from 40 college campuses," including representatives of 24 community groups, came together "to figure out constructive ways of grappling with men's power and their fears in order to work effectively in partnership with women" ("Where the Men Are: Historic Feminist Conference Convenes in Minnesota," by Shira Tarrant).

In joining or engendering a conversation about men from specifically Jewish perspectives, in some contexts it makes sense to speak of a specifically Jewish masculinity, while in other contexts it makes more sense to speak of specific Jewish masculinities, as these essays demonstrate. The academic field of men's studies or masculinity studies moved from speaking of masculinity in the singular to speaking of masculinities in the plural early in its development. To speak of masculinity or the male sex role in the singular simply paints with too broad a brush, leaving most men feeling that what is being discussed is an abstract caricature that does not really capture their own lives and the lives of the men they know. Masculinities are experienced and must therefore by analyzed as they vary according to race, class, ethnicity, religion, sexuality, region, age, physical and mental appearance and abilities, and many other hierarchical categories of difference.

In that context, Jewish masculinity is one among many forms. But, as this volume amply demonstrates, one can fine-tune one's analytical lens within the category of Jewish masculinity to discern different Jewish masculinities. To take only some among many examples from the following essays, Jewish masculinity meant something very different to Daniel Mendoza, the 18th century English boxing champion discussed by Sylvia Paskin, than to the contemporary Jewish boys whose moving accounts of their lives one can read in the lead essay by Michael Reichert and Sharon Ravitch. And the 19th century Eastern European scholars discussed by Israel Bartal had very different prescriptions for masculinity, as well as strikingly different enforcement mechanisms for those prescriptions, than did the boys on the Boston area streets in Jackson Katz's autobiographical reflections (although there may turn out to be more similarities here than one might initially suspect).

In my own thinking about the relationship between the concepts of masculinity and masculinities, I have found useful a concept developed by Ludwig Wittgenstein, the profoundly influential 20th century philosopher born in Vienna to Jewish parents who converted to Protestantism and whose complex relationship to his Jewish heritage either did or didn't influence his philosophy, depending on which of various contested interpretations of both his philosophy and his life one prefers. Wittgenstein argued against the traditional philosophic concept that things have a single essence, which makes them what they are, by introducing his concept of "family resemblances." If, for example, I were to show you a photograph of an extended family, you might well remark that yes, you saw the family resemblance. But there would most probably be no one single feature shared by all members of the family. Rather, some might share a certain body type, others might share a single facial feature, perhaps the set of the eyes, and still others might share the shape of the chin or the size of the ears, etc. But there would be sufficient overlap and continuity among these different sets of shared characteristics to create the impression that one was seeing a single family and to justify speaking of the presence of that family being apparent in the photograph. Analogously, there is sufficient overlap and commonality among diverse Jewish masculinities to present a coherent picture of Jewish masculinity while still acknowledging differences among Jewish masculinities.

Understanding other Jewish masculinities is essential for Jewish men to understand their own masculinity. First of all, and as a matter of general principle, I would say that I do not fully understand myself if I do not understand how my beliefs and practices are situated within the range of possible variations. Otherwise, the course of my life appears simply as given fact, as things that happened to me, rather than as the result of choices made and consequences lived with, as things that I did. If I do not understand my past choices as choices, then the result is that I disempower my ability to make future choices, because options will continue to not be visible to me as options. To put the point in more academic language, if I do not understand the "other," I lose agency over my own life.

Further, issues I may have thought were issues only for others often surprisingly turn out to be deeply implicated in my own life. For example, some years ago I accepted an invitation to give a talk on Jewish masculinity at the Reconstructionist Rabbinical College. In the course of that talk, I explained that I am one of many people who use more expansive versions of concepts of homophobia and heterosexism than do some others. For some of us, these concepts mean not only fear or hatred of gays or lesbians, but also more broadly fears of others of the same sex (stressing the etymological root of "homo-phobia," meaning fear of the same). For men this especially includes fears of or aversion to real same-sex closeness of any kind, including restrictions on one's own expressions of emotional or physical non-sexual intimacy with those of the same gender. Thus, homophobia creates in many heterosexual men a fear of deep personal intimacy or emotionally expressive connections with other men. Consider next that many of us, despite subscribing to theologies that tell us that God or the divine presence is neither male nor female, nonetheless at some emotional level still carry with us a traditional image of a male deity. Some of the most meaningful aspects of our prayer or spiritual lives require a sort of communicative communion with the divine presence, which demands exposure of the most intimate aspects of ourselves, a practice of deep and authentic self-disclosure and revelation. Most men, who have at some level internalized both an image of a male deity and a homophobia that makes them feel more comfortable with women than men at such intimate or self-disclosing moments, are therefore going to experience homophobically induced blockages to some of the most potentially meaningful aspects of their spiritual practice. Homophobia is thus a core issue for all, not just some, of us.

During the question and answer period at the end of the session in which I presented this analysis, I was asked my favorite question that I've ever received following a talk. "You said something about homophobia and prayer," said one young male rabbinical student. "I remember being very struck by it, and it must have been something that was personally extremely important for me to hear, because I've already completely blocked and forgotten what it was. Would you please repeat whatever it was you said?"

As a teacher, one lives for such moments. My greatest hope for this book is that for each reader it may contain one such moment, one new revelatory idea that is so personally important that one immediately forgets it but nonetheless remembers that one was so profoundly struck by something that it necessitates a rereading.

I now turn to provide a brief orientation to what follows in these pages, often using the words of the authors themselves, for which the editors wish to offer them our great thanks.

The first section, "The Boy Is Father to the Man," attempts to start at the beginning of the life course and our lives in families by considering the contemporary culture of Jewish boys, conceptualizations of relations between fathers and sons, sometimes crystallized in how we have understood the core rite of Jewish masculinity, circumcision, and the lived experience of growing up as a Jewish boy, especially in relation to issues of violence.

In "'Everything that Makes Us Human': Identity, Bonding, and Resilience Among Jewish Boys" Michael Reichert and Sharon Ravitch present their research showing that young men who had active, positive, and healthy Jewish identities described adaptations that were more independent of adolescent peer group norms and freer, especially in terms of masculine pressures, with more expressive communication styles and more intimate male friendships, than less Jewishly-identified boys. These boys treasured their relationships with other Jewish boys and found them to offer a refuge from anti-Semitism and their social position as members of an ethno-cultural minority. With each other they enjoyed rare opportunities, sheltered from normative homophobic teasing, to share common commitments and find understanding. The countercultural vitality of the masculine identities of these boys, reflecting their rootedness in community support, encourages hope for boys' ability to consider alternatives to restrictive and unhealthy masculine identities.

In "Circumcision and Masculinity: Motherly Men or Brutal Patriarchs?" Eric Silverman explores the rhetoric of masculinity in the contemporary debate over Jewish circumcision (*Brit Milah*). Voices pro and con within the Jewish community understand the rite to carve an image of manhood into the bodies and psyches of men. For some, the rite ideally shapes infant boys and their fathers into loving, caring, responsible men who, during the act, assume the role of mothers. The rite bonds father and son through its emotional, bloody anguish. Additionally, circumcision from this angle fosters male empathy toward women and circumscribes masculine sexuality within a moral framework. Here, the rite is a gesture of a kinder, gentler masculinity. But opponents of *Brit Milah* contend that the rite is best understood as a legacy of brutal patriarchy. Circumcision wounds the boy in his body and soul, coerces mothers into sacrificing their maternal instincts to protect their newborns, and requires adult men to deny both the pain they inflict and the pain they suffer. From this angle, the rite sustains a vision of masculinity that brutalizes fathers, sons, and mothers and often, later in life, results in psychic torments that lead to misogyny. If the debate over *Brit Milah* is clear about anything, it is that Jewish men today often attribute to the rite their anxieties, fears, tragedies, and triumphs as men.

Jackson Katz's "Not-So-Nice Jewish Boys: Notes on Violence and the Construction of Jewish-American Masculinity in the Late 20th and Early 21st Centuries" concerns the complex and conflicted role that violence plays in the construction of late 20th and early 21st century Jewish-American (*Ashkenazic*) masculinity. Katz weaves his personal history into a discussion of such matters as the role of assimilation in the toughening up of American-Jewish men in the past few generations, the reality of domestic and sexual violence in the Jewish community, and the role played by Israeli military prowess in Jewish-American men's gendered identities. He also argues for the moral and political necessity of exploring the gendered subtext of Jewish men's response to vulnerability embodied in threats to the Jewish state (e.g., Palestinian hijackers/suicide bombers, Iranian nukes) and highlights two very different ways that some Jewish-American men have responded to what Warren Rosenberg calls the *legacy of rage* (see Rosenberg's essay in this volume, page 160); on the one hand, with the armor of conservative masculinity and an unrestrained embrace of violence and, on the other, with a more nuanced and ambiguous orientation toward the legitimacy of violence. In the latter category, Katz offers some speculations about why a disproportionate share of prominent men involved in antiviolence "men's work" over the past three decades have been Jewish.

The next section, "Toward Embodiment: Wrestling with the Angel," considers Jewish male bodies in various forms in which they are experienced, viewed, contemplated, and constructed. Issues of sexualities often come to the fore here.

In "Virility and Impotence: From Traditional Society to the Haskalah," Israel Bartal demonstrates how traditional and prescriptive texts describing how Jewish familial and sexual relations should be conducted are found to be at odds with actual life as it was being lived by European Jews in the wake of the Enlightenment. In many different ways and senses, Jewish men struggled with challenges to the potency of their masculinity.

In "The Zionist Body: Nationalism and Sexuality in Herzl's *Altneuland*," Michael Gluzman examines the intertwined development of heterosexuality, queerness, nationality, gender, and Zionism. Gluzman's examination of Herzl's utopian novel reveals that the projected new land was also a project for a new man and that, in both cases, inherited traces of old outlooks made realization of these projects highly problematic.

In "National Troubles: Male Matters in Israeli Gay Cinema," Raz Yosef examines the relationship among sexuality, nationalism, and masculinity in the cinema of two leading Israeli gay male filmmakers: Eytan Fox and Amos Gutman. Describing a gay love affair of two Israeli army officers, Fox's film *Yossi and Jagger* (2002) is an example of the politics of normalcy characterizing the sexual agenda of the gay and lesbian community in Israel. The film represents an attempt on the part of its filmmaker to join the national heterosexual collectivity and attach himself to the myths that constitute it at the price of depoliticizing gay male identity. The film constructs the image of homosexuality as normal by maintaining it in the closet and by representing it as an open secret. This politics of the closet allows for homosexuality to be included in the national discourse within which the film wants to incorporate itself, while at the same time shaping a male homosexual identity that does not challenge, and indeed reproduces and perpetuates, oppressive hetero-normative practices. In contrast to the politics of normalcy of Fox's film, the films of Gutman—the first to make gay Israeli cinema—show contempt for the demand for idealized and sanitized depictions of (homo)sexuality. He refuses to provide consensual images of either gay or straight sex. Male (homo)sexuality is explicitly associated with power and domination as well as violence and death. His male heroes slip into passivity and an uncontainable agitation; they passionately and compulsively seek to lose their ego boundaries and to shatter their self-identity and the way it is constructed by national hetero-normativity. However, these new queer visions of such gay (*Ashkenazi*) filmmakers are marked by an absence of political awareness of ethnicity. Moreover, they repeat the colonial fantasy of the dominant discourse in which *Mizrahi* men are fixed into a narrow repertoire of types: the Eastern sexual stud, on the one hand, and the delicate exotic Oriental boy on the other hand. The disavowal of ethnicity in *Ashkenazi* gay sexual politics and the incorporation of *Mizrahi* men into stereotyping and sexual objectification enable the construction of *Ashkenazi* gay male identity as a Western identity.

In "'Restrain Your Impulse' Versus 'Break the Boundaries': From Whence Shall My Sexual Guidance Come?" Lawrence Bush juxtaposes the teachings about sexuality he received from Jewish tradition against those he received from contemporary culture as well as his own desires. His own questions and reflections inevitably provoke further thoughts from others, which he invites.

"Prosthetic Voice" is an exchange of letters between Marcus Fisher, Oreet Ashery's orthodox Jewish male alter ago, and Barnaby Adams, a writer. The exchange reveals, at times in an unexpected fashion, a series of musings on the nature of gender limits. The letters examine an attachment to preconceived notions of sex, nationality, religious observance, the body, and its politics. Playing on notions of fictional identity and reality, the conversation nonetheless manages to locate its own voice, and it is this voice, despite the authors' assertions to the contrary in the title, which offers heterogeneity as a potential alternative code for a post-Zionist Jewish male identity.

The third section, "Emasculation and Its Discontents," considers the vicissitudes of Jewish masculinities, with an emphasis on the dialectical interactions between positive and negative aspects of Jewish masculinities, both within Jewish cultures and in the context of the interactions between Jews and their surrounding non-Jewish environs. Here we see Jewish men's resistance to common cultural constructions of Jewish masculinities.

In "Trouble on Max Nordau Street: Michael Chabon Rewrites Jewish Masculinity," Warren Rosenberg shows how the novels of contemporary Jewish-American writer Michael Chabon dramatically rewrite the image of Jewish masculinity in our time. Chabon, fully aware of the mixed legacy that includes violent biblical figures such as Samson and David, Diaspora *Yiddishkeit's* gentle rabbis and *mentshes*, and Zionists, real and imaginary (such as muscular Jews Jabotinsky and Ari Ben Canan), creates a new kind of Jewish-American male hero. Protagonists of his two major novels to date, *The Amazing Adventures of Kavalier & Clay* (2000) and *The Yiddish Policemen's Union* (2007), embody the postmodern hero. The first, a refugee from the Holocaust who becomes a comic book writer in New York City, and the second, a hard boiled detective working in a Yiddish settlement in Alaska, combine masculine traits drawn from Jewish history that represent, for Chabon, what is most positive in that tradition. Chabon simultaneously interrogates a negative aspect of the tradition, the attraction to and use of violence, which he sees as antithetical to Jewishness. In this way, using his visionary imagination and gift for language, Chabon reconceptualizes what it might, and should, mean to be Jewish and male today and in the future.

Two key questions underlie Michele Aaron's "The New Queer Jew: Jewishness, Masculinity, and Contemporary Film": (a) How dependent on queerness is the representation of Jewishness in cinema? and (b) What are the meaning and value of queerness as it comes to describe contemporary representations of Jewishness? In order to address these questions, Aaron addresses more basic questions: (a) What is the relationship between queerness and Jewishness? (b) How is this relationship articulated by cinema? (c) Is the Jew still "queered"? (d) Is the queer still "Jewed"? (e) What's new about all this?

Sylvia Paskin's "Mendoza Forever" tells the story of Daniel Mendoza, the redoubtable Sephardi-Jewish bare-knuckle boxing champion who helped change the perception of Jews in late 18th and early 19th century England. Both his opponents and anti-Semitic stereotypes about the physical prowess of Jewish men fell before the new style of "scientific boxing" that he introduced.

In the fourth and final section, "Hearts and Souls," we end with the more personal aspects of Jewish masculinities, in essays ranging from personal reflections to ritual renewal.

"The Odyssey (of a Jewish Man)" by Rabbi Mordechai Liebling is a personal essay chronicling growing up Jewish, confronting violence and other life trials, and becoming a committed man of faith, a Jewish communal leader, and a social justice advocate.

In "Telling Our Stories: Liberation Work for Jewish Men," Billy Yalowitz looks at the detrimental effects of the loss of community among Jewish men from the generations of our fathers and grandfathers to the present day and describes ways that important connections may be regained.

In "Why Men Gather: The Jewish Men's Retreat Journey," Allen Spivack and Yosaif August tell the story of how the Jewish Men's Retreat, which just celebrated its 18th annual and most well-attended weekend at the Elat Chayyim Center for Jewish Spirituality, has brought together men from diverse backgrounds—age, sexual orientation, profession, religious observance—to create a weekend community that suspends the usual rules of male engagement and instead encourages men to share openly and honestly and to take risks and create a new personal vision of what is possible. This article also describes one man's journey through childhood into manhood and how attending this retreat enabled him to move beyond the constraints of his personal history and unleash his potential as a caring man, mentor, devoted husband, and father.

"Men and Dreams: Embracing Esau" by Rabbi Rami Shapiro explores a process of male spiritual maturation found in the story of Jacob and Esau, who represent two sides of the male psyche. Jacob is the feminine side, raised and protected by his mother and sent to live under the protection of his mother's brother. Esau is the masculine side, the red, hairy, hunter/warrior beloved by his father. The prenatal unity of the two is troubled as each seeks to dominate the other, and the tendency to assume a spiritual unity without the intermediary step of true separation would be no less violent. Jacob and Esau must separate from one another and achieve maturity on their own. Unfortunately the Torah only hints at this in the case of Esau. In the case of Jacob, however, the Torah goes into great detail, tracing his development from Jacob to Israel, the wounded warrior who both wrestles with God and cares for the nursing calves and children.

In "Finding the Light—*Kiddush Levanah*: A Ritual of Renewal for Jewish Men," Rabbi Kerry M. Olitzky borrows from the traditional ritual of *Kiddush Levanah* (consecrating the moon) to provide a context for men to get together that includes the regular celebration of an unusual and engaging ritual. While public rituals have been part of the core of Jewish life and living, few have been identified as decidedly for men only, although feminist critics will argue rightfully that was the main message of classical Jewish tradition for many generations. Through making this ritual available and providing easy access to the ritual of *Kiddush Levanah,* the goal of the chapter is to provide a means through which men can begin to reclaim their places in the Jewish community without eclipsing the progress made on behalf of women during the course of the last 50 years. The basic ritual is included and, in the spirit of the many things that have been creatively added to this ritual throughout Jewish history, additional suggestions are included throughout to enhance the experience.

In "When the Stories Stop..." Doug Barden builds on his 2006 monograph *Wrestling With Jacob and Esau: Fighting the Flight of Men*, which demonstrated that the disengagement of men from religious institutions is a real cultural phenomenon, one that has not only impacted one of the most liberal arms of Judaism, the Reform Movement, but nearly every religious institution in American society, be it conservative or liberal. While this disengagement is not necessarily new, since there is documented evidence from some religious denominations that this disengagement of men is at least 40 or almost 50 years old, what cannot be disputed is that there has been a marked increase in the rate of disengagement of men from religious institutions in the past 20 to 30 years. "When the Stories Stop..." summarizes the various reasons usually cited for men's disengagement and makes a number of suggestions that concerned congregational leadership can take to rectify the situation. One of Barden's key assertions is that this disengagement phenomenon has been obscured for, and by, various cultural, linguistic, and political reasons, including a profound misreading of progressive feminist ideology. He argues that this misreading has led to pressure to eliminate not only gender stratification but also gender differentiation. Within the liberal Jewish congregational community, for example, the leadership, lay and professional, to its individual and collective credit, has appropriately sought to eliminate gender stratification, that is, the uneven distribution of power, leadership, involvement, and recognition. For this, gender egalitarian-based religious institutions are to be applauded. Unfortunately, too many professional and lay leaders, men and women alike, have also mistakenly sought to eliminate gender differences. To deny that gender—whatever its origins—affects how adult men and women express themselves as individuals and as Jews, and to deny that gender is one of the key variables that shape an individual's gestalt is to deny human reality and is actually anathema to the goals of feminism. If it is desirable to stop men's flight from religious institutions, a major change effort will be necessary. In calling for this change effort, Barden's goal is not to turn the egalitarian clock back 30 years, to reverse women's gains, or to return to an imbalance of gender stratification. Rather, it is to establish a new equilibrium—an updated, truly profound balance of gender differentiation. The goal must be to create and maintain a cultural climate within the congregational community that fully respects and integrates the different spiritual and religious needs and wants of Jewish women and men.

The last chapter in this section, comprised of poems by Ed Stafman, Jacob J. Staub, and Simcha Paull Raphael, brings the book full circle in that many of the poems deal with the themes of fathers and sons with which this book began.

The book comes to completion with coeditor Shawn Israel Zevit's "Afterword: A Midrash for the Postmodern Man" in which he revisits and adds to the themes in a poetic fashion by using the book of Kohelet (Ecclesiastes) as a template, thus bringing the book through the spiral of exploration of Jewish men and masculinities into a view toward the horizon line of the future.

We extend our great and sincere thanks to the Men's Studies Press and its publisher Jim Doyle for enabling us to bring this work to publication.

As we pass from one Jewish year to the next, our progress is always simultaneously both linear and cyclical, as we move ahead in time while also repeatedly traversing the same ritual cycle. It is fitting that this book embodies this same structure, whereby it hopes to contribute to our ongoing collective journey.

I
The Boy Is Father to the Man

1

"Everything that Makes Us Human": Identity, Bonding, and Resilience Among Jewish Boys

Michael C. Reichert and *Sharon M. Ravitch*[1]

Concerns About Boys

This book on Jewish masculinities is well-timed. In recent decades there has been a revolution in how people think about male lives and a growing awareness that there are critically important questions—for men, boys, and societies—begging for answers. Early in the men's studies movement, Brod (1992, p. 1) wrote, "There is a need for men's lives to be re-cognized in some fundamental way." Up until that time, maleness was the normative standard to women's otherness; as such, the gendering of boys into masculine subjects was invisible. Gender realignment in areas like education, health, crime, and even procreation created "profound changes ... in the economic and social structure of many modern societies" (Whitehead, 2002, p. 57) and made it increasingly important to study males qua males: "the study of masculinity as a *specific male* experience" (Brod, p. 40). Conditions have changed to now permit a more thoughtful consideration of boys' lives, including a willingness to examine the impact of dominant ideas and images of masculinity on boys themselves.

The men's studies movement has prompted a growing body of scholarship on men's ways of being, the contexts and possibilities of their lives, and the problems posed by masculine identities. Methods and perspectives developed within men's studies—what Connell and Messerschmidt (2005) characterize as "ethnographic realism" (p. 833)—offered helpful tools and perspectives with which to explore boys' actual experience of boyhood. To grasp the actual nature of boys' lives and the day-to-day nature of their opportunities and pressures, researchers now understood that the masculine dimension of their experiences had to be discerned: the peer pressures and incitements, institutional norms, rewards and recognitional systems, family and school tacit man-making curricula, and structured world of opportunity as it is typically offered to boys. For too long, gendered developmental paths for boys had been imperceptible.

These tools and perspectives encouraged "voice-centered" methodologies in work with boys, which have helped researchers to hear boys' stories about the costs of the masculine identity process. In particular, a worrisome picture of the restrictive force of the dominant form of masculinity has emerged: "It is exclusive, anxiety-provok-

[1] The authors wish to express their appreciation to the Rose Community Foundation for supporting this study and to Moving Traditions and especially to Deborah Meyer, executive director, without whose initiative, guidance, and partnership this project would not have happened.

ing, internally and hierarchically differentiated, brutal and violent" (Donaldson, 1985, p. 646). Our own and a great deal of other research on boys' lives has established that boys' encounters with this dominant form of masculinity are unavoidable and often painful (Connell, 1989; Martino, 1999, 2008; Reichert, 2001; Reichert & Kuriloff, 2003; Reichert, Stoudt, & Kuriloff, 2006; Stoudt, 2006). This dominant form of masculinity and its ideals are promoted through valorization and institutionalized endorsement—accompanied by potent reward and recognitional systems—and are enforced by violence, bullying, and even ongoing threat. For a boy not to make some accommodation or show at least public complicity with the privileged identity invites substantial reaction, usually in the form of admonishment, exclusion, and peer policing. Ultimately, most boys and men square themselves with society's central ideas about manhood as much to realize their benefits, especially in terms of recognition and reward—the patriarchal dividend—as to avoid the punishments meted out to dissenters (Connell, 1995, p. 79).

In many key developmental areas, boys' accommodation to this masculine ideal reveals its distorting effect. For example, in terms of basic health outcomes, Waldron (1976), the U.S. Preventive Services Task Force (1996), and Courtenay (2003) all found that boys' choices and lifestyle practices imperil them at far greater rates than those of females. Brooks and Silverstein (1995), Pleck, Sonenstein, and Ku (1994), and Pleck (1995) determined that the greater the boy's conformity to narrow ideas about masculinity, the more likely he is to take risks related to alcohol use, drunk driving, and drug abuse. Similarly, in relation to mental health outcomes, O'Neil, Good, and Holmes (1995) compiled stunning testimony over many years to the detrimental effects—in terms of self-esteem, depression, anxiety, violence, and relationship success—of restrictive masculine norms. These damaging constraints take effect quite early in boys' lives, according to the work of Chu (2000), who studied elementary-age boys and found them to be sensitive to the cultural demands of masculinity, making deliberate compromises in personal authenticity to avoid going against the grain of masculine norms. The author felt that compromises were forced on her research subjects by the tacit and ever-present masculine pressures of school and community life, resulting in a loss of both voice and opportunity. Finally, and perhaps most problematic for societies, a strong relationship exists between these same male norms and uncivil behavior. Boys far more commonly than girls engage in behaviors that increase the risk of disease, injury, and death to themselves and others; they carry weapons more often, engage in physical fights more often, wear their seat belts less often, drive drunk more frequently, have more sexual partners as well as more unprotected sex, and use alcohol or drugs more often before sex (Centers for Diseaese Control and Prevention, 2006).

Schools, families, and communities have all sought better options for boys, to the point that Connell (1996) wrote, with a particular focus on schools: "It is clear from the responses to current debates about boys that many teachers and parents see these issues as urgent. Schools are launching 'Programs for Boys' whether researchers and policy makers give them guidance or not" (p. 207). The impulse behind many such programs has been the Aristotelian aspiration to transmit values to children, to teach boys how to be men. More recently, proponents of positive youth development and positive psychology, defined as "a science of human strength whose mission will be to understand and learn how to foster these virtues in young people" (Seligman & Csikszentmihalayi, 2000, p. 7), have adopted a curricular approach to cultivating positive traits. In this scheme, enabling institutions, such as schools and religions, that "facilitate the development and display of positive traits" (Seligman et al., 2005, p. 507) become central to the hope to instill a core set of values. Overall, these programs for boys promote a values-based or skills-based approach to a new masculinity.

But these organizations have confounding experiences with boys. Schools have struggled with their historic, embedded, "hidden" masculinity curricula, discovering that boys are learning from their experience of near-Darwinian school cultures much more effectively than they learn from any didactic programs (Berkowitz, 2002; Connell, 1996; Reichert, 2001; Reichert & Hawley, 2006; Swain, 2005). Poor school achievement, disciplinary problems, overdiagnosis and over-referral to special educational services, athletic over-injury, bullying, peer harassment, and school violence are some of the issues that raise concerns about the effectiveness of schooling for boys. Religions and cultures across society struggle with boys. Put simply, male adolescents in every religion included in a recent large study showed up less often and dropped out more dramatically (Smith & Denton, 2005).

With regard to Jewish boys, a particular sensitivity to continuity and assimilation has impelled religious and cultural leaders to seek better traction for their efforts (Langman, 1999). But patterns of Jewish male religious involvement mirror other religious groups. Leffert and Herring (1998) found significant differences between boys and girls in terms of their involvement in Jewish activities, for example, and concluded, "Adolescent males do not find the activities as meaningful as females do" (p. 59). Even more illuminating was the finding by Kadushin, Kelner, and Saxe (2000, p. v) that boys rejected Jewish supplemental education more decisively than did girls, demonstrating their greater disaffection in lower participation rates. Overall, in response to gender's effects on boys' connections to their community, Holzman (2007) captured the despair of many when he wrote, "The substance of Jewish traditions exists to add color to our lives, and without it too many young men will live in monochrome" (p. 21).

Listening to Boys Themselves

Concerns about boys led Moving Traditions, a Jewish organization that developed and conducts programs for adolescent girls across the country, to create something parallel for boys.[2] The organization takes gender seriously, as they explain in their lit-

[2] See www.movingtraditions.org

erature: "Gender serves as the framework for our activities because it shapes the way our culture defines who we are and can become" (Moving Traditions, 2008a). A clamor had arisen among the 200 or so congregations and youth-serving organizations that were sponsoring their program for girls and seeking a similar program for boys. There was a great deal of concern that boys are more likely to disappear from Jewish community life, especially post *Bar Mitzvah*. In response to this high level of concern, the organization has launched a Campaign for Jewish Boys and Young Men, which they frame as "a research and educational effort to help the Jewish community better meet the needs of pre-teen and teenage boys" (Moving Traditions, 2008b). It was to help launch this program that we were called.

To begin, they wisely commissioned a study of Jewish male teens' lives. Our research team includes a psychologist, who has worked clinically and in a wide variety of community contexts with boys, and a university-based educator who has previously conducted a number of studies of Jewish youth. This particular study was conducted in a Western U.S. city with a significant Jewish population. As an effort to describe the subjective experience and meanings of Jewish boys' lives, the study aimed to "hear" their stories. In this sense, precisely who was interviewed was less important than the conditions established in which interviewees could exercise their voices and speak about themselves (Way, 2004). We were guided by the insight that, though they are not conventionally thought of as a silenced group, boys do not necessarily find it easy to talk about their experiences as males (Brown & Gilligan, 1992). Enabling teens to speak honestly, especially in groups, requires the same sensitivity to dynamics of power as that governing qualitative inquiry generally (Tolman & Brydon-Miller, 2001).

For the research, we arranged through a local organizer in the fall of 2007 to gather groups of Jewish boys, their parents, educators, and community organizers for a semi-structured focus group and individual interviews. Capitalizing on the organizer's close connection to Jewish networks, the study's sample was comprised predominantly of boys who were affiliated with synagogues, Jewish camps, Jewish youth organizations, and/or other Jewish communal contacts, though there were also a number of boys who identified as presently unaffiliated. Overall, 41 boys were interviewed. The average age of the participants was 14.4, with two large groups of younger boys (sixth and seventh graders). The protocol for the interviews was semi-structured, loosely following a set of open-ended questions intended to elicit critical features of their lives (e.g., home, school, and neighborhood) and allowing room for them to tell stories as they might choose. Anonymity was assured, and agreement was reached with participants to record the interviews, which were then transcribed and coded for theme by the study's investigators by using an iterative coding process, with the first set of themes deduced separately and the second representing a synthesis of the previous two. In addition, the researchers' themes were explored in follow-up groups, including a final boys' group selected from previous groups; this member check process helped us to refine our conclusions and served to confirm the validity of our interpretations.

From this coding, thematic development, and member checking process, we deduced key themes about these boys' relationships with each other. These themes tell a story about boys of principle, willing to stand up for their beliefs and to fight for their hearts. We argue that such culturally supported commitments help boys to build deep connections with each other and, in the relationships they enjoy, to mitigate the more restrictive and deleterious aspects of dominant masculinity.

I'll Fight for People

The boys we interviewed were aware of their status position as members of a minority group. In their position as distinct minorities in their schools, they encountered wholesale misunderstanding and ignorance, outright anti-Semitism and the marginalization of their group. What was so striking was their confidence that it was their choice—not their fault—that they were not the most popular boys on campus. The masculinities that they adopted were often premised on values they embraced—for example, treating other people with kindness and respect—that set them apart from the "cool" boys in the high school hierarchy. We queried them about their difference from the mainstream.

> Interviewer: Are you the popular kids?
> Participant 1: Just about the furthest from it. I just don't identify with them. Like, I see them as, kind of, the beer-drinking bozos of the school, you know. They're also the kind of kids that I have seen as, like, they don't even really realize the implications of, like, them saying things.

It was as if their base in their community and its values emboldened them, allowing them freedom to strike their own course. Another boy exemplified the sort of independence we heard.

> I wouldn't say that, like, we couldn't be the most popular kids in our school, because there are, there's this one guy who's Jewish and he's pretty popular. I don't necessarily say we couldn't be. It's just that we don't want to be.

Among the values these boys adopted from their culture was a commitment to justice and fairness. This boy's comment illustrates how the priority he gave to a concern for social justice set him apart from his classmates.

> Well, I think that at my school I'm … at my school there's like five groups of kids and it all goes in order. I'm generally like the floater between all the groups. I'll hang out with some of [the], like, real nerdy kids, my group that I want to hang out with. Sometimes I'll hang out with the popular kids because the girls will be cool. And then I think I'm the only one who's really at my school, me and another Jewish kid, are the only people that are willing to stand up to the group. Like certain people will stand up to be cool, but I'll fight for people.

Being different by virtue of principles that were deeply embedded in their identities did not seem to trouble these boys. In fact, they seemed to welcome the distinction.

> I guess that I'd say that I'm different. When I'm around my friends, especially some of my friends who love football, love video games and things like that. I mean I also like it, but it's not really as big a part of my life.

In addition to a value of justice, boys' identities were premised on the commitment to taking themselves and their lives seriously; they believed that they had a social significance, a role in the world, a call to make a contribution. One boy, for example, so internalized this sense of purpose that he turned routine interactions into occasions for being good to people.

> [Being a] *mensch* is just being a good person. Like, if I'm going over to a friend's house, I'll always call them up … just do something cool, like pick up a drink while I'm on my way, you know? Just the little stuff, like holding doors or waiting for your friend outside, or anything like that. It's going the extra mile to be a friend. There [are] the small steps you can take. There's also, every year I volunteer at some kind of Jewish camp. One year, it was our shul's Hebrew day school camp here in the summer, and last year I worked as a CIT at the JCC. I mean, I donate money and it really is just a value that I want to keep, just, trying to do *tikkun olam*, repairing the world.

This calling to make the world better was directly attributed by the boys to their experience and identity as Jews. It was clear from students such as this one that boys drew deeply from their community, its religious and cultural teachings, its relationships, and its history.

> It's because of where he's been brought up and, just, his whole environment. It becomes automatic to him. Like, he doesn't even question, like, the fact of helping someone else. It's just the way he was raised and the way he was brought up to do these things. Like, it's just kind of this quality of, just the way that we do things. Like, we're very community oriented.

At the outset, then, we were struck by the boys' minority position and their confidence in the face of the prejudice, scapegoating, and pressure coming at them in this position. It was clear to us that they drew encouragement and support to fight for themselves from the history, ideals, and relationships of their Jewish community.

The Root of Everything, Like, that Makes Us Human

We discovered that those boys who had made a commitment to their identities as Jews were drawn to other Jewish boys. Many made a clear distinction between their

Jewish and non-Jewish peers, stating that their friendships with other Jews felt safer and more lifelong and were more substantive. These boys drew their Jewish friends around them in the same way they wore their stars and *kippah* or interrupted anti-Semitic remarks; it was another way to live within a Jewish identity and all that comes with it. That is, they seemed to claim the shared values and understanding, the relatively greater freedom to be themselves, as a social space within which to live out their chosen identities.

> Participant 1: My parents always taught me that you'd always have friends when you grew up, and you'd have people you called your friends, but the only friends that would really be there for life would be your Jewish friends.
> (Interviewer, to another boy: Have you singled out Jews to be friends with, the way Z. has?)
> Participant 2: Actually, kind of. I mean, yeah, I guess. I mean, not actually by choice, it just happened that way, I guess. Just because we're Jewish, we're friends. It wasn't that
> I was trying to be friends with them because they're Jewish. It just happens that a lot of my best friends are Jewish, just because that's how it worked out. Honestly, I guess we just have things in common. I think that we're Jewish.

It made sense to us that boys would turn to each other for relief from the "mis-recognition" of their non-Jewish peers, following Lacan (1981) to refer to the derogatory images minority groups find in the biased "gaze" of groups hostile to them, because here they could take a breather from having to defend their identity and could also deepen their own experience of it. Despite often living far from each other and coming from very different school and social contexts, many of the boys spoke heartily about how much they counted on getting together with other Jewish boys. As one of our informants put it, "It's nice to be with people like you."

> Participant 1: I think there is a safety to it. I think that, like, I don't know. Yeah, I definitely think you feel safe because, like, nobody's going to be, like, "Oh, you're Jewish!" Like, I don't know.
> Participant 2: I think he's absolutely right. Like, the whole, like, when you're around Jews, you're not "The Jew!" That's a big deal.
> (Interviewer: Say more.)
> I don't know. Well, I guess, like, I go to a school where I am, like, "The Jew" on campus. There's like 5, 10 of us maybe, and so, you know, you get a reputation. And, so from there on out, everybody knows you as, "The Jew"; you're "The Jewish kid." Whereas, like, I'm in a room like this where, like, everybody here's Jewish, I'm not "The Jew" anymore.

But more than simply being spared the mis-recognition of the majority, our informants openly expressed a longing for the common value system, the familiar culture, and the capacity for understanding they found possible when they were with other Jewish youth. We were moved by these stories of their search for recognition, relationships in which they could feel heard and tell that they were seen. We witnessed two boys, for example, who had not known each other before we placed them in a focus group together, who found understanding and compassion with each other, based simply on assumptions they made about each other's identities and commitments.

> It's the fact that I can relate to him on some level already. It's like there's some connection, there's some bridge that we already have with each other, just because I know he's here tonight, I know he's Jewish. I know that there's some connection.

As we pointed out what we observed of their connection, they explained further.

> If they would define themselves as Jewish, then that's already enough to view them as me. I mean, to view them as they're like me. See, I wouldn't sit down right here and tell him my whole life story just because somebody's Jewish. But I think I would be more inclined to get to know them more and be able to talk about these things, these kinds of things, a lot more quickly. Just because I think they'd be able to maybe relate more. I think they'll be able to understand more. Understand and feel, I guess.

That last thought, as we considered it in the context of other boys' comments, seemed quite important; the understanding the boys meant involved common reactions and interpretations, the sharing of an emotional connection.

> There's a level of understanding from Jew to Jew that exists. There's a level of understanding that makes you connected, whether it's the holidays, whether it's your belief system, whether it's your family values, whether it's your ethics, your morals, what you live your life by. There's definitely connections that you form there I don't think it's as much, like, people going to Judaism as some place for them to be put into sort of a category. But I think it's like the root of everything that, like, makes us human. It helps us bond together, so we can kind of better understand each other.

Most of the boys said that, in their schools where Jews were a very small minority, they spent most of their time in friendships and activities with non-Jews. But they made arduous efforts toward each other because they gained from being with each other and how important that was in the broader context of their lives as teenage boys. One boy alluded to this contrast, between his time with his Jewish friends and what it felt like with his other school friends:

> You have stuff in common with, like, people at school and all that stuff, but you're not, like, totally interacting with them. You don't totally know them. They could be totally different people than you. When you go to temple, the first time I went,

> I had so much fun. I didn't know anyone there. And it was cool because, like, I think we're all raised on the same values, like "don't steal." Even if it's not, like, the same real detailed values, it's still the same, you're raised the same way generally. That kind of all connects you. Like you may go into it thinking that you won't, but you'll like the people around you, because you just have this natural connection with them.

The boys were emphatic that they were Jews in an active, intentional way, not to satisfy their families or religious leaders, but because they could find safety, validation, and opportunity with each other. They were clear, in fact, about their affiliation: away from the flat and depressing masculinity of the mainstream, they could express themselves and experience "everything that makes us human."

We're Not Going to Make Fun of Him

Building on this sense of connection and freedom, our informants described relationships with each other that provided important opportunities for authenticity. They tended to talk more substantively about their lives and about the world with each other than they felt they could with non-Jewish peers. As one boy stated,"With the masses at [local high school], I mean, you just can't talk to them about serious things."

Being with other Jewish teenage boys allowed our boys to make certain assumptions. They described the contrast between their Jewish youth group contexts and the norms of high school: "It's just a really comfortable place. You don't feel like, if you say something and people disagree with it, they're going to think about you differently or they're going to, like, beat you up."

This brief dialogue between two boys illustrated their consciousness of the alternative possibilities offered by relationships with other Jewish boys, especially within the mainstream norms of peer policing.

> Informant 1: I don't know if I make the assumption that he's not going to ridicule me. I just make the assumption that he's like me.
> Informant 2: I might not, because he's Jewish. I don't know. That's what I'm saying.
> Informant 1: Jews have been ridiculed enough in history, that we don't need to ridicule each other to solve anything.
> Informant 2: We're not going to make fun of him, or anything.

For these males, among the important ways they would distinguish their interactions with each other from those of the mainstream was to refrain from the most common male put-down, the homophobic taunt: "Yeah, because there's nobody—'Oh, you're gay, you talk to each other!'—like, it just doesn't exist."

This cultural commitment not only offered these boys safe harbor in a peer world of masculine posturing, put-down, and hierarchical jockeying, it afforded them safety to deepen their relationships and to use those relationships to process their lives with each other.

> One of my favorite things in today's day and age is that we label people, like, "gay." We love that word. Boys love gay, which is funny because they're not. It's interesting. When I'm around my Jewish friends, it's like there's a level of connection that makes, like, "comfortable" is the perfect word. It makes me a lot more comfortable with anything that I say or do. And I can say I feel this way and know that it's a safe place to do that. There are serious things that we deal with on a regular basis, too, and to have a place where you feel connected and you feel comfortable is awesome, because it enables you to be able to talk about things that you wouldn't otherwise talk about.

This safety and mutuality created relational contexts in which boys both validated and deepened their sense of who they were. It enhanced their interest in being with each other and seemed to define the significance of their lives as Jewish males.

> I mean, it ("gay") definitely prevents you from going further with what you're talking about or what you're doing. I think your comfort level when you're around a bunch of Jews is something that's a lot easier to obtain than when you're around a group of people, whether you know them or not, that's non-Jews. It's people like you. You know immediately when you meet them you have connections with them: "I'm Jewish and you're Jewish." I know that the chance of you being a jerk, the chance of you being ignorant about how I feel, is a lot less because you feel some of the things I feel.

Their common cultural commitment to fairness and to civility, coupled with their conscious appreciation for the benefits of their relationships with each other, led to these boys' establishment of quite distinct norms for their male friendships and peer groups. These norms protected the social space they used to exercise authentic voice and allowed them a unique freedom within the larger society of high school boys.

You Feel Some of the Things I Feel

The participants in our focus groups, as they said, were less inclined to humiliate or make fun of each other; there seemed to be strong norms among them not to position themselves socially at someone else's expense. But our informants also claimed to enjoy an even greater freedom than this; they were less constricted generally by restrictive masculine norms.

> Guys have the stereotype of not being able to express their emotions or anything like that, and there's a general homophobia about expressing emotion. And, I think honestly at [local high school], there's a pretty massive homophobia. And,

> at [local Jewish youth groups], I don't think that really exists. Like, we can be comfortable with ourselves and still talk to each other and not, like, have an issue.

Perhaps the most noteworthy countercultural aspect of these boys' masculinities was the freedom of emotional expressivity available in their relationships. Our informants told a story of being able to reveal their hearts to each other within the shared assumptions and relative safety of their common Jewish commitments.

> With my Jewish friends, I'm a lot more likely to talk about politics or something like that, talk about your feelings, than I am with my non-Jewish friends. And the reason is, I think, just because you feel more comfortable.

As we have seen, restrictive emotionality is one of the hallmarks, and one of the most damaging outcomes, of traditional masculinity, signifying a "not feminine" constraint that boys enforce mercilessly on each other throughout boyhood's playgrounds, school hallways, and locker rooms. Males adhere to this crippling standard to such an extent that they are typified as stoic or "alexithymic," literally "no words for feelings" (Levant, 1995). Lane and Pollerman (2002) have identified opportunities to encode emotional experiences with language, in actual communication, as fundamental to the development of emotional intelligence. In their view, alexithymia represents "a developmental deficit consisting of a relative absence of emotional experience" (Lane & Pollerman, p. 284), so that children fail to develop a nuanced awareness of, or vocabulary for, their feelings. In this sense, boys' normative deprivation in the realm of emotional communication may be the most costly outcome of the dominant masculine paradigm.

The boys we interviewed were explicit about the effect on their relationships of not having to duck and cover when they got together; their groups were safe, affording them comfort to say how they feel. They appeared to appreciate the opportunity to develop this side of their lives, their emotional capacity. Another boy, the wrestler, contrasted what he could do with his Jewish friends with his more mainstream, non-Jewish friends: "Like, with my athletic friends, more like, the most emotions we probably get to is 'I don't like you. You're annoying.' We'll talk about girls. But that's all the feelings we really talk about."

In such moments in our groups, what we heard underscored how consciously boys valued what they were able to do with their Jewish friends, as if, in the desert of mainstream masculine adolescence, these relationships were their oases.

> But with, like, my friends who aren't Jewish, things like, the personal things like family, family stuff going on, or other stuff in your personal life, it's harder to talk about it with those guys than it is to talk about with these guys.

In addition to providing safety, understanding, and resonance for each other's values, these Jewish boys promoted the development of their emotional intelligence in the relationships they built with each other. By enabling them to acknowledge feelings, find words for what they feel, and refine the various skills of emotional communication, Jewish boys had relationships that defy the constrictive conventions of dominant masculinity and seem likely to make these boys stronger, more resilient, and more relationally effective. We have to believe boys find these opportunities intrinsically rewarding and that they must appreciate their relative freedom, particularly as they grow older and the impact of dominant masculinity takes deeper hold in their non-Jewish friends' lives.

Discussion

Men's studies theorists, like Connell (1995), have been somewhat gloomy about possibilities for boys to resist powerful pressures to conform to the dominant masculine identity. It is indeed stunning to hear boys in so many different contexts describe how their lives are hostage to the norms, incitements, and constraints of this ubiquitous man-making curriculum. But recent research on boys' relationships has had more hopeful news: boys are ever-creative in their efforts to build their lives and to construct a positive sense of self based on human needs for connection, meaning, and validation (Reichert, 2001; Reichert & Kuriloff, 2003). These boys sort through the resources and opportunities of their lives and often discover ways to assert new, freer ideas for being male. In particular, boys draw on their friendships with other boys for key qualities of support and understanding. The Jewish boys in our sample illustrated how boys' development can be positively affected when they find such peer acceptance and resource. In their intimate support and mutual regard, we observed males who shaped the course of their masculine development in healthier, more civil, and more authentic ways. It is our argument that it was precisely their affiliation with the Jewish community that afforded them the freedom and confidence to resist pressures to conform to mainstream masculinity and to construct counter-hegemonic identities.

These findings about Jewish boys fit with research conducted among other groups of minority boys. In Way's (2004) longitudinal study of adolescent friendships in working-class and poor urban environments, despite more stereotypic images of boys' relationships as shallow, action-oriented, or troubled, she reported finding deep connections, loyal support, and expressive sharing among many boys.

> Boys who have been portrayed in popular culture as more interested in shooting each other than in sharing their thoughts and feelings spoke to us about male friendships that "you feel lost without," about "deep depth" friendships, and about wanting friends with whom you "share your secrets," "tell everything," and "get inside." (p. 182)

Boys being able to achieve such positive connections with other males, Way (2004) felt, had a great deal to do with the cultural context surrounding the boys she studied: "The beliefs and values maintained at home and in the larger community in which adolescent boys reside most likely influence the ways in which boys befriend each other" (p. 186). In fact, Way found that groups that are more marginalized offer values to boys that support more meaningful friendships. By contrast with White middle-class boys whose friendships tend to be less intimate and more stereotypically action-oriented, her research discovered that ethnic urban boys are less apt to buy into dominant masculine norms: "They don't benefit from adhering to these dictates" (Way, p. 187). Way concluded that the "antagonistic" quality of adolescent peer policing "may lead adolescents to appreciate their close friendships even more than if the conflict did not exist" (p. 191).

Another researcher, Chu (2000, 2004), studied boys' relationships at different ages by using similar voice-centered methodologies. Her research focused in particular on the critical role relationships can play in boys' lives, helping them to resist masculine pressures and to establish authentic identities. In a longitudinal study among elementary age boys, Chu (2000) detailed how sensitive to the peer and institutional demands of masculinity young boys are, making deliberate compromises in their sense of who they are to avoid going against the grain of masculine norms. Constrained in these ways, these boys would lose any opportunity to be themselves. In a separate study of adolescent boys, Chu (2004) identified two general patterns for how boys respond to these masculine pressures. Some boys internalize societal definitions of masculine ideals, even "to the detriment of [their] own sense of self" (Chu, 2004, p. 100). Such boys not only hold back in order to fit in, they can even come to evaluate themselves, sometimes mercilessly, against this unrealistic masculine standard. In the second pattern, boys are better able to shield themselves from these external pressures and to establish senses of self that are more confident and independent. Boys exhibiting this second pattern typically enjoy relationships with other boys with whom they can talk honestly, find validation, and exchange support. Chu (2004) concluded that "boys' experiences of being validated and valued in relationships appear to be key to boys' resistance and resilience" (p. 101).

This insight about the role that male friendships can play in promoting greater resilience, by helping boys resist the more confining dimensions of masculinity, seems importantly related to the findings about the contribution that identity can make in positive youth development.

In our work on boys' development, we have been impressed by how influential a boy's identity can be, affecting the widest range of his choices, behaviors, feelings, and relationships (Reichert, Stoudt, & Kuriloff, 2006). For this reason, what we found among these Jewish boys was so encouraging; fueled by their cultural traditions, institutions and influences, boys created sanctuary from the harsher elements of adolescent masculinity. In these sheltered spaces, they afforded each other opportunities to be real, to be liked and understood, and to be respected. Thus emboldened, they forged principled, involved, and expressive identities as men. Their identities emerged from what they have found possible—modeled, encouraged, and supported—in their Jewish worlds. Conditions supporting such an alternative masculinity existed in their lives; it was that simple.

References

Berkowitz, M.W. (2002). The science of character education. In W. Damon (Ed.), *Bringing in a new era in character education* (pp. 43–63). Pala Alto, CA: Hoover Institution Press.

Brod, H. (1992). *The making of masculinities.* New York: Routledge.

Brooks, G.R., & Silverstein, L.B. (1995). Understanding the dark side of masculinity: An interactive systems model. In R. Levant & W. Pollack (Eds.), *The new psychology of men* (pp. 280–333). New York: Basic Books.

Brown, L.M., & Gilligan, C. (1992). *Meeting at the crossroads: Women's psychology and girls' development.* Cambridge, MA: Harvard University Press.

Centers for Disease Control and Prevention. (2006, June). Youth risk behavior surveillance—United States, 2005. *Morbidity and Mortality Weekly Report, 55.*

Chu, J.Y. (2000). *Learning what boys know: An observational and interview study with six four-year-old boys.* Unpublished dissertation, Harvard University, Boston.

Chu, J.Y. (2004). A relational perspective on adolescent boys' identity development. In N. Way & J.Y. Chu (Eds.), *Adolescent boys: Exploring diverse cultures of boyhood* (pp. 78–106). New York: New York University Press.

Connell, R.W. (1989). Cool guys, swots and wimps: The interplay of masculinity and education. *Oxford Review of Education, 15*, 291–303.

Connell, R.W. (1995). *Masculinities.* Berkeley, CA: University of California Press.

Connell, R.W. (1996). Teaching the boys: New research on masculinity and gender strategies for schools. *Teachers' College Record, 98*, 206–235.

Connell, R.W., & Messerschmidt, J.W. (2005). Hegemonic masculinity: Rethinking the concept. *Gender and Society, 19*, 829–859.

Courtenay, W.H. (2003). Key determinants of the health and well-being of men and boys. *International Journal of Men's Health, 2*(1), 1–30.

Donaldson, M. (1985). What is hegemonic masculinity? *Theory and Society, 22*, 643–657.

Holzman, M. (2003). *G'varim: Resources for Jewish Men.* New York: National Federation of Temple Brotherhoods

Kadushin, C., Kelner, S., & Saxe, L. (2000). *Being a Jewish teenager in America: Trying to make it.* Boston, MA: Cohen Center for Modern Jewish Studies, Brandeis University.

Lacan, J. (1981). The seminar of Jacques Lacan. Book XI. In J. Miller (Ed.), *The four fundamental concepts of psychoanalysis* (A. Sheridan, trans.). New York: Norton.

Lane, R.D., & Pollerman, B.Z. (2002). Complexity of emotional representations. In L.F. Barrett & P. Salovey (Eds.), *The wisdom in feelings* (pp. 271–296). New York: Guilford Press.

Langman, P.F. (1999). *Jewish issues in multiculturalism.* Northvale, NJ: Jason Aronson, Inc.

Leffert, N., & Herring, H. (1998). *Shema: Listening to Jewish youth.* Minneapolis, MN: Search Institute.

Levant, R.F. (1995). Toward the reconstruction of masculinity. In R.F. Levant & W.S Pollack (Eds.), *A new psychology of men* (pp. 229–251). New York: Basic Books.

Martino, W. (1999). "Cool boys", "party animals", "squids" and "poofters": Interrogating the dynamics and politics of adolescent masculinities in school. *British Journal of Sociology of Education, 20*, 239–263.

Martino, W. (2008). Male teachers as role models: Addressing issues of masculinity, pedagogy and the re-masculinization of schooling. *Curriculum Inquiry, 38*, 189–223.

Moving Traditions. (2008a). *Moving Judaism and Jews.* Jenkintown, PA: Moving Traditions.

Moving Traditions. (2008b). *Where have all the young men gone?* Jenkintown, PA: Moving Traditions.

O'Neil, J.M., Good, G.E., & Holmes, S. (1995). Fifteen years of theory and research on men's gender role conflict: New paradigms for empirical research. In R. Levant & W. Pollack (Eds.), *The new psychology of men* (pp. 164–206). New York: Basic Books.
Pleck, J. (1995). The gender role strain paradigm: An update. In R. Levant & W. Pollack (Eds.), *The new psychology of men* (pp. 11–32). New York: Basic Books.
Pleck, J., Sonenstein, F.L., & Ku, L.C. (1994). Problem behaviors and masculinity ideology in adolescent males. In R. Ketterlinus & M.E. Lamb (Eds.), *Adolescent problem behaviors* (pp. 165-186). Hillsdale, NJ: Lawrence Erlbaum.
Reichert, M. (2001). Rethinking masculinities: New ideas for schooling boys. In W. Martino & B. Meyenn (Eds.), *What about the boys?* (pp. 38–52). Philadelphia, PA: Open University Press.
Reichert, M., & Kuriloff, P. (2003). Boys' selves: Forging identities in the looking glass of school life. *Teachers' College Record, 106*, 547–576.
Reichert, M.C., & Hawley, R. (2006). Confronting the "boy problem": A self-study approach to deepen schools' moral stance. *Teacher's College Record,* 25. www.tcrecord.org ID Number: 12813.
Reichert, M.C., Stoudt, B., & Kuriloff, P. (2006). Don't love no fight: Healing and identity among urban youth. *The Urban Review, 38*, 187–209.
Seligman, M., Berkowitz, M.W., Catalano, R.F., Damon, W., Eccles, J.S., Gillham, J., et al. (2005). The positive perspective on youth development. In D.L. Evans et al. (Eds.), *Treating and preventing adolescent mental health disorders* (pp. 499–529). New York: Oxford University Press.
Seligman, M., & Csikszentmihalayi, M. (2000). Positive psychology. *American Psychologist, 55*(1), *5–14.*
Smith, C., & Denton, M.L. (2005). *Soul searching. The religious and spiritual lives of American teenagers.* New York: Oxford University Press.
Stoudt, B.G. (2006). You're either in or you're out. School violence, peer discipline and the (re)production of hegemonic masculinity. *Men and Masculinities, 8*, 273–286.
Swain, J. (2005). Masculinities and education. In M.S. Kimmel, J. Hearn, & R.W. Connell (Eds.), *Handbook of studies on men and masculinities* (pp. 213–229). Thousand Oaks, CA: Sage.
Tolman, D.L., & Brydon-Miller, M. (2001). *From subjects to subjectivities. A handbook of interpretative and participatory methods.* New York: New York University Press.
U.S. Preventive Services Task Force. (1996). *Guide to clinical preventive services* (2nd Ed.). Baltimore, MD: Williams and Wilkins.
Waldron, I. (1976). Why do women live longer than men? *Journal of Human Stress, 2*, 1–13.
Way, N. (2004). Intimacy, desire, and distrust in the friendships of adolescent boys. In N. Way & J.Y. Chu (Eds.), *Adolescent boys* (pp. 167–196). New York: New York University Press.
Whitehead, S.M. (2002). *Men and masculinities.* Cambridge, UK: Polity.

2

Circumcision and Masculinity: Motherly Men or Brutal Patriarchs?

Eric Kline Silverman

Prologue: Sometimes a Pickle Is Just a Salami

Shortly after the year 2000, to use a particular calendar, several groups of young American Jews self-consciously sought to push Judaism to the cutting-edge of contemporary culture. The New Jew Cool, as this dispersed movement is sometimes called, yearns to redefine Jewishness so as to challenge the reigning ideologies and institutions of mainstream American Jewry. These "hipster Jews" are politically progressive, post-denominational, witty, urbane, sometimes brilliantly insightful, but also, to be honest, occasionally pretentious, narcissistic, and parochial. They are, to repeat, bright kids in their 20s.

The New Jew Cool sees the hegemonic modes of Jewish identity as anachronistic and alienating, inert and dull, rooted in stale theology, and lacking resonance and relevance. This younger generation wants Jewishness to become central to the politics of identity and multiculturalism. They shun the tones and etiquette of conventional Jewry, and instead express their Jewishness as irreverent, sardonic, playful, jarringly aggressive, and scandalously erotic. With the in-your-face demeanor normally associated with hip-hop, the New Jew Cool wants Judaism to be fashionable.

The flagship venue for this movement is *Heeb Magazine*, a polished monthly periodical, perhaps best summarized as a borscht belt smorgasbord of *National Lampoon* and *People Magazine*. The publication received start-up funds in 2001 from an institution prominently seated in the front pews of the Jewish mainstream, namely, the Joshua Venture Fellowship, itself partly supported by Steven Spielberg's Righteous Persons Foundation and the Andrea and Charles Bronfman Philanthropies. Despite these conventional roots, *Heeb* aims to undermine the middle-aged authority and authenticity of the Jewish establishment.

Heeb delights in presenting humorous, bawdy, slightly offensive, and sophomoric self-advertisements. I recall one issue where a young Talmudic scholar, a *yeshiva bochur* with long *peyess*, large velvet *yarmulke*, and black suit, sits on a park bench with his face nervously buried in the magazine. To hide his shameful transgression of orthodox modesty, the student attempts to conceal his copy of *Heeb* behind a slightly smaller yet more palatable magazine: *Barely Legal.*

In the same issue of *Heeb*, another self-advertisement features a grim tableau of an anonymous New York City street. We see no people, only a grimy fire hydrant and a chewing-gum-bespeckled sidewalk on which some hapless soul has placed a few used books and miscellaneous items for sale. In the background rises the façade of a brick building besmirched with graffiti. One tag is prominent: All ethnic groups love our salami!!!

The middle-school innuendo is obvious but also ambiguous. Should we see the salami as bravado by Jewish men, or a as boast by Jewish women about their Jewish partners? Perhaps the salami refers *in general* to the idea of Jewish manhood. Or it might instead evoke a more *specific* bodily focus and thus point to the unique Jewish phallus—a phallus, of course, marked the signal bodily token of Jewish identity: circumcision.

Equally ambiguous is the cover of a rather different publication, the 1999 literary anthology *Neurotica: Jewish Writers on Sex*, which features a prominent pickle. On Amazon.com, Kirkus Reviews says, "Abundantly juicy. One bite and you're lost." But here, too, like the *Heeb* parody, the seemingly obvious pun is actually quite slippery. The pickle, of course, alludes to a broad sense of Jewish ethnicity through a culinary nod to the delicatessen. But the pickle also represents Jewish sexuality in general through the common cross-cultural equivalence of food and sexuality.[3] From this angle, the gustatory symbol on *Neurotica* alludes to the distinctive flavors of Jewish eroticism—whatever that means. From another angle, though, the pickle, like *Heeb*'s salami, suggests the specific sexuality of Jewish men. And on this point, the pickle finds itself in a bit of a semiotic pickle.

To the extent that the pickle represents the penis, it is a phallus detached from the body. Indeed, the *Neurotica* pickle is depicted against a plain white background. It is, dare I say it, a circumcision gone awry—a culinary representation of castration anxiety, we might say, or a symbol of male sexuality that also erases masculinity. From another angle, the pickle is the Jewish variant of male adolescent humor concerning women and cucumbers that, however misogynistic, also registers anxiety about the role and value of male sexuality. It is not unlike an old joke: "Did you hear that hospitals stopped doing circumcisions? No, why? They were throwing away the wrong part."

This leads me to my last point about the pickle illustrating *Neurotica*: for all of its Jewishness, this pickle is surprisingly *un*circumcised. It is whole. There is no bite. The *Neurotica* pickle thus triply erases Jewish masculinity: first, by representing most Jewish men as they are not; second, by severing the phallus entirely; and third, by alluding to Jewish masculinity through another ethnic body. No ethnic groups, as *Heeb* might put it, like our salami.

Yet both *Heeb* magazine and the *Neurotica* anthology, however much they may seem to emasculate Jewish manhood, also sustain the centrality of men within Judaism by allowing the male body to stand for *all* Jews, male *and* female. Here, to continue the culinary quip, there are only salamis and pickles, no bagels. To the extent that we could, or should, take these comedic efforts at representing Jewishness seriously, we can all likely agree that the salami and pickle resist any singular inter-

[3] Another example from the same milieu as *Heeb* is t-shirts sold on the Internet that proclaims "Eat Me I'm Kosher."

pretation. They lend voice to a wide-ranging ambivalence and anxiety over the definition of Jewish masculinity.

From Pickles to Penises

The same themes, albeit with far less humor and innuendo, animate current debates within Judaism over the meaning and relevance of ritual circumcision (*Brit Milah*). My interest here is narrowly focused. I want only to explore the dispute over *Brit Milah* for what it says about Jewish masculinity. Consequently, I refrain from assessing the respective merits of arguments pro and con; I stake no particular claim. Likewise, I do not here comprehensively review the rite historically or cross-culturally, nor probe the ongoing controversy over medical circumcision. I have covered all these topics elsewhere (Silverman, 2004, 2006). Rather, I want only to listen to voices within the Jewish community that construe the rite of *Brit Milah* as carving images of manhood into the bodies and psyches of men.

On one side, the rite ideally shapes infant boys and their fathers into loving, caring, responsible, and even motherly men. From this angle, too, *Brit Milah* bonds father and son through its emotional, bloody anguish and fosters male empathy toward women. Finally, the rite circumscribes masculine sexuality within a moral framework. All told, *Brit Milah* shapes Jewish men into a kinder, gentler masculinity.[4]

On the other side, however, *Brit Milah* is a sign and symptom of brutal patriarchy and misogyny. This mutilation cuts away any possible moral virtue. Circumcision wounds the boy in his body and soul and celebrates manhood by coercing mothers into sacrificing their natural maternal instincts to protect their newborns. *Brit Milah* arises from a cycle of inter-generational abuse whereby adult men deny the pain they both inflict and suffer. So deeply repressed is this psychic torment that most Jewish men refuse to confront their anguish directly and, indeed, deny their suffering entirely. But this same repression nonetheless compels circumcised Jews to reenact their trauma by traumatizing male infants. From this angle, the rite sustains a vision of masculinity that brutalizes all Jews—fathers, sons, mothers, and neglected daughters. The rite is simply wrong.

For the purpose of this essay, to repeat, I intentionally avoid questions of verification and validity. It is not my task here to validate or refute. Rather, I want to show how Jews today attach to the rite of circumcision a broad range of masculine anxieties, fears, tragedies, and triumphs. In Judaism, as in many cultures, circumcision is a powerful and, more significantly, tangible symbol of masculinity, whether monstrous or *mentsh*, on account of the sheer physicality of the rite—its potent juxtaposition of intimacy and infancy, joy and anguish, celebration and fear.

---

[4] Many readers will immediately trace the "kinder, gentler" phrase to the Presidential campaign of George Herbert Walker Bush, but, when I use the term in regard to Jewish masculinity, I draw instead on Boyarin (1997).

A Long Tradition

Appeals to history are common rhetorical strategies used to sustain Jewish circumcision, especially after the Holocaust or Shoah. To abandon the rite is tantamount to countenancing a posthumous victory for Nazism or to forsaking the blood of Jewish martyrs throughout history.[5] The rite, too, is often justified on the basis that Jews have unswervingly abided by *Brit Milah* for over 5,000 years. We have kept the covenantal ceremony, and it, in turn, has symbolically sustained us. To refrain from circumcising our sons is to shatter a chain of tradition that has persisted intact for centuries in spite of, or perhaps because of, the best efforts of our enemies. But lacking from these common, deeply held sentiments is the recognition that Jewish debates over *Brit Milah* also constitute an equally enduring tradition. For as long as we Jews have circumcised our sons, we have also registered discontent, anxieties, and qualms about the rite.

There is considerable evidence in biblical and rabbinic literature for Israelite and Jewish ambivalence toward *Brit Milah* (see Cohen, 2005, Click, 2005, & Silverman, 2006). For example, nearly all biblical references to the rite are connected to some act of terrible violence. In Genesis 34, for example, the sons of Jacob use circumcision to avenge the rape of their sister, Dinah, by a Hivite named Shechem. Afterwards, Shechem proposes marriage, but Dinah's brothers refuse to "to give [their] sister to a man who is uncircumcised, for that is a disgrace among [them]." Then they offer a compromise: if the Hivites collectively undergo the rite, "[they] will give [their] daughters to [the Hivites] and take [the Hivites'] daughters to [themselves] ... and become as one kindred." The Hivites agree, but while they are convalescing in pain after the circumcision, they are slaughtered. Dinah's brothers kill all the male Hivites, plunder their town, and take captive the women and children. In this biblical context, circumcision symbolizes deception and retributive slaughter—really, a moment of ethnic cleansing.

In Genesis 17, God commands the rite to Abraham and all subsequent male Israelites. Upon performance of the act, promises God, the Israelites will reap numerous benefits, including bodily and moral wholeness, nationhood, refuge from exile, and plentiful "seed." Given the propensity of ancient peoples to dramatically alter their bodies in religious devotion, one could reasonably expect that the Israelites would have celebrated the fact that the covenant required *only* the removal of the foreskin. Such a minor prick to receive such divine beneficence![6] What's more, circumcision was well known throughout the Near East. The rite was not, in its historical and cultural context, a big deal.

[5] Circumcision is famously central to the 1990 Holocaust film *Europa, Europa*, see Lungstrum (1998).

[6] The pun here on the word *prick* is, of course, intentional and ultimately derives from the famous speech by Shylock in Shakespeare's play *The Merchant of Venice* (see Katz, 1999; Shapiro, 1996).

Yet the biblical punishment for the non-performance of circumcision was severe: you were "cut off" (*kārēt*), a verb that refers not simply to death but to total family annihilation, that is, death without male heirs. Later Jewish texts are more explicit: Jews who forsake the rite, declares Jubilees 15, will be "destroyed and slain from the earth." Even Moses himself, the lawgiver and the liberator, apparently had qualms about the rite. At the very least, he simply neglected to perform it. Indeed, Moses would have suffered death by the Lord for this infraction had Moses's wife, Zipporah, not swiftly severed their son's foreskin (Exodus 4:24–26). All this suggests, I contend, that the ancient Israelites and early Jews in Late Antiquity registered at least *some* unease with circumcision. Why else would they so commonly connect circumcision with violence and death? And why would God, as well as His (pronoun intentional) human emissaries, namely, the prophets and rabbis, need so aggressively to enforce the rite—to bully, if you will, the Israelites and Jews into performing it?

Another historical moment that clearly evidences the lack of consensus among Jews on the relevance of *Brit Milah* occurs in the Maccabean literature. Most Jews today know these texts only vaguely through children's stories told during *Hanukah*. But the actual texts are rather more grim and revealing. In many respects, the conflict memorialized through *menorahs*, *latkes*, *dreidels*, and gift-giving was a bitter civil war that pitted Hellenized Jews against Jewish traditionalists. The Jews who embraced Greek culture, and so abjured circumcision, can be seen as reasonable reformers or vile apostates. Likewise for the traditionalists who repelled them: they are either gallant saviors who rescued our heritage, or fundamentalist fanatics akin to the Taliban. Either way, the traditionalists triumphed, whereupon they forcibly circumcised all the uncircumcised boys they found in Israel (1 Maccabees 2:46). However much the Jews of Palestine were thrilled with liberation and the restoration of traditional Judaism, they did not celebrate victory by reaching for the covenantal knife; the blade was imposed on them.

Even Maimonides, hardly a foe of circumcision, understood Jewish ambivalence and anxiety about the rite (Stern, 1993). Why, he asked, does circumcision occur in infancy? For one, adults would outright refuse the procedure. For another, parental love and affection increases over time, and so fathers would never allow the rite on an older child. On both accounts, Maimonides seems not altogether wrong.

In the mid-19th century, Jewish dissent over *Brit Milah* dramatically increased as European Jewry embraced modernity and welcomed the long-overdue invitation for full citizenship in the nation-state (Judd, 2007). Jews aspiring to assimilation, especially members of the burgeoning Reform movement originally based in Frankfurt, understood compulsory religious circumcision to violate the basic tenets of modernity: science, progress, individualism, secularism, hygiene, and rationality. Reform Judaism enacted many religious innovations in the late-19th century, including the abandonment of the dietary codes, mixed male and female pews, vernacular worship, bare-headed male prayer, and the education of girls. But no reform so enflamed traditionalists as the decentralization of circumcision to male Jewish identity. Reform Judaism never formally abandoned *Brit Milah*, however. Rather, the movement only shifted *Brit Milah* from a compulsory to an *optional* sign of Jewish masculinity. Circumcised Jewishness became a matter of free-choice, and thus male Jewish identity joined, rather than opposed, modern individualism.

Traditional Jews bristled at their reformist coreligionists. As they saw it, the whole point of circumcision was to cut *off* Jews from the wider society! Worse, reformist appeals to modern rationality and scientific hygiene undermined the authority of God and the rabbis. For them, the circumcised definition of Jewish manhood was beyond debate.

In the latter 19th century, many Jews and Gentiles, especially in the intelligentsia, increasingly saw Jewish circumcision as an antiquated violation of modern sensibilities. Ironically, the practice of circumcision as a medical, not Jewish, procedure gained currency in the very same era. From one angle, circumcision was dismissed as premodern. From another angle, the procedure exemplified modern medicine. By the 1880s, many American and British physicians enthusiastically promoted the routine circumcision of boys as a broad hygienic measure and a specific prophylaxis against syphilis.[7] The procedure, too, offered a defense against masturbation, a key site of moral panic in the Victorian era, and a curtailment of excess licentiousness. No longer did circumcision betoken Jewish separatism and barbarism or cut Jews out of European civilization.[8] Now the rite positioned Jews at the cutting edge of modernity. To non-Jews, the bodily sign of Jewish masculinity was now, after centuries of theological derision, good.

American and British medical journals suddenly published papers that lauded Jews for their (supposedly) superior health, a quality often attributed to the (supposedly) superior cleanliness of the circumcised Jewish penis. The benefits of the procedure were moral as much as medical. Jews, declared Brown (1896–1897) in *Journal of the Orificial Society*, rarely "figure in silly crimes, police or divorce courts" (p. 299). Of course, the medical practice was not promoted to create more Jews. Rather, it would guarantee pious, hard-working Christians (see Darby, 2005). The Jew's body was still different, much as it was throughout European history, but this difference was now worth emulating. The "old Mosaic rite," boasted Hirschfeld (1858) in the *American Medical Monthly*, "receives a confirmation, perhaps stronger and more binding upon [ones] age than that in which the Legislator lived" (p. 275). And so, by the early decades of the 20th century, the genitals of Jewish men shifted from an ethnic peculiarity at best, and a bodily affirmation of Jewish perfidy at worst, to the image of normal male health itself.

---

[7] For broader surveys of this issue, see Efron (2001), *Medicine and the German Jews*; Judd (2007) *Contested Rituals*; Gollaher (2000), *Circumcision*; and Silverman (2006), *From Abraham to America.*

[8] Gilman's (1991) book *The Jew's Body* remains the classic source on the somatic fantasies of the Jewish body in Europe (see also, Gilman, 1993, 1995).

A Hole in Masculinity

By the mid-1990s, circumcision reemerged as a popular issue in defining Jewish identity and masculinity. Major Jewish monthlies—*Conservative Judaism*, *Tikkun*, and *Moment*—devoted special issues to the topic. National Public Radio featured the debate on the program "All Things Considered," as did Jewish and non-Jewish newspapers, magazines, and Web sites. Anti-circumcision "intactivists" launched organizations and websites,[9] lobbied legislators, and even registered as nongovernmental organizations with the United Nations. References to the rite frequently appeared on television shows, such as "thirtysomething," "The Nanny," "Will & Grace," "Dharma & Greg," "L.A. Law," "St. Elsewhere," "South Park," and "Seinfeld."[10] Most significantly, Jews over the past decade have penned scores, if not hundreds, of articles, op-ed columns, and essays as well as several books, variously defending and especially deriding *Brit Milah*. Once again, Jews and non-Jews debate the status of the Jewish penis and the normal body of Jewish manhood.

A prominent figure opposing *Brit Milah* is Goldman (1997, 1998), author of *Circumcision: The Hidden Trauma* and *Questioning Circumcision: A Jewish Perspective*. Critics of infant circumcision, such as Goldman, see the procedure as directly causing severe social, sexual, and psychological traumas (see also Boyle et al., 2002; Hammond, 1999; and Rhinehart, 1999). The circumcised man is a traumatized man. Symptoms of his circumcisional distress may include low self-esteem, excessive rage, feelings of parental betrayal, anxiety disorders, sexual dysfunctions (including homosexuality), depression, shame, distrust, victimization, powerlessness, grief, withdrawal, teenage suicide, alcoholism, drug abuse, promiscuity, theft, hatred, genital insecurity, misogyny, and rape. Goldman suggests that some cases of Sudden Infant Death Syndrome (SIDS) may in fact be a type of infant suicide following the trauma of circumcision. Intactivists see the procedure as permanently damaging the neurological architecture of the infant's brain. Consequently, a circumcised man is more

---

[9] The more prominent online organizations include CIRP (Circumcision Information Resource Pages; www.cirp.org), NOCIRC (National Organization of Circumcision Resources; www.nocirc.org), NOHARMM (National Organization to Halt the Abuse and Routine Mutilation of Males; www.noharmm.org), Mothers Against Circumcision (www.mothersagainstcirc.org), ARC (Attorneys for the Rights of the Child; www.arclaw.org), and In Memory of the Sexually Mutilated Child (www.sexuallymutilatedchild.org). Elsewhere, I extensively discuss these organizations, as well as the anti-circumcision literature in general, with an eye toward discerning and thoroughly documenting the unfortunate retention of medieval caricatures of the Jew as a mutilated and mutilating threat to civilized society (Silverman, 2006, Chap. 10). One of the more egregious examples of this anti-Judaism is a book published in a medical series by Warner Books, a subsidiary of AOL Time Warner—one of the largest entertainment and media conglomerates in the world (Fliess & Hodges, 2002).

[10] An anti-circumcision Web site actually keeps track of these episodes; see "Treatment of Circumcision on TV," http://www.circumstitions.com/TVSitcoms.html. This and all Web sites were accessed in August 2008.

likely than his foreskinned counterpart to pursue deviant sexuality and sado-masochism, and to exhibit aggressive antisocial behaviors. The circumcised man is a wounded man, and he wounds others.

Self-declarations of circumcised woe, especially on Internet Web sites, punctuate anti-circumcision literature. Jed Diamond, a leading psychotherapeutic figure in the men's movement, connected circumcision to "irritable male syndrome." In a letter to *Moment* magazine (August, 1997), moreover, Diamond writes that he "would break into tears when [he] tried to write about shame" for his book *The Warrior's Journey Home: Healing Men, Healing the Planet* (1994). Why? Because he had "body memories of having been circumcised and realized that [he] carried a great deal of pain, even 50 years later."

In a progress report issued by the National Organization to Halt the Abuse and Routine Mutilation of Males, another Jewish man traces his adult and childhood anguish to his *Brit Milah*. He recalls recurrent boyhood nightmares of a "long bearded goat"—the *mohel*— "eating its way through the wall of the bedroom ... to take bites out of [his] flesh" (Traiman, 1994). He connects his loathing for alcohol to the failure of the *mohel*'s wine-soaked cloth to soothe the pain of the circumcision. The rite, too, explains his "earliest memories ... of terror, pain and helplessness."

Another popular Internet site advocating the abolishment of circumcision is titled "In Memory of the Sexually Mutilated Child" (http://www.sexuallymutilatedchild.org/levitt). On it, another Jewish man recounts his emotional response to reading Bigelow's (1994) book, *The Joy of Uncircumcising!: Exploring Circumcision.*[11] He "curled up in a fetal position ... and cried and grieved." Then grief turned to rage as follows:

> I denounce Judaism ... as sick, perverted and immoral.... I fantasize about revenge on the mohel who circumcised me.... One of the main reasons I'm active in the intact baby movement is to vent my rage in a positive way and not end up in prison. I've put a MOHEL = MENGELE sign across the back of my car.

So furious are some circumcised men at their foreskinlessness that they publically declare on the Internet their desire actually to kill their parents.

Let me examine in more detail some of the wounds allegedly inflicted by *Brit Milah*. Neonatal circumcision, including *Brit Milah*, irredeemably ruptures the mother-infant bond. By disrupting "the development of basic trust in infancy," the rite thwarts "the potential for intimacy in later life" (Goldman, 1998, p. 98). Circumcised men may thus approach all intimate relationships with guarded mistrust. Similarly, the circumcised child may grow into an adult man who experiences emotional withdrawal. Since most Jewish boys are circumcised, the inevitable conclu-

[11] Nonsurgical foreskin restoration typically involves the attachment of various weights, cones, and tapes that tug the skin around the shaft of the penis over the glans in order to simulate a prepuce.

sion is that most Jewish men are emotionally wooden—unable properly to express their emotions or to emotionally connect with others.

Infants are so profoundly traumatized by circumcision, aver intactivists, that they become adult men who can *only* function and protect the ego by repressing their psychic pain. But the trauma is so indelibly and overwhelmingly etched on the circumcised man's psyche that he is compelled to circumcise his own son as a way of repeating the ordeal. After all, reasons Goldman (1998), "we tend to act out our repressed feelings on those who are weaker" (p. 69; see also Goldman, 2004). In short, cut men like to cut. And they do so without acknowledging their own suffering or the suffering they inflict on others.

A recent paper from Hill (2007) offers a similar view of the psychic trauma experienced by circumcised men:

> Failure to grieve the loss of the foreskin function results in a cohort of men who are in denial about their loss. Traumatized persons tend to reenact and repeat their trauma. The compulsion to repeat the trauma and the emotional need to deny the loss result in a large cohort of circumcised men who seek to perpetuate the practice of non-therapeutic circumcision. Such men become the "adamant fathers" who insist on circumcising their sons despite medical evidence that the operation is injurious. (p. 319)

And here is a comparable assertion on the Web site for Jews Against Circumcision (www.jewsagainstcircumcision.org):

> The excruciatingly painful trauma we inflict on infant boys when performing circumcision rewires their brain[s] to be violent, and causes brain damage.... Males are violent due to circumcision. It is usually boys who go to school and kill people; they are violent since their brains are wired for violence from infancy. Rarely does a girl take a gun to class and kill people. (http://www.jewsagainstcircumcision.org/psycholo.htm)

From this angle, normative Jewish manhood rests on a brutalized psyche—a psyche so damaged that it can only seek resolution by terrorizing helpless infants.

Many opponents of *Brit Milah* dismiss Jews who adhere to the rite, especially proponents who find validation in classic rabbinic theology, as loathsome religious fundamentalists. More commonly, circumcising Jews are pitied for being what Goodman (1999a) calls the unwitting victims of a "culturally conditioned terror" (see also Sandel, 1996). Judaism is at fault—not individual Jews. Goodman and others explain the persistence of *Brit Milah*, which Goodman summarizes as "a wounded human being ... wounding another," as "compulsive behavior on the part of people who at some level do want to stop" (see also Goodman, 1999b). In this framework, the Jew is a victim and victimizer ultimately trapped in his own damaged psyche. Were it not for normative Judaism, Jews would otherwise grow into whole persons. Instead, the Jew suffers from a deep hole in his psyche—a wound attributed to *Brit Milah*.It is this masculine wound, suggests Goldman (1998), which best explains a key theological tenet of *Brit Milah*. Jews often connect the rite to "a desire for God's protection" (p. 69). Why? Because most Jewish men "received no protection when they were circumcised as infants" (p. 69). From this angle, one can also understand the source of the ancient yearning to appease God: the return of the repressed fear related to circumcision. In effect, Jewish men look to God for the parental nurture they never received. The rite thus doubly scars the psyche of Jewish men—first, by subjecting them to a ceremony that is routinely dubbed as child abuse and, second, by offering an illusory solution to their longing for nurturing parents.

But Jewish men experience yet another layer of psychological trauma. Despite the horrific trauma subjected to Jewish boys in the early days of life, most adults refuse to validate the subsequent psychic pain. At a time in history when the (civilized) world rightly condemns (uncivilized) female genital mutilation, the equivalent disfigurement of infant boys, so goes this argument, receives scant criticism—worse, it is even celebrated in Judaism! There is no patriarchy here but quite the opposite: the Jewish boy is brutalized, and the man later neglected, precisely because they are male. He is first abused by *Brit Milah*, and then by the denial of his trauma and adult dysfunctions.

Despite the multiple levels of masculine wounding inherent in *Brit Milah*, the ritual also violates motherhood, as befitting the overall patriarchal structure of biblical culture and traditional Judaism.[12] The rite cuts women out of the covenant. It shifts the early experiences of a newborn boy from his mother and her breast to men and their knife. *Brit Milah* not only arises from the fear of women it also arises from the fear of pleasure, especially the pleasure of emotional security, the pleasure of intimate human relationships first learned from the mother-infant bond, and the pleasure of sexuality (Pollack, 1995, 1997). As Pollack (1995) writes, the covenantal rite has the effect of "psychosexually wounding the manhood still asleep in the unsuspecting baby boy" (p. 185).[13]

Brit Milah reproduces religious patriarchy by consecrating male (not female) bodies and masculine (not feminine) procreative potency. *Brit Milah* celebrates the paternal phallus—yet Judaism offers no comparable ritual exaltation of motherhood. In this sense, the rite endows men with hegemonic privilege even as it carves a hole in Jewish men's psyches, damages Jewish men's (and women's) sexuality, and cuts

[12] See, for example, Karsenty (1988); Kimmel (2001); Moss (1990). For scholarly accounts of the role of mothers in the history of *Brit Milah*, especially in regard to rabbinic texts, see Cohen (2005) and Margalit and Tziraki-Segal (2006). I do not challenge the idea that circumcision threatens motherhood—and, indeed, I make this very argument in my own book on the rite—but I think it fair to say that most critics of *Brit Milah* who make parallel claim have simply failed to read carefully the relevant literature, either scholarly or rabbinic.

[13] The claim that circumcision severely damages male sexuality is crucial to the opposition to routine medical circumcision but less pronounced in the debate over *Brit Milah*.

apart a child's first and most important relationship: that with the child's mother. But the rite also causes a more direct brutalization of Jewish women.

Many intactivist or non-cutting covenantal Jews affirm that *Brit Milah* gives rise to a vicious Jewish misogyny since men are angry at their mothers for the ceremonial abandonment. This sexism takes the mild but biting form of popular jokes that mock the stereotypical Jewish-American mother and her daughter, the Jewish-American Princess.[14] But some critics, such as Goldman (1998), understand circumcised Jewish misogyny to go much further than sexist, bawdy humor. The rite explains the serious problem of Jewish domestic violence. "It may be," proposes Goldman, "that, from the infant's perspective, while he is having his penis cut, he is experiencing a betrayal by his mother" (p. 64)—a betrayal he later unconsciously avenges through misogynistic rage and a general distrust of women. In turn, women respond with reciprocal suspicion and anger. In this cycle of terror, the rite of *Brit Milah* cuts men and women off from each other, while sustaining and causing male violence toward women.

Nonetheless, the indelible mark of *Brit Milah* ultimately marks men, and not women, for potential death in the event of anti-Jewish violence. The typical martyrology of *Brit Milah* is misconstrued. Jews should not see the rite as inscribing past tragedies into men's bodies. Critics of *Brit Milah* strenuously reject the common rhetorical trope by proponents that Jews should circumcise their sons to honor those Jews who died while upholding the covenant. Rather, Jews should see the rite as branding Jewish men so they are more easily identifiably by their enemies (Pollack, 1997). For all of Judaism's patriarchy, Jewish men are ultimately disposable.[15] Additionally, asserts Hayward (1993), executive director of Men's Rights, Inc., Sacramento, California, *Brit Milah* denies men the same "sovereignty over their bodies that women have long enjoyed," and causes men to voice "the same sense of outrage when their bodies are violated" (p. 12).

Finally, *Brit Milah* can explain Jewish xenophobia. The Walking Stick Foundation is an "educational organization dedicated to the restoration and preservation of aboriginal Jewish spirituality, occasionally sharing events with teachers indigenous to Native American and other earth-honoring traditions" (www.walkingstick.org). In a 1992–1993 issue of the now-defunct newsletter of the Walking Stick Foundation, *Pumbedissa*, a writer called attention to Jewish anger at non-Jews, parents, and even Judaism itself. Often, Jews attribute this anger to their "collective history of oppression." But they are wrong. Rather, Jews are angry from "personal histories of betrayal ... by [their] parents to the *mohel*" (Susskind, 1993).

[14] For a more nuanced account of American Jewish humor and derision toward mothers and daughters, see Prell (2000).

[15] Not incidentally, the men's movement offers the very same argument against medical circumcision. The discarded foreskin, writes Farrell (1993, p. 355), represents the "disposability" of modern men "as soldiers, workers, dads." Keen (1991, pp. 30–31), for example, is bitterly critical of medical circumcision.

In a similar vein, Rothenberg (1989) affirms that, because "people who have been imposed upon are conditioned to impose upon others" (pp. 22–23), *Brit Milah* explains Jewish oppression of the working classes and Israeli oppression of Arabs. Even the internationally celebrated Egyptian feminist and human rights advocate el Saadawi (1999, Introduction) connects "overtaking the land of Palestine and the cutting of boys' foreskins."[16] Of course, all these references to Jews really concern circumcised Jews—that is, Jewish *men*. Here, again, conventional Jewish manhood is construed as a form of brutality that assaults non-Jews, women, infants, and blue-collar workers—as well as Jewish men, women, and children.

What does all this rhetoric against *Brit Milah* say and imply about Jewish manhood? What are the overarching implications of *Brit Milah* for the psyches of Jewish men? There are two overarching trajectories of innuendo. On the one hand, Jewish masculinity appears brutalized—wounded in psyche, deficient in eros, tortured, anxious, slightly paranoid, emotionally stilted, and suspicious of all intimacy. The Jewish man is a lesser man, a damaged man, a man whose severe psychological pains are severely denied by his own parents and people. On the other hand, Jewish masculinity appears brutal. The Jewish man is hyper-masculine, a monster of manhood who views the world through flat affect and wrathful eyes. He directs his anger at everybody—women, mothers, children, non-Jews, even himself. He is cut off from the world and reacts with unsurprising viciousness. Above all else, the average Jewish man is unaware. So dreadfully has *Brit Milah* ruined his psyche that he is unable to access his own tortured, torturing soul.

A Cut of Wholeness

Jewish circumcision has a long history of derision. Greek and Roman satirists, such as Martial and Petronius, delighted in mocking the foreskinless Jewish penis (e.g., Stern, 1974/1984).[17] In the latter first-century ACE, Paul construed circumcision as the fundamental impediment to the globalization of faith in Christ (e.g., Romans 4:9–12; see Boyarin, 1994).[18] The early Church Fathers bested Paul, at least rhetorically, and scoffed at circumcision as a grave theological error and, worse, divine punishment for the betrayal of Christ (e.g., Origen, Homilies on Luke 5:8, mid-3rd century). In the imagination of medieval Christendom, *Brit Milah* served to anchor several anti-Jewish obsessions, including the blood libel and the belief that Jewish men menstruated (Silverman, 2006, pp. 62–68). In England, during the 1753

[16] This statement occurs in el Saadawi's (who is not, I should add, Muslim) "Introduction" to the Arabic edition of a scholarly and widely-hailed yet at times ludicrously anti-Jewish book by Aldeeb Abu-Sahlieh (1999).

[17] The classic source for ancient writers on the Jews is Stern (1974/1984), *Greek and Latin Authors on Jews and Judaism.*

[18] No mention of Paul on circumcision and the Jews can fail to cite, and read carefully, Boyarin's (1994) masterful *A Radical Jew: Paul and the Politics of Identity.*

tumult over the "Jew Bill" or Jewish Naturalization Act, opponents vilified Jews as the clippers of coins and not just penises (Wolper, 1983). Throughout European history, non-Jews attached a knife to Jewish manhood—a blade that either armed the Jew as aggressively dangerous or unmanned him as dangerously effeminate.

To all this scorn, the classic rabbis, especially in *midrashim*, offered many responses. I want here to mention some common rejoinders. First, the rabbis steadfastly rejected any insinuation that circumcision mutilated Jewish manhood. They did quite the opposite: they saw circumcision as a means of shaping masculine *wholeness* (see Silverman, 2006, pp. 62–63).[19] The rite ensured moral-bodily perfection, refined nature, and domesticated man's innate wildness. After all, God introduced Abraham to the covenant of circumcision by inviting the patriarch to "walk in my ways, and be blameless [*tamim*]," a word that also means whole and perfect (Genesis 17:1). In effect, the rite *created* masculinity. The rabbis were no Rousseauists. They had little nostalgia for the natural, foreskinned state of man.

A second rabbinic defense of circumcision arose within Kabbalah. The Jewish mystics understood *Brit Milah* to bring about an intimate union between men and God. The rite cut away an excrescence that barred manhood from the divinity. *Brit Milah* was a wedding between man and God (Boyarin, 1994, pp. 128-129).[20] What's more, the mark of circumcision literally inscribes the divine name into the male body and so hews masculinity into the *imago dei* (Wolfson, 1987).

Third, the rabbis viewed the act of circumcision as representative of a key ambition of rabbinic masculinity. The *removal* of the foreskin (called *milah*), and the subsequent *peeling back* of the underlying mucous membrane that covers the corona (called *periah*), mirrored the mystic's goal of uncovering the hidden meaning of Torah to gain access to divine revelation (Wolfson, 1994, 2003). From this angle, circumcision molded Jewish men into scholars attuned to the mysteries of God.

The rite also represented the circumscription of manhood within the Law. In Exodus 24, Moses, beneath Mount Sinai, officiated over sacrificial offerings of well-being to the Lord. Moses then read aloud the record of the covenant and dashed the sacrificial blood on the people, saying, "This is the blood of the covenant that the Lord now makes with you concerning all these commands" (Exodus 24:8). The rabbis interpreted Moses's declaration as equating circumcision with *all* the commandments in the Torah (Cohen, 2005, p. 232).[21] Thus construed, *Brit Milah* shapes Jewish men into law-abiding citizens—especially, as I now show, in matters of sexuality.

Last, the rabbis understood *Brit Milah* to offer erotic restraint. Opponents of circumcision often set the rite against erotic joy. But even a cursory exploration of classic rabbinic texts reveals the naiveté of this claim. The rabbis not only endorsed matrimonial sexuality, they *mandated* it. Indeed, the rabbis interpreted Exodus 21:10

[19] The connection of circumcision with moral and somatic wholeness occurs in numerous *midrashim* (e.g., *Genesis Rabbah* 46:3).

[20] See also, for example, *Numbers Rabbah* 12:8.

[21] See also, for example, M. Shabbat 19:3.

as a divine decree that required husbands *regularly* to pleasure their wives.[22] Moreover, the erotic tones of Kabalistic discourse, especially concerning the circumcisional intimacy between man and God, *clearly* undermine any suggestion that rabbinic culture preserved *Brit Milah* in order to cut off erotic delight from masculine experience.

Circumcision foes often cite the great 12th century philosopher Rabbi Moses ben Maimon, better known as Maimonides, as the authoritative voice for Judaism in regard to the real intent of *Brit Milah*. Maimonides offered several justifications for circumcision. Perhaps most controversial is his statement that the rite weakens, or diminishes, the erotic drive of men—and also constrains female lust since it "is hard for a woman with whom an uncircumcised man has had sexual intercourse to separate from him" (Maimonides, 1963). I have no desire to endorse Maimonides on this point. But it seems somewhat clear that he defended circumcision as a curtailment of "violent concupiscence," to use his phrase, and *not* as a means to celibacy or renunciation. Moreover, his plea for erotic moderation takes root not in Jewish theology or culture but in Hellenistic philosophy, especially Platonic idealism. Maimonides, moreover, does not univocally speak for Judaism; his is not the sole official voice. He speaks as a Jew from a particular philosophical orientation.[23] Still, it is clear that the rabbinic tradition understood *Brit Milah* to restrain masculine lust—and female desire—while nonetheless preparing Jewish men for reproduction.

In summation, the rabbis understood *Brit Milah* to create a particular kind of man. Circumcision perfected Jewish manhood both morally and bodily. The rite, too, represented several goals of rabbinic masculinity: scholarly erudition, intimate union with God, sexual restraint, and the siring of sons.

Devout Jews today, as in the past, generally abide by *Brit Milah* on the basis of faith and biblical conviction. For them, the rite is a divine commandment—perhaps the signal commandment of monotheism. But most contemporary Jews who uphold the rite do so through more diffuse appeals to religious authority—say, a general commitment to the covenant while rejecting the everyday strictures of Orthodoxy (the very rules that Orthodox Jews believe the covenant entails). Many Jews today also typically connect circumcision to fuzzy notions of hygiene, aesthetics, conformity, and father-son identification. For them, the force of the rite is largely emotional, not cosmological. They see *Brit Milah* as sanctifying new life, commemorating tradition, and renewing community. The ceremony defies tyrants past and present. It acknowledges the weight of history. And *Brit Milah* indelibly etches a Jewish identity into the body of a baby boy.

But some contemporary supporters of *Brit Milah* also call attention specifically to masculinity. They see the rite, as did the classic rabbis many centuries ago, as creating not just a male Jew but a particular kind of man. For example, the rite carves a

[22] See M. Ketubot 5:6; B. Ketubot 61b.

[23] Philo, in *On the Special Laws* 1:1-11, anticipated Maimonides's argument for circumcision.

sense of communal and covenantal obligation into the boy (Roth, 1992), and symbolizes the Jewish ethos of self-sacrifice (Kletenik, 1998). In other words, the mark of circumcision serves to remind the Jewish boy—and, later, the Jewish man—that he inherits responsibilities neither of his own making nor his own choosing. The rite affirms the male Jew's obligations to his community and makes the community responsible for his masculine identity. The rite shows that the boy is needed for something grander than either himself or his immediate family (Cohen, 1998; Gordis, 1998; Landes & Robbin, 1990; Levenson, 2000; Neusner, 1987). It imbues Jewish manhood with significance that expands beyond the romantic images of individual desire.[24] Because the community has bestowed on him a Jewish identity that he cannot erase, the Jew must assume an obligation to the community. In this way, *Brit Milah* contains manhood within a moral framework.

Opponents of circumcision perceive the rite as terribly violating a cherished premise of modernity, namely, the inalienable right of each person to freely choose his or her religious affiliation and bodily shape. Individuals alone, in the absence of coercion, should define themselves by shopping, in a sense, in the marketplace of ethnicity. Advocates of the rite agree. *Brit Milah* does breach this modernist assumption of personhood. But the rite does so precisely to craft a form of manhood that expressly opposes, or at least constrains, the modern ideologies of individualism and the self-made man—a man who, more often than not, mainly pursues material expressions of superficial self-interest (Kimmel, 1997).[25] The *Brit Milah* ceremony—precisely because it imposes an identity onto the child rather than asks the child later to choose his own identity—enfolds manhood within a tradition and a historical community.

Sokobin (1976), a rabbi, tells that the bodily location of *Brit Milah* effectively domesticates male sexuality and thwarts masculine hubris. How? By reminding men that God, not man, is the ultimate creator of life and by intimately uniting man with the Creator.[26] The location of the covenantal sign also represents a key choice for the Jewish man: he can use this organ for "a life of debauchery or—if he pays close attention to the deeper meaning of the sign—to a life of procreative holiness" (Kletenik, 1998, p. 59). The implication here is clear: *Brit Milah* shapes Jewish men into better, more ethical men. To cut to the chase, they will use their penises wisely.

A brief essay by Landes and Robbin (1990) elaborates on this ethical vision. The physical placement of *Brit Milah* carves a moral boundary, or "fence" to use a rabbinic concept, around the natural proclivities of men. The rite transforms intercourse between Jewish men and non-Jewish women from sexuality into a covenantal viola-

---

[24] The rite imbues birth, as a biological affair, with profound social significance. Similarly, the ceremony resists the modern ideal of family privacy.

[25] For the history of the self-made man in America, see Kimmel (1997).

[26] When I write here and elsewhere in this essay with a masculine phrasing, it is not to universalize manhood and so erase women but to intentionally convey a particular gendered nuance that seems appropriate to the underlying meaning of the ceremony.

tion. The rite, too, thwarts the very modern principle that erotic desire is the prerogative of individuals—and thus positions Jewish men outside the Enlightenment tradition and its valuation of individual will and free-choice. *Brit Milah* converts male sexuality from a private, personal affair into a public, communal obligation.

Likewise, the performance of the ceremony encloses mother and son within an intergenerational group of friends, kin, and religious leaders. Rather than seeing *Brit Milah* as brutally shattering the mother-child bond and so wounding women and men, the rite incorporates motherhood and nascent masculinity within a loving community. The ceremony enmeshes parents and child in a network of enduring social ties. In effect, the rite resists the very individualism that opponents endorse. It creates a sense of communal manhood in which the message is precisely that one is *not* his own man and his penis is *not* his alone. Rather, a man is part of a community in which, like it or not, his masculinity is everybody's responsibility—just like his responsibility is to reproduce the moral order of the community. As anthropologists would put it, the rite carves a sense of sociocentric identity into the boy, thus preventing him from later embracing a wholly egocentric mode of personal identity. It is, from this angle, a tribal rite that resists the ideology of individualism.

Through circumcision, the masculine self becomes permanently plural. Jewish manhood is defined from the start, but it is not defined in terms of loss and longing, as critics contend, but in terms of "belonging" (Raul-Friedman, 1993, p. 33). And through the bestowal of a name during the ceremony, manhood is connected to a long heritage, thereby tethering masculine individualism to a communal identity.

Landes and Robbin (1990) construe *Brit Milah* as a bodily protest against the natural propensity of men to succumb to carnal desire and, worse, to exercise sexual violence against women. The rite "affirms the value of sexuality through restraint" (Landes & Robbin) and thereby hampers phallic aggression. This way, Brit Milah "seeks to set both women and men free from all bondage" (Landes & Robbin)

In this view, *Brit Milah* emancipates men from their own masculine desires. Critics argue that circumcision assaults free choice and thus denies men their autonomy. But Landes and Robbin (1990) turn this argument to claim that *Brit Milah* liberates men from their animalistic urges so they can pursue meaningful, moral endeavors. They can expand the definition of manhood beyond brute phallic power and sexual conquest. For conservative Jews, such as Levenson (2000), the expansion or constriction of masculinity represented by circumcision includes "the sanctity of marriage" as well as the "traditional virtues of sacrifice, discipline, and obedience" (p. 36).

The political left and right disagree on what precise merits circumcision inscribes in men, but they both agree that *Brit Milah* creates or stands for masculine virtue. And both views understand the rite through an egalitarian lens. By trimming away dangerous masculine desires and self-delusions of phallic potency, *Brit Milah* enhances trust between men and women. The rite does not glorify phallic potency and submerge women within an enduring, muting misogyny. Rather, circumcision protects Jewish men and women from the dangers of an unfettered, raw, natural masculinity. That is, the rite shapes Jewish men into a kinder, gentler manhood.

Some Jews, as discussed, denounce ritual circumcision as an unjustifiable infliction of agony onto a helpless infant in violation of Jewish ethics and basic human rights. Why do Jewish fathers tolerate the intentional infliction of pain onto their sons? What sorts of defense mechanisms permit this torture (Hezbrun, 1991)? What, in short, is wrong with Jewish men? The answer, of course, is psychological: normative Jewish manhood presupposes a wounded psyche—an otherwise normal personality destroyed, and in turn destroying, by circumcision.

Advocates of the rite do admit to the pain, but they seek to harness this pain to moral purposes. The sting of *Brit Milah* expresses tough love and, furthermore, "most pain leads to growth" (Kletenik, 1998, p. 59). Far from wounding boys, *Brit Milah* is simply one of many painful events characteristic of childhood through which parents soothingly guide their sons. The rite thereby strengthens, not dilutes, parental bonds (Kletenik, 1998). The ceremony does *not* celebrate a hard, cruel, affectless version of manhood. Instead, it teaches boys from the beginning to work through their pain together with a loving family and community. The trials of manhood are not yours to suffer alone.

In its biblical setting, Israelite circumcision resembled male initiation ceremonies in Melanesia (see Silverman 2001. Both rites defined masculinity against—yet in terms of—motherhood. The ceremonies detached youthful masculinity from femininity by gifting men religious significance not bestowed onto women. But the ceremonies also celebrated male reproduction by symbolically connecting men to a bloody menstrual and parturient fecundity that, when associated with women, was cast as polluting. Circumcision thus transformed Israelite men into mothers while denying that identification, lest men admit to themselves and, worse, to women, the primacy of female fertility (Kletenik, 1998).

One of the central figures in the Jewish Renewal movement, Rabbi Waskow (1984), tacitly recognizes the validity of this post-Freudian interpretation. Anthropologically, however, he erroneously romanticizes the masculine emulation of female fertility that is so pervasive in many premodern, or pre-state, tribal societies—and in Judaism. But the contours of his argument mandate some consideration. Waskow argues that certain categories of men—priests, rabbis, monks, and mystics—pursued psychological wholeness by nurturing the community and ritually experiencing feminine mystery. In other words, male leaders sustained their authoritative positions by experiencing and expressing femininity. Waskow offers the same analysis for *Brit Milah*: "This moment of intense physical and emotional connection binds the father to his son in a way analogous to the mother's physical and emotional connection through the birth canal." The father appears poised to murder his son but instead becomes "motherly" and hallows the boy's genitals, thus "nurturing the cycle of the generations." The rite also removes the "tough outer casing" of the boy's genitals in order symbolically to make him "more vulnerable, more open, more 'womanly.'" The menstrual imagery of the rite only enhances this ritual transformation.

For politically conservative proponents of *Brit Milah*, such as Levenson (2000), the rite restores and defends traditional gender roles and the separation of male and female. But for Waskow (1984), *Brit Milah* transcends normative gender through ritual androgyny. The rite emulates women so men can access their otherwise suppressed abilities to nurture the community. Circumcised Jews are not brutal patriarchs who dominate others but tender figures of masculo-feminine empathy and care.

Rabbi Zaslow (2003) similarly sees *Brit Milah* as fostering empathetic fatherhood, thus transforming men into nurturers (see also Kozberg, 1984). The rite is "the once in a lifetime chance for the souls of father and son to bond in the deepest way imaginable" (Zaslow 2003, p. 196). When Zaslow administers over the rite, he counsels "the dads to hold the hands of their sons, and to whisper blessings of love to them" (p. 196). He implores fathers to carry the pain of their sons and to weep "for all the pain their sons will experience in their lives" (p. 196). For him, then, *Brit Milah* engenders male love and compassion. The ceremony also attaches this sense of generative fatherhood to femininity because "our mothers, sisters, wives and daughters experience the awesome spiritual bonding power of blood every month" (p. 196). Men can do so only during circumcision.

Jews commonly see circumcision, as well as the near-sacrifice of Isaac by Abraham, called the *Akedah* in Hebrew, as a defining moment in human history that also demonstrates the compassion of Judaism. When fathers in other ancient cultures still "killed their firstborn sons as a sacrifice to a bloodthirsty deity" (Meyer, 1992, p. 45), Jews (or Israelites) were guided by God and their own keen moral compass to offer a substitute: animals and foreskins. Of course, this argument is simply run-of-the-mill ethnocentrism. All cultures tend to create their collective self-worth by exaggerating the savagery of their neighbors.

But several recent commentators on *Brit Milah* also take this argument in a different direction—particularly two rabbis who circumcised their very own sons. The first rabbi, Meyer (1992), highlights the fact that fathers and *mohels* do not, despite the knife, kill Jewish sons. *Brit Milah*, then, mobilizes the tension, anxiety, and potential horror of the rite to the forging of a loving, trusting union between father and son. The second rabbi, Hammerman (1994) understands the rite to transform every Jewish father into a potential murderer. *Brit Milah* is tied to the primal anger unleashed by the sight of another male—in this case, a son—in physical intimacy with one's wife. The rite, too, continues Hammerman, adheres to a primal anxiety elicited when a man confronts his own death in the guise of his son since, in traditional Judaism, a male offspring is called one's *kaddish*—the person who will recite memorial prayers over one's grave. The father envies his son, yet fears his own death. But then Hammerman tells of gazing into the trusting eyes of his son as he cut the foreskin:

> I finally understood that the knife transforms the father … into a shield. The breast provides, but the knife protects. It channels a father's natural anger and

> jealously into one controlled but he takes off one small part in order to preserve—and love—the whole. (p. 29)

However cruel *Brit Milah*, the rite nonetheless accomplishes two redemptive tasks. First, it allows the father ritually to act on aggressive emotions he would otherwise be loath to admit, never mind express. Second, *Brit Milah* arouses a passionate desire to never again allow those emotions to potentially harm the child: "For it is from the father's hand," writes Hammerman (1994, p. 29), "that Abraham's knife dangles, every moment of every day." A instant of brutality, in other words, affords Jewish men a rare yet therapeutic glimpse into the dark side of manhood that immediately transforms them into loving, protective fathers.

In a complex but fascinating essay, Boyarin and Boyarin (1995) paint a heroic yet kindhearted image of the circumcised Jew. The rite challenges dominant Euro-Christian—ultimately, Hellenistic—bodily notions of natural perfection and unnatural mutilation. Likewise, the rite proudly allows Jews, as I hinted earlier, to push against the homogenizing, theologically foreskinned, universal spread of Christianity. Finally, as I also stated earlier, the rite opposes the very American ideal of the self-made man. In each instance, *Brit Milah* creates a sense of Jewish manhood that resists hegemony. Jewish men thus stand for all ethnic groups that celebrate difference against the wider, pervasive forces of mute conformity. Jewish men, since the rise of Christianity, can point to their circumcised penises as the original emblem of multiculturalism.

But the Jewish penis, for all of its resistance, does not—and should not—shape Jewish men into martial men. Christendom often defined the circumcised Jew as grotesquely monstrous—or as grotesquely emasculated, a wimp, virtually castrated, lacking full phallic puissance, and so barred by his own chosen effeminacy from the warrior ideal of European manhood. In late 19th-century Vienna, in fact, the clitoris was dubbed "the Jew" (Gilman, 1993, p. 39). A masturbating woman was "playing the Jew." Circumcision, in this sense, created not an alternative form of manhood but simply an illegitimate one. The Jew was negatively feminized.

This caricature is not entirely wrong, as Boyarin (1997) recognizes; it is only misguided. Within Jewish culture, circumcision *did* feminize Jews, at least in comparison to the wider society. But the feminine infliction of manhood *within* Judaism nonetheless constituted a *legitimate* form of masculinity, one in which Jewish men clearly succeeded at the two endeavors that the wider Euro-Christian society coded as quintessentially male: attracting women and siring sons. Circumcision was *not* castrative in rabbinic culture because masculinity was *not* defined in terms of phallic aggression. Rabbinic culture inverted Euro-Christian norms but still favored men. The rite (to use Boyarin's felicitous phrase) is counter-phallic. It celebrates manhood over femininity, but it does so not through the exercise of aggressive power. Rather, *Brit Milah* privileges men because they remain men (at least within Judaism) as well as a type of woman.

Most proponents of *Brit Milah*, when thinking about manhood, see the rite as shaping Jewish men into better men—into loving, nurturing, caring, compassionate, sexually restrained men. Circumcised men are better fathers and better husbands who, moreover, resist hegemony by standing up for the right and duty to be different—but they stand, however heroically, with an ennobled pacifism.

A Return to Comedy

Despite the counter-phallic inflection of *Brit Milah*, many Jews today internalize a phallic ideal of masculinity and see circumcision as a mark of ambivalent or lesser manhood.[27] Gilman (1991, p. 29) offers a wonderful example of this ambivalence. After the cancellation of Jackie Mason's short-lived 1989 television show, "Chicken Soup," Mason commented to the effect: "Well, at least Americans now know what a Jew looks like." To this, a columnist in *Gentlemen's Quaterly* (Merkin, 1991) replied, "If Jackie Mason is even remotely like a typical Jew, then I'm in the market for a used foreskin in a medium—um, make that a medium large."

Jackie Mason, of course, exemplified one stereotypical image of the male Jewish body. Woody Allen does likewise and, indeed, plays the role fittingly in his 1977 comedy *Annie Hall*, where, in the guise of Alvie Singer, Allen obsesses about foreskins and anti-Semitism. Jackie Mason is apparently more comfortable with his circumcision. But Merkin evidently is not, as Gilman (1991) brilliantly recognizes. Merkin responded to his anxiety by voicing, in response to Jackie Mason, a fantasy for a longer, more powerful, seemingly non-Jewish phallus.

Some Jewish proponents of circumcision believe that the rite creates a docile form of manhood. Opponents of the rite reject this argument, yet they subscribe to the very same logic when asserting that circumcision creates a hostile Jew. Clearly, the adult imagination about circumcision is equally as powerful, dare I say it, as the infant's experience of the rite. It will surely be more enduring.

References

Bigelow, J. (1994). *The joy of uncircumcising!: Exploring circumcision: History, myths, psychology, restoration, sexual pleasure, and human rights.* Aptos, CA: Hourglass Book Publisher.

Boyarin, D. (1994). *A radical Jew: Paul and the politics of identity.* Berkeley: University of California Press.

Boyarin, D. (1997). *Unheroic conduct: The rise of heterosexuality and the invention of the Jewish man.* Berkeley: University of California Press.

[27] Many contemporary theorists offer a similar explanation for the martial stance of Jewish manhood celebrated by Zionism and the state of Israel (see Boyarin, 1997) and Breines (1990). For a different take on Jewish aggressiveness, especially as evidenced by 20th century Jewish-American male literature, see Rosenberg (2001).

Boyarin, J, & Boyarin, D. (1995). Self-exposure as theory: The double-mark of the male Jew. In D. Battaglia (Ed.), *Rhetorics of self-making* (pp. 6–42). Berkeley: University of California Press.

Boyle, G. J., Goldman, R., Svoboda, J.S., & Fernandez, E. (2002). Male circumcision: Pain, trauma and psychosexual sequelae. *Journal of Health Psychology, 7*, 329–343.

Breines, P. (1990). *Tough Jews: Political fantasies and the moral dilemma of American Jewry*. New York: Basic Books.

Brown, S.G.A. (1896–1897). The Mosaic rite of circumcision: A plea for its performance during childhood. *Journal of the Orificial Society, 5*, 299–304.

Cohen, R.A. (1998). Bris mila, desire and Levinas. *SHOFAR, 16*, 63–70.

Cohen, S.J.D. (2005). *Why aren't Jewish women circumcised?: Gender and covenant in Judaism*. Berkeley: University of California Press.

Darby, R. (2005). *A surgical temptation: The demonization of the foreskin and the rise of circumcision in Britain*. Chicago: University of Chicago Press.

Diamond, J. (1994). *The warrior's journey home: Healing men, healing the planet*. Oakland, CA: New Harbinger Publications.

Efron, J.M. (2001). *Medicine and the German Jews: A history*. New Haven: Yale University Press.

Farrell, W. (1993). *The myth of male power: Why men are the disposable sex*. New York: Simon & Schuster.

Fleiss, P.M., & Hodges, F.M. (2002). *What your doctor may not tell you about circumcision: Untold facts on America's most widely performed—and most unnecessary—surgery*. New York: Warner Books.

Gilman, S.L. (1991). *The Jew's body*. New York: Routledge.

Gilman, S.L. (1993). Mark Twain and the disease of the Jews. *American Literature, 65*(1), 95-116.

Gilman, S.L. (1995). *Freud, race, and gender*. Princeton, NJ: Princeton University Press.

Glick, L.B. (2005). *Marked in your flesh: Circumcision from ancient Judea to modern America*. Oxford: Oxford University Press.

Goldman, R. (1997). *Circumcision: The hidden trauma*. Boston: Vanguard.

Goldman, R. (1998). *Questioning circumcision: A Jewish perspective*. Boston: Vanguard.

Goldman, R. (2004). The growing Jewish circumcision debate: A psychosocial critique. In G.C. Denniston, F.M. Hodges, & M.F. Milos (Eds.), *Flesh and blood: Perspectives on the problem of circumcision in contemporary society* (pp. 171–194). New York: Kluwer Academic/Plenum.

Gollaher, D.L. (2000). *Circumcision: A history of the world's most controversial surgery*. New York: Basic Books.

Goodman, J. (1999a). Open Letter to Fourth International Symposium on Sexual Mutilations, Lausanne, Switzerland, August, 1996. In: Syllabus of Abtracts. Reproduced online at http://www.cirp.org/pages/cultural/goodman.html

Goodman, J. (1999b). A Jewish perspective on circumcision. In G.C. Denniston, F.M. Hodges, & M.F. Milos (Eds.), *Male and female circumcision: Medical, legal, and ethical considerations in pediatric practice* (pp. 179–182). New York: Kluwer Academic/Plenum Publishers.

Gordis, D.H. (1998). The power of ritual. Response to Dr. Ronald Goldman's "Circumcision: A Source of Jewish Pain." *Jewish Spectator, 62*, 61–62.

Hammerman, J.J. (1994, March 13). Birth rite. *The New York Times Magazine*, 28–29.

Hammond, T. (1999). A preliminary poll of men circumcised in infancy or childhood. *British Journal of Urology International, 83*, 85–92.

Hayward, F. (1993, April). A kinder, more genital nation. *Jewish Spectator*, 9–15. Reprinted online at http://www.noharmm.org/kinder.htm

Herzbrun, M.B. (1991). Circumcision: The pain of the fathers. *CCAR Journal, 38*, 1–13.

Hill, G. (2007). The case against circumcision. *Journal of Men's Health and Gender, 4*, 318–323.

Hirschfield, J. (1858). The Jewish circumcision before a medical tribunal. *American Medical Monthly, 9*, 272-275.

Jews Against Circumcison. http://www.jewsagainstcircumcision.org/

Judd, R. (2007). *Contested rituals: Circumcision, kosher butchering, and Jewish political life in Germany, 1843–1933*. Ithaca: Cornell University Press.

Karsenty, N. (1988, Summer). A mother questions brit milla. *Humanistic Judaism 16*, 14–21.

Katz, D.S. (1999). Shylock's gender: Jewish male menstruation in early modern England. *Review of English Studies, 50*, 440–62.

Keen, S. (1991). *Fire in the belly*. New York: Bantam.

Kimmel, M.S. (1997). *Manhood in America: A cultural history*. New York: Free Press.

Kimmel, M.S. (2001). The kindest un-cut. *Tikkun, 16*, 43–48.

Kletenik, R.P. (1998). It's Brit Milah, not circumcision: Response to Dr. Ronald Goldman's "Circumcision: A source of Jewish pain." *Jewish Spectator, 62*, 59.

Kozberg, C.D. (1984). A father performs a berit milah. *Journal for Reform Judaism, 31*, 3–9.

Landes, D., & Robbin, S. (1990). Grateful pain. *Tikkun, 5*, 72–74.

Levenson, J.D. (2000). The new enemies of circumcision. *Commentary, 109*, 29–36.

Lungstrum, J. (1998). Foreskin fetishism: Jewish male difference in *Europa, Europa*. *Screen, 39*, 53–66.

Maimonides. (1963). *The guide of the perplexed* (S. Pines, Trans.). Chicago: University of Chicago Press.

Margalit, O., & Tziraki-Segal, C. (2006). Circumcision: Man's obligation and woman's praxis. *Nashim, 12*, 10–38.

Merkin, R. (1991, February). The bad and the beautiful. *Gentleman's Quarterly*, p. 66.

Meyer, D.J. (1992). Doing it myself. *Moment, 17*, 45.

Moss, L.B. (1990). Circumcision decision. A painful case. *Tikkun, 5*, 70–72.

Neusner, J. (1987). The rite of circumcision: The "others" who come to celebrate. In *The enchantments of Judaism: Rites of transformation from birth through death* (Chap. 3). New York: Basic Books.

Pollack, M. (1995). Circumcision: A Jewish feminist perspective. In K. Weiner & A. Moon, (Eds.), *Jewish women speak out: Expanding the boundaries of psychology* (pp. 171–187). Seattle: Canopy Press.

Pollack, M. (1997). Redefining the sacred. In G.C. Denniston & M.F. Milos (Eds.), *Sexual mutilations: A human tragedy* (pp. 163–173). New York: Plenum.

Prell, R-E. (2000). *Fighting to become Americans: Assimilation and the trouble between Jewish women and Jewish men*. Boston: Beacon Press.

Raul-Friedman, E. (1993). A rebuttal—Circumcision: A Jewish legacy. *Midstream, 38*(4), 31–33.

Rhinehart, J. (1999). Neonatal circumcision reconsidered. *Transactional Analysis Journal, 29*, 215–221.

Rosenberg, W. (2001). *Legacy of rage: Jewish masculinity, violence, and culture*. Amherst: University of Massachusetts Press.

Roth, J. (1992). The meaning for today. *Moment, 17*, 41–44.

Rothenberg, M. (1989). Being rational about circumcision and Jewish observance. *M.E.N.*, 4, 22–23. Accessed online at http://www.noharmm.org/rationaljew.htm

el Saadawi, N. (1999). Introduction. In S. Aldeeb Abu-Sahlieh's *Male and female circumcision in the Jewish, Christian, and Muslim communities* (M. Sarkis, trans; ed by E. Tennis). online at http://www.fgmnetwork.org/authors/samialdeeb/nawal.html

Sandel, M. (1996). Brit Milah: An inscription of social power. *The Reconstructionist, 61*, 49–58.

Shapiro, J. (1996). *Shakespeare and the Jews*. New York: Columbia University Press.

Silverman, E.K. (2004). Anthropology and circumcision. *Annual Review of Anthropology, 33*, 419–445.

Silverman, E.K. (2006). *From Abraham to America: A history of Jewish circumcision*. Lanham: Rowman & Littlefield.

Silverman, E.K. (2001). *Masculinity, motherhood, and mockery: Psychoanalyzing culture and the Iatmul Naven rite in New Guinea*. Ann Arbor: University of Michigan Press.

Sokobin, A.M. (1976). A belated response to a responsum on circumcision. *CCAR Journal*, 67–72.

Stern, J. (1993). Maimonides on the covenant of circumcision and the unity of God. In M.A. Fishbane (Eds.), *The Midrashic imagination: Jewish exegesis, thought, and history* (pp. 131–154). Albany: SUNY Press.

Stern, M. (1984). *Greek and Latin authors on Jews and Judaism* (Volumes 1–3; Edited with Introductions, Translations, and Commentary). Jerusalem: The Israel Academy of Sciences and Humanities. (Original work published 1974)

Susskind, J. (1992-1993). A discussion of circumcision. *Pumbedissa* (Newsletter of the Walking Stick Foundation), *1*(5). Accessed online sometime during 1993–1994 at www.walking-stick.org

Traiman, L. (1994). My story of ritual abuse. NOHARMM Progress Report 3. Reprinted online at http://www.noharmm.org/mystory.htm

Waskow, A. (1984). The Bible's sleeping beauty and her great-granddaughters. *Tikkun, 4*, 39–41, 125–128. Reproduced online at http://www.theshalomcenter.org/node/577

Wolfson, E.R. (1987). Circumcision and the divine name: A study in the transmission of esoteric doctrine. *The Jewish Quarterly Review, 78*, 77–112.

Wolfson, E.R. (1994). *Through a speculum that shines: Vision and imagination in medieval Jewish mysticism*. Princeton: Princeton University Press.

Wolfson, E.R. (2003). Circumcision, secrecy, and the veiling of the veil: Phallomorphic exposure and kabbalistic esotericism. In E.W. Mark (Ed.), *The covenant of circumcision: New perspectives on an ancient Jewish rite* (pp. 58–70). Hanover: Brandies University Press.

Wolper, R.S. (1983). *Pieces on the "Jew Bill" (1753)*. The Augustan reprint society, publication No. 217. Los Angeles: William Andrews Clark Memorial Library, University of California.

Zaslow, D. (2003). A covenant above reason. In E.W. Mark (Ed.), *The covenant of circumcision: New perspectives on an ancient Jewish rite* (pp. 94–96). Hanover: Brandies University Press.

3

Not-So-Nice Jewish Boys: Notes on Violence and the Construction of Jewish-American Masculinity in the Late 20th and early 21st Centuries

Jackson Katz[28]

Every Saturday morning before my high school football games, our team would meet at the local Catholic Church, St. John the Evangelist, where the monsignor would give us a talk about life, manhood, and football. I don't remember much about what the grandfatherly Irish-American priest actually told us back in the late 1970s, but I do remember the discomfort I felt every week when I walked up the aisle to the first four or five rows of pews where all the guys gathered. It was at that moment when, as one of only a handful of Jews on the team, I was forced to announce my Jewishness publicly. Most of my teammates and coaches were Catholic, and they invariably kneeled as they entered the pews. I wanted to fit in with my fellow football players, but there was no way I was going to make that gesture under their watchful eyes in a sacred space that felt both foreign and vaguely threatening. Still, as one of the best players and a team leader, I felt exposed and self-conscious about thus declaring my outsider status.

Being Jewish coded me not only as "other," but also potentially raised questions about my masculinity. In my hometown just north of Boston, as elsewhere in the United States, I was more than aware of the prevailing stereotypes about middle-class Jewish boys (and girls) in the post-war era, i.e. that we were pampered and entitled, academically strong but physically weak. As an outwardly confident but covertly anxious adolescent, I wanted nothing more than for my friends, their parents and others in the community to accept and respect me, both for my intellectual abilities and as a three-sport varsity athlete. Most of all, I coveted the respect I would gain—especially among non-Jews—if I could prove on the football field that I was as tough as the Irish and Italian boys whose families ruled in my small-town suburban "jockocracy." Academic accomplishment was valued in my family, in the local Jewish community, and in our school system as a whole. But before my own bar mitzvah and long before I even knew the meaning of the word *assimilation*, I had learned that the quickest way to popularity in the larger culture was to prove myself not in the classroom but in violent physical competition with other boys.

This essay is about the complex and conflicted role that violence has played in my life as well as more generally in the construction of late 20th and early 21st century Jewish-American (*Ashkenazic*) masculinity. It is an attempt to draw from and build on important foundational work in this area in the past couple of decades. Several pieces

[28] Thanks to Mark Mlawer for input and assistance in this essay.

in Brod's (1988) groundbreaking collection *A Mensch Among Men* included discussions about violence done both to and by Jewish men. Breines's (1990) study *Tough Jews* outlined three major developments that helped shape 20th-century Jewish-American masculinity: the development of Zionism as a nationalist ideology in the late 19th century, the Holocaust, and the Six-Day War. Violence is a central theme in each of these momentous events, both as a material reality and in its symbolic importance to Jewish-American manhood. Talmudic scholar Daniel Boyarin's (1997) *Unheroic Conduct* was an attempt to uncover the roots of nonviolent masculinity as a Jewish ideal, one deeply rooted in ancient and more recent Jewish texts. And Rosenberg's (2001) literary study *A Legacy of Rage* examined the Biblical sources of Jewish masculine violence and featured a detailed discussion of the role of violence in the work of several mid-to-late 20th-century mostly Jewish-American male writers, including Norman Mailer, David Mamet, and Tony Kushner.

These studies of Jewish masculinity have been part of an outpouring of scholarship—and to some extent popular discussion—over the past two decades about various aspects of multicultural masculinities. This work has contributed to the long-term feminist project of putting the intersectionality of gender and ethnicity/race under a critical spotlight, not only by focusing on women's lives but also by applying a critical gendered lens to men's lives. The purpose is not to push women aside and put men back on center stage but to understand better how masculinity is constructed within various ethnic, racial, and religious minorities. The special promise of this work is that it can inform efforts to resist ethnic/racial/religious oppression at the same time that it contributes to the process of breaking down gender and sexual inequality within minority groups. R.W. Connell's concept of hegemonic and subordinated masculinities provides a useful framework toward this end. Simply stated, Connell maintained that, within a given society at a given moment in history, there is an idealized and dominant (hegemonic) form of masculinity, which in our culture is White, Christian, middle- and upper-class, and heterosexual, and is further characterized as aggressive and competitive. There are also, at any given time, a series of subordinated masculinities, all competing with each other and vying for social position vis-à-vis the hegemonic masculinity. In our society these include ethnic, racial, and religious minorities and poor and working-class men as well as gay and bisexual men and others.

The usefulness of this sociological framework is that it gives us a way to think about Jewish-American masculinity and its relation to violence from the point of view of a minority culture (the Jewish people) that has been and continues to be profoundly influenced by the dominant American culture, which it in turn helps to shape. Numerous questions about Jewish men and violence arise from this dialectic, some of which have long been the subject of academic inquiry and others of which have arisen more recently: To what extent is violent masculinity an ancient part of the Jewish tradition, and which features of contemporary Jewish- American men's violence owe more to the influence of American notions of manhood? What, if anything, can be considered "Jewish" about men's violence and men's responses to it?

What, if anything, can be considered "American" about the same topics? How do various Jewish religious traditions differ from each other in their interpretations of Jewish law and custom when it comes to violence, and how do those interpretations compare and contrast with those from Christian, Islamic, Buddhist, and Hindu traditions? What are some of the differences and similarities between secular and religious Jewish men and how they regard violent perpetration and victimization? *Ashkenazim* and *Sephardim*? When Jewish men physically abuse their Jewish wives, is it because they have taken on some of the unpleasant characteristics of the larger Gentile culture? Or are they better understood as contemporary representatives of a long-standing problem in Jewish culture, which has only come to public light in recent years because of the bold leadership of Jewish women in the battered women's movement? To what extent has historical Jewish victimization, and the profound 20th century trauma of the Holocaust, played a role in some Jewish men's (and women's) identification with projections of American and Israeli military power? In what ways have the Jewish people's historical and contemporary experiences with violence—in Europe, the Middle East, and the United States—contributed to the emergence, in recent decades, of American-Jewish conservatism? In the decades after the Six Day War in 1967, what sorts of influences has Israeli-Jewish masculinity had on American-Jewish masculinity, both in a personal and a political sense? What have been the effects on ideas about Jewish masculinity of the gay liberation and civil rights movements, especially when you consider that American Jews have played central and often highly visible roles in those movements? On a related note, why have Jewish men (and women) been overrepresented for many years in the leadership of organized efforts to oppose men's violence, including various antiwar movements as well as the ongoing struggle to reduce men's violence against women and children? Have these Jews been drawing on, as *Tikkun* editor Rabbi Michael Lerner and others have argued, something exemplary in the Jewish cultural tradition? Looking forward, what are some of the ways that violence in its many forms will continue to impact Jewish people in the United States and around the world, and what in Jewish traditions past, present, and future can be mobilized to respond to and counteract it?

What follows are a series of vignettes and recollections through which I hope to draw out and personalize some of the themes raised by these sorts of questions. But as the breadth and depth of the aforementioned questions make clear, this discussion is intended merely to suggest directions for further research, study, and autobiographical works in these areas, rather than to reach any definitive conclusions about the critical place of violence in contemporary Jewish-American masculinity.

Hypermasculinity as a Response to Victimization

As long as I can remember, and perhaps like most members of my species, I have had ambivalent feelings about violence. One of my earliest memories of the world beyond my relatively sheltered suburban enclave is reading media accounts of the My Lai Massacre in Vietnam. As a nine-year-old boy in 1969, I read *Time* magazine with revulsion and morbid fascination about the slaughter of innocent Vietnamese women, children, and elderly men by American soldiers. Just a year or two before at Jewish summer camp, I had seen one of those classic black and white newsreel films about the liberation of the death camps in Germany and Poland. For me, as for so many of my fellow Jews who were born in the 1950s, 1960s, and 1970s, those images of all-but-unimaginable Jewish victimizations were forever imprinted on my young and fragile psyche.

At the same time that I was awakening to the extent of violence in the world and specifically to the suffering of Jews, I began to learn, especially on the football field, that standing your ground and fighting back was not only physically satisfying but also a way to win friends and potentially to attract the attention and interest of girls. I didn't know many Christian kids who actually believed in turning the other cheek, and, if any of my Jewish friends rejected in principle the use of force to establish manhood, I was unaware of it. There is a famous passage in *The Interpretation of Dreams* where Freud (1955) recounts a story his father told him when he was 10 or 12 years old. It was 19th century Austria. His father was walking down the street one Saturday, wearing his new fur cap, and a Christian man approached him, knocked his cap off into the mud, and shouted: "Jew, get off the pavement." The young Freud asked his father what he did, and his father replied, "I went into the roadway and picked up my cap." Freud was deeply disappointed in his father's response and in his (to Freud) antiquated sense of Jewish manhood. Instead of idolizing his own father, Freud recounted that he began to fantasize about a scene where the father of the great Carthaginian general Hannibal made his boy swear before the household altar to take vengeance on the Romans.

Boyarin (1997) argues that the westernization process for European Jews in the late-19th and early 20th centuries was "one in which *mensch* as Jewish male ideal became largely abandoned for a dawning ideal of the 'New Jewish Man,' 'the Muscle-Jew,' a figure almost identical to his 'Aryan' confreres and especially the 'muscular Christian' also born at about this time" (p. 37). For thousands of years, the rabbinic tradition praised humility before adversity, and interpreted Jewish victimization as a punishment from God for insufficient adherence to his commandments. But instead of embracing a nonviolent masculine ideal rooted in Talmudic texts and a long Jewish cultural tradition, more and more Jewish men were finding themselves attracted to the idea of becoming real men, as defined in physical terms by Gentile culture—a development, not coincidentally, that informed and was contemporaneous with the birth of Zionism as a response to the plight of the Jews.

As a Jewish boy growing up in the 1960s and 1970s, I was oblivious to any of these gendered currents in Jewish life, even though years later I began to make sense of some of my own family dynamics only after I began to study these features of Jewish history. But while I might not have been privy to a larger sociocultural analysis of Jewish masculinity and violence, I was aware that I embodied a certain set of contradictions. From childhood, I empathized with the victims of bullying, harassment, and other forms of mistreatment, even though as a young teenager I sometimes found myself perpetrating the petty cruelties against which I later defended others. As I moved through adolescence and into college, I found myself pulled inexorably toward movements for social justice—such as the Civil Rights Movement and feminism—that were rooted in principled nonviolence. All the same, I continued to feel a strong sense of identification with oppressed people—men and women—who fought back with their fists and guns or by any means necessary. It seemed to me then, as now, that violence was sometimes justified, especially in self-defense or the defense of others.

These tensions and contradictions surfaced again in the 1980s, when I first learned about the Jewish Defense League (JDL), which was founded by Rabbi Meir Kahane in New York City in 1968. The JDL is a racist and fanatically right-wing organization with a controversial history that includes a string of actual and alleged terrorist incidents over the past 40 years, but its original rationale had a crude simplicity: you mess with Jews and we will mess with you. You mug an elderly Jewish woman on her way home from the grocery store, and we will show up on your doorstep with baseball bats. You vandalize a synagogue? You'd better watch your back. I was never a Charles Bronson fan, but in my gut I get the popularity of 1970s vigilante films like the *Death Wish* series. I readily admit that I have long enjoyed indulging in the fantasy of Old Testament style eye-for-an-eye justice—especially from a safe distance. As the organization theorist Levy puts it, this sentiment "resonates with major themes in our culture and religion—perpetual victimhood, humiliation, but occasional moments of triumphalism when we rise up to smite our enemies" (personal communication, June 20, 2008). A friend of mine relates the anxiety he felt as a young teenager on Long Island walking home from school, when he had to walk past a certain block and would face taunts and verbal abuse from an aggressive group of Christian boys. He says that he felt a certain kind of pride when he first heard about the JDL. Leon Wieseltier, literary critic of *The New Republic*, actually joined the JDL for a short time in 1969 as a 17-year-old student at a yeshiva high school in Brooklyn. In a classic article,Wieseltier (1985) wrote that Rabbi Meir Kahane's appeal "was not to our minds," that he and his fellow young Jews were caught up in a great Jewish melodrama where "the whole world is against [them]" (p. 24).

Where and when I grew up, I rarely had to worry about being physically assaulted because I was Jewish, but throughout my childhood and adolescence I heard stories from older relatives who told of being taunted, threatened, and sometimes attacked by Polish, Irish, and Italian boys on the streets of Brooklyn or Boston in the 1930s, 1940s, and 1950s. And of course the newsreel footage of Jewish corpses being bulldozed into mass graves at Auschwitz and Bergen-Belsen were running permanently in the movie theater in the back of my brain. As a progressive young Jew, I never had any illusions about JDL's authoritarian, antidemocratic nature, along with the vicious racism and unreconstructed sexism and homophobia of its founder and members. Nonetheless, I was invigorated by the raison d'etre of this extremist organization: the idea that Jews did not simply have to be victims and take the sort of abuse we had been dealt for thousands of years. We could fight back—we could even beat the *goyim* at their own brutal game. As Kahane once said, "a Jewish fist in the face of an astonished gentile world" (Weiseltier, 1985, p. 24). Only later did I come to understand that my identification with Jews who stood up to bullies had roots even closer to home.

I went to see Kahane speak in a hotel in Brookline, Massachusetts, on a snowy winter evening about a year before he was assassinated in Manhattan in 1990. I was well-informed about Kahane's racism and right-wing political and theological beliefs, but I wanted to get an up-close feel for his personal charisma. What drew people to him? What drew Jewish men to him? I was also curious to see what sorts of Jews in my outwardly liberal community actually supported this political and religious demagogue. There were about a hundred chairs set up in the long, rectangular room, which was about two-thirds full. Men in suits, standing with their arms folded, were posted every 25 feet around the perimeter. These right-wing Jewish men conjured images of the Fruit of Islam, the African-American men in the Nation of Islam whose public performance as bodyguards of their people similarly consists of standing erect and motionless and appearing vaguely menacing. The major difference was that the Jewish men didn't wear bow ties. A big sign behind the podium said *Koach*, Hebrew for strength.

The putative topic of Kahane's talk was the demographic crisis in Israel and his belief that the Jewish state is doomed unless Israel expels the Palestinians from Israel proper and the West Bank. But what I witnessed in that room had more to do with Jewish masculine pride than anything to do with Arabs. The JDL and Kach, Kahane's political party that was banned from the Israeli Knesset, are infamous for their anti-Black and anti-Arab racism. But to focus only on JDL's racism is to miss the deeply wounded Jewish masculinity that lies at the heart of its appeal, both for its members and their closeted sympathizers. The long shadow of the Holocaust hangs over everything they say and do. The symbol of the JDL is a clenched fist inside a Jewish star, and its statement of principles reads like a manual for reasserting Jewish male aggression in the face of a dangerous and hostile world. The five principles of the JDL set out the organization's beliefs, including standard features of ethnic pride rhetoric: love of the Jewish people and pride and knowledge of Jewish tradition, faith, culture, land, history, strength, pain, and peoplehood. But principle three is the ideological core of the JDL: *barzel,* or iron. The principle of barzel is as follows:

> [Jews] need to … change the Jewish image through sacrifice and through all necessary means … even strength, force and violence. The Galut image of the Jew as a weakling, as one who … does not fight back is an image that must be changed … because if a Jew runs away or because a Jew allows himself to be stepped upon he guarantees that another Jew in the future will be attacked because of the image he has perpetuated. JDL wants to create a physically strong, fearless and courageous Jew who fights back. (JDL Web site, 2008)

The JDL's use of iron as a symbol of Jewish strength is especially revealing of the extent to which 20th century right-wing Jewish militarism—including, arguably, Israeli policy—is discontinuous with Jewish tradition. As noted by the historian Yaakov Rabkin (2006), "The rabbis often pointed to the biblical injunction against using iron, the instrument of murder par excellence, to hew the stones for the Temple (I Kings 6:7), to illustrate that a truly spiritual attitude required pacifism" (p. 1).

The JDL has rightly been condemned by virtually all reputable Jewish organizations. But for anyone who is concerned about the future of the Jewish people, and especially the fate of Israel, it is a mistake simply to dismiss the JDL as political and religious extremists without trying to understand the roots of their violent anger. For one thing, they speak for a not insubstantial sector of the American-Jewish public. In 1984, the National Survey of American Jews found that 24% of respondents had a generally favorable view of the JDL. Extremist movements characteristically provide useful insights into dynamics at work in the larger society, in part because of the virulence of their beliefs and because they use blunt and uncompromising language. The JDL is no different. Most American Jews want nothing to do with them. But if you want to understand the visceral appeal to some Jewish men (and women) of right-wing rhetoric about getting tough on Islamist terrorism, not to mention the support among some neoconservative intellectuals and others for preemptive wars in the Middle East, there are few more interesting places to start than a Jewish organization whose murdered leader (Kahane) used to close his standard speeches with the following: "If I have succeeded in instilling fear in you, I consider this evening a success" (Anti-Defamation League, 2001, p. 1).

Peace at Home?

I didn't grow up in fear of Cossacks and Arabs. I grew up in fear of my late stepfather, a working-class Jewish man who embodied the antithesis of the gentle, contemplative Jewish masculine ideal. He was a big man, six feet tall and 200 lb, with large, powerful hands that were perpetually rough and calloused from his work as a carpenter and truck driver. He was emotionally distant and physically intimidating. He in turn had been beaten down emotionally and physically by his Jewish father, who had immigrated to this country from London with his eastern European parents early in the 20th century. My step-grandfather was an outstanding athlete and coach, and a decorated veteran of World War I and II. He was a semiprofessional football player and an amateur boxer, part of a generation of Jewish boxers that was documented in Bodner (1997). I still have my step-grandfather's 8 oz. boxing gloves in a box in my garage. In his time, my *Zadie* [grandfather] developed a reputation as a protector of other Jews, or "King of the Jews," as my stepfather called him, because he never backed down from a fight and would come to the assistance of Jewish boys in distress. At a social gathering once I was told by an older cousin of a friend of mine how much he had admired my grandfather for this very reason. But, sadly, among the Jews my step-grandfather failed to protect were members of his own family, whom he failed to protect from his own violence.

In the course of my work in the movements to end men's violence, as well as in my personal life, I have known many Jews who have family histories of violence, including domestic violence and child abuse. I used to think my family was atypical, in part because I had bought the stereotype of violence as something the *goyim* engaged in—not those nice Jewish men. It was only when I started to hear stories from Jewish friends about their fathers' explosive tempers, or incidents where their fathers beat them or verbally and physically intimidated their mothers that I began to regard as wishful thinking my earlier assumption about Jewish men's gentleness. The stories people shared with me about abuse and violence perpetrated by Jewish men sounded awfully similar to the stories I regularly heard about non-Jews. It seemed that being Jewish in mid-to-late 20th century America most definitely did not inoculate Jewish men against the internalization of some of the worst features of American masculinity, which included the propensity to violence.

And yet, if being Jewish didn't prevent Jewish-American men from being violent, was it possible that something in the Jewish experience itself might have actually contributed to the violence, or something in Jewish history? For example, to what extent did my step-grandfather's—and my stepfather's—violence have its roots in anti-Semitism, in the survival strategies developed by Jewish boys raised in the midst of overt discrimination and violent pogroms in Czarist Russia in the late 19th and early 20th century, who then found themselves in the tough ethnic working-class neighborhoods of northeast American cities? Isn't it likely that some Jewish men have enacted the classic pattern where men from oppressed and despised minority groups bring home the violence and degradation they experience from members of the dominant group at work and on the streets and visit it on their own families? And what was the role in all of this played by my great-grandparents? They were 19th century European peasants whom I never met and whose names I can scarcely recall. My life is vastly more privileged than was theirs, but their hard lives have had a dramatic impact on my own. Was it possible that my step-great-grandfather was abusive to his wife and/or to his son, my step-grandfather? Will we ever know? How many generations back did the abuse go in my family and others'?

Moving into the early- to mid-20th century, what is known about the relationship between Jewish men's service in the two world wars and their later mental health issues or their problems with violent and/or self-destructive behaviors? More than 500,000 American Jewish men and women served in World War II, a remarkably high percentage of the total Jewish population at the time, which was less than five million. Approximately 11,000 were killed, and more than 40,000 were wounded. We know from scholarship since the Vietnam era that a much higher percentage of combat veterans suffer the effects of posttraumatic stress disorder than previously thought. My own father, a medic in the U.S. Army who served in France and Germany, dropped dead of a heart attack at age 37 when my mother was pregnant with me. I'll never know the true source of his cardiac problems, but my aunt—his sister—always maintained that my father was never the same after he came home from the war. Many returning working-class Jewish veterans of World War II, themselves the sons of poor immigrants, headed straight to college with the help of the GI Bill, got married, in the late 1940s and 1950s bought houses with Federal Housing Administration-backed loans, and ascended rapidly into the expanding middle- and upper-middle class. They brought with them their wartime experiences in the armed forces, which often included incidents of overt anti-Semitism, as well as socialization into a militarized and authoritarian form of masculinity. A central part of military training involves the acceleration of a process that takes place in our culture under the guise of "normal" male socialization: conditioning empathy out of young men in order to equip them with the ability to kill other human beings. In recent years a growing body of work in men's psychology has sought to explore the relation between this sort of conditioning and men's struggles to forge and maintain intimate connections and refrain from acting out in violence to themselves or others.

I have nothing but respect for my father's and stepfather's service in World War II, along with other members of their generation. Many Jewish men, including my late uncle, eagerly devised schemes to sign up when they were underage so they could go and help fight the Nazis. But many of these men and their families paid a terrible price for their service, even the majority of those who came back alive or with their limbs intact. To this day I can get misty-eyed when I see footage of the triumphant return of veterans of World War II, kissing their sweethearts and sometimes seeing their children for the first time. But some of those young men were traumatized by the violence they both endured and inflicted in the war. They carried with them the scars and symptoms of post-traumatic stress disorder for the rest of their lives and also carried them into their relationships with those same wives and children in the Jewish enclaves of the leafy and superficially tranquil suburbs of cities like New York, Philadelphia, Boston, Baltimore, Cleveland, Chicago, and Los Angeles.

Violence and Silence

I recall hearing the phrase *domestic violence in the Jewish community* for the first time in the early 1990s, when I attended a program in Boston organized by a coalition of Jewish women's groups. The timeline here is notable in part because, when I first began to think seriously about Jewish men's violence, I had already been doing gender violence prevention activism for a decade. But, like many others, I had never focused on men's violence against women as a Jewish issue. Today, after 20 years of pioneering work by Jewish women around the issues of domestic violence and sexual assault, few people would argue that these problems do not exist in the Jewish community. When Jewish women advocates first began to raise the issues of domestic and sexual violence in the Jewish community, they had to contend with the myth of the "nice Jewish boy" and the widespread disbelief that Jewish men would ever behave like those brutish goyim. It remains unclear whether Jewish men were less emotionally, physically, and sexually abusive than non-Jewish men in the past, whether accelerated assimilation in the 20th and 21st centuries in countries like the United States is responsible for a shift in Jewish men's attitudes and behaviors, or whether

Jewish men were in the past and/or are now less abusive than non-Jewish men; there are no reliable data that speak conclusively to these issues. What is clear is that in the light of contemporary consciousness and what is known, it seems hopelessly naïve to suggest that Jewish men possess some sort of absolute ethnic exemption from sexist abuse.

At that first Jewish domestic violence event that I attended in Boston, there were a number of speakers, including one Jewish woman who was identified as a survivor. Until that moment, like many other Jews, I reflexively assumed the term survivor referred to someone who had survived the Holocaust. Now the word had taken on an entirely new meaning, and I began to think about the Jewish women who were survivors of violence at the hands of their own Jewish (and non-Jewish) husbands and boyfriends. Just a few years before, in a high-profile trial in 1987, Joel Steinberg had been convicted of killing his 6-year-old daughter. In what seems in retrospect to be willful naiveté, many people I know, myself included, were shocked to see pictures of Steinberg's wife Hedda Nussbaum's bruised and battered face. They and I had never before seen the face of a battered woman as a Jewish woman's face. Just as poignantly for me, when I heard the terms "wife-beater" or "batterer," I had never before imagined a Jewish man.

Today, the women-led movement against domestic and sexual violence in the Jewish community has achieved a historic breakthrough. These crimes are no longer talked about only in hushed tones and private conversations; there are regular national and international conferences on the topic, and many synagogues and Jewish community centers have literature available in their foyers and on their Web sites. But, as in the broader movement against domestic and sexual violence, most people in the Jewish community see these issues as women's issues that men only get involved with if they're "good guys" or supportive partners who want to help out. There are a number of Jewish men who are prominent in antisexist men's work outside the Jewish community, but, within the community, few Jewish men have distinguished themselves in this area. These men include the pioneering activist and author Paul Kivel, who has long maintained that the concept of *tikun olam* (repairing the world) applies to interpersonal relationships as well as to abstract social justice issues, and the Orthodox Rabbi Mark Dratch (2005), who founded JSafe, The Jewish Institute Supporting an Abuse Free Environment, whose mission is "to create an environment in which every institution and organization across the entire spectrum of the Jewish community conducts itself responsibly and effectively in addressing the wrongs of domestic violence, child abuse and professional improprieties" (p. 1). Still, with the exception of the work of some feminist scholars in Jewish studies programs, the occasional profeminist men's article in *Tikkun* magazine, or collections like this one, there is little critical discussion in the Jewish world of issues of Jewish masculinity, much less a shifting of the paradigm about domestic violence away from an exclusive focus on women as victims and toward a culturally sophisticated discussion about why some Jewish men are perpetrators and what can be done about it.

The feminist pioneer and author Letty Cottin Pogrebin and others have pointed out that the number of Jews who are victims of domestic violence is far greater than the number of victims of anti-Semitic acts. Silverstein (2006) cited Pogrebin when she said, "Think how quick Jews are to decry anti-Semitism in France and how intense and widespread our community's outrage was when Jesse Jackson and Louis Farrakhan insulted Jews. Now think how long it's taken to acknowledge the abuse happening in Jewish families. Just imagine how our community would respond if Jewish men were assaulting each other instead of their wives. Would the community ignore the black eyes and broken bones? Would they proceed as if nothing were wrong? I don't think so" (Paragraph 17).

In spite of the overall success of American Jews in the 20th and 21st centuries, it is tough to avoid the conclusion that, when it comes to acknowledging the problem of men's violence against women within this ethnic group, they have a lot in common with other historically oppressed or marginalized populations. More than a century after the shtetl, many Jews retain a strong sense not only of disbelief that they have these problems but of the need to keep their dirty laundry private. When one combines that impulse with the sexism that still runs deep in Jewish (and American) culture, one has a prescription for inaction.

One strategy I have developed to engage more Jewish men in the struggle against men's violence—and all forms of sexism, including emotional abuse and financial deprivation—is to link key aspects of Jewish identity to the imperative of speaking out against sexist violence. For example, I am sure that being Jewish helped motivate me to get involved in efforts to reduce the incidence of domestic and sexual violence. Concern and compassion for one's fellow human beings is woven deeply into the pages of the Talmud and other sacred Jewish texts; religious and secular Jews alike are profoundly influenced by the moral sensibility that infuses our tradition. And then how many times did we learn as young Jews that, throughout history, horrible things happened to Jews in part because "good people" remained silent? This is one of the main reasons why Jews have been overrepresented in virtually every progressive social justice movement in this country in modern times: identification and solidarity with the underdog and a deeply held belief that to be silent in the face of oppression is to be complicit in it.

Why should men's silence in the face of other men's violence be any different? This concept animated the approach to gender violence prevention that I developed in the early 1990s, along with my colleagues at Northeastern University's Center for the Study of Sport in Society. The chief curricular innovation of the Mentors in Violence Prevention (MVP) program was a focus on men not as the perpetrators or potential perpetrators of violence but as bystanders. The term bystander is familiar to students of the Holocaust; in the MVP context it refers to anyone (man or woman, boy or girl) who is not abusive or being abused but who is in the same peer culture as someone who is in that situation. The idea is to encourage friends, teammates, coworkers, and other family members to speak out and not remain silent, and hence complicit, in the face of emotional, physical, or sexual violence. In male culture, if enough men made it clear to each other that sexist abuse is unacceptable—as well as the harassment of gays and lesbians and the bullying of other boys/men—they would begin to see a diminution of abuse, because most boys and men who abuse girls and women are not sociopathic or mentally ill; they care deeply about what their fellow men (and women) think of them.

In his research into the motivations of heroic helpers of Jews in Nazi-controlled Europe, social psychologist Staub (1997) found that many of these non-Jews had been asked for a favor by a Jewish friend or colleague or an acquaintance: Can you host this family overnight? Can you provide some money for safe passage? Sometimes that was all they did, but other times, as they came to feel more personally connected to Jews and their predicament, the helpers did more, and their sense of responsibility often deepened. The social conditions in this country are radically different from those in Germany in the Nazi period. Women are not being rounded up by a fascist state and taken to death camps, and no one is looking for men to be heroic helpers. But men's violence against women is widespread, and people need to find ways of encouraging more men to take up this struggle. I used to think that men should be asked simply to speak out about domestic and sexual violence, rather than being told they should. Once they took that first step, some would become more deeply involved. But instead of asking men to help out, I now believe that the next stage of this work involves defining men's participation in gender violence prevention—inside and outside the Jewish community—as a leadership issue. In other words, Jewish men with influence in their families or in the larger Jewish community—not to mention Rabbis—by definition of their leadership status should have working knowledge of the issues surrounding domestic and sexual violence, including the special issues that arise in Jewish populations and across all denominations. Then, with an enhanced understanding of the scope of the problem and its relation to myriad other social problems, they would have a responsibility to figure out what they can do to help prevent the abuse—not because they're nice guys who want to help the women and children out but because they are leaders. Fortunately, the audacious and prophetic work of Jewish women has already set a fine example of how enlightened, committed, and passionate Jewish leaders can begin to bring peace to the world by first working for *shalom bayit*, or peace in the home.

Don't Mess with the Jewish State

Early in the hit 2007 Judd Apatow movie *Knocked Up*, the main character Ben and his friends, all twentysomething Jewish men, are sitting in a nightclub. Ben tells them he just saw *Munich* again, "and it was, like, mind-blowing." His friend Jonah says "*Munich* fuckin' rules." Jay says "*Munich* is awesome." Ben says "That movie was Eric Bana kicking fuckin' ass!" They all agree, and then Ben says, "Dude, every movie with Jews, we're the ones getting killed. *Munich* flips it on its ear. We cappin' motherfuckers." Jonah responds, "Not only killing, but fuckin', like takin' names." "If any of us get laid tonight," Ben says, "It's because of Eric Bana in *Munich*."

As this scene from *Munich* makes clear, Israel is important to Jews in the United States and around the world for many reasons. My purpose here is to suggest some of the ways that the Jewish state—the idea of Israel as much as the nation itself—plays a role in how contemporary Jewish-American men see themselves. For the past 40 years, Israel has played a major role in our violent fantasies and in our very identities—not only as Jews but as Jewish men. The defining event in this process was the Six Day War in June 1967. Something profound shifted in the American-Jewish male psyche when the Israeli armed forces defeated the armies of Egypt, Jordan, and Syria in less than a week. Jewish men all over the world were "remasculinized" by proxy. Wieseltier (1985, p. 24) reported that, a few weeks after the war, he and his friends hung a large poster of a Hasid changing into a Superman costume in a telephone booth.

Breines (1990) explored the profound effect that the Six Day War had on the American Jewish community. Because his study is so rich, I have chosen to quote from it extensively:

> What occurred in the Middle East in early June 1967 transformed the way American Jews thought not only about Israel but about the Holocaust, politics, their parents, grandparents, children, Jews, non-Jews, and, not least, themselves and their bodies. And that is an understatement. (p. 58)

The implications of the Israeli victory for American-Jewish men's identities as men were clear:

> The encounter of American Jews with the stunning Israeli victory over a coalition of Arab armies that had threatened to obliterate the Jewish state constituted a fantastic turn in what was becoming the central Jewish American fantasy: the vulnerability of the Jews destroyed by Nazism was easily transferred to Israel's vulnerability on the eve of the Six Day War; the Nazis were easily replaced by Arabs. (p. 71)

Jewish men had proven that they could defend their women and children, and themselves! The great tragedy for the Palestinians was that, in the face of this historical drama—backed by American military muscle and legitimated by anti-Arab racism—their counternarrative, however compelling, took second billing.

While the Jewish shift from victim to victor was transformative, not everyone in the American-Jewish community was thrilled about this embrace of hypermasculine militarism. For example, Breines (1990) discussed the ideas of the author Michael Selzer, who argued that militaristic enthusiasm in the face of Israeli victory indicated the extent to which the Jewish inferiority complex was as strong as ever. Selzer further argued that the American Jewish embrace of the Israeli warrior is a form of "self-rejection," since the true Jewish self is anchored in Eastern European history and resembles the timid and gentle Jewish tradition" (p. 62).

I do not believe there is such a thing as a true Jewish self or an essential Jewish masculinity, only different ways Jewish masculinity is configured in various historical circumstances, informed by complex historical lineages and individual psychological needs and desires. For example, my generation of American Jews was the first to come of age with Israeli military power as a given; I learned about the Holocaust and historic Jewish victimization at roughly the same time that I became aware of Israel's technological and military mastery over its Arab enemies. And because Israeli power is in many ways an extension of American power, there is no doubt that Israel's military success provided many right-leaning American-Jewish men of my generation and after with a kind of double-barreled arsenal from which to draw parts of their masculine identity. (A journey through the archives of *Commentary* magazine over the past four decades or *The Weekly Standard* since its founding in 1995 will supply ample documentation of the extent to which the politics of masculinity infuse debates about American and Israeli foreign policy.) Of course, the euphoria from 1967 was short-lived. After all, that was the year the disastrous occupation of the West Bank and Gaza began. And shortly thereafter, the United States debacle in Vietnam punctured the mythology of American omnipotence, just as the 1972 Munich Olympics hostage massacre, the 1973 Yom Kippur War, and more recently two decades worth of the Palestinian intifada and suicide bombings have underlined Israel's vulnerability.

Breines (1990) lamented the fact that American Jews went along as American culture in the late 1960s and early 1970s increasingly offered up the message that "life is a battlefield where only the tough, icy-veined and well-armed survive" (p. 66). Rabbi Michael Lerner (2006) calls this approach, especially in relation to Israel, "domination as the path to security," a legacy of what he refers to as "the Right Hand of God" (p. 2). The Jewish neoconservatives who rose to prominence in recent decades certainly regarded the threat of violence at home and abroad as central to their world view; it is revealing that Kristol, one of the founding figures of that influential movement, famously described a neoconservative as "a liberal who has been mugged by reality."

By contrast, Breines (1990) wistfully recalled what Jean-Paul Sartre had said about Jews in his famous 1946 essay "Anti-Semite and Jew":

> The Jews are the mildest of men … passionately hostile to violence. That obstinate sweetness which they conserve in the midst of the most atrocious persecution, that sense of justice and of reason which they put up as their sole defense against a hostile, brutal, and unjust society, is perhaps the best part of the message they bring to us and the true mark of their greatness. (quoted in Breines, p. 45)

Breines (1990) argued that the national turn toward toughness and violent imagery in American society, beginning in the late 1960s, was a turn away from the nonviolent ideals of the early Civil Rights and antiwar movements as well as the initial expression of women's liberation and a more general loosening up of the culture. In addition, he wrote, "The 1960s Jewish American revival of Yiddishkeit, with its scholars, storytellers, and schlemiels; the stateless vulnerability of the shtetl; the absence of soldiers and military norms; the pale and often delicate look of shtetl children; was part of an American flirtation with gentleness that in our male-dominated society was inevitably perceived as being insufficiently manly or simply effeminate" (p. 67). And so Jews, along with other groups such as African-Americans, participated in a counterattack "in the name of manliness and toughness against the threat of gentleness perceived as feminization" (p. 67), a process that persists to this day.

In fact, the response by many Jews to the 2009 films *Defiance* and *Inglourious Basterds* suggests that a generational shift may be underway in how Jewish-American men (and women) approach the topic of historic Jewish victimization: by constructing and nourishing a counter-narrative of violent Jewish resistance to Gentile (including Arab and Muslim) violence.

Defiance (Zwick, 2009) is a Hollywood drama based on the true story of the three Bielski brothers, who successfully saved themselves and 1,200 of their fellow Jews from the Nazis and their collaborators in the Belorussian woods during the early years of World War II. The Bielskis are depicted as physically tough and brave and more than willing to kill to defend Jewish lives. The film's release was accompanied by an educational curriculum that was distributed to Jewish and secular schools by the Jewish Partisan Educational Foundation, a San Francisco-based group founded in 2000 whose purpose is to counteract popular perceptions of Jewish passivity during the Holocaust by celebrating the stories of heroic Jews who fought back against the Nazis.

Quentin Tarantino's film (Tarantino & Bender, 2009)—a worldwide box-office hit—tells the fictional story of a group of American Jews who parachute behind enemy lines during the war and mercilessly kill Nazis, crushing their skulls, scalping, disemboweling, and degrading them. Tarantino, who is famous for his cinematic depiction of brutal violence that is—in the words of the cultural critic Giroux (1995)—voyeuristic and "emptied of its social consequences" (p. 308)—explains that he chose to tell his story by using not only Jewish but Jewish-American soldiers in part because their violence would send a powerful message to the Nazis.

> The basterds are like, "Our European relatives could do nothing when the Hun pounded at their door, but we're the American sons, and we don't have to endure pain—we can inflict it. We've got the right to do that, because we're fucking Americans." (Pfefferman, 2009, p. 2)

Tarantino denies that his film is a Jewish revenge fantasy, although many Jews experience it that way. Eli Roth, the extreme horror film director, who played the part of one of the basterds, sees his character Donny as "a Jewish guy from South Boston who is fighting on behalf of Jews who can't. He uses his baseball bat to pummel Nazis, so he can physically feel that sensation of cracking their skulls in" (Pfefferman, 2009,

p. 7). In a widely quoted comment, Roth described his experience on the movie as "Kosher porn. It was an orgasmic feeling to swing that bat" (Pfefferman, p. 7).

Where does all of this leave us? How do the Holocaust and the character and behavior of the Israeli state affect American-Jewish men in the 21st century? As the scene from *Knocked Up* that discusses *Munich* makes clear—and the popularity of *Defiance* and *Inglourious Basterds* notwithstanding—the theme of Jewish masculine inadequacy and vulnerability to Gentile violence continues to resonate, even as the Holocaust recedes further into memory and the number of living survivors diminishes daily. One of the most psychologically complex as well as politically challenging aspects of the Israeli-Palestinian conflict for American Jews is the extent to which most of us continue to see Jews in Israel as embattled victims, even as much of the rest of the world sees Israel as the dominating regional power and merciless bully. The duality in American-Jewish masculinity between the gentle, sensitive mensch and the muscle Jew helps to explain why American Jews tend to be liberal and progressive on domestic issues but more right-wing on Israel: they satisfy both sides of their dual identity in a way that seems right to many Jewish men. However, an entire generation has grown up since the Six Day War and is now raising its own children, children who will be even further removed from a time when Jewishness was defined as gentleness and the Jewish state was not the dominant military power in the Middle East.

Conclusion

Boyarin (1997) makes a powerful case that Jewish capitulation to Gentile notions of strength that rely on brute power and violence is a tragic development in Jewish history, and it may be so. Yet, it is also true that Jews, like other peoples, have a right to defend themselves, although not a right to disguise aggression as self-defense. The grim reality is that the 20th century was the bloodiest in history, and the 21st is not starting out very peacefully either. If one follows the news these days in this country and from the Middle East, it is hard to be optimistic about the prospect that nonviolent forms of masculinity might supplant the more aggressive ones that have long been a feature of our species. But there is, I would argue, at least some basis for optimism that is based in generational change on a familial level, as well as the prospects in coming years of an acceleration of nonviolent social justice activism, in which American Jewish women and men will continue to play an important part.

I can illustrate the point about generational change with reference to my own family. Sadly, my stepfather, who died a few years ago, passed down to his children some of the damage he had experienced, but his son, my stepbrother, together with his wife, raised two sons in a peaceful Jewish home. My own young son will inevitably have struggles in life, but one of them will not be emotional or physical abuse at the hands of his loved ones. And my nephew's children, and any subsequent children in his generation, will be fully two generations removed from the trauma. People can, and do, make a conscious choice that the violence will stop with them. In this society there are millions of family stories like mine, among Jews and Gentiles alike.

In spite of the brutalizing trends in this country and Israel that I discussed earlier in this piece, there are many American Jewish men who are as committed as ever to social justice and nonviolent social change. My own work on men's violence is planted firmly in these traditions. In fact, Jewish men (and women) are disproportionately represented in activism against violence toward women, in the movements against gay-bashing and for gay civil rights, against racism and other forms of oppression, and in the small but growing field of pro-feminist men's studies. There are also many Jewish-American men (and women) whose principled opposition to state violence leads them to reject the idea that whatever violence the state of Israel inflicts on Palestinians is justified in the name of greater Jewish claims to victimization. Although their efforts are often out of the spotlight and far from the mainstream of organized American Jewry, progressive Jewish groups in the United States have, for example, organized speaking tours for Israeli Defense Force officers who love Israel but refused to serve in the West Bank, and they have also raised money for peace groups within Israel.

Jews have suffered a great deal of violence in their history. They were the victims just a few decades ago of one of the greatest crimes in human history; it will be a very long time before the scars heal. As a result of these injuries, they are the inheritors of, in Rosenberg's (2001) evocative phrase, a legacy of rage. Jewish men have a choice about how to respond to this rage. On the one hand, they can respond with the armor of conservative masculinity and an unrestrained embrace of violence. On the other hand, they can champion nonviolence, even as they continue to wrestle with the question of when and where violence might be necessary or even appropriate. One can only hope that, in coming years, more of them will be drawn toward the path of courageous nonviolence that Sartre said was the best part of their message to the world.

References

Anti-Defamation League. (2001, December 12). ADL Applauds FBI for arrest of JDL leader Irv Rubin for alleged acts of terrorism. Retrieved April 3, 2008, http://www.adl.org/PresRele/Teror_92/4016_72.htm

Apatow, J (Producer/Director). (2007). *Knocked up* [Motion picture]. United States: Universal Pictures.

Bodner, A. (1997). *When boxing was a Jewish sport.* Westport, CT: Praeger Trade.

Boyarin, D. (1997). *Unheroic conduct: The rise of heterosexuality and the invention of the Jewish man.* Berkeley: University of California Press.

Breines, P. (1990). *Tough Jews: Political fantasies and the moral dilemma of American Jewry.* New York: Basic Books.

Brod, H. (Ed.). (1988). *A mensch among men: Explorations in Jewish masculinity.* Freedom, CA: The Crossing Press.

Connell, R.W. (1987). *Gender and power*: Stanford: Stanford University Press.

Dratch, M. (2005, May 2). Rabbi Mark Dratch launches JSAFE. *Domestic Abuse in the Jewish Community.* Retrieved October 11, 2008, *http://www.imakenews.com/eletra/mod_print_view.*

cfm?this_id=394154&u=jewishwomeninternational&issue_id=000079559&show=F,T,T,T,F,A rticle,F,F,F,F,T,T,F,F,T,T. The Official Jewish Defense League Web site http://www.jdl.org/information/five principles.shtml (Retrieved July 13, 2008).

Freud, S. (1955). *The interpretation of dreams. The standard edition of the complete psychologicval works of Sigmund Freud* (J. Strachey & A.Freud, ed. and trans.). Reprint, London: The Hogarth. (Original work published 1900)

Giroux, H. (1995). "Pulp Fiction" and the culture of violence. *Harvard Educational Review, 65*(2), 308.

JDL Web site. (2008). http://www.angelfire.com/ma3/jdlboston/about.html. Retrieved 3-27-08.

Kristol. (2009, September 18). "Irving Kristol, Godfather of modern conservatism, dies at 89." Barry Gewen, *New York Times.*

Lerner, M. (2006). *The left hand of God.* New York: HarperCollins.

Pfefferman, N. (2009). "Revenge of the Jews, Tarantino style." The Jewish Journal of Los Angeles, Aug. 18. Retrieved on 12-4-2009 from http://www.jewishjournal.com/articles/print/revengeof_the_jews_tarantino_style_200908

Rabkin, Y. (2006). The use of force in Jewish tradition and Zionist practice. *Tikkun Magazine Online,* http://www.tikkun.org/magazine/specials/article.2006-05-03.0871880066//, p.1 (Retrieved July 13, 2008).

Rosenberg, W. (2001). *Legacy of rage: Jewish masculinity, violence and culture.* Amherst, MA: University of Massachusetts Press.

Silverstein, M. (2006). Author seeks to combat aura of "shame" among domestic violence victims. New Jersey Jewish News. Accessed April 4, 2008.http://www.njjewishnews.com/njjn.com/111606/pmbAuthorSeeksTo.html.

Staub, E. (1997). The psychology of rescue: Perpetrators, bystanders and heroic helpers. In J.J. Michalczyk (Ed.), *Resisters, rescuers and refugees: Historical and ethical issues* (pp. 137-149). Kansas City, MO: Sheed & Ward.

Tarantino, Q. (Director), & Bender, L. (Producer). (2009). *Inglourious basterds.* United States: Universal Pictures.

Wieseltier, L. (1985, November). Kahane: The making of a Jewish monster. *The New Republic, 11,* 15-25.

Zwick, E (Producer/Director). (2009). *Defiance.* United States: Paramount Pictures.

II
Toward Embodiment: Wrestling with the Angel

4

VIRILITY AND IMPOTENCE: FROM TRADITIONAL SOCIETY TO THE *HASKALAH*

ISRAEL BARTAL

1

The European Enlightenment's attitudes on political, social, and economic questions was filtered through and modified by various intermediaries before it reached Jewish society in Eastern Europe. The passage of ideas, images, and fashions from Western Europe to the Pale of Settlement in the Russian Empire or to Austrian-ruled Galicia frequently created a totally new version of the French or German original. In some cases, a student of the French Enlightenment cannot recognize Eastern Europe *Haskalah* (the Hebrew name of the Jewish enlightenment movement) phenomena as having anything in common with their parallels in the western half of the continent. What is more, because of the heterogeneous nature of the European Enlightenment and the broad diversity of attitudes in various domains, incomplete segments of the cultural inventory of the Enlightenment made it to the east, while others were held back at the border between Germany and the partitioned Polish–Lithuanian Commonwealth or crossed it only decades later to become a later accretion to social and cultural phenomena that had already existed for many years. Consequently, researchers should not be astonished that almost all Eastern European *maskilim* (members of the Jewish Enlightenment movement) adopted a similar stance on issues of the family, conjugal life, and male-female relations, at least until the 1860s—a stance that represented only one of the several options that figured in the vigorous debate conducted over these topics by the Enlightenment in Western Europe.[29]

> The universalistic claims made for human liberty and equality during the Enlightenment did not inherently exclude the female half of humanity. Nature had to be searched, if men were to justify their dominance of the public sphere, whose distinction from the private world increasingly came to be figured in terms of sexual differences. (Laquer, 1990, p. 194)

This is an excerpt from Thomas Laquer's book *Making Sex* where he noted that the biological explanation of sexual differences could have been used to justify dominance by men on account of their greater power in spirit and body, to paraphrase John Locke, but also to explain the inverse case of female control of family or state.

[29] On the progress of scholarship in recent years on various aspects of sexual life and sexual differences and the debate about questions of gender during the Enlightenment, see, for example: Gilman (1989); Goldberg (1984); Hauser (1992); Maccubbin (1987); Rousseau & Porter(1988); Salvaggio (1988); Steinbrugge (1995).

If a researcher looks through the writings of Jewish *maskilim* from Galicia, Lithuania, and Volhynia, however, he/she finds only the position that ascribes superior strength to the man and views the patriarchal family as the social, political, and ethical ideal—an attitude that is compatible with Jewish religious values. Statements of the sort that Montesquieu (1899) placed in the mouth of one of his fictional travelers in his *Persian Letters,* a work known to early 19th-century Galician *maskilim,*[30] cannot be found in the writings of the advocates of *Haskalah* in Eastern Europe:

> Another much-discussed question is, whether women are intended by nature to be subject to men. "No," said a very gallant philosopher to me the other day; nature never dictated any such law. The dominion which we exercise over them is tyrannical; they yield themselves to men only because they are more tender-hearted, and consequently more human and more rational. These advantages, which, had we been reasonable, would, without doubt, have been the cause of their subordination, because we are irrational.
>
> Now, if it is true that it is a tyrannical power which we have over women, it is none the less true that they exercise over us a natural dominion—that of beauty, which nothing can resist. Our power does not extend to all countries, but that of beauty is universal. Why, then, should we have any privilege? Is it because we are stronger than they? But that would be the height of injustice. We use every possible means to discourage them. Our powers would be found equal if we were educated alike. Try women in those gifts which education has not weakened, and we soon will see which is the abler sex. (Montesquieu, 1899, Letter 38)

In contrast to Montesquieu's (1899) criticism of men's repression of women, the *maskilim* of Eastern Europe justified male control of society and the family. Consider, for example, the attitude toward the woman's role in the family and relations with her husband taken by a *maskilic* textbook (*Imrei Shefer*) the various editions of which were committed to memory by several generations of Jewish pupils in Galicia and other provinces of the Austrian Empire. This volume was also a state-sanctioned text, written by an author (Homberg, 1802) on whose writings Jewish couples had to be tested before receiving a marriage license.

> The husband's obligations include loving his wife very much—showing her respect, arranging all the needs of the house for her as she wishes. And even though

[30] Montesquieu's work exerted a major influence on the satirical epistolary literature of the eighteenth century. The Persian Letters were imitated in Hebrew at the very beginning of the Haskalah in Germany (Isaac Euchel's Iggerot Meshullam ben Uriyyah ha-Eshtemo'i) (see Peli, 1993, pp. 545–562). According to Werses (1971), "There are grounds for assuming that Perl and his associates, the Galician maskilim, closely followed this genre of the Persian Letters and its avatars in German literature." Werses notes that on certain issues (political topics, for instance) that were central for Montesquieu, the Galician maskilim were quite remote from the French original (see Werses, pp. 11–12).

> the husband is the master of the house, he should not treat her like a serving girl, but always be gracious to her and speak to her cordially. Sometimes he should ask her advice about his business, even though he does not need her opinion, in order to demonstrate his fondness and trust—for he conceals nothing of his business from her. And in this way her love and confidence and security in him will increase. Should he see something improper in her, he should rebuke her in private, with good sense and discretion, and assure her that he does not love her any less, but a gracious lady like her ought to remove every stain of unseemliness and always endeavor to ascend higher and higher in the degrees of perfection. (pp. 156–157)

As for the gracious lady's obligations toward her husband, Homberg continues:

> The wife's obligations to her husband include loving him, showing him respect, and arranging for him everything he needs in food, drink, and clothing, so that he does not have to wait and lose any of his business. Supervising the household affairs wisely, watching over her children lovingly, and keeping an eye on the members of the household, so that the custom of the house will be in the best order and her husband will not find anything contemptible that might anger him. She should always speak to him gently and with good sense, so that his love for her will increase from day to day. She should be modest in her words and deeds and not address other men. Her eyes should always be on him, for he is her lot, to whom she dedicated the first fruits of her love, and she should never abandon the love of her youth. (pp. 159–160)

Homberg's (1802) *Imrei Shefer* was a textbook for boys and girls attending the new *maskilic* schools. Homberg had served as superintendent of the German-language Jewish schools in Galicia and assistant censor of Jewish books in the late 18th century and who earned eternal infamy among traditional circles as an inveterate foe of the Jewish religion. Homberg's statements about how a Jewish family should be run sound just as conservative as the guidebooks for young brides that circulate today in Orthodox circles in Israel and the United States.[31] These same ideas recur, in various formulations, in Homberg's other works—see Augsburg (1812, pp. 155–157). These ideas appear in the context of loyalty to the absolute monarch and the ideal hierarchical social order in a chapter about relations between parents and children and between masters and servants, with the benevolent despot in miniature, the *maskilic* husband, at its center. He is a man who is loyal to his king and country, conducts an ordered and rational life that hews to the middle course, engages in a dignified occupation that provides him with a decent income, and rules unchallenged over his

[31] For example, The Book of Respect for One's Husband, to teach and strengthen wives how to respect their husbands and try in various ways to give him joy and strength and expand his knowledge, so that wondrous domestic harmony may prevail between them ... (Hebrew), published by the Braslaver hassidic sect (Jerusalem, 1991, 5761).

household and his spouse. This amalgamation of the social and political order of the Austrian state, with its rigid class structure, with the ideal of the Central European bourgeois family, which Homberg tried, through his textbooks, to transplant into the Jewish youth of Galicia, was based on 18th-century German moral texts that circulated widely among the *maskilim* in Eastern Europe and influenced their views of family life and relations between the sexes.

Much like the writings of Homberg, *maskilic* mentality and writings combined the notions of traditional Jewish society and the classical Jewish texts with the German bourgeois model of family life and its place in the centralized state. This combination, influenced prominently by German writers like von Campe,[32] nurtured the idealized image of the reformed Jewish family, a family with a clear distinction between the tasks of husband and wife and explicit definitions of social activity and sexual roles. It is true that the *maskilim* did not write extensively about what was deemed taboo by the bourgeois ethos, which influenced them and which they transmitted to Eastern Europe. Nevertheless, from the little that can be extracted from the *maskilic* texts, one can reconstruct the men's ideal image of the *maskilic* family, a family in which economic control goes along with sexual potency, and these together endow the *maskilic* male with absolute dominance. As Biale (1992, pp. 149–175) has shown, this image was as far from the reality of family life in Eastern Europe as was Berlin from Shnipishok (a suburb of Vilna) in Lithuania.

2

The *maskilic* discourse presented an ideal family situation that was almost unattainable in Eastern European Jewish society, with its customs and conditions. What is more, the *maskilim* indicted the traditional milieu for the failure of their own family lives and linked their own sexual dysfunction to a series of social phenomena that cried out for repair. They believed that traditional society was warped, because it confronted young couples with emotional, physical, and economic difficulties they were not equipped to deal with. Beyond all this, however, the *maskilim* who documented their own sexual experiences argued the case for the restoration of male dominance, of which they had been deprived by the socioeconomic conditions in which they lived. Consider the autobiography of the Lithuanian-born *maskil* Guenzburg (1864), who had no reservations about sharing his most intimate experiences with his readers. Guenzburg's description of his marriage includes the three plagues of family life that all the *maskilim* of Eastern Europe inveighed against: (a) early marriages of prepubescent youngsters; (b) the custom of *kest,* whereby the newlyweds lived with the wife's parents so that the husband could devote several years to intensive Torah study (this custom was, of course, practiced mainly by bet-

[32] The influence of German moral literature, except for children's literature, on the Haskalah in Eastern Europe has not yet been adequately studied. The latter served as a conduit for channeling the bourgeois ethos from Germany to Eastern Europe, including notions of sexual roles in the family (see Bartal, 1990; Bartal, Turniansky, & Mendelssohn, 1993, pp. 193–207; Feiner, 1993).

ter-off socioeconomic classes); and (c) unrestrained sexual activity, typical of the traditional Jewish family in Eastern Europe. On the surface, these three "evils" were fundamental values of the Jewish elite in Eastern Europe: marriage at a young age allowed parents to be involved in molding the next generation and minimized premarital sexual activity. Kest subsidized the training of an intellectual and economic elite and preserved its framework. Finally, the "exaggerated" sexual activity that supposedly took place within the family guarded the stability of the family unit.[33] But Guenzburg viewed all three as irrational conduct, incompatible with common sense and physical health. Furthermore, they undermined the ideal of male dominance of society and family and subjugated the husband to his wife in both the economic sphere and conjugal life.

Guenzburg (1864) reports candidly that his wife attained puberty before he did. As he saw it, this was nature stood on its head:

> My wife was given the endowment of a man, in terms of force, strength, and promptness, so that her fruit of love ripened before its time, and when she was thirteen years old she was a heifer able to satisfy a man, whereas [nature] was slack and behindhand in molding me, so that even in my fourteenth year I was a calf who could not satisfy a woman in physical love. As a result, the masculine female shamed this feminine male in the ways of the world. (p. 90)

A man-like woman, who is the dominant partner in sexual relations, was the antithesis of the ideal of the German bourgeois wife. A woman who achieves sexual satisfaction not according to her partner's physical prowess and not in keeping with his pace of activity provokes fear and constitutes a moral peril. A woman with strong appetites who does not achieve sexual satisfaction exposes the monstrous nature of the sexual urge, uncontrolled eruption of which, on the one hand, or its unreasonable repression, on the other, destroys the body's equilibrium and impairs the social order. Disease, dementia, prostitution, and poverty are the lot of those who loosen the chains of unrestrained female sexuality or, by contrast, do not satisfy a woman physically. Nor is a man-like woman productive, since some 19th-century physicians believed that a woman could not become pregnant if she did not achieve orgasm. A woman who did not coordinate her orgasm with the man's was, in a certain respect,

---

[33] On the Jewish Ashkenazi family at the start of the modern age see Katz (1945, pp. 21–54). Late eighteenth-century non-Jewish observers explained the stability of the Eastern European Jewish family in terms diametrically opposed to Guenzburg's; they viewed sexual relations and married life among the Jews as rational and productive. For example, Polish authors of the prepartition age of political reform saw the controlled sexual activity within the Jewish family unit as one of the factors contributing to the strength of Jewish society. Even the most fervent opponents of the Jews noted the stability of the Jewish family, including the Polish priest Stanisław Staszic (1755–1826), one of the most important Polish reformers of the late eighteenth century: "[Among the Jews], there is fidelity between the spouses and a stronger love of children for their parents and parents for their children" (Goldberg, 1979, 25–33).

a prostitute or masturbator. According to the medical wisdom of Enlightenment Europe, a man-like woman was someone whose uncontrolled sexual appetite, focused in her clitoris, was stronger than the rational control exerted by the male intellect. A man's sexual appetite, though it too is "monstrous," is productive, because it is focused in the male organ, which makes sperm, whereas there is no direct link between the center of female passion (the clitoris) and fertility and childbirth. Hence a sound social, political, and physiological order require that the man restrain the woman's irrational sexual desire and direct it into a beneficial, moral, and healthy channel.[34] The Eastern European *maskilim* absorbed some of these views, as can be learned from the written sources available. The *maskilim* replaced the traditional fear of passionate women with the 18th-century medical explanation of the dangers of uncontrolled female sexual desire.

It is interesting to note that Lilienblum (1970), who did not write much about his first marriage in his autobiography, reveals in a letter to the writer Gordon that he suffered from impotence: "I too experienced the situation of M.A. Guenzburg, as happened to him in his book on his wedding night ..., and after that, too, I engaged in cures for this (one of them was to drink nonkosher wine, which the rabbi of Vilkomir permitted me to do on the basis of the book *Mif'alot Elohim*)" (Breiman, 1968, p. 152). Here Lilienblum alludes, with marked irony, to the unscientific popular cures that came instead of a rational scientific approach to his impotence. Not only had traditional society created the problem, the solutions it proposed were of no value.

3

In general, *maskilic* writings of a personal vein contain clear expressions of a sense of vulnerability and physical weakness (of which impotence is one part)—a weakness that stands in stark contrast to their wives' sexual potency and strength. A prominent example is Abraham Mapu's complaint in a letter to his brother Matityahu, who lived in Kovno (1970). The latter's wife was suspected of infidelity, and the wronged husband had divorced her. Mapu writes pessimistically about the frailty of men: "Haven't I always told you, my brother, how happy we should be that we only have a few sons, because sickly men father sons who themselves know sickness" (p. 133). The practice of *kest* exposes young husbands to the joint authority of the domineering mother-in-law, who rules the house, and his new wife, who makes sexual demands of her impotent husband. When he cannot satisfy her, his lack of virility is exposed in front

[34] On these medical concepts, the legacy of the eighteenth century, see Gilman (1989), Sexuality, pp. 200–203 after the 1844 work by the German anatomist Georg Ludwig Kobelt. In the period corresponding to the Haskalah in Eastern Europe, the image of female sexuality made a 180-degree turn: rather than being possessed of an excessive sexual appetite, women came to be viewed as totally devoid of passion. The new image was internalized by women themselves and also reflected the internalization of the bourgeois ethos by male physicians (see Cott, 1978; Degler, 1974; Smith-Rosenberg & Rosenberg, 1984).

of the entire household. And as Lilienblum (1970) reports in his memoirs, it was the mother-in-law who lorded it over the young man, instead of his dominating his wife:

> It is no wonder if an accursed woman like that expanded her sway to include the naïve lad of 15 that I was then and embittered my life with her curses and imprecations, with the fiery coals she spat from her mouth, her curses and screams directed against my young wife, against me, and against my father-in-law. It seems most likely that this thing too, which continued for many years, made a strong impression on my personality and led to, or at least reinforced, the dull spirit and weak heart from which I suffer greatly today. (p. 108)

Guenzburg's mother-in-law went even further and played an active role in the attempt to restore her young son-in-law's sexual potency, resorting to old-wives' remedies—or, as he described it in his memoirs: "When she saw that as long as I could not function in bed her daughter would not love me, she was stirred to pour manliness into me through medicinal means" (1864, p. 94). Here Guenzburg explicitly identifies love with male sexual potency, which leads a woman to be subordinate to her husband. His premature marriage, instigated by his parents, and his abandonment to a girl whose sexual capacity exceeded his own and to his domineering mother-in-law irremediably disrupted the model of the ideal *maskilic* family.

> I asked myself why my father vainly hurried to have me married before I was capable of making love.... As a result my wife got into the habit of viewing me as weaker than herself. Who knows how difficult it will be for me to prove to her that a man is like his virility. The physician enjoined me many times to conduct myself in moderation—to hoard my meager semen lest I waste away. On top of all this the love that unites me and my wife is a cupboard love and not an innocent one, for our hearts have already parted and we shall never be one flesh. This is a twisted situation that cannot be made straight. (pp. 127–128)

Guenzburg's ideal *maskilic* household repeats almost word for word the description that students of the government schools in Galicia learned by rote from the books of Homberg (1802):

> And even though it is simple to give the man dominion over his wife, as reason and Scripture enjoin ... and after I had hoped to establish a house like my father's, a place full of love, where there is neither lordship nor domination, but a household conducted serenely according to the husband's reason and the wife's sense, a house that stands firmly on a strong foundation of inner love, with no need to support it from the outside by the pillars of lordship and domination. (Guenzburg, 1864, p. 64)

This passage appears in a description of the Polish Jewish custom that the groom treads on the bride's foot before giving her the wedding ring, so that he will rule the house. He juxtaposes the man's control of the house, in accordance with reason and Scripture, with the irrational traditional custom, which he compares to the behavior of horse traders. His inevitable conclusion is that the *maskilic* way guarantees married life in which love means that the man rules the house and the bedroom, "according to the husband's reason and the wife's sense" (Guenzburg, 1864, p. 64), whereas the traditional way, based on empty customs and superstitions, is contrary to reason and turns male control, if it exists, from a consensus based on reason to a matter of compulsion.

The *maskilic* perception of appropriate sexual activity, as expressed in Guenzburg's (1864) memoirs, combines a number of medical concepts and economic ideas that prevailed in 18th-century Europe. First of all, male sexual capacity is limited and must be shepherded and subjected to a strict regime; it is productive, so it is morally wrong to waste it lightly or without rational planning. The German Jews, who wait to marry until they are old, are mistaken. In bold and picturesque language, full of biblical allusions, Guenzburg describes the enfeebled male organ that has trouble achieving an erection ("a king that cannot stand up"—playing on the obscure text of Prov. 30:31) and cannot overcome the potent female sexual organ (a hilltop citadel, a fortified mound, a high and protected place). The exhausted organ, whose potency was wasted mindlessly, has no strength and cannot stand up.

> After they have wasted their youthful vigor in the bosom of harlots and prostitutes and given their virility to adulteresses, their youthful vigor sinning and sinking in their corrupt way, until their strength dries up like a shard and their sins are on their bones—then they gather to approach the hilltop citadel, the lovely lass, and the king who cannot stand is with them. He prepares to make himself a family, but, without strength, leans on his house but does not stand. (p. 75)[35]

Unlike the Jews of Germany, who have carried the bourgeois sexual ethos to its absurd climax, the Jews of Poland offend by marrying off their children too young. Both groups thereby deviate from the golden mean. Love, according to Guenzburg (1864), is sexual compatibility between partners who have grown up and achieved puberty: "For young men in their twentieth year and girls of fifteen, for at those ages the body has reached its final stature and nature has refined the pleasant produce of semen into sparks of love, the time has come to frolic in the mighty pleasure of first love—oh! how good and beautiful it is" (p. 76).

It is interesting to note that, in another *maskilic* autobiography, Gottlober (1976) writes of the love that developed between himself and his wife five years after they were married, when they had finally reached sexual maturity:

---

[35] "Leans on his house but does not stand" plays on Job 8:15, with awareness of the Talmudic sense of "house" as "wife." The second half of that verse, which Guenzburg does not quote, can be rendered as "he takes hold of it but it will not stand up."

> There was also something new in my bedroom: The wife that God had given me, through my father, when I was 13½ and she a year younger—I did not love her, though indeed I did not hate her, either, because my heart still did not know what love was. For how could such a boy know what divine love is? But this time, when I returned to my father-in-law's house, by now eighteen years old, the spirit of love began to stir in me. It also descended on my wife and she loved me, too. For us it was as if we were newly married. (p. 244)

4

The implication is that the *maskilic* view of conjugal relations assigned a larger role to the erotic side of family life (Biale, 1992, pp. 149-175). The truth is that Eros stood in the strong shadow of order, economy, and strict regimen. The Eastern European Jewish male, as already noted, was afraid of female unrestrained sexual activity, even within the family. It held that husband and wife should limit themselves to reasonable sexual activity—that middle ground between what Guenzburg (1864) called a "beast in the field" and "innocent" with regard to men and between a "gracious woman" and "dominant harlot" for women (p. 75). Too much sexual desire is immodest in a woman, and woe betide the man whose wife demands that he "slake her ardent craving" and cannot satisfy her "lusty spirit" (p. 75). What is more, the *maskilim* associated the sexual demands of the Eastern European woman with her social and economic roles in the bourgeois family. Unlike the *maskilic* ideal, in Lithuania and Volhynia women exercised firm control of the domestic economy, while their husbands were subordinate to them in this realm. Her activities in the marketplace and streets and contact with the world had an immoral character, which sometimes came close to seducing her non-Jewish customers. *Maskilic* writings associate women's economic activity with inappropriate sexual activity and a division of roles that is antithetical to social order and common sense. The successful merchant in Israel Axenfeld's novel *Dos Shterntikhl* (Miron, 1979, p. 213) subdues his wife both economically and sexually as he transfers his household and business from feudal-style money-lending to modern capitalism. Gordon's (1956) poem about *Bat Shua*, is mistakenly lauded as the key to understanding women and their needs (see Biale, 1992, p. 160),[36] is supposed to be transferred from the traditional economic model of Eastern Europe to the German economic model favored by Gordon the man. And what is the significance of this transfer in the eyes of a man of the *Haskalah*?

> Fabi decided when he completed the work
> to go on and build railroads
> and transfer his residence to the capital
> where he would establish his home in praiseworthy order.
> All this he told her and did not keep secret.

[36] In fact, Gordon's poem is written from a distinctly male point of view, for which the ideal woman internalizes the bourgeois ethos and especially the husband's unchallenged primacy in the family (see also Stanislawski, 1988, 124–128).

She too intended to build on his idea
and give her children to a trained teacher
and prepare to be a housewife in due time
and fill the large hole in her schooling,
studying music and writing, languages and literature.
(Gordon, 1956, p. 164)

The man Fabi, the industrious and mobile economic entrepreneur, who builds the railroads that are part of Russia's transition to a capitalist economy during the reign of Alexander II, will become a wealthy businessman. His wife, by contrast, will be an educated housewife, fluent in languages and able to play the piano. Bat Shua, the heroine of the poem, was in fact married according to the old kest custom. According to the Eastern European male *maskil*, reforming the economic and social distortions wreaked on women by traditional marriage customs means returning them to their parlor and severing them from the business world outside the house, which is the exclusive province of the husband. A comparison of the ideal conduct of Bat Shu*a*, who returns the love of an energetic and productive economic entrepreneur, with a real woman who did not act this way in similar circumstances and was turned into a figure of infamy in the letters of Mapu, is instructive. The wife of his brother Matityahu—who, like Fabi, Bat Shua's fiancé, was preoccupied with the business affairs of Guenzburg and spent most of his time away from home—did not pine away waiting for him to visit home once a year but carried on love affairs in the boarding house run by her parents in Vilna. Bat Shua was the daughter of a boarding house keeper in the fictional town of Eilon (a stand-in for Vilna) and conducted a romance with a railroad magnate. Matityahu Mapu's wife, too, was romantically involved with railway tycoons in the Vilna region and refused to put up with her husband's protracted absences from home. With her mother as her accomplice (again the threatening sexual combination of mother-in-law and demanding wife!), she slept with other men. In his letters, Abraham Mapu wrote a dirge for the family honor and his brother's profaned male dignity and hurled fire and brimstone at the woman who sought her satisfaction in the beds of other men, describing her as a "dominant harlot" and even "Lillith."[37] By contrast, Mapu (1970) wrote calmly, "many rich men live here for their business and do not go home for a year, yet no one protests. The railroad will be finished soon, and then you will be able to see your family more frequently" (p. 30).

For a woman to have a greater sexual appetite than the man is thus disastrous, and Eros is the enemy of reason. Hence the *maskil* should be wary of both of these, lest he lose his control of his wife. Gordon (1960) molded his ideal enlightened physician, Albert, in accordance with the *maskilic* model. All his actions and thoughts are the embodiment of pure rationalism—until he meets the beautiful Sarah. Then, "He sat

[37] On the figure of the active and seductive woman, characterized as the succubus Lillith in Abraham Mapu's work, and the realistic context of this characterization, see, in detail, Cohen (1990, pp. 167–213).

... like a man stupefied and at a loss for what to do; his heart wavered, his spirit was bruised, his thoughts were caught in chains. For long moments he paced back and forth in his room, unable to calm down" (Gordon, 1960, p. 32). For a brief instant, erotic desire escapes the control of male reason but is quickly restored to its place in the bourgeois institution of marriage. The remedy for the momentary loss of equilibrium in the maskil's mind and body was to make Sarah his wife. This is the "happy end" of the Russian *Haskalah*—an idyllic conclusion in which reason's domination of passion merges with the appropriate division of roles between the dominant husband and the submissive wife. Sarah supervises domestic affairs and dabbles in music but stays away from public matters. When the new family unit is established, sexual desire is channeled into its appropriate place and reason once again reigns supreme in the physician's life: "Albert no longer sat by himself chasing a fleeting shadow, but rested quietly in his place, his heart and peace restored, his dream solved" (Gordon, p. 76).

It was not women's liberation, in the sense of gender equality, which was imagined by the *maskilim* of Eastern Europe when they molded their social vision but putting the woman where she belonged: in her husband's bed, in the kitchen, and in the salon. The Eastern European *maskil* was terrified of women who had their own minds and an uncontrollable sexual appetite. The man, lacking in confidence, sought to place the strong and passionate woman under the control of male reason and under the aegis of the ideal political and social order. In the ideal vision of the *Haskalah*, sexual power and economic power were the province of the man. The reality of Eastern European Jewish society, however, struck the *maskilic* man as topsy-turvy: the man found himself powerless—both biologically and economically. The traditional fear of female passion was replaced by concepts drawn from medicine and by economic metaphors borrowed from the European Enlightenment. The appearance of notions of women's liberation on the horizons of the Eastern European *Haskalah* in the second half of the 19th century, under the influence of the new currents in Russia and Poland, added a new fear to the old terrors and a new threat to the ideal political and social order. The menacing figures of the passionate and demanding wife and of the domineering mother-in-law, the nightmares of the men in traditional Polish-Jewish society, were supplemented, from the 1860s, by the radical revolutionary woman, who rebelled against the rule of the men in her life. The *maskilim* of Eastern Europe, who recoiled both from the traditional threatening woman and her radical sister who rejected the conventions, continued to find solace in the idealized gracious woman of the German bourgeois environment. This gracious woman, whom they pictured in their mind's eye and modeled in their masculine discourse, was ultimately the literary compensation for the fear, weakness, and sense of inferiority that were the lot of so many *maskilim*.[38]

[38] On the maskilic male's fear of the modern woman, in whom they identified "superficial acculturation, shallow education, lack of familiarity with the Hebrew language and the Jewish religion, and sexual permissiveness," see Hyman (1995).

References

Bartal, I. (1990). Mordecai Aaron Guenzburg: A Lithuanian *maskil* confronts modernity. In F. Malino & D. Sorkin (Eds.), *From East and West: Jews in a changing Europe* (pp. 128-129). Oxford: Oxford University Press.
Bartal, I., Turniansky, H., & Mendelssohn, E. (Eds.). (1993). *According to the custom of Ashkenaz and Poland: Chone Shmeruk jubilee volume.* Jerusalem.
Biale, D. (1992). *Eros and the Jews: From Biblical Israel to Contemporary America.* Berkeley: University of California Press.
Breiman, S. (Ed.). (1968). *Letters of M. L. Lilienblum to J. L. Gordon* (Hebrew). Jerusalem.
Cohen. I. (1990). *Hypocrites and honest men, Goddesses and Lilliths: Studies in the work of Abraham Mapu* (Hebrew). Tel Aviv.
Cott, N.F. (1978). Passionlessness: An interpretation of Victorian sexual ideology, 1790–1850. *Signs: Journal of Women in Culture and Society, 4*(2), 219-236.
Degler, C.N. (1974). What ought to be and what was: Women's sexuality in the nineteenth century. *American Historial Review, 79*, 1467-1490.
Feiner, S. (1993). The modern Jewish woman: A test case in the relations between the Haskalah and modernity (Hebrew), *Ziyyon, 58*, 453–499.
Gilman, S.L. (1989). *Sexuality: An illustrated history.* New York: Wiley.
Goldberg, R. (1984). *Sex and enlightenment: Women in Richardson and Diderot.* Cambridge: Cambrige University Press.
Goldberg, Y. (1979). Jewish marriages in old Poland in the public opinion of the enlightenment (Hebrew), *Galed, 4–5*, 25–33.
Gordon, J.L. (1956). The point of the Yod (Hebrew). In *Writings of J. L. Gordon: Poems.* Tel Aviv.
Gordon, J.L. (1960). After joy comes sadness (Hebrew). In *Writings of J. L. Gordon: Prose.* Tel Aviv.
Gottlober, A.B. (1976). *Memories of youth* (Hebrew). In *Memoirs and travels.* Jerusalem.
Guenzburg, M.A. (1864). *Aviezer.* Vilnius.
Hauser, M. (1992). *Gesellschaftsbild und Frauenrolle in der Aufklärung.* Vienna.
Homberg, H. (1802). *Imre Shefer.* Vienna
Homberg, H. (1812). *Im Verlagsgewölbe des k. k. Schulbücher-Verschleisses.* Augsburg.
Hyman, P. (1995). *Gender and assimilation in modern Jewish history: The roles and representation of women.* Seattle: University of Washington Press.
Katz, J. (1945). Marriage and marital life at the end of the middle ages (Hebrew). *Ziyyon, 10*, 21–54.
Laquer, T.W. (1990). *Making sex: Body and gender from the Greeks to Freud.* Cambridge: Harvard University Press.
Lilienblum, M.L. (1970). *Hatte'ot Ne'urim.* In S. Breiman (Ed.), *Autobiographical writings* (Hebrew). Jerusalem.
Maccubbin, R.Pr. (Ed.). (1987). *'tis nature's fault: Unauthorized sexuality during the enlightenment.* Cambridge: Cambridge University Press.
Mapu, A. (1970). *Letters of Abraham Mapu* (Hebrew). Jerusalem.
Miron, D. (1979). The wimple, or on the advantages of forgery: The reality principle in Israel Axenfeld's *Dos Shterntikhl* (Hebrew). In *Vision and truth: The buds of the Hebrew and Yiddish novel in the nineteenth century.* Jerusalem.
Montesquieu, C. de S. (1899). *Persian letters* (J. Davidson, Trans.). London: Chinswick Press.

Peli, M. (1993). Utopian models of the Judaism of the future in the vision of Isaac Euchel (Hebrew), *Tarbiz, 61*, 545–562.
Rousseau, G.S., & Porter, R. (Eds.). (1988). *Sexual underworlds of the enlightenment.* Chapel Hill: University of North Carolina Press
Salvaggio, R. (1988). *Enlightened absence: Neoclassical configurations of the feminine.* Urbana: University of Illinois Press.
Smith-Rosenberg, C., & Rosenberg, C. (1984). The female animal: Medical and biological views of woman and her role in nineteenth-century America. In J.W. Leavitt (Ed.), *Women and health in America* (pp. 12-27). Madison: University of Wisconsin Press.
Stanislawski, M. (1988). *For whom do I toil? Judah Leib Gordon and the crisis of Russian Jewry.* New York: Oxford University Press.
Steinbrugge, L. (1995). *The moral sex: Woman's nature in the French enlightenment* (P.E. Selwyn, Trans.). New York: Oxford University Press.
Werses, Sh. (1971). The satirical methods of Joseph Perl (Hebrew). In *Sippur ve-shorsho: Iyyunim be-hitpathut ha-prozah ha-ivrit.* Ramat Gan.

5

THE ZIONIST BODY: NATIONALISM AND SEXUALITY IN HERZL'S *ALTNEULAND*

MICHAEL GLUZMAN

The idealization of masculinity is the foundation of nation and society.
— George Mosse (1985, p. 17)

1

In his seminal book, *Imagined Communities*, Anderson (1983) contends that "in the modern world everyone can, should, will 'have' a nationality, as he or she 'has' a gender" (p. 14). This equation, Sommer (1991) suggests, reveals just "how universal both nationality and discrete genders are today ... everyone not only 'has' a nationality and gender in the same imagined way, but these imaginings constitute us as modern subjects" (p. 40). While Sommer directs attention to the "interchangeability between sex and nation" (p. 40) in Anderson's formulation, it is also true that the two sides of Anderson's equation are not entirely symmetrical. Although he carefully construes nationality as a possible, desired, and yet potentially transient state, he seems to view gender as a natural given.

The Jewish condition in late 19th century Europe, however, challenges Anderson's (1983) formulation. For both nationalism and gender are experienced by Jews as categories outside of their possession. Against the foil of modernity, Jews were perceived—and perceived themselves—as a people deviating from European national and gender ideals. The wandering Jew's anomalous state among the nations was often regarded as pathological. Similarly, the Jew was viewed as someone tormented by severe gender trouble. Thus, the advent of Jewish nationalism in the *fin-de-siècle* offered a solution not only to the anomaly of Jewish homelessness but also to the alleged pathological nature of the Jew's gender identity.

In imagining a Jewish homecoming, Zionism had to fashion its national, social, and cultural ideals, including its perceptions of gender and sexuality. This is evident in Theodor Herzl's (1902/1960) novel *Altneuland*, in which Herzl offers a detailed description of the social, political, and cultural structures of the imagined New Society in Palestine. While these aspects of Herzl's text received close scrutiny,[39] the

[39] The debate over the political-economic-social-cultural structures advanced in *Altneuland* began immediately after the novel's publication. Ahad Ha-am (1961), for example, viciously attacked Herzl. Nordau came out in defense of Herzl and attacked Ahad Ha-am, who was forced to respond to Nordau's arguments (see Ahad Ha-am, pp. 313-325). For a comprehensive description of the political debate that accompanied the publication of *Altneuland*, see Laskov (1991).

novel's sexual politics have remained largely unexplored.[40] My reading of Herzl's *Altneuland*, informed by feminist criticism and queer theory, exposes the ways in which the discourses of nationalism and sexuality intersect and inform each other in this text. Thus, in what follows, I read *Altneuland* not only as a political utopia but also as a sexual one. The political program, which lies at the center of the text, I argue, is framed by an erotic narrative that turns the novel into a narrative of sexual redemption. Yet, before I focus on this novel, I want to turn attention to the medical and cultural discourse on gender and sexuality that emerges precisely at this historical moment and that underlies the national narrative of Zionism in general and of this text in particular.

In the first volume of *The History of Sexuality*, Foucault (1990) argues that homosexuality as an identity is a modern invention: "The nineteenth-century homosexual became a personage, a past, a case history, and a childhood, in addition to being a type of life, a life form, and a morphology with an indiscreet anatomy and possibly a mysterious physiology. Nothing that went into his total composition was unaffected by his sexuality" (p. 43). The invention of homosexuality as an identity, rather than a sexual act, was part of a larger reshaping of sexual categories. For Foucault, the distinction between sodomy and homosexuality is not merely a linguistic distinction but rather a historical one: "Homosexuality appeared as one of the forms of sexuality when it was transposed from the practice of sodomy onto a kind of interior androgyny, a hermaphrodism of the soul. The sodomite had been a temporary aberration; the homosexual was now a species."

The invention of homosexuality as a category of sexual identity was inextricably entangled with what Katz (1995) terms "the invention of heterosexuality." Although at times it seems that the concepts homosexuality and heterosexuality have always existed, they are in fact new terms (Halperin, 1990). The word homosexual was first coined in 1868 and became widely circulated only in the beginning of the 20th century. The word heterosexual is new as well, and its initial meaning in psychiatric writings differed from present usage. In an article published in a Chicago medical journal in 1892, the American psychiatrist James Kiernan uses "heterosexual" to denote a perversion, one of several "abnormal manifestations of the sexual appetite" (quoted in Katz, 1995, p. 20).

Foucault (1990) argues that the invention of the homosexual/heterosexual opposition was part of a new discourse on sex and sexuality. This "discursive explosion," which emerged in the 18th century, invented new modes of surveilling bodily pleasures as the body and sexuality were brought under the domain of the new science of sexology. This science did not merely focus on the individual, but as Foucault explains:

[40] An exception is Jacob Press's (1997) "Same-Sex Unions in Modern Europe: *Daniel Deronda*, *Altneuland* and the Homoerotics of Jewish Nationalism."

> [I]t claimed to ensure the physical vigor and the moral cleanliness of the social body; it promised to eliminate defective individuals, degenerate and bastardized populations. In the name of a biological and historical urgency, it justified the racisms of the state, which at the time were on the horizon. It grounded them in "truth." (p. 54)

The medicalization of sexuality in 19th century Europe served as a means to subordinate the others—Jews, Gypsies, vagrants, and homosexuals—in the name of state and society. This new pseudo-objective medical gaze measured skulls, noses, feet, and sexual organs in order to formulate differences between races and nations. This "scientific" production of difference turned the body into an "object and target of power" (Foucault, 1979, p. 136). Europe's others "provided a countertype that reflected, as in a convex mirror, the reverse of the social norm" (Mosse, 1996, p. 56). The Jew had a central place in the European discourse on the others. Anti-Semitic discourse described the Jew as ugly, stooped, dirty, and in possession of an ill-proportioned, pathological body (see Gilman, 1989, 1994, 1995). In this context, Almog (1992) argues:

> In the Age of Science the beliefs concerning the pathological tendencies of the Jews did not lose their potency. On the contrary: the pseudo-scientific approach validated and reinforced these prejudices even further.... The specific emphasis was laid upon mental illnesses and sexual pathologies, and created a picture of a genetically flawed and degenerated creature. (p. 250)

Additionally, as I suggested earlier, the Jew's predisposition to special forms of mental illness was said to have a distinct gender component. Medical literature throughout the 19th century repeatedly describes male Jews who suffer from hysteria, a disease typically associated with women.[41] Jean-Martin Charcot, one of Europe's most celebrated physicians at the turn of the century, contended that male Jews have a special disposition for hysteria (see Gilman, 1989, p. 265). The Jew's body was understood to destabilize the very anatomical distinction between man and woman. Gilman traces this analogy between male Jew and woman in a Christian tradition, which constructed the Jew as inherently and biologically different. As Gilman (1994) reports, the epitome of this mode of thinking can be found in discussions of male menstruation:

---

[41] It is no accident that Freud's first lecture in the University of Vienna in 1886 was on male hysteria. Freud sought to destabilize the racist accusation that male Jews suffer from hysteria, and he thus attempted to show that hysteria could be found among men of all races. Freud, who writes about this incident in an autobiographical essay, recounts that, upon hearing Freud's hypothesis an old physician angrily commented: "Isn't the name 'hysteria' itself, which is derived from the Greek word for womb, sufficient to demonstrate that only women suffer from it?" (see Gay, 1988, p. 53).

> Thomas de Cantimpré, a thirteenth-century anatomist presented the first "scientific" statement of this phenomenon (calling on Saint Augustine as his authority). Male Jews menstruated as a mark of the "Father's curse," their pathological difference. This image of the Jewish male as female was introduced to link the Jew with the corrupt nature of the woman (both marked as different by the same sign) and to stress the intransigence of the Jews. (p. 97)

This was by no means an isolated view. Gilman (1989) documents a widespread tradition that lists Jewish male menstruation as part of specifically Jewish maladies.

This conflation of male Jew and woman, which originated in blatant anti-Semitic texts, became so widespread that, in turn-of-the-century European culture, there are repeated descriptions of effeminate male Jews. Leopold Bloom, the Jewish protagonist of James Joyce's *Ulysses*, is described in the novel by Dr. Mulligan, an expert on sexuality, as "abnormally bisexual" (Reizbaum, 1999). He is also portrayed as the "new womanly man," and as the plot unfolds he becomes—in his fantasy—a woman and gives birth to eight sons. Joyce, who imagines Bloom imagining himself, presents his protagonist, a Jewish Odysseus, in clearly gendered terms (see Reizbaum, pp. 51-88). At the end of the 19th century—when the binary opposition between heterosexuality and homosexuality becomes the organizing principle of the discourse on sexuality—the effeminate male Jew is viewed as having pronounced homosexual tendencies. As the sexual terminology changes from sodomy to homosexuality—and homosexuality is understood as psychological hermaphrodism—the European imagination turns the Jew into a homosexual. In fact, there are similarities in the ways Jews and homosexuals are described at the turn of the century: both disrupt the natural order of gender and sexuality, both are described simultaneously as hyper-sexual and as neurasthenic, and both have a pathologically feminine body. It is precisely against this background that Marcel Proust (1982), homosexual and half-Jew, draws the analogy between Jews and homosexuals in his *Remembrance of Things Past*. The medical and cultural discourse of the period, which dealt extensively with hysteria, perversions, and degeneration, repeatedly drew a double analogy between male Jew and woman and between male Jew and homosexual (See Garber, 1992, pp. 224-233).

However, the analogy between male Jew and woman does not appear only in texts written by non-Jews. This analogy gradually infiltrates two prototypically Jewish discourses: psychoanalysis and Zionism (Boyarin, 1997). Otto Rank, a Jewish psychoanalyst, and among the founders of the Viennese Psychoanalytic Society, wrote a 1905 essay entitled, "The Essence of Judaism," in which he determines that Jews have a primitive sexuality: "Like women, they have remained unchanged" (Gilman, 1994, p. 176). According to Rank, Jews are less repressed. Although he uses the word "primitive" in a positive sense, and in so doing inverts the value assigned to the male Jew's femininity, he does not challenge the analogy itself.

In a footnote to the case history of "Little Hans," which in recent years has attracted much critical attention, Freud (1909/1955) discusses the analogy. Freud attempts to explain European anti-Semitism in psychoanalytic terms, suggesting that the anti-Semite's fear stems from his misunderstanding of circumcision. Freud interrupts his explanation of Little Hans's fear of castration to speculate on the roots of anti-Semitism:

> The castration complex is the deepest unconscious root of anti-Semitism; for even in the nursery little boys hear that a Jew has something cut off his penis—a piece of his penis, they think—and this gives them a right to despise Jews. And there is no stronger unconscious root for the sense of superiority over women. Weininger (the young philosopher who, highly gifted but sexually deranged, committed suicide after producing his remarkable book, *Geschlecht und Charakter* [1903/2005], in a chapter that attracted much attention, treated Jews and women with equal hostility and overwhelmed them with the same insults. Being a neurotic, Weininger was completely under the sway of his infantile complexes; and from that standpoint what is common to Jews and women is their relation to their castration complex. (p. 36)

For Freud, then, anti-Semitism is first and foremost a sexually motivated fear: the fear of castration. Because of the practice of circumcision, the Jew is perceived as castrated, a condition or lack he shares with women. Oddly enough, while Freud attempts to explain non-Jews hatred of the Jew, the Jewish Weininger is his most salient example.[42] Freud's interest in Weininger (1903/2005)—who claimed that "Judaism is saturated with femininity to such an extent that the most manly Jew is more feminine than the least manly Aryan"—is part of a wider cultural reception of Weininger's pseudo-scientific text. This notorious text was, as Robertson (1998, p. 23) argues, "one of the most influential doctoral theses ever written. It was admired by Strindberg, Karl Kraus, Kafka, Broch, Musil, Doderer, Schoenberg and Wittgenstein."

2

The Zionist discourse of both Herzl and Nordau, the two most prominent leaders of Political Zionism, similarly engaged and grappled with the stereotype of the Jew as woman.[43] Nordau (1980) expresses a desire for a new, more masculine breed of Jews and argues that the Jew needs to exercise in order to counter his characterization as feeble and weak as follows:

> Two years ago, during a committee meeting at the Congress at Basle, I said: "We must think of creating once again a Jewry of muscles." Once again! For history

[42] Boyarin (1997) has already shown that Freud ignores Weininger's Jewishness and thus fails to take into account Weininger's self-hatred.

[43] Many critics have pointed out the similarity between anti-Semitic and Zionist discourses. In a chapter entitled, "Jewishness as Illness: Anti-Semitic Stereotypes and Self-Image," Almog (1992) discusses the ways in which Jews internalized anti-Semitic stereotypes: "Together with European culture, modern Jews also absorbed the abundant anti-Semitic residues contained within it" (p. 250).

> is our witness that such a Jewry had once existed. For too long, all too long have we been engaged in the mortification of our own flesh. Or rather, to put it more precisely—others did the killing of our flesh for us.... In the narrow Jewish street our poor limbs soon forgot their gay movement; in the dimness of sunless houses our eyes began to blink shyly; the fear of constant persecution turned our powerful voices into frightened whispers, which rose in a crescendo only when our martyrs on the stakes cried out their dying prayers in the face of their executioners. But now, all coercion has become a memory of the past, and at least we are allowed space enough for our bodies to live again. Let us take up our oldest traditions; let us once more become deep-chested, sturdy, sharp-eyed men. (p. 435)

The desire or even longing to rehabilitate the Jewish body is grounded in a national vocabulary and phrased in masculine terms. As quoted in my epigraph, Mosse (1985) has already noted that the "idealization of masculinity [is] the foundation of the nation and society" (p. 17). Indeed, it seems that Nordau's (1980) exhortation "let us once more become deep-chested, sturdy, sharp-eyed men" (p. 435) is a typical example of the ways in which the male body becomes an emblem of the new society, as well as a means of nation building.[44] Nordau was influenced by the founder of German fitness and exercise, Friedrich Ludwig Jahn, who intertwined the culture of the body with national heroism.[45] Nordau (1937) draws an analogy between physical and national renewal (as well as between normative masculinity and normal nationalism). Against this background, it is easy to understand his euphoric description of the first Jewish immigrants to Palestine in the 1880s: "They were stronger than the students of Rabbi Yochanan Ben Zakkai, as big as the legendary warriors of Bar Kochba, the same man who fought not only for the sake of Israelite culture ... but also ... for the national existence on the land of the patriarchs" (Nordau, 1937, p. 7). A year after the publication of "Jewry of Muscle," in a speech at the fifth Zionist Congress in Basle, Nordau revisited the subject of the Jewish body and described the reasons, mostly economic, that brought about the "bodily degeneration of our people." Nordau's solution to the Jewish problem is phrased in bodily terms:

[44] Numerous scholars, of course, have noted the bodily characteristics of the New Hebrew. Shapira (1984), for example, describes the ideal of the new Jew as follows: "No longer a Yeshiva student attending to his Talmud, but instead a mentally and physically healthy young man, daring and ready for battle" (p. 28). Nevertheless, the gender dimension of the Zionist discourse has not, in my opinion, been adequately discussed.

[45] Breines (1990) notes: "While the club's name [Bar Kokhba] revived and honored the ancient Jewish warrior, its prototype was not Jewish at all. In 1810, Friedrich Jahn, patriot and poet, established a network of gymnastic clubs for German students in the wake of Prussia's defeat at the hands of Napoleon's troops. Since then, youth-centered sports and physical culture programs had become a common and important component of nationalist movements in much of Europe" (p. 142).

> To those Jews, who have some money and spare time, we can suggest once more, to exercise diligently ... the idea of educating muscle Jews emerges here, the educated Jewish youth understands this, and there is no doubt that the youth will fulfill such an idea more and more ... we make it our goal that each Zionist organization that has the means will establish a department of fitness and exercise. (Nordau, 1920, p. 85)

Herzl dealt even more extensively with the physical rehabilitation of the male Jew. In a 1895 diary entry, he recounts his conversation with the French writer Alphonse Daudet about his (Herzl's) desire to write a book for and about the Jews.

> Sometime before Easter I became acquainted with [Alphonse] Daudet. On one occasion, we got on the subject of the Jews. He confessed himself an anti-Semite. I explained to him my own standpoint and once again grew ardent... . When I told him that I wanted to write a book for and about the Jews, he asked: "A novel?" "No," I ventured, "preferably a man's book." To which he said: A novel reaches farther. Remember *Uncle Tom's Cabin*." (Lowenthal, 1962, p. 11)

This dialogue is interesting in several ways. Most important in this context is Herzl's telling comment about the question of genre. On the surface, Herzl seems to refer to the correlation between genre, gender, and audience, implying that the novel is read first and foremost by women. Yet Herzl's reply has wider ideological and cultural connotations, which are the subject of this essay. Herzl's Zionist discourse can be read as a discourse about masculinity or, more precisely, as a discourse about a longing for masculinity. Boyarin (1997) describes Herzl's Zionism along these lines:

> To a not inconsiderable extent, the project of these Zionists (known as political Zionists) was to transform Jewish men into the type of male they admired, namely, the ideal "Aryan" male. If the political program of Zionism was to be a nation like all other nations, on the level of reform of the Jewish psyche it was to be men like all other men. The Zionist catchphrase, *kekhol hagoyim*, "like all of the nations," thus has a double meaning since in its popular acceptance it would have meant rather "like all of the (male) gentiles." (p. 277)

Boyarin's reading is supported by an array of textual evidence—for example, the following entry in Herzl's (1925) diary:

> In the course of twenty years, "until they feel it," I need to educate the youth and turn them into military men. But a real army, only 10% of the men—less would not be enough for internal matters. But the rest I should educate to become free and brave men, and in a time of trouble, they join as volunteers. Education through songs of the homeland and the Hasmoneans, religion, plays, heroes in the theater, honor, etc. (pp. 39–40)

Military training and education are perceived here as means for creating "free and brave men" (Herzl). Although this educational program is located within a military framework, it is noteworthy that not only soldiers but all men will participate in this process of educational reformation. The institutionalized teaching of masculinity relies on military and national values, which are now (re)constructed from selected moments in Jewish history. These inextricably entangled values are disseminated through texts—songs of the homeland, religion, plays—in the hope that Zionist education will produce a new type of Jewish masculinity. In one of his letters Herzl argues that "a half-dozen duels will significantly improve the social standing of the Jews" (Locker, 1948, p. 5).

It is against this background that one should understand the senseless plot of Herzl's 1894 play "The New Ghetto," the protagonist of which chooses to duel unnecessarily, a decision that leads to his death. But this death is justified in Herzl's eyes, because through it the protagonist realizes the valued (un-Jewish) code of manly, chivalrous behavior. Herzl concludes his programmatic book, *The Jewish State,* with an impassioned call for the creation of a powerful, brave Jewish man: "Therefore I believe that the wonderful Jewish race will rise from the earth. The Maccabees will live again" (Locker, 1948, p. 75). *Altneuland*, Herzl's (1902/1960) utopic novel, is also preoccupied with the Zionist masculine code, which is both a bodily and ethical code. Herzl's Zionist novel is not simply a political manifesto for the New Society but also, as I argued earlier, a narrative on gender and masculinity.

3

Herzl's *Altneuland* (1902/1960) centers on a cultural attempt to cure the feminized, melancholic male Jew. It is no accident that the novel's first sentence describes Dr. Friedrich Loewenberg as "sunk in deep melancholy" (p. 3). Freud (1913/1955) tacitly suggests, in his early writings, that melancholy is a gender-related state, a "mourning over the loss of libido" (p. 201), while libido itself is construed as masculine. In another theoretical context, Butler (1995) argues that melancholia stems from the repression of homosexual identifications.[46] Despite their obvious differences, both readings point to a gender component in melancholia. Friedrich's melancholia is described as part of the decadent Viennese malaise. The "sickly, pale waiter" or the "equally pale girl cashier" who serve Friedrich in the cafe embody the sickly *fin-de-siècle* Vienna. Friedrich's melancholia, which is a state of permanent mourning, is explained from the start in terms of his difference from other Jews, a difference phrased in phallic terms. While other young men make "bold strokes with their long poles" as they play billiards, he is mostly occupied in "solitary musings," that is, day-

[46] Butler relies here, in part, on the analogy Kristeva makes between motherhood and melancholia, as well as on Irigaray's (1985) argument that Freudian psychoanalysis draws a parallel between melancholia and femininity (see Irigaray, pp. 66-73).

dreaming. Although everybody in Vienna seems to be pale or sickly, Friedrich's emotional problems are clearly related to gender; that is why his friends say to him, "get thee to a nunnery, Ophelia," an address that marks him as both feminine and melancholy. As the plot unfolds the reader learns that Friedrich's melancholia worsens when his beloved Ernestine gets engaged to another man. The loss of Ernestine intensifies Friedrich's distress, but it is noteworthy that the narrator emphasizes Friedrich's melancholia even before he learns of Ernestine's engagement.

Although these events ostensibly occur at the text's margins (namely, in the novel's first chapter), they set the plot in motion. Friedrich's disappointment causes him to answer an ad in the paper that reads: "*Wanted*, an educated, desperate young man willing to make a last experiment with his life. Apply N.O. Body, this office" (p. 8). Friedrich accepts the invitation and joins the man who published the ad, an eccentric Prussian nobleman named Kingscourt, on an exodus from Europe. This libidinal attachment to the non-Jewish man who signed an ad "N.O. Body" (which reads as both "nobody" and "Mr. Body") deserves close critical attention. It is by no means accidental that the non-Jewish Prussian nobleman Kingscourt is called by Herzl "Mr. Body." Herzl, who internalized the anti-Semitic view of the Jew as having a defective body, describes the diasporic Jewish body as grotesque. Numerous minor Jewish characters who appear at Ernestine's engagement party are described in precisely this way. Thus Weinberger, Ernestine's future husband, has a "decided squint and very damp palms" (p. 10). Schlesinger, the confidential representative of Baron Goldstein, is described as a "lean man with the staring eyes" who is "obnoxious, but very popular" (p. 11). And Mr. Gruen is characterized as a "long, lanky man with a reddish beard and ears that stood off from his head" (p. 12). These ignominious Jews cannot but remind us of Mauchel, the horrifying figure of the Jew portrayed by Herzl (1928) in a blatant anti-Semitic essay. Unlike Weinberger, Schlesinger, and Gruen, whose appearance seems to violate the aesthetics of the "proper" body, Kingscourt is described as a "tall, broad-shouldered" man (p. 28).[47]

Not everything Kingscourt seeks is explicitly mentioned in the Prussian nobleman's ad. Kingscourt is looking for a desperate man, but the ad does not specify the cause of this desperation. In their first meeting Friedrich learns that Kingscourt, who was betrayed by a young woman, is looking for a male companion to join him on an island in the "South Seas where one is truly alone" (p. 31). Without saying it explicitly, Kingscourt has chosen men who suffered bitter disappointments in their relationships with women, so much so that they no longer seek the company of women. They will be served on the island by a mute African and a Tahitian "whom [Kingscourt] pulled out of the water in Avrua harbor when he tried to drown himself over an unhappy love affair" (p. 31). Kingscourt says: "I want to take a companion back with me—so that I shall not unlearn human speech, and so that there may

[47] On the emergence of the aesthetic and ethic standard of the male body in European culture, see Mosse (1996).

be someone by me to close my eyes when I die. Do you want to be that someone" (pp. 31–32)? Kingscourt tells Friedrich that a "yes" would mean a lifetime commitment: "I must remind you that you are undertaking a life long obligation.... If you come with me now, there will be no going back. You must cut all your ties" (p. 32). It is impossible, of course, to ignore the wording "a life long commitment," which draws an analogy between Ernestine's engagement and Kingscourt and Friedrich's contract. After Friedrich recounts his own life story, Kingscourt is appeased: "Now I believe that you will not leave me once I have you upon my island" (p. 33).

On their way to the island, Kingscourt and Friedrich make a stop in Palestine, which they find desolate. After 20 years on the island, they make their way back to Europe only to discover that Palestine has in the meantime turned into a world center. The encounter with the prosperous land is, of course, at the heart of the novel. About the 20 years the two men spent on the island the reader learns practically nothing, except for the following dialogue:

> "Well, our island did not disagree with you, Fritz. What a green, hollow-chested Jewboy you were when I took you away. Now you are like an oak. You might still be dangerous to the women."
> "You are quite mad, Kingscourt," laughed Friedrich. "I think too much of you to infer that you are dragging me to Europe to marry me off."
> Kingscourt was convulsed with laughter. "Carrion! Marry you off! You don't think me that kind of an ass, I hope! What would I do with you then?"
> "Well, it might be a delicate way of getting rid of me. Haven't you had enough of my society?"
> "Now the carrion's fishing for compliments," shouted the old man, who expressed his good humor best through epithets. "You know very well, Fritzchen, that I can no longer live without you. Indeed, I arranged this whole trip for your sake. So that you would be patient with me for a few years longer." (p. 54)

Herzl describes the radical transformation of the Jew's body, and implies that Friedrich's exodus from Europe facilitated this physical rehabilitation, renewed vigor, and reshaped masculinity. From an effeminate male, "a green, hollow-chested Jewboy," Friedrich becomes strong as "an oak." This transformation brings Friedrich closer to Herzl's ideal of the rehabilitated body, but the stay on the island brings about only a partial recovery of the effeminate male Jew, because Friedrich's physical recovery cannot be fully realized before he reaches Palestine. This dialogue is interesting in yet another way, for it reveals a deep homoerotic subtext that informs the relationship between the two men. What the dialogue reveals, in fact, is that the men's relationship and a heterosexual relationship are in their eyes mutually exclusive. The libidinal attachment between the two men to which this dialogue gives voice reveals that, prior to arriving at Palestine, Friedrich does not want to marry a woman. When he suspects that Kingscourt wants him to get married, Kingscourt denies such plans, because marriage would make their relationship impossible. Interestingly enough, on their way back to Europe, Friedrich draws an analogy between his lack of interest in marriage and his apathy regarding news from Europe. Thus he says that, when he received a shipment from Europe wrapped up in newspapers, he "rolled the papers into a bundle and burned them unread" (p. 55). Friedrich's stay in Palestine, the new-old land, rekindles both an interest in society and a dormant heterosexual desire. Looking back at his years on the island, Friedrich suddenly feels he may have wasted 20 years of his life:

> "How did we spend twenty beautiful years? Hunting and fishing, eating, drinking and sleeping, playing chess." Upon hearing that Kingscourt adds: "And with an old donkey, what?" But Friedrich assures Kingscourt of his loyalty: "Drop the 'old donkey' stuff .... I could not and would not live without you any more." (p. 84)

Friedrich's recovery from his melancholia, a process that culminates in Palestine, has two aspects. On the one hand, he expresses a new interest in social issues and a desire to be a productive member of society. On the other hand, he begins once again to experience heterosexual desires. Kingscourt understands well before Friedrich that joining the new society may threaten their special relationship. But at this stage, Friedrich still chooses to remain loyal to the older man, without whom he could not and would not live.

As the plot unfolds, however, land and woman become entirely enmeshed in Friedrich's imagination: his budding desire to be a useful member of the New Society and his nascent heterosexual desire for Miriam are linked time and again. Following is a scene where Miriam woos Friedrich and tries to persuade him to join the New Society. Friedrich says

> "You really think it is not too late, Miss Miriam?" He was overjoyed. "Could I still become a useful human being?"
> "Of course," she smiled.
> Hope stirred within him. He felt suddenly rejuvenated. New perspective opened before him. But after a moment he recalled his situation, and sighed once more.
> "Ah, no, Miss Miriam. It would have been too beautiful. I cannot do as I choose. I cannot remain here. I am not free."
> She paled slightly as she repeated in a voice that trembled, "Not free?"
> "No, I am tied to someone for life."
> "To whom, if I may ask?" She spoke tonelessly.
> "To Mr. Kingscourt." He explained his relation to the old man. He had given his word of honor never to leave him. (p. 157)

Miriam, who does not understand the intensity of Friedrich and Kingscourt's relationship, is relieved to hear Friedrich's answer, but Friedrich's route to heterosexuality is by no means simple. Even after this episode Friedrich reconfirms his unfailing loyalty to Kingscourt. Kingscourt, who already wants to move on, asks Friedrich if he wants to stay in Palestine. Friedrich then replies: "Why ask me, Kingscourt? You know very well that I belong to you, and go with you wherever and whenever you choose" (p. 181). Here, too, the contract tying Friedrich to Kingscourt cannot but remind one of the language of a marriage contract.

The process of Friedrich's heterosexualization is a slow one. Even when Kingscourt agrees to stay in Palestine due to his love for little Fritzy (Zionists David and Sara's baby), Friedrich does not allow himself to express explicitly his heterosexual desire:

> Friedrich still did not know whether the old man was in earnest. To remain was his own most ardent wish. To become a member of the New Society, to participate in its high enterprises, to join hands with his valiant men. There was something else, besides, but he dare not admit it to himself. (p. 269)

Friedrich's deep commitment to Kingscourt generates self-censorship, which prevents him from saying why he truly wishes to join the New Society. Kingscourt, at the same time, instructs, perhaps sarcastically, both Friedrich and Miriam to resist their mutual attraction:

> When Friedrich shook hands with Kingscourt, the latter said, "Do you know, Fritze, that this is the first day that we have spent apart in twenty years? Don't get lost on a byroad .... And you, Miss Miriam, please don't take advantage of the opportunity to turn this boy's head. He's forty-three years old. The most dangerous age!" (pp. 234–235)

Despite this homoerotic attachment, however, the novel does end with marriage. But even this moment, which signifies the successful completion of the task of transforming the effeminate male Jew into a "healthy" heterosexual, is a rather passive moment. Friedrich is almost forced to say yes to Miriam on her mother's death-bed. The dying mother urges them to hold hands:

> "I thought—so—at once. Then ... when you—on the balcony ... outside here ... children!" She groped blindly. "Miriam—has told—me ... nothing. But a mother ... sees! Children! Give ... each other ... your hands. My blessing—my blessing!"
>
> Miriam and Friedrich had to reach out their hands to each other, but they were so hesitant that she [i.e., the mother] took notice. She looked anxiously from one to the other, and whispered, "Or? ... or?"
>
> "Yes, indeed," said Friedrich fervently, and pressed the girl's hand. "Yes," repeated Miriam softly. (p. 293)

Normal masculinity is perceived in the novel as a precondition for nation-building.

Friedrich, who at the beginning of the novel is called "Ophelia," turns into an "oak" on the island, and later on in Zion becomes a man capable of taking a woman and raising a family. Friedrich's maturation is presented as a shift from a pathological state (melancholia) to a normal state (heterosexual masculinity). As the novel ends, Friedrich and Miriam assume proper gender roles. Thus, it is no accident that Friedrich, after all his hesitation, says yes fervently, while Miriam, despite her active wooing of Friedrich, utters her yes softly. Herzl is interested here in what I call gender polarization, an ideology that presents man and woman not only as essentially different, but also as diametrically opposed.

The narrative on sexuality and gender, which I presented here linearly, appears in the novel in a decidedly fragmented way, at the margins of the detailed account of the political, social, and cultural structures of the new society. But the reconstruction of this narrative—which starts from Friedrich's disappointment with women, continues with his decision to share his life with an older man, and ends with his return to a normative, heterosexual model—seems necessary for a full understanding of this utopian novel.

Herzl's (1925) choice to end the text with Friedrich's and Miriam's engagement turns marriage—and heterosexuality—into a central theme of the novel. Herzl's decision to have Friedrich marry Miriam should not be explained away as a resort to a literary convention, for the importance of marriage appears in Herzl's diaries time and again: "We will give those who have families bigger salaries. We will make numerous, i. e., cheap, furniture for wedded couples, and for other groups as a prize for 'diligence and industriousness' etc. Our goal is marriage." In an equally revealing passage, he writes

> As a stipend for my brave warriors, aspiring artists, and faithful, talented officials, I will use the dowries of our wealthy girls. I must drive a marriage politics. To the leading bankers, who will curry my favor, I shall say: I should be happy if you give your daughters to vigorous and ambitious young men. I need it for the State. It is the self-fertilization of the nation. (p. 40)

Herzl's ideological interest in marriage is anchored in an assessment (voiced, for example, by the Zionist Swiss psychiatrist Rafael Becker, as well as by A. D. Gordon) that the late age in which male Jews get married contributes to the outbreak of sexual nervousness (Biale, 1992). But a crucial question imposes itself: why does Herzl frame his detailed political, economic, social, and cultural plan with an unconvincing romantic narrative ending in marriage? After all, on June 11, 1895, he wrote in his diary that "it would be below my honor to sweeten my plan with a love story" (1925, Hebrew translation, p. 74).[48] Herzl's resort to a love story should be read in light of Sommer's (1991) observation that "eroticism and nationalism become figures for each other in modernizing fiction" (p. 31). Following this insight, I argue that Herzl indeed intertwines the erotic healing of the protagonist and the national restoration of the people. Thus, to quote Sommer, "the rhetorical relationship be-

[48] This is omitted from the English translation. See Hebrew translation (p. 74).

tween heterosexual passion and hegemonic states functions as a mutual allegory, as if each discourse were grounded in the allegedly stable other."

In a way, *Altneuland* signifies a reversal in Herzl's position. As I mentioned earlier, Herzl refused to write his book in the form of a novel, fearing that it would be read only by women. This refusal led to the writing of the programmatic, nonfictional book, *The Jewish State* (1896/2006). Sommer's (1991) formulation may explain the modification of Herzl's position. He now chooses the feminine genre of the novel precisely because it allows him to mesh the national and the erotic into a single narrative. The heterosexual narrative and the national narrative are inextricably entangled, so that the shift from homoeroticism to heterosexuality functions as an allegory for the shift from political powerlessness to national strength. And at the same time, renewed national vigor functions as an allegory for heterosexual desire. The novel's ending is generated by the crucial link between the love of Miriam and the love of Altneuland.

Friedrich's transformation is by no means accidental, because almost everyone who reaches Palestine is presented as undergoing a physical and psychological change. Although the classification of the Jewish body originated in anti-Semitic discourse, it has come to serve Zionist ideology as well. In his diaries Herzl (1925) expresses his desire for a place in which the Jewish body will cease to bear a particular meaning: "The Promised Land, where we can have hooked noses, black or red beards, and bandy legs without being despised for it" (p. 46). But a reading of *Altneuland* reveals that the novel advances a prescriptive hermeneutics of the body. The analogy between the body and the body politic (and the question which physical body will represent the new national body politic) haunts Herzl throughout the entire novel. When Friedrich revisits Palestine after his stay on the island, he discovers that Palestine has transformed from a desolate land into a prosperous place. David Littwak, the one time miserable Viennese beggar, has turned into a public figure of the new society. He is now described as "a tall, vigorous man of thirty, whose sunburnt face was framed in a short black beard" (p. 60). He welcomes Friedrich and Kingscourt and explains the transformation Zionism has brought about in the Jew.

> We are merely a society of citizens seeking to enjoy life through work and culture. We content ourselves with making our young people physically fit. We developed their bodies as well as their minds. We find athletic and rifle clubs sufficient for this purpose, even as they were thought sufficient in Switzerland. We also have competitive games—cricket, football, rowing—like the English.... Jewish children used to be pale, weak, timid. Now look at them! The explanation of this miracle is the simplest in the world. We took our children out of damp cellars and hovels, and brought them into the sunlight. Plants cannot thrive without sun. No more can human beings. Plants can be saved by transplantation into congenial soil. Human beings as well. That is how it happened! (pp. 79–80)

David Littwak's words cannot but remind one of Nordau's (1980) description in the "Jewry of Muscle." Both Herzl and Nordau are interested in negating the anti-Semitic stereotype of the effeminate male Jew, yet they do not reject the stereotype's accuracy but rather present it as a direct consequence of materialist conditions in the diaspora. The effeminate Jewish body does not signify a racial essence but is instead a symptom of national and social distress. It should come as no surprise then that immigration to Palestine brings about an almost immediate change in the Jew's body. In Palestine not only David Littwak turns into a tall, vigorous man but also his father, whose existence in Vienna aroused Friedrich's pity, is described as a transformed man.

> The dignified old man who carried himself so well—could he be the wretched peddler to whom he [Friedrich] once tried to give alms in a Viennese cafe! What a remarkable transformation! And yet it had happened in the most natural way in the world. The Littwaks had been among the first to hasten to Palestine at the beginning of the great new national enterprise, and reaped the rewards of the prosperity the helped so faithfully to create. (Herzl, 1902/1960, p. 160)

The entire land is presented as a site of national health, both mental and physical. In their visit to the Neudorf (new village) they are welcomed by Friedman, "a sturdy farmer of about forty" and by another farmer who is "a robust, sunburned man" (p. 133). Moreover, the new form of commerce is described in terms of bodily health: "We had a social-political motive: that is to say, we wanted to cure our small tradesmen of certain outworn, uneconomic, and injurious forms of trade" (p. 100). Even the "penal colony," the modern jail, is described as a site where people "are restored to physical and moral health" (p. 240).

Ahad Ha'am (1961), who published a sardonic review of *Altneuland*, was perhaps the first to recognize the cultural priorities forwarded by Herzl. He wrote ironically

> In Haifa there are, of course, good schools, and Miriam, David's sister, teaches French and English in one of the schools for women. If Hebrew and other Jewish subjects are taught—we do not know. Because in all matters dealing with education, David tells us only that [schools] attempt to strengthen children's bodies through various sports as is common in England.

Ha'am adds that, during the guests' stay in Neudorf, two of them visit the school as well as the library. "But among all they see there they tell us nothing except that in the school they saw useful and beneficial things for physical and spiritual education, and in the library many books on popular science." Ahad Ha-am recognizes here not only the lack of specific Jewish content in the New Society but also Herzl's longing for everything essentially unJewish, including the longing for a culture of the body. Thus, he angrily summarizes Herzl's national vision as "a monkey's mimicry lacking any independent national characteristics, reeking of 'slavery within freedom,' the result of [the] diaspora in the west, spreading in all directions" (Ahad Ha-am). It is perhaps no coincidence that Herzl confesses in a letter to Nordau that his first impulse after reading Ahad Ha-am's review was to "smack the head of this blabbering extremist. But then they would see the hurt writer in me." The hidden impulse to strike Ahad Ha-am is in accordance with Herzl's view of manly honor, a view best demonstrated by his advocacy of the duel.[49]

The question that has concerned me here is how Herzl imagines national recovery in terms that are clearly drawn from the field of gender and sexuality. Upon reading *Altneuland*, it becomes clear that Herzl aspires to what he considers to be normal masculinity. This normalcy is based on the repudiation of femininity in the Jewish man. Another Viennese Jew, Sigmund Freud (1909/1955), argued that the "repudiation of femininity can be nothing else than a biological fact, a part of the great riddle of sex" (p. 252). Yet, as we have seen, Herzl's and Freud's need to define masculinity as the repudiation of femininity did not stem from a biological fact, but rather from the social matrix that identified the male Jew as woman. Their construction of masculinity is thus based on negation: the negation of femininity.

Herzl's desire for normal masculinity, which is in essence a non-Jewish masculinity (represented in the novel by the figure of Kingscourt), brings him to describe Zionism as a process of gender/sexual redemption that culminates in marriage. Paradoxically, however, the protagonist's heterosexualization is achieved through homosexuality. Although the relationship between the two men is not portrayed as sexual, the description of their friendship is that of a married couple, bestowing on it a homosexual flavor or undercurrent. Herzl relies here on two different cultural perceptions of homosexuality. On the one hand, this relationship is based on Friedrich's femininity, in which case a parallel is drawn between homosexuality and femininity. On the other hand, it is precisely this homoeroticism that turns Friedrich into a sturdy oak. In other words, homosexuality is viewed as producing intensified masculinity.[50] Herzl who focuses in *Altneuland* on the heterosexualization of the male Jew, advances an ideology of gender polarization. Gender polarization is in fact the ideological basis of heterosexuality, because the opposite sexes are perceived as complementary. Gender polarization does not allow for any similarity between men and women, and it comprehends the sexes as essentially different.[51] In Herzl's (1925)

---

[49] Herzl was not the only Zionist to view Jews' avoidance of duels as a cowardly stance. The Zionist ideologue Birenbaum writes, "The cowardice that drives us away from military service and from the masculine duel, and our appearance which gives rise to mockery and strangeness—this list of virtues and good qualities has one origin: our Semitic race" (Quoted in Doron, 1968).

[50] It is not insignificant, of course, that the gentile Kingscourt represents normal masculinity, while Friedrich acquires his masculinity only gradually. This view of homoeroticism as a means of acquiring masculinity is based on the Greek model (See Halperin, 1990, pp. 56-57).

[51] It is noteworthy that the view of the sexes as essentially different, as in the phrase *the opposite sex*, is relatively new. Until the 18th century the male and female bodies were perceived as very similar, and female anatomy was understood as a mirror image of male anatomy (See Lacqueur, 1990, pp. 1-25).

diary, the desire for gender polarization is phrased as follows: "A novel. The male protagonist is a blonde type, blue eyes, a piercing gaze. His love is a Sephardic Jewess, tall, black hair, of noble stock. He sees her first as the commander of a battleship. He dreams about her [being] in his tent." Man and woman represent total opposite, both in complexion—he is blonde, she has black hair—and in behavior—he is a commander and she, at least in his dream, is subdued in his tent. Heterosexuality, for Herzl, is not simply a matter of object-choice; it is an ideological matrix requiring absolute difference between the sexes.[52]

One of the ideological tensions that surfaces in *Altneuland* and deserves critical attention stems from the incommensurability of two opposite desires: On the one hand, Herzl describes the Zionist project as a rehabilitation of masculinity, a process that can be achieved only through a polarization of the sexes. On the other hand, Herzl argues in the novel that one of the purposes of Zionism is the liberation of women. Biale (1992) has already observed that these two objectives are at the heart of the Zionist project: "Zionism promised an erotic revolution for the Jews: the creation of a virile New Hebrew Man, but also the rejection of the inequality of women found in traditional Judaism in favor of full equality between the sexes in all spheres of life" (pp. 176–177). While Biale sees these two tasks as complementary, I suggest that Herzl's two objectives are in contradiction with one another. Can the longing for gender polarization coexist with sexual equality? Can these two goals be achieved simultaneously? Let us look at the ways in which the longing for heterosexual masculinity affects the status of women in the New Society and how it relates to other aspects of his utopian vision.

4

Herzl's belief that women should be granted equal rights is part of a larger liberal-humanist ideology voiced by the character David Littwak:

> [M]y associates and I make no distinctions between one man and another. We do not ask to what race or religion a man belongs. If he is a man, that is enough for us.... I can tell you that the fundamental principles of humanitarianism are generally accepted among us. As far as religion goes, you will find Christian, Mohammedan, Buddhist, and Brahmin houses of worship near our own synagogues." (pp. 66–67)

The words that Herzl puts in David Littwak's mouth give the impression that the discourse on minorities is exceptionally tolerant and progressive. The New Society is presented as a place where not only Jews but all religions live in harmony. The de-

[52] I am referring to heterosexuality not as an object choice (of someone from the opposite sex), but rather as an ideological construction that views sex between man and woman as a union of opposites (See Rubin, 1975).

sire to liberate man and to demonstrate the interconnectedness of all types of racial discrimination is expressed in the novel by Steineck. Meditating on the "Black problem" in Africa, he says:

> The depth of the problem, in all their horror, only a Jew can fathom.... Don't laugh Mr. Kingscourt. Think of the hair-raising horrors of the slave trade. Human beings, because their skins are black, are stolen, carried off, and sold. Their descendants grow up in alien surroundings despised and hated because their skin is differently pigmented. I am not ashamed to say, though I be thought ridiculous, now that I have lived to see the restoration of the Jews, I should like to pave the way for the restoration of the Negroes. (p. 170)

During Herzl's own lifetime, his progressive vision was already considered unrealistic. Ludwig Gumplovitch, a law professor at the University of Gratz, and one of the fathers of modern sociology, wrote to Herzl in 1899 (quoted in Elon, 1972, p. 164): "You are endowed with a political naiveté that can be forgiven only in poets," and he adds, "You want to establish a state without bloodshed? Where have you ever seen such a thing? Without force or cunning? Simply like that, in broad daylight and in honesty—with easy monthly installments?" But is Herzl's vision indeed so egalitarian and progressive? Do the repeated descriptions of harmonious coexistence between Jews and Arabs, or for that matter men and women, actually portray a society without rifts and internal violence? In this last section I want to demonstrate how Herzl's apparently progressive representation of minorities is undermined by a subtext that relegates both the woman and the Arabs to the margins of the symbolic order of the New Society.

One of the most interesting moments in Herzl's novel emerges when David and his guests discuss the status of women in the New Society. On hearing that Miriam teaches French and English in a girls' high school, Kingscourt grovels: "So the poor girl has to drudge at giving lessons." Kingscourt perceives equality between the sexes as an unnecessary burden for women. David's conversation with Kingscourt is worth quoting at length.

> "She does not do it for livelihood. I don't have to let my sister starve, thank Heaven. But she has duties and performs them, because she also has rights. In our New Society the women have equal rights with the men."
> "All the Devils!"
> "They have active and passive suffrage as a matter of course. They worked faithfully beside us during the reconstruction period. Their enthusiasm lent wings to the men's courage. It would have been the blackest ingratitude if we had relegated them to the servant's hall or to the harem." (pp. 74–75)

David's reply reveals the ruptures and fissures in Herzl's thinking about the place of women in the New Society. This passage gives voice to two contradictory ideological positions. As a universalist, Herzl gives equal rights to all members in the

New Society (Muslims, Christians, Jews, men, and women). Yet his insistence on gender polarization relegates women to the margins of the social and symbolic order.[53] That is precisely why Miriam's work is not described in financial terms and why she is still presented as her brother's dependent. Against the background of David's own financial prosperity, the description of Miriam's work as divorced from any economic meaning is all the more remarkable. David's statement about equality between the sexes is anchored in hierarchical, polarized language, which underlines the difference between men and women. Moreover, the woman is presented here in strictly patriarchal terms. The Zionist idea is presented as a male project, and women's participation is restricted to lending "wings to the men's courage" (p. 75). Even women's suffrage is presented in terms of men's decision not to relegate woman to an inferior position in "the servant's hall" or in "the harem" (p. 75). Women enjoy equal rights, but men expect them to restrict their desire for political power voluntarily. Although their political participation and visibility is limited, women are expected to be satisfied with the truncated role granted to them by Herzl's liberal humanitarianism.

Interestingly, David Littwak's views on the place of women are inextricably entangled with his stance on the place of the Arab in the New Society. Both women and Arabs are viewed as minorities who, in return for equal rights, accept their marginal status within the male Jewish hegemony. Thus as they speak about the place of women and as they mention the harem, Friedrich asks about the place of the Arab in the New Society: "You told us on our way here," he tells David, "that Reschid Bey is also a member of your society" (p. 75). David replies:

> No one is obliged to join the New Society. And those who do join are not compelled to exercise their rights. They do as they please. In your own day you must

[53] Such contradictions surfaced, in various forms, in other schools of Zionism. Although the Socialist Zionism of Hashomer Hatsair was markedly different from Herzl's Liberal Zionism, one cannot ignore a similar view on the question of women. Consider, for example, the 1936 statement by left-wing leader Meir Ya'ari. Ya'ari's fierce statement attests to the opposition within Hashomer Hatsair to full equality between men and women: "Some find justification for a female member that has no interest in politics. Woman was not created for this. A song of praise is sung for women's deep understanding of educational matters and for establishing friendly relations within the Kibbutz. In this realm of social relations it is customary to draw a line between natural qualities of men and women. The men's strength is in public affairs, as it were, and women's strength is in intimate relations .... I object in this matter to all 'but' and 'indeed,' just as in the agrarian question so it is with women's liberation. Socialism cannot be satisfied with partial solutions. We must demand full equality without limits" Interestingly enough, Ya'ari himself confesses to the change in his own views since the 1920s, as well as to the masculinist ideology underlying Zionism: "We carried within ourselves a burden of the psychology of Weininger, Freud, and Nietzsche. In this anti-feminist literature woman appeared as a passive receptacle, bound to a specific time and place. As someone lacking imaginative creativity, who limits the storming conquest of the male fighters" (Rosner, 1969, p. 3).

> have known men in Europe who were not interested in elections, who never took the trouble to vote, and who could not by any means have been persuaded to take office. So it is with our women and their rights. Don't imagine that our women are not devoted to their homes. My wife, for instance, never goes to meetings. (p. 75)

This surprising shift from the place of the Arab in the New Society to women's rights emphasizes the link between different kinds of social otherness. The Others in the new society are grateful for their legal equality, but they don't demand that this equality be put into practice. In fact, it appears that legal equality serves as a mechanism to silence resistance. Thus, David explains in a patronizing manner that his wife stopped being politically active once she married him and gave birth.

> She nursed our little boy, and so forgot a bit about her inalienable rights. She used to belong to the radical opposition. That is how I met her, as an opponent. Now she opposes me only at home, as loyally as you can imagine, however. (p. 75)

It is Kingscourt, the *outsider-within*, who sees through this patriarchical trap of co-optation. He ironically says: "That's a damned good way of overcoming an opposition. It simplifies politics tremendously" (p. 76). Marriage and motherhood result in a depoliticization of women, who now cease to oppose the existing social order. The shift from radical opposition to obedient co-optation is based on a very sharp distinction between the private and the public spheres. The woman's place is in the home, and her main activity is within the domain of the family. Thus David argues: "I must make it clear to you gentlemen, that our women are too sensible to let public affairs interfere with their personal well-being. It is a common human trait—not only a feminine one—not to concern ourselves with things we already possess" (p. 76).[54]

Herzl's fantasy is exposed in the description of Fatma, Reschid Bey's wife, who doesn't join her husband and his guests when they take a day trip.

> Reschid was already waiting in front of his house. They greeted him cordially. From behind an upper-story lattice a lovely feminine hand waved a handkerchief.
>
> "Good-bye, Fatma!" called Sara smilingly to the invisible one. "We shall bring your husband back safely. Don't worry!"
>
> "Kiss the children for me, Fatma" cried Miriam.

[54] Similar patriarchal views appear in Herzl's (1925) diary: "Prizes for fertility, and a good, patriarchal education for the children" (p. 59) And in another entry, writing about a solution for prostitution, he adds: "A patriarchal family, helping young people get married ... we employ many young people, we pay them well, and we let them conduct a family life" (p. 94).

> Reschid's bags were stowed in the car, and he took a seat beside David. The white hand waved a last farewell. And the motor ark wheezed forward.
> Friedrich turned to Miriam. "So that poor lady must remain at home alone."
> "She is a happy and contented woman," replied Miriam. "She wants her husband to enjoy this little trip, I'm sure. He would not have thought of coming with us if it had annoyed her. They are both very fine people." (p. 116)

In order to understand the complexity of this scene it is worthwhile to read it against the initial appearance in the text of Reschid Bey himself.

> A handsome man of thirty-five was standing beside a wrought iron gate as they drove by. He wore dark European clothing and a red fez. His salute to them was the Oriental gesture that signifies lifting and kissing the dust. David called to him in Arabic, and Reschid replied in German with a slight Northern accent. "Wish you much joy of your guests!"
> Kingscourt stared. "Who's the little Muslim?" he asked.
> "He studied in Berlin," replied David laughingly. "His father was among the first to understand the beneficent character of the Jewish immigration and enriched himself, because he keeps pace with our economic progress. Reschid himself is a member of our New Society." (pp. 68–69)

Both scenes seem to respect the cultural otherness of the Arab. Yet it is noteworthy that only the male Arab is allowed to assimilate. Reschid Bey, who wears a European suit, and who speaks excellent German with a Northern accent, expresses his Arabness only superficially. He does not express any national aspirations, and the red fez and Arabic salute are the only expressions of his ethnic identity. However once Friedrich and Kingscourt arrive at Reschid Bey's house and encounter Fatma, we realize that Reschid's life is strictly divided between the public and private spheres. In the public sphere the Arab is an assimilated European who describes his Arab village during the pre-Zionist era in Orientalist terms, while in the private sphere of the home he remains an Arab who adheres to the traditional division of gender roles in Arab society.

There is no doubt that Herzl, who allows Jewish women to participate in the day trip, posits the Jewish woman as superior to the Arab woman, who lacks both body and subjectivity. The Arab woman is nothing but a floating hand waving silently goodbye, cut off from the body that it represents synecdochically. Her total absence—seeing but not seen—and absolute passivity are manifested also by lack of voice: she does not greet but is rather greeted; she does not utter a word but serves as an invisible receptacle to the greetings sent to her from afar. But is the difference between the Jewish woman and Arab woman as significant as it first appears? Friedrich says patronizingly: "I admire a woman who remains obediently behind her lattice. On a morning like this ladies" (p. 117). The Jewish woman then replies: "Isn't it delightful?... Spring days like these come nowhere but in Palestine. Life has a better savor here than anywhere else" (p. 117). This fascinating dialogue delineates the boundaries of freedom granted to women in the New Society. Unlike the Arab woman, the Jewish woman enjoys subjectivity and freedom, but both of them are relegated to the private sphere, which is represented by the home. The greeting that Miriam sends Fatma to kiss the children for her expresses the limited and depoliticized solidarity between women. Motherhood and home define both woman and femininity. Friedrich's provocative comments remain unanswered, and Sara, David's wife, who turns to speak about the weather is a living example of the political passivity to which women are relegated once they get married.

It seems that in his thinking about the status of minorities in the New Society, Herzl relies heavily on the father of Reform Judaism, Moses Mendelssohn's formulation: "Be a Jew at home but a man on the street." This formulation coerces the minority subject into an existence split between the public and private spheres. Such a dual subjectivity explains Reschid Bay's decision to be a devout Muslim at home but an assimilated western citizen in the public domain. The equality the Arab enjoys is based on his cooperation and co-optation within Jewish hegemony, because in the public domain he is required to erase his Arabness. In other words, only male Jews are allowed to be whole, unsplit subjects. But it seems that the woman's position is even more inferior, because, while the Arab is allowed to be an Arab at home and a man outside, the woman is encouraged to relinquish her right to leave home altogether. The Arab in *Altneuland* is encouraged to assimilate; the woman cannot but remain a woman.

As a political and sexual utopia, *Altneuland* does not simply represent reality; instead it constructs a reality. If *Altneuland* is a foundational fiction, it is because it has come to be perceived as a text that foreshadowed the birth of the State of Israel. Laskov (1991) thus argues that "it is well-known that many of Herzl's prophesies, which at the time seemed completely illusory, have turned into a reality." Yet the realization of Herzl's dream should not blind us to the problematic aspects of his political plan. It seems that today, over a hundred years after the advent of political Zionism, we should reexamine the political implications of the Zionist longing for "normal," heterosexual masculinity and gender polarization.

References

Ahad Ha-am (1961). *Collected writings*. Tel Aviv: Dvir.

Almog, S. (1992). *Nationalism, Zionism, anti-semitism* (Hebrew). Jerusalem: Zionist Library.

Anderson, B. (1983). *Imagined communities: Reflections on the origin and spread of nationalism*. London: Verso.

Biale, D. (1992). *Eros and the Jews*. New York: Basic Books.

Boyarin, D. (1997). *Unheroic conduct: The rise of heterosexuality and the invention of the Jewish man*. Berkeley: University of California Press.

Breines, P. (1990). *Tough Jews*. New York: Basic Books.

Butler, J. (1995). Melancholy gender/refused identification. In M. Berger, B. Wallis, & S. Watson (Eds.), *Constructing masculinity*. New York: Routledge.

Doron, Y. (1983). Classical Zionism and modern anti-semitism: Parallels and influences (1883–1914). *Journal of Israeli History, 4*(2), 169-204.
Elon, A. (1972). *The Israelis* (Hebrew). Jerusalem: Shocken.
Foucault, M. (1979). *Discipline and punish.* New York: Vintage Books.
Foucault, M. (1990). *The history of sexuality* (Vol. 1; R. Hurley, Trans.). New York: Vintage.
Freud, S. (1955). Analysis of a phobia in a five-year-old boy. In J. Strachey (Ed. & Trans.), *The standard edition of the complete psychological works of Sigmund Freud* (Vol. 10). London: The Hogarth Press. (Original work published 1909)
Freud, S. (1955). Mourning and melancholia. In J. Strachey (Ed. & Trans.), *The standard edition of the complete psychological works of Sigmund Freud* (Vol. 14). London: The Hogarth Press. (Original work published 1913)
Garber, M. (1992). *Vested interests: Cross dressing and cultural anxiety.* New York: Harper.
Gay, P. (1988). *Freud: A life for our time.* New York: Norton, 1988.
Gilman, S. (1989). *Sexuality. An illustrated history.* New York: Wiley.
Gilman, S. (1994). *The case of Sigmund Freud: Medicine and identity at the fin de siècle.* Baltimore: The Johns Hopkins University Press.
Gilman, S. (1995). *Freud, race and gender.* Princeton: Princeton University Press.
Halperin, D. (1990). *One hundred years of homosexuality.* New York: Routledge.
Herzl, T. (1925). *Diaries* (Hebrew). Tel Aviv: Mitzpeh.
Herzl, T. (1928). Mauchel. In *Before nation and world* (Hebrew) Vol. 1. Tel Aviv: Mitspe.
Herzl, T. (1960). *Altneuland: Old-new land* (L. Levensohn, Trans.). New York: Bloch Publishing Company and Herzl Press. (Original work published 1902)
Herzl, T. (2006). *The Jewish state.* Minneapolis: Filiquarian Publishing. (Original work published 1896)
Irigaray, L. (1985). *Speculum of the other woman.* Ithaca: Cornell University Press.
Katz, J.N. (1995). *The invention of heterosexuality.* New York: Penguin.
Lacqueur, T. (1990). *Making sex: Body and gender from the Greeks to Freud.* Cambridge: Harvard University Press.
Laskov, S. (1991). The debate over *Altneuland* (in Hebrew). *Ha-tsiyonut, 15*, 35-53.
Locker, B. (1948). Introduction to "The Jewish state" (Hebrew). In T. Herzl, *Zionist writings.* Jerusalem: The Zionist Library.
Lowenthal, M. (Ed.). (1962). *The diaries of Theodor Herzl.* New York: Grosset's Universal Library.
Mosse, G. (1985). *Nationalism and sexuality: Middle-class morality and sexual norms in modern Europe.* Madison: University of Wisconsin Press.
Mosse, G. (1996). *The image of man.* New York: Oxford University Press.
Nordau, M. (1920). *Selected writings* (Hebrew). Tel Aviv: Mitzpeh.
Nordau, M. (1937). *Political writings* (Hebrew). Tel Aviv: Mitzpeh.
Nordau, M. (1980). Jewry of muscle. In P. Mendes-Floher & J. Reinharz (Eds.), *The Jew in the modern world* (pp. 547-548). New York: Oxford University Press.
Press, J. (1997). Same-sex unions in modern Europe: *Daniel Deronda, Altneuland* and the Homoerotics of Jewish Nationalism. In E.K. Sedgwick (Ed.), *Novel gazing* (pp. 299-329). Durham: Duke University Press.
Proust, M. (1982). *Remembrance of things past* (Volumes 1-3). New York: Vintage.
Reizbaum, M. (1999). *James Joyce's Judaic other.* Stanford: Stanford University Press.
Robertson, R. (1998). Historicizing Weininger: The ninteenth-century German image of the feminized Jew. In B. Cheyette & L. Marcus (Eds.), *Modernity, culture and "the Jew."* Standford: Stanford University Press.

Rosner, M. (1969). *Changes in the perceptions of women's equality in the Kibbutz* (Hebrew). Givat Haviva: Institute for the Research of Kibbutz Society.
Rubin, G. (1975). The traffic in woman: Notes on the political economy of sex. In R. Reiter (Ed.), *Toward an anthropology of woman* (pp. 157-210). New York: Monthly Review Press.
Shapira, A. (1984) *Walking on the horizon*. Tel Aviv: Am Oved.
Sommer, D. (1991). *Foundational fictions: The national romances of Latin America*. Berkeley: The University of California Press.
Weininger, O. (2005). *Geschlecht und Charakter* [*Sex and character*]. Bloomington: Indiana Unerversity Press. (Original work published 1903)

6

National Troubles: Male Matters in Israeli Gay Cinema

Raz Yosef

The political project of Zionism of liberating the Jewish people and creating a nation like all other nations was intertwined with a longing for the sexual redemption and normalization of the Jewish male body. In fin-de-siècle, anti-Semitic, scientific-medical discourse, the male Jew body was associated with disease, madness, degeneracy, sexual perversity, and femininity as well as with homosexuality. This pathologization of Jewish male sexuality had also entered the writings of Jewish scientists and medical doctors, including Freud (see Boyarin, 1997; Gilman, 1993; Gluzman, 1997). Zionist thinkers such as Herzl and Nordau were convinced that the invention of a stronger, healthier heterosexual Jewry of muscles would not only overcome the stereotype of the Jewish male as a homosexual but also solve the economic, political, and national problems of the Jewish people. Unlike the passive, ugly, femme, Diasporic Jewish male, the new Zionist man would engage in manual labor, athletics, and war, becoming the colonialist explorer in touch with the land and with his body. This notion of a new Jewish masculinity became the model for the militarized masculine Sabra—the native born Israeli.

These gender and sexual aspects of the Zionist project brought the (formal and nonformal) exclusion of gay men and lesbians from Israeli society. In the end of the 1980s and 1990s, a series of legal and social struggles[55] of the Aguda—The Association of Gay Men, Lesbians, Bisexuals and Transgenders in Israel—led to the provision of a degree of civic legitimacy for gays and lesbians in the central institutions of Israeli society—the army, family, and motherhood—that define the limits of membership and participation in the Israeli collectivity (see Gross, 2000). Aguda members fought for the expansion of their civic rights and the right of representation of sexual orientation and criticized the absence and marginality of gay men and lesbians in Israeli society. The successes of these struggles also promoted the visibility of gay men and women in mainstream media as well as allowed for the rise of an urban queer culture that confidently took its place within the heterosexual national consensus. Emphasis was placed on the normality of the community's members and their being good citizens and on the fact that gay men and lesbians are like everybody else. As Walzer (2000) writes: "The Aguda was pursuing a very mainstream strategy

[55] These struggles achived the repeal of Israel's antisodomy law in 1988; the banning workplace discrimination based on sexual orientation; the first sitting of the Knesset to deal with homo-lesbian issues, in 1993; and a Supreme Court of Justice decision in favor of Yonatan Danilowitz, an El Al flight attendant, who demanded that the airline recognize his boyfriend as a partner. For a more detailed description see Walzer (2000) and Kama (2003).

and image at that time—demonstrating that gays and lesbians are 'just like everyone else,' serving in the military, and living in committed long-term relationships" (p. 41).

Although the homo-lesbian struggle led to increased tolerance toward queers and challenged the heterosexual privilege of participating in dominant social institutions, they did not question the very hegemonic position of those institutions or their privilege of deciding who would be or who was a proper ability to determine national subject. Indeed, the sexual politics of the gay community in the 1990s reinforced the discourse by which those institutions are seen as the key to receiving equal rights in society. Entrance to those institutions was limited to an exclusive group, largely made up of Ashkenazi (Jews of Eastern European origin) and financially secure gays and lesbians who could adapt themselves to the normative model of citizenship.[56] Members of the community who did not fit this normal and hegemonic image and who were not interested or were unable to join the heart of the Israeli consensus (Mizrahim [Jews of Arab and Oriental origin], Palestinians, effeminate gay men, butch lesbians, transsexuals, and so on) found themselves excluded not only from heterosexual society but also from the gay community itself.

In this article, I would like to examine the relationship between sexuality, masculinity, and nationalism in the cinema of two leading Israeli gay male filmmakers—Eytan Fox and Amos Gutman. Fox's film *Yossi and Jagger* (2002) describes a gay affair of two Israeli army officers. The film was very successful in Israel as well as in Europe and the United States, winning a number of international awards. Its great popularity among the Israeli gay community as well as with heterosexuals and its critical success in both the gay and straight presses in and outside Israel have made it the central text in the cultural visibility of Israeli gay people in recent times. *Yossi and Jagger* is an example for the politics of normalcy characterizing the sexual agenda of the gay men and lesbian community in Israel. The film represents an attempt on the part of its filmmaker to join the national heterosexual collectivity and attach himself to the myths that constitute it at the price of depoliticizing gay male identity. I argue that the film constructs the image of being gay as normal by maintaining it in the closet—by representing it as an open secret. This politics of the closet allows for gays to be

[56] In the context of the incorporation of gays in the Israeli army, Gross (2000) writes: "Not only does this approach strengthen the discourse of Israeli citizenship that conditions it on military service, but it is also entirely based on a conception of equality that demands that [gays] show they are 'normal' citizens 'like everybody else.' This approach is problematic in that it makes equal treatment conditional on realizing the ambition to be 'like everybody else,' thus issuing entrance tickets only to those [gays] who can most closely fit themselves to the model of standard masculinity. Thus this approach excludes those gays and lesbians who cannot or do not want to adapt themselves to that model. Those who support this approach are actually forging a coalition with normative heterosexual men, in the name of which they can continue to discriminate against anyone who does not belong to that group, and anyone who cannot buy himself a ticket to the heart of the Israeli security conception" (p. 176).

included in the national discourse within which the film wants to incorporate itself while at the same time shaping a gay male identity that does not challenge, and indeed reproduces and perpetuates, oppressive heteronormative practices.[57]

In contrast to the success of Fox's film, the official discourse of the Israeli gay men and lesbian community rejected the films of Gutman. Gutman—the first to make gay Israeli cinema—was accused of depicting a depressing, alienating, and even homophobic imagery of gay social existence. Indeed, he shows in his films an obvious contempt for the demand for politically correct—which is to say, idealized and sanitized—depictions of gay sexuality. He refuses to provide consensual images of either gay or straight sex. On the contrary, male gay sexuality is explicitly associated with power and domination, with violence and death. His male heroes slip into a delicious passivity, into an uncontainable agitation; they passionately and compulsively seek to lose their ego boundaries and to shatter their self-identities and the way they are constructed by national heteronormativity.

However, these new queer visions of such gay (Ashkenazi) filmmakers are marked by an absence of any political awareness of ethnicity. Moreover, they repeat the colonial fantasy of the dominant discourse in which Mizrahi men are fixed into a narrow repertoire of types—the Eastern sexual stud, on the one hand, and the delicate exotic Oriental boy, on the other hand. I suggest that the disavowal of ethnicity in Ashkenazi gay sexual politics and the incorporation of Mizrahi men into stereotyping and sexual objectification enable the construction of Ashkenazi male gay identity as a Western identity.

The Politics of Normality

The film *Yossi and Jagger* portrays the "forbidden love" story of two Israeli army officers—Yossi (Ohad Knoller) and Lior (Yehuda Levi), better known by his nickname, Jagger—serving in a snowy base in the Israeli-Lebanese border. The lovers' sexual orientation remains secret. Jagger, who tries throughout the film to persuade Yossi to publicly express their love, dies in battle—a moment too late to hear Yossi succeed in saying the words, "I love you." The only other person present at this tragic moment is Ofir (Assi Cohen), another officer, who is much more likely to interpret Yossi's confession as the expression of love between brothers in arms and not as romantic—especially since Ofir thinks that Jagger is having an affair with Yaeli (Aya Koren), a female soldier with whom he himself is in love. Also, in Jagger's parents' house during the Shiva (the Jewish weeklong mourning period), Yossi cannot publicly declare his love, known as that which dare not speak its name. While Yaeli, who was in love with Jagger, lies to his mother by telling her that they were having a romantic relationship, the only thing that Yossi can say to his lover's bereaved mother is that Jagger loved the song "Your Soul" by the famous Israeli singer Rita. Thus Yossi

[57] For a full discussion of the film, see Yosef (2005).

shares his secret with the film viewers alone, the only witnesses—apart from the gay protagonists, of course—who know throughout the film about his queer affair. Homosexuality, therefore, remains at the level of cinematic narrative, trapped in the closet, deeply buried in the coffin together with Jagger's mutilated body.

"The closet," claims Sedgwick (1990), "is the defining structure of gay oppression in the present century" (p. 71). In explaining the dynamics that construct the institution of the closet, Sedgwick formulates two views for the representation of homosexuality in Western society—the universalizing view and the minoritizing view—which function simultaneously. The minoritizing view argues that only certain people are gays, and so the definition of "homosexuality" is important only for those people who are interested in adopting a gay identity. On the other hand, the universalizing view claims that homosexuality is only one part of a more general phenomenon of intimacy between people of the same sex, which everyone can experience and which does not belong to a singular and distinct minority group. According to this view, homosexuality signifies sexuality in general and defines heterosexuality through a binary formula of "homosexuality/heterosexuality" that informs our entire culture. These two views exist simultaneously and construct an incoherent definition of homosexuality in modern culture. This incoherence explains the workings of the closet and the forces through which it is regulated. The closet, argues Sedgwick, is the apparatus that allows for the denial of incoherence between "real" homosexuals and the idea of fluidity of identity that sees homosexuality as a structural element in heterosexual identity. Heterosexuality needs knowledge about homosexuality in order to construct its own self-definition, but, at the same time, it must disavow this knowledge—to convince itself that it does not know what it does not want to know, even though it knows it all along—out of a fear of too dangerous a proximity between heterosexuality and homosexuality, which is supervised by policing the knowledge of the closet. The closet, therefore, is a kind of transit point between revelation and concealment, a play between knowledge and ignorance that constructs homosexuality as an open secret.

Knowing about the protagonist's gay love affair while the straight characters do not know about it allows the viewer of *Yossi and Jagger* to take pleasure from reading certain comments and situations in the film in a queer context. For example, right after a scene in which the gay officers have sex in the snow, the regiment commander (Sharon Reginiano) questions Ofir about their being in the outpost. Ofir tells him that they had gone out to patrol the positions, and the commander responds, "What? Didn't they do it already?" The viewer derives pleasure from reading the queer meaning latent in the sentence, pleasure made possible by the knowledge and the ignorance of others. On another occasion, in response to Yossi's opposition to setting out on an ambush because his soldiers are tired and there is a full moon, the commander says, "What's up with you? Have you become a faggot? Don't be a sissy!" A similar thing happens in the conversation between Ofir and Yaeli. Yaeli is in love with Jagger. Like Ofir, who is in love with her but afraid to show his feelings to her, Yaeli does not know that Jagger is gay. Ofir says to Yaeli: "I don't think you'd have a chance … with him. I think that you're just not his type. So what if you're not his type. It only says something about him." Ofir tries to persuade Yaeli to stop thinking about Jagger in the hope that maybe she will turn her affections to him. The viewer, aware of Jagger's sexual identity, reads into Ofir's words an additional (queer) meaning that is hidden from Ofir and Yaeli.

At certain moments the viewer joins up with Yossi and Jagger in carrying out queer readings. For instance, spectators and protagonists can read the lyrics of Rita's song "Your Soul," which Jagger sings during one of the scenes, in the context of Jagger's insistent pleading that Yossi come out of the closet and admit their love: "Come let us banish the smoke screen/ Let us stand in the light and not in the shade/ For how long will you keep running away/ Into power games/ You may cry sometimes/ When something inside you breaks/ Tell me a bit about moments of fear/ It is much easier to be afraid together." In addition, Jagger performs a self-conscious queer parody of the song when he replaces the words "Tell me a bit about moments of fear/ It is much easier to be afraid together" with the lines "Tell me a bit about moments of fear/ It is much easier to stick it up the rear."

Again through the figure of Jagger, this double meaning is expressed in the homoeroticism of the Israeli male military group. In an episode in the mess hall, Jagger says to one of the soldiers, nicknamed Psycho (Yuval Semo), "Say, Psycho, what would you do if I told you I'm a faggot?" and Psycho replies, "Man, you are as pretty as a girl. Of course we'd fuck you." Psycho's use of the word "we" and not "I" indicates that Psycho thinks he is not the only one who could contemplate having sex with a man, or even male group sex, with Jagger being penetrated. The viewer's epistemological privilege, and the fact that within the framework of the narrative, the protagonists' homosexuality remains secret, allows for the inclusion of the homosexuality of characters who are seemingly signified as heterosexual. If Psycho can be suspected of homosexuality, then Adams (Hanan Savyon) can be, too. Adams is a soldier who practices Zen Buddhism and who leaps to the defense of the "faggots from Tel Aviv" when he says to another soldier, "You would kill to get laid like those faggots from Tel Aviv. They get laid like you guys won't all your life." Psycho replies, "You've been man-drilled, huh? I noticed you walk funny." The film emphasizes Adams' different and eccentric behavior; he seems to live in his own private and secret world, separate from the violent and hypermasculine military homosociality. This representation creates a signifying relation between Adams and Yossi and Jagger that allows the spectator to read Adams as a gay man in the closet.

The construction of homosexuality as an open secret allows the viewer to read the film according to the universalizing view, which holds that homosexuality is a constitutive element in any sexual identity. By knowing more about the protagonists' sexual identity than anyone else, the spectator actually controls and regulates the representation of homosexuality in the film. Thus the film lets the viewer apply the category of homosexuality to various comments and certain straight characters and so blurs traditional sexual boundaries. However, the film also allows the viewer to deny the presence of homosexuality in a male military group and to confine it to the bodies of Yossi and Jagger. Thus the film distinguishes between those who are really homosexuals and those who are not. And the spectator can even read Adams, the prime suspect of being gay, as straight, especially when Goldie (Hani Furstenberg), the unit's loosest woman soldier, erotically places a snack in his mouth, while he licks her fingers with evident pleasure. Yossi and Jagger are the only characters clearly signified as homosexuals. This strategy, which characterizes the minoritizing view—homosexuality is the domain of a specific and distinct group of people—is made possible because the protagonists' homosexuality remains locked in the closet, constructed as an open secret, and revealed only to the viewer. The film's insistence on constructing Yossi and Jagger's gay identities as closeted constructs homosexuality as simultaneously contagious and absent.

When the doors of the closet are closed, heterosexual viewers can peek at homosexuality without any fear; they can even show sympathy toward it. However, because of their exclusive epistemological privilege, they can also "not know"; that is, they can keep homosexuality as a secret only they know about, thus making sure it is contained in the bodies of others. Locking homosexuality in the closet protects heterosexuals not from knowledge about homosexuality but from the necessity of acknowledging that knowledge. By constructing homosexuality as an open secret, the film guarantees these viewers a narrative of sexual coherence, protects them from homosexual desires, and ultimately marks the sexuality of gay men as destined to be eternally closeted. If the protagonists' sexuality came out of the closet, heterosexual viewers would lose the choice of ignorance, would have to read the sexual comments made in the film, as well as in the whole military male group, in a queer context. In other words, releasing the protagonists' homosexuality from the regime of secrecy would expose the repressed homosexual foundations of the entire male heterosexual military homosociality. This would challenge the accepted sexual boundaries of both the straight characters in the film and the heterosexual viewers themselves.

For gay viewers interested in signing up to the heterosexual national consensus, the film sells them the normative fantasy of being like "everybody else," of being "normal," but at the price of leaving the protagonists' and their own gay identity in the closet. The epistemological privilege afforded to gay viewers allows them, like heterosexual viewers, to identify with the closeted gay protagonists while enjoying a comfortable position of ignorance. In this way homosexuality can be incorporated into the framework of military society without the threat of proximity between homosexuality and heterosexuality. Thus conservative gay viewers can pass as heterosexuals and be assimilated into normal heterosexual society without having to challenge the sexual polarity that constructs it.

The subversive, troublesome potential of homosexuality is embodied in the film by the character of Jagger. His captivating, challenging sexuality produces erotic ambivalence between all the other characters. He subverts sexual conservatism through his desire and his uncompromising demand that Yossi come out of the closet. In other words, Jagger is the queer who defines himself, as Warner (1993) puts it, through resisting "regimes of the normal" (p. xxvi). It is for this reason precisely that he represents such a threat to the politics of the normal for both Yossi and the film itself. The film gives Jagger his unsettling signifying power, but it must simultaneously get rid of him in order to construct an appropriate and respectable image of homosexuality. Paradoxically, queer sexuality is a subversive element that sabotages the construction of gay identity as normal, while at the same time being essential for its self-definition.

Jagger is the outcast other who must remain outside the sexual field of vision—must stay invisible—but at the same time is present through the very fact of his denial so that he can be assimilated into the film's sexual conformist politics and the national discourse in which the film participates. To do this, the film associates itself with one of the central myths in national cultures, that of the "living-dead" soldier. The ideal national body is that of the fighter whose physical body is absent (dead) but that is present (alive) in the imagined national consciousness.[58]

In *Yossi and Jagger* the politics of death is interwoven with the politics of the gay closet. Just before setting off for a dangerous ambush, the protagonists have a conversation that signifies a crisis in their relationship. Jagger tests the strength of Yossi's love for him: "Say, Yossi. Will you stay with me if I lose a leg?... And what if my face gets all burnt and I only have one eye left?... What if I die and you haven't even told me today that you love me?" Jagger imagines his mangled body as a precondition for Yossi's public admission of their love. In this context, coming out of the closet is identified with mutilation, death, and self-nullification. Later on Jagger again sings his version of Rita's song, "Tell me a bit about moments of fear/ It is much easier to stick it up the rear," but this time he adds the sighs of a dying man to the end of each line.

The identification between death and the gay closet is further reinforced when Jagger asks Yossi to come out of the closet with him and meet his parents. Yossi, feeling threatened, refuses: "Let me remind you, I never promised you it would ever be different. So you've got two choices: either live with it, or get out of my life." In this sentence, the binary oppositions of being in or out of the closet are identified with the opposites of life and death. For Jagger to come out of the closet, he must get out of Yossi's life, which in fact happens when he dies in battle. For Yossi, coming out of the closet is like going into battle, as is seen when he rubs camouflage paints on his face while looking in the broken mirror that represents his fractured sexual identity. In the following scene, Yossi tells his soldiers, "Be professional and be alert, because I don't intend to meet any of your mothers soon." Ironically, having just refused to meet Jagger's mother for one reason, Yossi soon meets her for another.

---

[58] Hever (1986) identifies the myth of the living dead in Israeli society: "The myth of the living dead is a solution that culture formulates in order to bridge the poignant paradox of a society that sacrifices the lives of its sons in the name of collective values, of which the preservation of life is a central one. This myth is aided by the individual who lost his life in order to strengthen the ideological and collective binds of a society deep in a struggle over its existence" (p. 190).

The film thus constructs the drama of coming out of the closet as tragic and impossible because Jagger's demand for sexual visibility arouses anxiety not only in Yossi but also in the film itself. For the two to come out of the closet would deny the viewer the privilege of ignorance, forcing the recognition of the overt presence of homosexuality within the military framework. This endangers the film's project of sexual normalcy and threatens to frustrate its desire to include homosexuality in the national collective by adopting the practice of the open secret. The film points to Jagger's sexual subversiveness—his desire to shatter the regime of the open secret—but it must also do away with the undermining force because of the threat posed to the film's sexual politics. Therefore, the film chooses for its rebellious protagonist, Jagger, the second option that Yossi offers: to get out of his life. Jagger's departure from the dramatic sphere cannot be a nonconformist exit from, but must be incorporated into, the film's sexual politics. That is, the possibility of his leaving the army and carrying on a free sexual lifestyle far from the closeted life that Yossi offers is unacceptable from the film's point of view, because such an act would throw critical light on the film's politics of the normal, as realized in the open secret. Jagger's subversive identity, therefore, must be excluded but in such a way as to justify the conformist sexual logic that shapes the film. So Jagger's removal from the narrative through nationalistic death is not coincidental but necessary. The politics of national death justifies the fighter's death by giving it a higher transcendental meaning. In his heroic death, Jagger becomes part of the imagined national community. He is absent yet present, dead yet alive, in the collective national memory. It is not by chance that the image of Yossi bending over Jagger's recumbent and bleeding body toward the end of the film mirrors a Pièta. Like Christ, who in dying underwent a religious-metaphysical transcendence, Jagger in death is also metamorphosed and comes to embody a national collective meaning.[59] Again, it is no coincidence that, in one of the film's final scenes, a mourning notice reveals Jagger's surname—Amichai (literally, "my nation lives"). The film dismisses Jagger's troubling presence while justifying his death, through his representation as a living-dead character, by giving it a national meaning. Thus his death is included in the film's nationally imaged sexual politics. Homosexuality, then, remains mute, silenced, and buried deep in the darkness of the coffin—Jagger's coffin, the national coffin, or rather the national closet.

Desire Unlimited

Gutman died of an AIDS-related disease in February 1993. In his brief filmic career he made three short films: *Repeat Premiers* (1977), *A Safe Place* (1977), and *Drifting* (1979). *Drifting* was also made as a feature film (1983), followed by three

[59] Hever (2001) shows that the myth of the living dead rests on the notable male tradition of male sacrificial victims—such as Isaac, who is saved from sacrifice, and Jesus, who was crucified and then resurrected—who in death undergo a process of transcendence: "The subject of the sacrifice is the result of a transcendent mechanism that converts the lack of meaning in

more features: *Bar 51* (1986), *Himmo, King of Jerusalem* (1987), and *Amazing Grace* (1992). Representations of homosexuality in his films do not offer any sort of redemption. The protagonists are caught in vicious circles of sexual and emotional exploitation from which there is no hope of escape. The characters are dependent on each other for their social, economic, and emotional existence—for their very identities—but cannot bear the incursions of others into their lives. They are oppressed, manipulated, and betrayed but at the same time exercise power and domination over others. Ilan (Ami Traub) in *Drifting* (feature version) is a married gay man who has sex with his wife ("You close your eyes and think about the national anthem") only because he is afraid to be without economic support, yet he mocks his one-night-stand soldier lover who "gets a dick up his ass and immediately talks about a relationship." In another scene, at a gay club, Robby (Jonathan Segal), a young filmmaker who wants to make "the first Jewish gay movie," follows an attractive man into the bathroom, hoping for casual sex. Rejected on the spot, he gives a blow job to another young man whom he does not desire and whom he himself rejects a minute later. Robby finds out that the old man who had promised to sponsor his new film never had money to begin with. "He asked me not to leave him because he doesn't have anyone," Robby tells. "He asked me to sleep with him.... I slept with him. I don't know how." In *Amazing Grace* Yonatan (Gal Hoyberger) falls in love with Thomas, who constantly rejects him but eventually has sex with him. He then returns to New York, leaving Yonatan alone and infected with the HIV virus. In the same film, Miki (Aki Avni), an army defector who tries to commit suicide after his mother hands him over to the military police, says sadly, "Whatever I do I am always left alone."

This unbearable pessimism, inflated to the point of self-annihilation, is interspersed with flashes of ecstatic optimism and sexual fantasies, most of them unattainable. Gutman depicts aggressive and threatening emotional situations as well as moments of self-sacrifice and unconditional love in esthetically pleasing, camp forms that make psychic and social existence tolerable. Most of his films present a dancing ritual that dramatizes the power relations of sex. In these rituals of subjection and possession, men challenge and fight one another, seduce and touch one another, and play games of domination and submission and of weakness and dependency, performing the mechanisms of control expressed in the sexual act. In *Drifting*, Robby takes into his home three runaways, convincing them that he will give them roles in his new film if they will obey him. Sitting masterfully in his director chair, he orders them to take off their clothes and perform oral sex. In this scene, the hierarchy and authority inherent in cinematic production dramatizes the power relations and self-abasement in sexuality itself. In other words, Gutman rejects the illusory, redemptive account of sexual desire in favor of what Bersani (1988) terms "the inestimable value of sex as—at least in certain of its ineradicable aspects—anticommunal, antiegali-

private, physical death into an alternative, higher meaning. Ultimately, the victim is saved from death and he undergoes a transformation. After his death he comes back to life though a process that includes divine, metaphysical, religious or national justification" (p. 36).

tarian, antinurturing, antiloving" (p. 215). Contrary to the Zionist project of redeeming the Jewish male body, male homosexuality is associated in his films with power and domination, with violence and death. Fantasies of power and control give way, in anticipatory excitement or in the orgasmic shattering of the body to degrading self-abolition. Representations of sex emphasize the sexual act as a symbolic embodiment of abdication of mastery, of a desire to abandon the self in favor of communicating with what Bersani calls "'lower' orders of being" (p. 221).

In *Drifting*, subversive sexual politics is dramatized through the sexual relationship between Robby and two Palestinian "terrorists," as his grandmother calls them, whom he invites into his home. He feeds them, bandages the wound of one of them (it is implied that they are running away from the Israeli police), and even pleasures them by summoning a female prostitute to his house. In the middle of the night he wakes one of them, an attractive, hypermasculine male, leans against the wall, pulls down his underwear, and asks the Palestinian to fuck him.

Gay anal receptivity is associated in phallocentric culture with abdication of power, with insatiable feminine sexuality. Gay men who embrace this cultural understanding of anal sex represent to others, according to Bersani (1988), a desire to abandon positions of mastery and the coherence of the self: "Male homosexuality advertises the risk of the sexual itself as the risk of self-dismissal, of *losing sight* of the self, and in so doing it proposes and dangerously represents *jouissance* [enjoyment] as a mode of ascesis" (p. 222). Robby willingly renounces his self-mastery, submitting himself to the domination of the racial other, and positions himself as an object of an Arab male's anal penetration. He yearns for dissolution of the psychic boundaries of the self, forfeits his authority as the oppressor, relinquishes his sovereign status, and attempts to become the other rather than the colonizer. For Robby, only at the moment of merging—at the sexualized political and racial moment of mixing, in the terrible and pleasurable shattering of the subject—is jouissance to be found. By willingly submitting in this way, he passionately and compulsively is seeking for the anti-redemptive self-shattering of his ego boundaries and national identity, thereby demonstrating his hostility toward the Israeli political and national order.[60] At the same time, by celebrating the sexual pleasure found in anti-identificatory self-annihilation, the film challenges the Aguda's sexual identity politics and its imperious demand for a respectful representation of homosexuality. In *Drifting*, Gutman's most autobiographical film, Robby says, "Even the Gay Association doesn't want to hear about the short films that I made. They're not positive films. They don't put the homosexuals in the desired light."

Gutman's queer cinema presents a vision of a disintegrated and debased nuclear family. Fathers are absent (with one exception in *Drifting* in which the father appears in a short scene "in an impulse of sentimentality," as Robby describes), and the male heroes are associated with their mothers, who are usually depressed and suicidal.

[60] For certain problems in the representation of Arab men in Gutman's film *Drifting*, see Yosef (2002, pp. 553-580).

The great divas of the silver screen—such as Anna Magnani, Marlene Dietrich, Greta Garbo, and Joan Crawford—are a source for a primal identification with the maternal and femininity. Gay men's identification with maternal rather then paternal figures, argues Silverman (1992), "negate[s] the most fundamental premise of male subjectivity—an identification with masculinity—and in so doing … obstruct[s] paternal lineality" (p. 362). By refusing to identify with the father, male gays relinquish phallic power and mastery positions and embrace features, such as lack, specularity and receptivity—in short, castration—that the phallic construction of manliness disavows and externalizes. However, as Farmer (2000) noted, though the "gay male subject may make a foundational identification with psychic femininity—whether by accepting those tropes of castration culturally defined as feminine, or by identifying with 'femininity' of the maternal image—'he' is still required to negotiate a psychocultural relation with the category of masculinity that, by definition, plays a determinative role in the organization of *male* homosexuality" (p. 202). In other words, phallic manhood is a repudiated structural element within gay masculinity.

Bersani (1988) took such a notion even further and claimed that "the logic of homosexual desire includes the potential for loving identification with the gay man's enemies" (p. 208). Gay men's internalization of certain codes of cultural masculinity, specifically the gay hypermasculine style, "is in part constitutive of male homosexual desire, which, like all sexual desire, combines and confuses impulses to appropriate and to identify with the object of desire" (p. 209). For Bersani, gay men's adoption of these codes arises from the fact that "a sexual desire for men can't be merely a kind of culturally neutral attraction to a Platonic Idea of the male body; the object of that desire necessarily includes a socially determined and socially pervasive definition of what it means to be a man" (pp. 208–209).

The hypervirile male Sabra appears in Gutman's films as the loved object of desire. His idealized muscular body is a source of sexual excitement for the gay protagonists who, despite their alienation from the straight hypermasculine culture, never stop feeling uncontrolled fascination and attraction to it. The lack of interest of the gay hero in participating in gym class in the film *A Safe Place* express his rejection of the Zionist body culture and its compulsive demand for heterosexual masculinity. However, in the locker room he produces erotic pleasure by touching the fetishized items of clothing of his classmates. Identification with straight masculinity takes place in the hero's fantasies, where the phallic male is stripped, literally and figuratively, of his masterful virility and pictured in passive, vulnerable eroticized positions. The hero of *Repeat Premiers* is a puppeteer who imagines that his desired masculine coworker moves his arms slowly as if he is pulled by invisible threads. In *Amazing Grace*, as Yonatan lies in his bed masturbating, he fantasizes that muscular underwear male models in a magazine advertisement come to life, tenderly and sensually caressing one another with he among them.

The gay man, Bersani (1988) argues, "never stops re-presenting the internalized phallic male as infinitely loved object of sacrifice" (p. 222). This psychic identification is literalized in both *Repeat Premiers* and *A Safe Place*, in which the protagonists fantasize the phallic man lying naked, bathing in chiaroscuro lighting, in a pose that recalls the iconography of Saint Sebastian. This process of identification and incorporation means that paternal masculinity is figured in the libidinal construction of male homosexuality as a site of transgression and negation. Phallic masculinity in Gutman's films is a primary source of desire for gay men; however, this desire is structured by constitutive ambivalence of cathexis and displacement. "Gay men," to quote Bersani, "'gnaw at the roots of a male heterosexual identity' … because, from within their nearly mad identification with it, *they never cease to feel the appeal of its being violated*" (p. 209).

In Gutman's cinema, gay male sex is depicted as an orgasmic shattering of the body and self. Tragically, AIDS literalized this fantasmatic potential of gay sex as an actual death. In heterosexual media, the epidemic is figured as somehow caused by gay sexual practices. Homosexuality itself is imagined as death-bearing practice; however, this is hardly new. Nunokawa (1991) argues that, long before the AIDS era, the history of the homosexual man for the dominant culture has been one of death, doom, and extinction. This long-standing discursive tradition figured the gay man as already dying, as one whose desire is incipient dying. For the straight mind, Nunokawa claims, "AIDS is a gay disease, and it means death, because AIDS has been made the most recent chapter in our culture's history of the gay male, a history which, from its beginning, has read like a book of funerals" (p. 312). However, according to Nunokawa, this construction of the gay man is not restricted to the lurid heterosexism but also reproduced by gay culture itself: "The gay community is thus taxed during its sad time by a double burden: the variegated regime of heterosexism not only inhibits the work of acknowledging the loss of a gay man, it also exacts the incessant reproduction of this labor, by casting his death as his definition" (p. 319).

Rather than expelling the figure of the doomed gay man, the film *Amazing Grace* confronts it. The film stages such a confrontation by critically linking the recent queer history of AIDS and Israel's national culture of death. More than any other social group in the Israeli national community, mothers—who did not actively participate in wars and whose husbands and sons were killed in combat—were forced by the Israeli national ideology to read their loss in terms of national redemption. It is not surprising that in *Amazing Grace* Gutman gives voice especially to Thomas's mother, who expresses the pain of her son's coming death from AIDS, her personal history of loss as a Holocaust survivor, and Israel's national history of death:

> I wanted to keep together what was left from our family.… I tried to take care of Thomas as much as it is possible. I didn't want that he would experience the things that I experienced. This is why I wanted that we would come to Israel. But there is always something going on: war, new diseases. No, I'm not sorry that Thomas has no children.… But it hurts me, if I think about it, that I cannot do anything for him. I don't know how I can help him. I don't know what I can do.

By blurring the private material death of European Jews in the Holocaust with Israeli soldiers on the battlefield, the official cultural discourse produced and legitimized the Israeli national collectivity. Specifically, the disavowal of the materiality of AIDS was needed to invent and enforce the image of a heterosexual Israeli national community. Male gays, who in the dominant imagination were associated exclusively with the disease, were not only left outside of the national discourse but were also imagined as not existing at all. By marking and linking the death from AIDS with official national deaths, Gutman not only resists the dematerialization and decontextualization of all deaths in Israeli nationalism and the imagined community it produces but also specifically challenges heteronormative ideology and the way it polices death in national culture.

Throughout Gutman's films, the dominant national discourse was a prime target for his critique of the "redemptive reinvention of sex." In *Drifting*, a group of gays walking in Independence Park—a site for gay male cruising in Tel Aviv constituting a sharp contrast to the idealized Zionist dream—ironically sings a famous Israeli folk song about the "beautiful and blooming land of Israel." Communal singing, one of Israel's distinctive cultural marks, is critiqued in *Bar 51* for producing an imagined national solidarity by disavowing not only the expression of (sexual) individualism but also for eliding the pain, loss, alienation, and despair that are part of the Israeli existence.

In one scene in the film, Marianna (Smadar Kalchinsky), a naïve homeless orphan girl who is involved in a forbidden love relationship with her brother, watches on television Sara'le Sharrone, a famous Israeli *Kibbutznic* folk singer in the 1980s, who says in an excited voice: "There are those days that you think all sorts of thoughts, and you want to cry, and instead of crying you sing, and when you sing together, you feel good." In *Drifting*, Robby says: "There was a war and the only thing I was scared of was that again they will start making positive films to raise the morale, and again there will be no place for my film." *Drifting* is Gutman's most autobiographical film. In the opening sequence, the diegetic and extra-diegetic filmmakers (Robby/Gutman) present this critique at the outset, when the protagonist addresses the camera in a monologue. Complaining about the lack of support his new movie has received from gay and straight establishments, Robby shifts in his monologue from the third to the first person, from talking about the hero of his forthcoming film to talking about himself:

> If the film dealt with a social problem, or if the hero at least had a political opinion: If he were a soldier, if he were a resident in a developing town, if he served on a naval destroyer, if he become religious, if he were a war widow. But if you must have him be a [gay], then at least he should suffer; he shouldn't enjoy it. The state is burning; there's no time for self-searching. There's a war now. There's always a war. He left the army of his own will, without any reason. The viewers won't accept it. There are too many dead relatives. He's not sympathetic, not thoughtful; he scorns all those who want the best of him. He's not even a sensitive soul, a composed intellectual. Why should [the viewers] identify with me? Why should they identify with him?

According to Robby/Gutman, gays do not have a right to representation, not only because they do not serve national interests but also, in the rare cases when they are represented, they must be constructed as sad suffering people. Obviously, Gutman is not arguing for a positive image of gay men; in fact, he sharply critiques it in the monologue. Gutman is aiming for something completely different. When Robby/Gutman argue that gay men, according to the straight mind, cannot be happy and enjoy life, it is because gay sex, that would make gay men smile, is intolerable in heterosexual culture because of its threatening appeal of loss of ego and of self-debasement. Gay people must suffer—they must not get it and certainly they must not enjoy it—because male-male sexual desire threatens the traumatic undoing of the psychic and national self on which heterosexuality is based.

In *Amazing Grace*, Yonatan advertises and celebrates the risk of loss of ego boundaries by having sex with the AIDS body of Thomas. In one episode, he imagines himself sick, cared for by Thomas's mother who lays him down on the bed in a posture that evokes the Christian imagery of the Pièta. He submits to the sentence of death that culturally defines his gay subjectivity, but, by this self-sacrifice and subjugation, he also evades it. Bersani (1988) wrote that "if the rectum is the grave in which the masculine ideal ... of proud subjectivity is buried, then it should be celebrated for its very potential for death.... It may, finally, be in the gay man's rectum that he demolishes his own perhaps otherwise uncontrolled identification with the murderous judgment against him" (p. 222). In the rectum, as in a grave, Yonatan puts to rest an identity which is before all else the mark of death. In the last image of the film, Yonatan is seen lying on an armchair in his backyard, a beam of light illuminates his face, and he smiles. Yonatan finds jouissance in the ecstatic suffering of self-annihilation and experiences grace in self-shattering, an amazing grace.

Queer Orientalism

A more complete analysis of the sexual politics of the Israeli gay community must also consider its effects on the construction of the Mizrahim. In the Zionist discourse Mizrahim, men and women alike, were represented through Orientalist perspectives.[61] Specifically, the construction of Mizrahi men as violent savages and primitives reproduces certain Zionist-Ashkenazi ideological fictions and psychic fixations about the sexual nature of Oriental masculinity and the otherness it is constructed to embody. Assigned the role of embodying ethnic/sexual difference within an Ashkenazi metaphorics of representation, the Mizrahi man becomes for the Ashkenazi man the repository of his repressed fantasies, similar to the way in which the Western colonialist projected his own desires onto the native man, as Fanon (1967) described: "The civilized white man retains an irrational longing for unusual eras of sexual li-

[61] Shohat (1987) was the first to critically expose Zionism's colonialist Orientalism and the exclusion of Eastern subjects—Jews and Arabs—from Israeli Ashkenazi nationalism.

cense.... Projecting his own desires onto the Negro, the white man behaves 'as if' the Negro really has them" (p. 165). Those fictions about Mizrahi manhood were fabricated in order to allay the Ashkenazi subject's own fears and desires as well as to provide a means to justify the regulation of the Mizrahi men's bodies and absolve any sense of guilt.

The Ashkenazi colonial fantasy fixed Mizrahi males to a narrow spectrum of sexual stereotypes. The Mizrahi male is represented as a sexual savage and a hypersexual stud who "does it more" and even better, hence the Ashkenazi fear of engulfment, of being swamped by "the primitive." The myth about over-reproduction and hypersexuality locked the Mizrahi male into his body, reinforcing the racist notion that Oriental males are inferior in mind and morality on account of their bodies. Along the image of the hypervirile Mizrahi male, the Isareli-Ashkenazi gaze was also fascinated by the delicate, noble, and exotic beauty of Mizrahi male bodies. One of the Jewish Agency emissaries in Libya described the male Arab-Jew as if he were trading in horses: "They are handsome as far as their physique and outword appearance are concerned, but I found it very difficult to tell them apart from the good quality Arab type" (Segev, 1986, p. 170). The Mizrahi man was invented and classified as a type of racial man, a racial form, with recognizable psychological and physiological qualities and morphology (for a full analysis of this discourse, see Yosef, 2004).

Israeli Ashkenazi gay cultural discourse repeats the colonial fantasy of the dominant discourse in which Mizrahi men are fixed into a narrow repertoire of types—the Eastern sexual stud, on the one hand, and the delicate exotic Oriental boy, on the other hand. While the Israeli queer culture addressed questions of homophobia and gay subjectivity, it remained silenced on issues of race and racism, especially when it concerns the interethnic tension between Mizrahim and Ashkenazim. The Aguda's Ashkenazi middle-class sexual politics left Mizrahi gays no alternative but to identify with a Eurocentric gay identity that ignored the ethnic diversity of the Israeli gay community. The Israeli gay mainstream culture refused to acknowledge that not all the gays are Ashkenazim and that Ashkenazi gay sexuality itself is informed by ethnicity. The Aguda's use of the pink triangle to advertise its cultural activities challenged, on the one hand, the dominant national discourse by associating the gay Holocaust and the Jewish Holocaust, linking homophobia and anti-Semitism. On the other hand, it also submitted Mizrahi gays and lesbians to a Western narrative of homophobia, which excludes ethnicity in the formation of sexual identity. By emphasizing homophobic society as the enemy that all gays should fight against, Ashkenazi queer culture disavowed the racism that Mizrahi gays and lesbians confronted in and outside the gay community.

Furthermore, in the narrative of the pink triangle, Israeli gay identity is constructed against an anti-Semitic enemy, a role assigned in the modern history of Jews to the Arabs, therefore leaving no legitimized cultural space for Mizrahi queers to express their Arab culture and heritage, which was structurally eliminated from gay identity discourse. In this discourse, Jewishness and Arabness are perceived as binary oppositions and the Mizrahi gay man as representing a kind of sexual and national anomaly. Ironically, the term *Gay Pride* adopted by the Aguda from the Euro-American Gay Pride is originally derived from American *Black Power* and *Black Pride* of the 1960s. If Ashkenazi gay activism were more aware of the history of its own queer terminology, it would recognize that race and ethnicity are structural elements within its sexual politics while also acknowledging that people with a history of oppression can organize without ignoring different forms of identity. Israeli queer culture simply did not want to talk about the complexities that arise at the junctions of multiple identity categories, especially in regard to race and ethnicity, for the fear of losing Ashkenazi hegemony and authority of defining *gay identity*—a term often masking the struggle for power over representation.

In his documentation of the Israeli gay community, Walzer (2000) describes the denial by both gay Ashkenazim and Mizrahim whenever the issue of ethnic discrimination is raised as "denial that there ever was a problem and denial that such a problem exists today" (p. 48). However, the rhetorical formulation that Walzer uses to discuss the subject indicates his very own disavowal of ethnic oppression. Beyond the fact that Walzer enforces Orientalist stereotypes and racist explanations for the "problem of the gap" (p. 48) between Mizrahim and Ashkenazim[62] and avoids exploring the issue critically, his discussion is also characterized by splitting levels of arguments, which structure the logic of denial in Freudian fetishism. He writes, for example: "The problems between Ashkenazim and Mizrahim are not primarily race- or color-motivated, *although* [emphasis added] such prejudice also exists," or "gaps in education and income levels between Mizrahim and Ashkenazim have narrowed, *although* [emphasis added] they are still too wide" (p. 49). Walzer's fetishistic disavowal can therefore be rendered thus: "I know that ethnic discrimination against Mizrahim exists in Israel, but in my narrative it does not exist." Through this disavowal, Walzer fetishizes the Ashkenazi gay identity as the norm.

Ethnic disavowal also characterizes the films of Gutman. Despite Gutman's subversive sexual politics, his films have nothing to say about the intersectionality of sex and ethnicity. While the social margins in his films are sexualized and form a critique of the homophobic dominant discourse, they are rarely figured in terms of ethnic oppression and racism, despite the fact that some of his characters are Mizrahim. The ethnic identity and the social marginality of the Mizrahi heroes are exploited and manipulated to serve Gutman's radical vision of sexuality, using Orientalist types, stereotypes, and images, whose racist quality is often masked by the claim that they are part of gay camp subculture, or what has been called *gay sensibility*, with its harmless joyful play of stereotypes. The film *Bar 51*, for example, rehearses the colonial stereotype of the Oriental feminine boy in the figure of Aranjuez (Alon Aboutoul), a sissy Mizrahi gay man with orange hair, extravagant dress, and effeminate talk,

[62] Walzer (2000) reproduces the Orientalist imagery of Mizrahim as primitives, backwards, and conservatives, contrary to the Zionist modern and enlightened society: "They came, in the main, from tradition-minded backgrounds to a revolutionary society," and "some of them arrived illiterate in any language" (p. 48).

working in a sleazy striptease bar as a dresser. His character decorates the film's camp aesthetic and dramatizes the idea of the performativity of identity, because Aranjuez is actually Israel Azulay, who left with his sister Sara—known in the bar as Zara—their home in the suburbs of Tel-Aviv. However, the ethnic identity of *Aranjuez* as a Mizrahi gay man plays no role in the film. By erasing ethnicity from his sexual politics, Gutman assumes that all gays share the same experience of oppression. In other words, Gutman uses sexuality as a metaphorical substitution of ethnicity. This kind of ahistorical analogy between sex and ethnicity has the effect of obscuring and concealing the specific form of oppression experienced by Mizrahi gay men. Furthermore, by constructing such an analogy, Gutman implicitly posits Ashkenaziness as the norm.

The Israeli new queer cinema produces and enforces Ashkenazi gay normative identity through the repetition of a colonial fantasy that confines Mizrahi men to a rigid set of ethnic roles and identities. The exotic Oriental boy and the hypermasculine Mizrahi male are major images through which Mizrahi men become visible in the Ashkenazi urban gay subculture. This colonial fantasy attempts to fix the position of Mizrahi male subjectivity into a space that mirrors the object of Ashkenazi needs and desires. Fox's short film *Gotta Have Heart* (1997) is an attempt by the new queer cinema to ally with and be part of the Ashkenazi middle-class consensus and the national ideology. The film describes the lives of two Ashkenazi gay men, Gur (Chak Barkman) and Neahav (Uri Omanoti), who share a dream to find a husband, get married, and live happily ever after (the Hebrew title of the film is translated *Husband With a Heart*). Contrary to Gutman's "alienating" imagery of homosexuality, Fox presents a different vision of male homosexuality that conforms to the dominant national discourse. When Neahav says that he does not wish to join the army, Gur, a paratroop unit veteran, scolds him in the name of his civic duty. Gur hopes to get admitted to Bezalel Art Academy and to be an architect, while Neahav dreams to dance with his lover at the Eurovision Song Contest (a major camp cultural event for gay people in Israel).

But everybody's object of desire is Marito (Sami Huri), a dark, muscular, over-sexualized Mizrahi man, the central dancer in folk dancing evenings held at the settlement where they live. The Mizrahi male is objectified into otherness by the Ashkenazi gay gaze that inscribes on his body fears and fantasies of the wild, animalistic nature of Oriental sexuality. This stereotypical convention of racial representation is especially manifest in the scene where Marito invites Gur to his apartment, waiting for him dressed only in his underwear, sitting on the bed, sensually eating a watermelon with his hands. Fear of aggressive sexuality shifts to desire as Marito calms his threatened lover while unbuttoning his shirt: "[Sex] is my art .... Don't be afraid boy." Such a representation of Oriental sexuality, which governs the gaze of Ashkenazi gay culture, not only continues the pattern of the Zionist colonial exploitation and objectification of the Mizrahi male body but also leaves no space for the institution of Mizrahi gay identity as well as blocking any attempt for queer Mizrahi-Ashkenazi social and political interaction.

Surprisingly, in the anal sex between the two, Marito takes the passive position. This may be seen as a counterimage to the racist construction of Mizrahi man as hypermasculine stud. Immediately after the sex, however, Marito is seen in the shower, vigorously scrubbing his body with soap, washing away the "filth" of gay sex. He is depicted as a man who feels uncomfortable with his sexuality, incapable of being emotionally attached to either a gay or straight partner, in contrast to the Ashkenazi gay man who accepts his sexual identity. Marito is destined to be trapped in his troubled sexual body, while Gur and Neahav aspire to goals beyond sexuality unattainable to the Mizrahi male. Thus, it seems neither surprising nor important that one knows nothing about Marito's life. He has no history or future plans; he functions only as a fantasized sexual object of the Ashkenazi homosexual man. (His fictive name—Marito—echoes romantic fantasies of the Latin lover, not his Jewish-Mizrahi origin, as opposed to the Hebrew names of Gur and Neahav.) After he understands that Marito is not good husband material, Gur rejects his offer for a last dance and instead joins Neahav for a dance, fulfilling his Euro-vision dream as well as the film's Euro-vision of an Ashkenazi gay identity.

Additional problems in the representation of Mizrahi gay men arise in Eytan Fox's Israeli TV series *Florentin*. The show tells the story of Israeli twentysomethings living in a south Tel-Aviv neighborhood of Florentin. The two main gay protagonists are Iggy (Uri Bannay), an effeminate openly Mizrahi gay man and Tomer (Avshalom Polak), an Ashkenazi straight-looking closeted gay. By constructing the Mizrahi gay man as already "out," Fox can conveniently avoid addressing the specific experience of coming out for Mizrahi queers, therefore assuming a common narrative of gay identity formation, which is always Ashkenazi. While the show describes in detail Tomer's coming out drama and his complex relationships with his family, Iggy's family ties are rarely mentioned. Confessing to his family about his sexual orientation, Tomer destroys the illusionary harmony of the patriarchal, middle-class, nuclear family and finds comfort and support among his friends.

The assumption of this narrative is that everyone comes out the same way and that all families are the same. However, unlike the stereotypical Ashkenazi nuclear family, the extended Mizrahi family provides a necessary source of support against ethnic discrimination, which cannot be so easily replaced by other social systems. Economically, moving out of your parents' house is not an easy task for many Mizrahim after army service, especially if you are one of the providers of the family. Further, the Ashkenazi narrative of coming out privileges gay identity as the most important task of any gay person. It might also be true to argue that, for Mizrahi gays coming from working-class background, gay identity is not always the prime target. There is a desire to do other things, and coming out is not the only important thing in the construction of Mizrahi identity. The Israeli queer urban culture, dominated by middle class Ashkenazim, never addressed those issues of class in the construction of sexual identity.

Florentin enforces the notion that true identity may be revealed in sexuality. The secret hidden truth of sexuality must be confessed because sex is a natural basic element in human identity. Coming to terms with his queerness, Tomer becomes a more free, open, complete, in-touch-with-his-body person, as Iggy is, with whom he will couple at the end of the series. This essentialist notion of sex, as Mercer and Julien (1988) have argued, "is in fact based on the prevailing Western concept of sexuality which *already contains racism*" (p. 107):

> Historically, the European construction of sexuality coincides with the epoch of imperialism and the two inter-connect ... the person of the savage was developed as the Other of civilization and one of the first "proofs" of this otherness was the nakedness of the savage, the visibility of the savage's sex. This led Europeans to assume that the savage possessed an open, frank and uninhabited "sexuality"—unlike the sexuality of the European which was considered to be fettered by the weight of civilization. (pp. 106–107)

Florentin repeats this colonial concept of sexuality though the relationship between Tomer and Iggy. Returning from a postmilitary service trip to India, Tomer moves to live with his old friend Toti and her gay roommate, Iggy. Still silent about his sexuality, Tomer feels uncomfortable with Iggy's queer extravaganza, especially the sounds of lust that Iggy makes during sex, which Tomer overhears through the walls. For his part, Iggy is indifferent to Tomer's criticism and even enjoys teasing his stuffy new friend. As the process of his coming out progresses, Tomer finds himself sexually attracted to Iggy and jealous of his natural, authentic unmediated relation towards his body, dramatized in the scene in which Iggy belly dances to the music of the famed Egyptian singer, Om Kolthom. Later on, when he finds himself alone in the apartment, Tomer plays the music of Om Kolthom and belly dances, erotically touching his body. The seductive, exotic Eastern music unbuttons the rational Western-Ashkenazi gay man, opening him to a different, unfamiliar realm of the senses that he had never experienced. This Orientalist fantasy is extended to the sexualized body of the Mizrahi gay man, who becomes an object of study and desire of the Ashkenazi gay subject. The identity of the Mizrahi queer man is reduced to his corporeality and to his natural, thus uncivilized, sexuality in a way that enables the Ashkenazi gay culture not only to control and regulate the representation of Mizrahi homosexuality but also to construct a Eurocentric gay consciousness underlying assumption of which is the naturalness of sexuality. In other words, rather than not being part of Ashkenazi gay culture, the oppressed image of the Mizrahi gay man is implicated in Ashkenazi queer sexual politics and its claim for a liberation of the gay person through sexuality. Thus, the Israeli gay community can no longer deny its own discursive oppression of Mizrahi gays and must question the ethnocentric assumptions behind its sexual agenda.

References

Bersani, L. (1988). Is the rectum a grave. In D. Crimp (Ed.), *AIDS: Cultural analysis, cultural activism*. Cambridge, MA: The MIT Press.

Boyarin, D. (1997). *Unheroic conduct: The rise of heterosexuality and the invention of the Jewish man*. Berkeley: University of California Press.

Fanon, F. (1967). *Black skin, white masks* (C.L. Markmann, Trans.). New York: Grove Press.

Farmer, B. (2000). *Spectacular passions: Cinema, fantasy, gay male spectatorship*. Durham: Duke University Press.

Gilman, S.L. (1993). *Freud, race and gender*. Princeton: Princeton University Press.

Gluzman, M. (1997). Longing for heterosexuality: Zionism and sexuality in Herzl's *Altneuland* [Hebrew]. *Theory and Criticism, 11*, 145-163.

Gross, A. (2000). Sexuality, masculinity, military and citizenship: Gay military service in I.D.F. in comparative view [Hebrew]. *Pelilim*, 95-183.

Hever, H. (1986). Alive are the dead and dead are the living [in Hebrew]. *Siman Kria, 19*, 190.

Hever, H. (2001). *Suddenly, the sight of war: Nationality and violence in Hebrew poetry of the 1940s* [Hebrew]. Tel Aviv: Hakibbutz Hameuchad Publishing House.

Kama, A. (2003). *The newspaper and the closet: Israeli gay men's communication patterns* [Hebrew]. Tel Aviv: Hakibbutz Hameuchad Publishing House.

Mercer, K., & Julien, I. (1988). Race, sexual politics and black masculinity: A dossier. In R. Chapman & J. Rutherford (Eds.), *Male Order: Unwrapping masculinity* (pp. 97-124). London: Lawrence & Wishart.

Nunokawa, J. (1991). "All the sad young men": AIDS and the work of mourning. In D. Fuss (Ed.), *Inside/out: Lesbian theories, gay theories* (pp. 311-323). London: Routledge.

Sedgwick, E.K. (1990). *Epistemology of the closet*. Berkeley: University of California Press.

Segev, T. (1986). *1949 – The first Israelis* (N. Weinstein, Trans.). New York: Henry Holt.

Shohat, E. (1987). *Israeli cinema: East/west and the politics of representation*. Austin: University of Texas Press.

Silverman, K. (1992). *Male subjectivity at the margins*. New York: Routledge.

Walzer, L. (2000) *Between Sodom and Eden: A gay journey through today's changing Israel*. New York: Columbia University Press.

Warner, M. (1993). Introduction. In M. Warner (Ed.), *Fear of a queer planet: Queer politics and social theory*. Minneapolis: University of Minnesota Press.

Yosef, R. (2002). Homoland: Interracial sex and the Israeli-Palestinian conflict in Israeli cinema. *GLQ, 8*(4), 553-580.

Yosef R. (2004). *Beyond flesh: Queer masculinities and nationalism in Israeli cinema*. New Brunswick, NJ: Rutgers University Press.

Yosef, R. (2005). The national closet: Gay Israel in *Yossi and Jagger*. *GLQ, 11*(2), 283–300.

7

"Restrain Your Impulse" Versus "Break the Boundaries": From Whence Shall My Sexual Guidance Come?

Lawrence Bush

The Talmud tells a story about Eliezer ben Dordia, a rabbi who loves to have sex with prostitutes, so much so that he crosses seven rivers to get to a new one with a hot reputation. "During the foreplay of the sexual act, she broke wind," the text (*Avodah Zarah* 17a) narrates. Perhaps seeing surprise and horror on the rabbi's face—*by God, she's an actual human being!*—the prostitute curses him: "As this wind will not return to its place, so Eliezer ben Dordia will never be received in penitence" (Bialik & Ravnitzky, 1992, p. 560). This throws him into a frenzy of sobbing repentance, until he eventually dies from grief—whereupon a divine voice goes forth announcing his acceptance in the world-to-come.

For me, one moral of this story, and perhaps the most essential and useful teaching about sexuality in the Jewish religious tradition, is that the harmful potential of sex lies in objectification: in treating a human being as a tool of gratification, a notch in the belt, an elixir, or even an object of worship. While objectification may be active during a sexual encounter (that's me, not the Rabbis, speaking), it should not motivate or dominate the encounter, lest one indulges in sin by failing to treat others as creatures *b'tselem elohim* (made in God's image)—that is, as vessels of consciousness, will, and emotion. The positive power of sex, in the eyes of most Jewish religious authorities, is dependent on intention. If it is driven by an intent other than *devek* (cleaving, or intimate emotional attachment), it tends powerfully to cultivate one's *ta'ama d'issura* (taste for the forbidden), which is seen as a path to spiritual downfall.

As a Jewish man who is deeply committed to my wife of 36 years, I have been intrigued and occasionally inspired by such teachings. In small ways, they have helped this nonobservant Jew cultivate my ongoing desire for the woman with whom I've made love more than 3,000 times. They have also helped me to cope with the siren song of our sexualized commercial culture and the parade of near nudity on the street, and to define my sexual manhood without a body count.

Nevertheless, when my own son turned 15 and I began wondering seriously about what he was making of girls, my concern was not that he was objectifying them as sex objects—but that he wasn't.

He seemed easygoing and brotherly with them, not at all shark-like and intent on sexual conquest. With his own girlfriend, he seemed to spend a lot more time television watching in our living room than making out in the privacy of his room. When he and I watched the tube together and a sexy model popped up in a commercial, his finger never hesitated on the remote; one ad seemed as useless to him as the next. And while he had a wild variety of posters and graffiti on the walls of his room, only one was a glamor-babe image—which he took down after his mother made a face.

I was pretty sure that my boy was heterosexual, yet his interest in the female body seemed very low-key. While I could have claimed this as a Jewish and feminist parenting victory, I found myself fretting, instead, and spinning theories about my son's slo-mo sexuality. My operative values were not those of Judaism but of the sexy 1960s: not *devek*, but *do it!* Not *restrain your evil impulse*, but *break the boundaries!*

Reminiscing about my own youthful experiences during that powerhouse decade would probably have been a good way to cajole my son into sharing confidences with me, but when I thought about my actual memories of adolescent lust, they seemed too embarrassing to recount. *Yes, my boy, I used to glance every 20 seconds at what's-her-name's cleavage in homeroom class. I used to watch reruns of* Bye, Bye Birdie *just to see young Ann-Margret's belly-baring dance. I would thrill to that rare discovery of a* Playboy *magazine at a friend's house or in a trash pile. Hell, I used to ogle the voluptuous women characters in comic books!*

It wasn't much of a resumé, since there were only slim pickings for titillation back then—and maybe that was a good thing. My sexual progress, I realized, had never been exceeded by my sexual exposure. Nothing had been shown to me that I hadn't hoped to see, and nothing had happened to me that I hadn't thought about for months in advance. By contrast, I wondered now, if the vulgarity of contemporary culture and especially the ubiquity of hard-core pornography on the Internet had traumatized my son with images raw and intense beyond his imagining. Could it be that his casual disinterest in nudity and sexual experience was an effort to slow things down, to stay in the comfort zone of an adolescent?

If so, why was I eager to incite my son to sexual riot?

I made a couple of weak conversational sallies but didn't get close to exploring my hypothesis with him. Instead, I began speculating about it with the guys in my Jewish men's group and other friends. Invariably, these conversations would prove to be as embarrassing as the one I'd hoped to have with my son, since they always turned into a discussion of our own involvement with Internet porn.

To me, pornography has always been a secretive and shameful thing, associated with loneliness, seediness, masturbation, alienation, and being a loser. To confess even to the occasional use of porn, especially as a middle-aged man, is to confess to not being a rock star, to not having all of my sexual desires met, to suffering from spiritual and ethical corruption — and to being a faux feminist, a man who has not fully mastered his impulse to view all women as sex objects.

These days, however, it seems to be my embarrassment about porn, rather than my use of it, that makes me a loser. Porn has become mainstream and way wicked cool. Teens wear "porn star" tee shirts and sweatpants. Jenna Jameson's (2004) *How To Make Love Like a Porn Star* was a bestseller, and porn actresses have replaced Dr. Ruth Westheimer as our country's leading sex advisors. Burlesque is making a comeback in small, behomian theaters. Casual blowjobs and group gropes are a standard part of adolescent culture, at least according to urban legend.

How did this happen, this spillage of shamelessness from the closets, basements, and dresser drawersof my childhood? Certainly, as a young man, I applauded every breakthrough, from the films *Portnoy's Complaint* to *I Am Curious, Yellow*, from Lenny Bruce to George Carlin, from birth control pills to miniskirts to gay bathhouse orgies. The fact, however, that contemporary porn seems to be the *momser* (bastard) of the "free love" and anticensorship mores of that liberatory period, and that the spirit of sexual liberation and license has been corrupted into endless commercial tiillation and loveless, misogynistic imagery has forced me to have second thoughts about the very meaning of "liberation."

In fact, the ubiquity of porn has me worried about America as a whole. I worry that young Americans are having their sense of sexual norm and sexual expectation defined by it and are therefore growing up with feelings of inadequacy or compulsion. ("I'm supposed to be *that* big?" "I'm supposed to shave it all and wear a thong?" "I guess all girls want to get it in the ass." "I guess if I were cool I'd get drunk and give blowjobs to strangers.") I worry that American men are using porn to inure themselves to the demands for personal growth and maturity that their relationships and their civic responsibilities require. I worry that the thousands of young American women who appear naked on the Internet are wallowing in victimization, degradation, rape and coercion, in order to earn some "easy money." I even worry that the Muslim world is looking across the Internet at the United States and concluding that the *burka*, the *hijab*, and the confinement of women are the only alternatives to whoredom.... All of these anxieties aside, however, however, I do periodically shift away from my work at my home computer to cruise Internet porn sites. The opportunity to see naked women for free usually proves to be far more compelling than all of my worries about it. I have my favorite free sites bookmarked; I know the names, real or pretend, of a few of my preferred models; I have a good sense of what I like to see and what I like to avoid seeing.

I'm a porn user.

Does this emerge from some lewdness gene? From an unhappy childhood? From my socialization in a society that makes a fetish of the female form? From spending too much time in front of a computer? Who knows, maybe, probably, sure. All I can say with absolute certainty is that the porn habit is by no means uniquely mine. A General Social Survey of 2002 found that 14 percent of respondents had visited a pornographic website in the previous month (25 percent of men and 4 percent of women) (www.christiancentury.org/article.lasso?id=3629). A Barna Research Group study released in February 2007 pegged it at 35% of American men and 17% of American women (http://www.umportal.org/article.asp?id=2967). An online survey of more than 10,000 Americans by the Kinsey Institute a few years ago found close to 80% of the respondents had used porn over a 30-day period (Paul, 2005, p. 13). Whateer the accurate numbers, Internet porn use is clearly widespread—and among the Jewish men I've spoken with and even formally interviewed, there are very few who have not explored it at least a few times.

Their responses are wildly varied. "Everything about porn, from the moment it flashes on the screen, is luridly unnatural," complains Ted, 58, an athlete and artist. "It announces to me a world of ill health—'You are now injuring yourself!' Everything that's going to happen is going to be deeply artificial, inauthentic, toxic. Porn confirms just how detestable I find artifice, especially the manufacturing of sexuality that is so clearly false."

"Porn shows a very interesting cross-section of the part of American life that nobody wants to talk about," says Andy, 25, a public relations guy. "There are men who are into animals, men who are into fat women, men who are into voluminous breasts, men who are into anal sex, and so on. And, based on the quantity of this kind of porn or that kind of porn, you can get a sense of numbers, too, of how many tastes are very marginal, how many are very mainstream. Another thing porn has taught me is that no matter what you look like, somebody will love the way you look. There's someone out there who will think that you are amazing to look at!"

"I guess porn has made me more willing to indulge in anything that I feel might be remotely kinky," observes Philip, 27, a playwright. "Since there's so much kink and craziness in porn, it kind of normalizes whatever I might do. It makes my desires seem normal, instead of my feeling that they're something I'm not supposed to be feeling. In my college days, I assumed that everyone was a rather extreme feminist. I erred too much on the side of caution. Now that I'm a little older, I've become comfortable with the idea of sex as an exchange that can involve some domination or submission, and I'm more willing to try things that I wouldn't have tried."

"Even though I use it, in general, I don't approve of it," concludes Mel, 70, a psychotherapist. "The pervasive obscenity and vulgarity of pornography is destructive to our culture. I would actually eliminate it if I could. It draws men into jerking off rather than engaging in life as it should be lived. Porn exploits a vulnerability that we'd be better off not having exploited. So I limit it for myself, and I fantasize giving it up. I don't want to be sitting in front of my computer screen with my dick in my hand. That's not who I am—it's only part of who I am. And it's not who I want to be."

A prod to outrage, a window into American sexual tastes, an instructional manual, an addictive time-waster—clearly, porn is more than an aid to masturbation for these men and, presumably, for the great number of people who frequent porn sites during working hours. For me, at least—still chasing my wife around but without much testosterone to spare at age 58—the draw is the lurid intensity of the sites, the combined sense of thrill and repulsion, "search" and "trespass," that they evoke, far more than any urge to masturbate. Like computer solitaire (with its satisfying shuffling sound), or *Seinfeld* reruns (with their satisfyingly predictable routines), or a physical itch that I need to scratch (with that satisfying surge of relief), porn-surfing stimulates some primitive pleasure center of my brain and evokes the crass joke men tell about dogs: Why do they lick their balls? Answer: Because they can.

Still, I do not turn my computer volume all the way down when playing computer solitaire; I do not hurriedly turn off *Seinfeld* when my wife comes into the room; I do not scratch my itches for 20 minutes at a time without seeking medical assistance. It seems obvious that pornography has a far more complicated influence than many other distractions in life because its stock-in-trade is sex, that primordial human drive, with its many compelling elements of desire, pleasure, elation, power, shame, frustration, taboo, degradation, and more. Although pornographic imagery is often gross, garish, formulaic, and disturbingly misogynistic compared to the rich and varied emotional reality of actual sex, it draws its addictive power from what the Talmud recognized as the allure of sexual fantasy for men: "Thoughts about illicit copulation are more exciting than the act itself," intones Yoma 29a, "the analogy being the aroma of meat" (Bialik & Ravnitzky, 1992, p. 542).

Ah, that aroma. Even after 36 years in the kitchen with my beloved wife, I have not driven it from my nostrils.

Like the great majority of guys I know, I have been plagued for much of my life by a sex drive that runs contrary to civilization's rules. I have wanted to have sex with far more women than I've had access to. I have wanted to have sex with strangers based just on the visuals and the pheromones. I have wanted to participate in orgies. I have wanted women to make this possible by wanting me just as I want them, without the need for lengthy conversation, psychic intimacy, the breakup of my marriage, the disruption of my life. But most women are not like that—or, if they are, they have rarely clued me in about it, and in most cases I have been too shy to ask.

Besides, my partner has not been able to handle the stresses and jealousies of a sexually adventurous, open marriage, and I have not wanted either to torture her or lie to her to indulge my lusts, fantasies, and ego needs. We once tried an open arrangement, for a few months, after one of my frequent objects of desire clued me into the fact that she was, herself, in an open marriage and was interested in taking me to bed. I said to my wife: "We've done it your way, monogamous for all of these years. Now we have to try it my way. The sixties way!" While the tension and insecurity of the situation helped to heat up the eroticism of our own marriage, it also pulled my wife into enormous emotional upheaval, until we called off the experiment.

I might nevertheless be tempted to take on occasional lovers and deal honestly with the consequences, but there are not many opportunities to do so in my life as an isolated, hard-working writer living outside the city. I'm also too obviously domesticated to appeal to most women interested in a fling, and I'm too decent to seduce them with falsehoods. Now that I'm middle-aged, fairly secure in my ego, and no longer in the unrelenting grip of hormones, I feel much less restless than at earlier stages of my relationship—yet the aroma persists and is wafted my way by our shamelessly sexualized, commercial culture and, of course, by easy access to porn.

Does my time at porn sites make my de facto monogamy feel better or worse? By fostering the illusion that there are gazillions of thong-clad women out there who are constantly in heat but forbidden to me, worse.

By stealing minutes from my various forms of sublimation—my writing, my art—worse.

By distracting me from the cultivation of intimacy and intensity with my true love, worse.

By feeding my dissatisfaction when I'm feeling dissatisfied, worse.

By making me feel guilty for participating, in my own small way, in the exploitation of women and the cultivation of sexism, worse.

It is not a healthy habit. I can't find much positive to say about it beyond praising the steaminess of my favorite models.

And yet ....

If I could, at least, share my porn discoveries with my partner without making her jealous or judgmental toward me, the habit might have some positive role to play in our life together. My ideal of an open marriage, after all, was never a "don't ask, don't tell" policy but one of complete disclosure: Let's share adventures, let's tell each other every detail, let's psychoanalyze it together, and let's have it all become part of our intimacy and our bond of trust. There's no way, however, that my wife has been interested in handling all that complicated emotional stuff—and there's actually very little in the monotonous and alienated sexuality of the porn world that could serve as a proxy for what I've wanted in real life.

Still I cling to my porn habit, as though it embodied some vestige of the 1960s message: that the path to fulfillment and authenticity is not a body of received wisdom from the past but a modern superhighway of exploration and discovery. Never mind restraint—restraint means repression! Explore your desires! Lead with your imagination! Question authority! Wake up! Have an orgasm! Have two or three! It's good for you! Then thoughtfully digest it all, preferably with a good therapist.

Karene Howie (August, 2009), an Australian sexologist who propounds what she calls an "Evolutionary Philosophy of Human Sexuality," offers a different excuse for my mouse-clicking (http://sexuality.spaceandmotion.com): "Men are so attracted to porn," she says, simply because of "our evolutionary ancestry." Her argument is not the classic one about women's hard wiring for monogramy and men's hard wiring for promiscuity (what Bette Davis called "God's joke on human beings"). To the contrary, Howie believes that women "evolved to have sex with a series of males in succession" (http://sexuality.spaceandmotion.com/evolution-promiscuous-behaviour.htm#female.promiscuity). How else can we account, she asks, for the female capacity for multiple orgasms as well as for the spermicidal properties of semen and "the shape of the penis, [which] causes it to act as a sperm pump ... to displace other male sperm?" Howie believes that women, at the dawn of humankind, sought to secure reproductive success for their meager batch of eggs through serial sexual encounters—which means that men spent a lot of time "standing around watching a woman have sex with a man while ... waiting for their turn" (http://sexuality.spaceandmotion.com/evolution-male-sexuality.htm).

Ahh, so my attraction to watching goes back to the cave ....

Howie also reports on a Canadian study that "pinpointed areas of the brain that become active" (http://sexuality.spaceandmotion.com/human-brain-male-female-right-left.htm#sexual.arousal) when men watching pornographic videos were asked to avoid being stimulated—"In evolutionary terms," she writes, "these regions of restraint are newer than the more primitive areas where the sexual urges arise in the first place.".

Ahh, so my attraction to porn is lodged in my lizard brain ….

Hey, I believe in evolution, and I will take my excuses wherever I can get them …. But then my Judaism comes storming back! *Wait a minute, Lizard Man! Isn't it our capacity to overcome our animal instincts that makes us distinctive, perhaps even unique, as human beings? And isn't the mobilization of our higher human nature the very essence of Judaism?*

Why else are Jews instructed by Jewish law to drain the blood from their meat before eating it, to separate the yummy dairy stuff from the yummy flesh stuff for six hours, to say a blessing before or immediately after every experience, to practice cleanliness and modesty in appearance, and to handle sexual lust as a live bomb? The common thread of all of these rules is the postponement of gratification, the disciplining of our instincts, the mastering of our animal impulses. In the words of Rabbi Mordecai Kaplan (1948), my favorite contemporary theologian, human nature "not only makes for the survival of the fittest, but aims to make the great possible number fit to survive" (Kaplan, p. 253). This has made us "exempt from the law of natural selection," he concluded, and "subject to the law of spiritual selection" (Kaplan, p. 247).

All well and good—but I do not obey the specifics of Jewish culinary law, and I rarely pause to say a Jewish blessing before indulging in an experience. My engagement with Judaism, overall, is far more cerebral and emotional than behavioral. Why should I regard Jewish sexual law any differently—especially when those Jewish communities most obedient to *Halakha* (Jewish law) seem least interested, among Jews, in eros, in the aesthetics of the physical world, or even in their own bodies?

Judaism is a system of thought produced, moreover, exclusively by men who seemed possessed, at least in part, by the idea that women are weak-willed carnal creatures, while the ideal Jewish man is of a spiritual nature and keeps his beast well-sublimated. ("Rabbi Yohanan said: A man has a small member. If he starves it, it is satisfied; if he satisfies it, it is starved"—*Sukkot* 52b) (Bialik & Ravnitzky, 1992, p. 629). This hardly inspires my trust in *Halakha* as a useful source of sexual guidance. Indeed, so fearful were the rabbis of male sexual need—and the power it concedes to women—that a few passages in the Talmud resemble nothing so much as an "XXX" spread-eagle porn shot: "A woman is a leather bag full of excrement, her cunt full of blood," says *Shabbat* 152a, "yet all men run after her" (Bialik & Ravnitzky, p. 629).

And even when it's celebrating and honoring sexuality, Judaism tends to confine sexual tastes, orientations, and desires to a narrow box. Fantasizing while having sex, lewdness while having sex, rough sex, make-up sex, sex during an emotional crisis, drunken sex, and, of course, non-heterosexual and extramarital sex—all of these shades of experience are, for better or worse, banished under traditional Jewish law (Friedman, 1996, pp. 60–64).

But hold on again there, Lizard Man! How can you have the audacity, the sheer khutspe, *to critique Judaism—while clinging to your taste for pornography!!—on feminist grounds?*

Okay, okay, I hang my head in shame. I admit to I having little doubt that the boundaries are porous between the world of porn and the worlds of prostitution, sex trafficking, and other sources of misery for women and children worldwide. I have little doubt that the formulaic world of porn, in which beautiful, insatiable women will do every imaginable sexual practice with any muttering, angry man in the room, has helped cultivate a new wave of American sexism and degraded the culture at large. These facts make my porn use seem unconscionable: Here I am, not only damaging my soul but consuming a product (I never pay for it, but I guess that's beside the point) that hurts women and sets back progress on healthy gender relations.

Equally harsh condemnations can be levied, however, against a whole range of consumer products. Drinking soda helps destroy water resources in poor countries. Eating industrial meat and farmed fish helps degrade the planetary environment. Driving cars feeds the oil industry and all of the war and pollution it spawns. Watching movies breeds a tolerance for violence in the culture as well as illusions about romantic love and the size of the average middle-class apartment. I resist many of these politically incorrect products, of course; I try to be a socially responsible consumer. Somehow, though, the chain of social irresponsibility linked to porn seems to warrant special condemnatory judgment. I mean, I would not hesitate to say in an article that I occasionally drink a Coke or rent a thriller from Netflix! But admitting in writing to porn use may place my entire political and moral reputation at stake.

"I was never discriminated against for any reason, at any time, by anybody, until I self-identified as a sex worker," said Nina Hartley, a porn actress, businesswoman and sex educator of vast experience, in a speech to the California branch of the National Organization of Women in April 2008 (Kernes, 2008). However, while the work can be utterly disastrous for many women, Hartley said, it can be a journey of self-discovery and a fine way to make a living for others. In her own case, she observed, working in nearly 300 porn films has enabled her to answer such questions as "What are my values, what are my boundaries, what are my limits, what are my desires, what do I want to get out of my sexual life?" Porn has enabled her to understand, she said, "men's humanity and men's pain over sex" and how "women are amputated from their vulvas and men are amputated from their hearts." "Feelings are not action," Hartley concluded. "Thoughts are not action. And I give everyone complete freedom of mental activity. I believe in freedom of speech and I believe freedom of thought... . [W]hatever gets that little tingle going, think it, think it, think it; wallow in it."

I love Nina Hartley—for her mind, of course.

She is actually the one who "popped my cherry" back in the late 1980s, when she was interviewed by a mutual acquaintance, Sheldon Ranz, in *Shmate* magazine. Because she came across so powerfully in that interview as a feminist, socialist Jew, I gave myself permission to overcome my political guilt and watched a porn flick for the first time—one of hers called *Debbie Does Dishes* (1987). Then, as a Jewish magazine editor myself, I briefly corresponded with her about my own feminist objections to porn. ("It's strange to write to you having just seen you stark naked, but here goes ...")

It is neither feminist nor accurate, Nina Hartley responded to me, to believe that women have no power or choice in the porn industry. Nor do women require our protection from false portrayals of their sexuality, she said; instead, they need opportunities to create real portrayals. Both she and a porn star named Candida Royale, Hartley told me, were planning on doing just that. Her hope was for a liberated kind of porn that might serve as an aid to intimacy and adventurousness, knowledge and shamelessness—as well as orgasms galore.

From my limited explorations of the porn world, however, I don't see her hopes realized: Porn sites generally horrify me more than they titillate. The sexuality of the 1960s was not about hedonistic degradation and garishness, not about pretending women are nymphomanics, not about anger and domination—it was about non-possessive, multivalent love, about the affirmation of pleasure, about experimentation with the boundaries of emotion and experience in order to gain self-knowledge and move away from fear. When porn sites start cultivating *that* sensibility instead of the retrogressive sexuality they peddle, I'll be the first to pull out my credit card—and I'll pay for accounts for my son and daughter.

So where do all these confessions and perturbations leave me?

I may have given up on an open marriage, but I still like to have open discussions, especially about important, taboo topics. I'd like to discuss, for example, whether people were wrong to pursue "free love" in the 1960s? Are we responsible for today's vulgarity? Did we mistake immorality and idolatry for liberation?

I'd like to discuss whether miniskirts then and outrageously revealing clothes today are an expression of social oppression—or power—for the young women wearing them.

I'd like to discuss why a lot of men actually seem to get off on scenes of cold-heartedness and control in explicit sexual scenes. Why do so many men seem ambivalent about sexual mutuality and warmth?

I'd like to discuss what it is that people really wish to see in the way of sexual films and art. How can artists be inspired to lift eros out of the gutter?

And what about Judaism: Is it a path to sexual happiness or sexual repression? Is the key to sexual happiness that human beings, especially men, exercise restraint or set themselves loose?

In short, I'd like to talk about turning "Fuck you!" into a friendly greeting rather than a curse.

References

Bialik, H.N., & Ravnitzky, Y.H. (1992). *The book of legends/Sefer Ha-Aggadah.* New York: Schocken Books.
Friedman, A.P. (1996). *Marital intimacy.* Northvale, NJ: Jason Aronson Books.
Frykholm, A. (2007, September 4). Addictive behavior: Pastors and pornography. *The Christian Century.* http://www.christiancentury.org/article.lasso?id=3629
Howie, K. Evolutionary philosophy of human sexuality (Web address, p. 40).
Jameson, J. (2004). *How to make love like a porn star.* New York: Regan Books.
Kaplan, M. (1948). *The future of the American Jew.* New York: MacMillan Company.
Kernes, M. (2008, May 13). Nina Hartley speaks at NOW meeting. *AVN Media Network.* http://avn.com/performer/articles/30170.html.
Paul, P. (2005). *Pornified: How pornography is transforming our lives, our relationships, and our families.* New York: Times Books.

8

Prosthetic Voice

Oreet Ashery and *Barnaby Adams*

A while ago my close friend in Israel became an Orthodox Jew, the friendship ended, and I lost him. In looking for ways to reconnect with him, or maybe make sense of his conversion and my feelings about it, I made a series of photographic stills of myself (a woman) dressed as an Orthodox Jewish man. These black and white stills were the starting point of a visual and performative research into the appropriation of the frameworks defining my cultural heritage. Researching the stills involved following orthodox men in Jerusalem and discussing, with my father, the various dress codes and their meanings. With time, the right look was created by diving under cover into Stamford Hill, the orthodox Jewish neighborhood in London. I did not want to follow a specific dress code and hence associate myself with a particular sect within Jewish orthodoxy; I simply wanted those unfamiliar with these codes to identify me as an Orthodox Jew—not a specific one, rather, a signifier, an image, a simulacrum.

Following a number of photo shoots, I found myself wanting to walk outside the door dressed up. I loved the way I felt being dressed up, as if something was corrected inside me—a homecoming, I guess. So was born my alter ego, Marcus Fisher. "Mar-Cus" translates in Hebrew to "Mr. Cunt." The homecoming feeling is not merely connected to a generalized desire or a playful pleasure taken in cross-dressing, it is undoubtedly culturally specific; it is my way to be visibly Jewish. It is my way into Judaism.

As a small girl wandering the streets of Jerusalem with my father, I would stop with him outside *yeshivas* or *heders* (men or boys only spaces dedicated to Jewish studies) and listen to the murmurs. At the time I experienced a deep sense of exclusion and injustice, felt with utter conviction that only a child can sustain: Why can't girls go in? Why can't I be part of it? I was haunted and yet drawn to the barely heard voices and to the sense of secrecy and importance oozing out of the stone walls and soaking into my porous physical and mental existence.

I was brought up in Jerusalem, somewhere between the Arab village Shoafat and the orthodox Jewish neighborhoods beginning with Bar Ilan Boulevard. As a girl, I felt not only excluded from both territories, the Arab and the orthodox Jewish, but also from the political conflict itself.

In many of my teenage dreams, I was running with an Arab boy held in my arms, saving him from the bullets of the Israeli soldiers; however, my dream-state sense of heroism was quickly deflated by the arrival of a dream-figure Israeli army officer telling me that my actions were futile. This recurring dream expressed not only common Israeli guilt and sense of impotency regarding the political situation but an equally frustrated and gendered desire to be heard as a female voice in this conflict.

It also occurred to me that, since my mother ran away from her orthodox family in Jerusalem, the character of Marcus suggests a queer return to that family. It is a way to connect to this lost family whom I would be pushed to recognize if encountered face to face in a street in Jerusalem.

I am Oreet Ashery. I am an interdisciplinary visual artist. I work with art forms such as videos, photography, and performances.

Marcus Fisher is my alter ego; I dress up to perform him. He is a man, he is an art object, he is real.

Between 2000 and 2003, Marcus conducted a series of performances in curators' bedrooms. This project was called "Say Cheese." Audiences, who were participants, entered the bedroom one at a time to spend three minutes with Marcus. Their interactions prompted any form of exchange between Marcus and themselves: conversations, various forms of play, for example, pillow fighting, mutual primal screaming, sexual and physical exchange (but never ones that might include physical pain), and confessional exchange of various sorts. Through the intimacy of the event, "Say Cheese" constructed Marcus as an open-ended space for participants' projection. The bedrooms included ones in London, New York City, Zagreb, Liverpool, and Ljubljana.

In 2003 Marcus visited Meron Mountain at the north of Israel to take part in the yearly celebration of *Lag Ba'Omer*, commemorating the death of Rabbi Shimon bar Yochai. This was a carefully planned intervention. On his deathbed Rabbi Shimon ordered his disciples not to mourn his death but rather to celebrate it with laughter and dance. Indeed, the celebrations are similar to outdoor rave events yet are fuelled by religious ecstasy alone. Only men may dance. Marcus danced among hundreds, perhaps thousands, of Orthodox Jewish men. Marcus' intervention in the celebration was personally risky. If Marcus had been outed as Oreet, an impostor, the consequences would not have restricted themselves to an exposition of (anatomical) gender in a men-only space: At the time two suicide bombers were operating in Israel posing as Orthodox Jewish men. The video documentation of this intervention is called *Dancing with Men*. It was shown extensively internationally in art cinemas and venues.

Oreet Ashery recently introduced her alter-ego Marcus Fisher to another man. Barnaby Adams, who she/he met at a public lecture, delivered by Oreet. Although not Jewish, Barney felt that he and Marcus had much to learn from each other regarding the subject of masculinity. They became friends and exchanged the following series of letters.

Dear Barney,

During the Q&A part of Ashery's presentation, you asked a question in relation to atheist rituals and the sacred; you also asked something about why can't I, Marcus,

be declared real? I would like to probe you further and ask you to expand a little on those questions.
Marcus

Dear Marcus,

The initial attraction to the work was the immediately apparent complexity in your examination of a hierarchical structure, that of Orthodox Judaism.

The examination seemed to utilize tools of blasphemy and/or heresy to prise open the intimacies of this structure. However—and this is where I felt that I had something to learn from your investigations as well—it also became apparent that these tools, or methods, were actually far more complex in their application than I had first guessed. A "shock-art" reading of your work is clearly one of gross oversimplification, if not just plain wrong. Your performative methodology revealed itself, in the course of the lecture that you delivered, as a mode of (self?) address that seemed to reinhabit a heretical approach as a way of assembling from the structures and strictures of Orthodox Judaism a series or set of meanings that were neither contemptuous or dismissive (and so not conventionally blasphemous) but of a subjective value to you yourself.

I had for some time been personally interested in the potential for organised religion as a fertile ground for the reaping of meaning: possibly negotiated by the adoption of ritual behaviors, rituals that drew their resonance from organized religions yet contextualized themselves within a secular approach to daily existence. Your approach, which seemed intent on a reinhabitation of Orthodox Judaism as much as the reinhabitation of a heretical critique seemed to allow—actually encourage—the sort of contradictions and impossibilities that assemble themselves in front of anybody who wishes to engage themselves in a pursuit of meaning that concerns the sacred, whether they be practicing Jew or Atheist.

The question that I posed (and I can't remember how I put it) was related to the aspect of your performance art where you don the costume of an Orthodox Jewish man. Many aspects of what I saw that evening left unresolved issues with me. I was curious as to whether the performative aspect of your work was simply performance: theatre. Or perhaps whether your wearing of this costume initiated a process, a trajectory, a movement within. Your answers to public questions seemed to indicate a contradiction ... or to put it another way there remained as many unresolved issues for you as there were for me. Personally, I think that this lack of resolution indicates interesting art!

Your talk introduced your actions as Marcus within a context of alter egos and fictional identities. Yet even within the context of organized religion—where one is required to suspend many disbeliefs—I felt under no particular obligation to disbelieve that you, Marcus, did not self-constitute as a man. We all have our particularities, singularities, and preferences. I felt you should be treated no differently. However, the fact that you are not (biologically) conventionally equipped as a man provoked more problematics, particularly if there is an obligation to recognize a movement between you and Oreet Ashery, your alter ego in the condition of gender (and identity): a state of *fluctuation.*

If this is so, it sites your examination of the sacred through its transgression firmly in a topography of the body: but it is a map of movement with barriers and breaches, walls of and against self-realization. As a Jewish Israeli artist this shares obvious connotations and metaphors with contemporary geopolitics in Israel and Palestine. Do you think these are relevant?

Yours,
In Fraternity

Barney

Dear Barney,

Thank you for your reply.

It will be misleading to present under the banner of art my actions—which have included, for example, public interventions, performances, very intimate interactions with audience/participants and photographs—as fully pre-considered at the time or place them at the conscious service of political or cultural agendas. Those art actions have been fairly intuitive and self-fulfilling and derived from biographically placed notions of geographical and artistic (or art-world) de-territorialization impulses.

What I am writing to you at present is an interpretation, or a contextualization, of impulsive art actions that took place in the past.

During those events I was always an empty canon, a theater, as you called it, a structure waiting to be filled with meaning induced by the interfacing of my orthodox Jewish male clothing, which covered my non-phallic body and the nature of the art actions that took place.

Another set of meanings was produced by the tensions, or the *fluctuation*, as you named it, between myself and Oreet: she, a secular Israeli female artist, and me, an orthodox Jewish male concept. These tensions reached their peak in her attempts to kill me in self-defense, most directly in her performance and film *Marcus Fisher's Wake,*[63] where she fictionalized my life in order to induce my immanent death. That

[63] Foremost example of this is in Spike Lee's film *Bamboozled* (2000), where a White adman uses the term "n...." because "[his] wife is black so it's okay." The scene is superbly directed with Lee milking it for all its excruciating potential.

sense of an impossible witnessed self-annihilation or self-sacrifice is at the core of our relationships and at the core, I suspect, of Jewish-Israeli subjectivity.

I am a concept. But you are absolutely right that what is at stake in this fluctuation between Oreet and me, is a body, or the gaps and overlaps between the two bodies: a female body and an imaginary male body. Me, a body? It is becoming clear to me as I am writing to you that this conversation between us intensifies the movement into, but also against, embodied self-realization. However, your proposal during the public talk that I could be declared real and hence we could grant me a voice and the temptation to have a man-to-man conversation using this voice is irresistible on my part, so I am going to try and embody myself with you as I go along. I can already feel that the attempt to create an emancipated alternative self is doomed to fail from the onset, and this is perhaps where the "Jewish story" comes into being.

The image of the Eastern European Orthodox Jewish male, which I mirror, signifies the western Jewish meta-narrative of Exile reflected in the Zionist gaze; that is, of Jewish life outside the Promised Land. This 2,000 years of Jewish life "in exile" is intrinsically linked to a sense of a temporary existence, a disregarded one, an economy of lack, and one in need of correcting; a body without a land, a land without a body. It is important to note that the Hebrew words for Diaspora (*Galuyot*) and Exile (*Galut*) share the same linguistic root. And so embedded in the Hebrew language and Israeli psyche is this notion that even contemporary Diasporic Jewish identity cannot be separated from that formed at the time of the historical dispersal of Jews by the Babylonian occupiers, at least until the visionary return to the land will readdress this wrong doing. Amnon Raz-Krakotzkin is one contemporary thinker who densely charts the Israeli psyche and its persistently negative preoccupation with the exilic Jewish identity: An identity synonymous with passivity, vulnerability, and, hence, femininity, this exilic Jewish identity also includes Oriental Jewish identity. This persistent relegation of the Oriental Jewish identity (the term Oriental is also sometimes called *Mizrachi*, or *Safardi*) parallels Israeli priorities toward Palestinian residents of a land "empty" of inhabitants, according to the early Zionist mirage.

So when Oreet attempted to kill me or free herself from me, among a performance of a number of forces at play, she was also executing the Israeli ritual desire to annihilate the exilic Jew in an attempt to create an independent identity based on Jewish national and sovereign values.

In gender terms, the Zionist rejection of exilic Jews (Oriental and Western) and Palestinians alike can also be seen as an abjection of the feminine, the secondary, the lesser, the weak. However, to complicate matters, there is the interplay between the masculine over-determinate Israeli Jew and the lacking exilic Orthodox Jew—a man without a land, without a gun, without a phallus. Both in turn represent different patriarchal structures that undoubtedly favor men, one within a secular militant hypermale mentality, the other within organized religion. These coexist in the gaps and overlaps between the bodies of Marcus Fisher and Oreet Ashery.

The sacred and the rituals of transgression performed in those art actions in which I take place lie precisely in that signified fluctuation between different masculinities:

female masculinity (that of women who perform what might be considered masculine roles, for example, a Jewish woman dressed as a man); effeminate masculinity (that could be a dandy—Daniel Boyarin talks at length about Jewish men being dandies in the eyes of the "European Knights" because they don't work or go to war, they only study); and Middle-Eastern, Oriental, and western masculinities.

Of course, geographical zones prescribe their own specific gender behavior, so, for example, in Israel an Oriental man can be seen, from a racist perspective, as more aggressive or more "primitive" in his attitude to women. Exilic masculinity and Jewish men outside Israel are viewed as less manly than their Israeli counterparts since they don't go to the army (or have a direct connection to the notion of "pioneering").

See you soon,
Marcus

Letter to Marcus 24 February 2008

Dear Marcus,

I agree that there is fluctuation in your performance work, yet it is precisely the immanence of this fluctuation, an ever-present and oscillating sense of ambiguity—one might also be tempted to call it a perpetual undermining or irony—that mitigates against the erection of binary opposites such as the ones that you articulate in your letter ... specifically your hilarious name.

Meeting Mr. Cunt brings both extremes of male and female into an encounter. Yet there is always a sense that *you* exist somewhere—at no fixed address—between these extremes. This sense resembles a perception of a high frequency nomadism. But it is a nomadism between two opposite poles.

However, a real danger lies in the assignation of values such as "strength" and "weakness" to the conventional, simplistic normative gender "opposites." Even the assignation of the value of a positive to "strength" and a negative to "weakness" is a radical misjudgment, and one that—conceivably—could rest at the core of contemporary "Middle East crisis" problematics.

There seems to me to be a particular irony that, at the precise point that the Western art world was abandoning the necessity for an art object, the Jewish Diaspora was "gifted" by the British and the United Nations the object of its statehood. Contemporary art discourses have examined in detail the relative strengths and fragilities of the object versus the concept, not least the enslavement of the artist by the persistence of form. These discourses dismantled conventions of aesthetic approach toward paintbrush, canvas and sculpture in the 1950s and 1960s and in turn enabled a wider liberation struggle against the roles that objects play in aspects of gender. But the examination of the concept of statehood as an unwelcome enslavement of a people by an object has probably been overlooked because of its relative exclusivity to the Jewish people and now, of course, consequently, to the Palestinians.

I recognize the potential for gross oversimplification of an incandescently controversial subject. Much of your work, however, makes just this point, albeit with more subtlety. It militates toward a far more nuanced examination and critique of gender ... and by implication offers a similar critique of the potential hyper-fragile-masculine reading of Zionist elements in the Israeli industrial-military complex. But where does my insistence that you, Marcus, have a right to exist *in the body that you choose*, equipped with the prosthetic and portable penis, yet breasts, fit into this paradigm?

And what of the brittle patriarchy to which this tradition belongs? The latter part of the 20th century revealed it in the West to be largely a parody. Effectively it died as an unambiguous, non-fragile concept together with Rock Hudson. Hyper-masculinity, probably more than any other gender construct, reveals itself as inherently weak because it places itself at a limit. This male, taciturn cowboy has nowhere else to go and insists that he is accepted on his own terms. He has offered a self-restriction that has placed himself in jeopardy.

Nonetheless, as is apparent from your last letter, a self-produced male identity is complicated (and thus strengthened?) by your identification of the Orthodox Judaic male with (conventional) notions of femininity. Again there is the undermining, Marcus—a take and give back—or a coexistence between two binary oppositions. It makes my assertion of your right to exist an additional, yet not irrelevant, complication. It is a complication that Oreet has been complicit in recognizing, inasmuch as she attempted a sacrificial killing of you. But that is something else, for another letter, as I think establishing limits in a relationship such as ours makes for enough work in one day!

Yours in fraternity,

Barney

Dear Barney,

I have the feeling that Oreet would want to write much of this response to you. However, I can tell she will be using my name at the bottom of the letter as a signature, as if it was my voice all along, as if it was written by me.

This act perhaps illustrates the trajectory between gender binaries you were referring to, in its most effective performative state; the invested fictive distribution of a voice, a signature, a name.

Mostly, the instant we encounter another human being, the first thing we register is their gender. It is a matter of a split second and usually an unconscious and, dare I say, a universal reflex.

I am trying to assign to this instantaneous moment of recognition, this performative reflex, a visual shape. I am trying to get away from a visual or cognitive representation of gender binaries as two parallel fields with a "third way" movement in between. This mode of operation referred to in much discourse on gender as "that which is simultaneously neither, both and in-between" to describe gender fluidity has been and still is very useful; however, it seems that I am looking for another shape, another field of reference.

Something like a pyramid comes to mind. The tip of the pyramid could be the moment of gender recognition, or mis-recognition (a "double take"), the signature. Below the tip of the pyramid are stacks of the expanding field of multiple gender forms of existence, as they interplay within the one person. Instead of placing the male/female binary at parallel or opposite ends, I guess I would like to place gender at the tip of the structure as one piercing construct, whilst everything underneath carries the reality weight of gender multiplicity. The relationship I have with Oreet sits well within this structure; at the tip are the two different dressing codes of a western secular woman and an orthodox Jewish man alongside the manipulation of gender-specific body parts. These are the points of recognition, below: all that you and I are attempting to articulate.

I very much agree with your comment that Western hyper-masculine behavior failed because its proposition of masculinity was set at its limit and hence weakened by default. In the context of Jewish Israel I would place hyper-masculinity as the tip of my proposed pyramid, the point of recognition: the indexical register in which everything else is measured against yet increasingly fails to pass. This specific form of hyper-masculinity is today not the cowboy but the man-machine legacy better known as the Israeli combat soldier of the elite brigades. This model citizen is the Israeli Jewish point of register. It could be argued that the Israeli combat soldier/citizen as a register is not primarily a gender construct but essentially a non-gender nationalistic construct, as the actual male bodies who engage in fighting are only arbitrary cogs in the propaganda machine of this symbolic order. Excluded from this register are Orthodox Jews, Arab Israelis, foreign workers, non-Jews, objectors, and the mentally ill. But even those who could pass register are struggling, and increasingly so.

At 60 years of age, the figure of the Israeli combat soldier is gradually being replaced by technology—morally emptied out by the oppression of another nation, further compromised by a lack of professionalism and corruption in the army, and dated within a post-Zionist and a postmodern existence—all within a backdrop of an increased religious fundamentalism on all fronts. The possibility of holding the certainty-torch of the "true Israeli," the "true new Jew" is becoming a fiction.

This increasing fiction, played out on my body-in-performance, invites metaphorical readings of art-object, gender ambiguity, and Israeli State substitution as an inevitability. (I suppose the concomitant "lack of resolution" you identified reflects this.)

Does the exilic effeminate, stateless Jew hold more power as a concept then his counterpart Israeli fighter/object of desire? Does the Jewish man without a state, without an object to hold and protect, last longer? Is he more historically sustainable? Or is the increasing impotency and emptying out of the figure of the Israeli military hyper-male creating a space for a Jewish Israeli manhood that is allowed to be vulnerable without feeling that his core survival mechanism is at stake? Perhaps gender fluidity can be used as a model for a positive mingling between the figures of the exilic Jewish man and the Israeli Jewish man? And what of the mingling potential of Jewish male identity with other border-crossing possibilities?

And me with a putative penis and invisible breast, where do I fit into these questions? Do I offer a future possibility for the Jewish male in any way? A metaphor, a model? A redemptive lack of objecthood (penis, state)? A way out of war?

Perhaps conceptually I could imply a suggestion of mobility, but biologically I have met the limits of my hidden bodies and parts and the fixidity that this imposed on me. I have met my physical limits not arm wrestling among strong men or combat soldiers but among a display of homoeroticism of Orthodox Jewish men.

In 2003 I went to the north of Israel dressed as an Orthodox Jewish man (as myself, Marcus) to take part in the celebration of Lag Baomer all over Meron Mountain.** At the annual celebration hundreds of thousands of Orthodox Jewish men mingle, following Rabbi Shimon bar Yocahi orders to dance, smile, and be happy as a way of commemorating his death. However, only the men danced in male-only outdoor dance-floor areas; the women wailed, mainly gathered under a passageway that according to common belief leads to bar Yochai's grave. I noticed that there were two main dance areas, one for "black Jews" with prayers sampled into techno sounds and rave dancing and a second area where masses of men dressed like me danced: traditional Eastern European Jewish dancing, holding hands in a strudel-like pattern, whilst sporadically some would burst out of the chain and swirl whilst clapping. I danced among the Eastern European Jews who looked like me, holding the hand of a teenager in order to hide my small hands and limited height. I did not know the dance and kept looking around for clues, mimicking.

During the event, which is staged very much like an outdoor festival, while I walked in the crowded passageways from one dance floor to the next, I could feel an undeniable homoerotic charge. Then I felt the (Orthodox Jewish) man behind me touching me up. First I thought that he had realized I was a female in disguise, but then I realized that this was happening all around me. I was terrified at the offer of physical intimacy: my cup B breasts were bound in tight rustling cling film, in my pants a pair of crunched up large socks. What hope did I have of successful subterfuge? What would happen to me? All around men were groping; some went to the sides of the mountain, hidden by trees, plants, and bushes, quickly touching or sucking each other off. I have never felt so vulnerable as a Jewish man, so lacking in a Jewish penis, and so over equipped with Jewish breasts than I did among those gently sensual, merry, homoerotic males. I had met a limit where clothes and an art-concept would no longer suffice. I desperately wanted a penis, I desperately wanted to be accepted as a man without one, but mostly I was terrified that I would be discovered, outed. Not just a breach of security and morality bothered me, it was a pure fear of humiliation, the humiliation of being found out pretending to be someone you are not. Yet the fantasy of being accepted unconditionally into the tribe, to be accepted as male without being one, to transcend or mobilize biological limits, or to be embraced just on the merit of my sheer intentions and desires kept me going for a few intense hours.

Yours without a penis,
Marcus

Letter to Marcus March 30

Dear Marcus,

What a profound sense of regret I felt on your behalf from your last letter. It is tempting, however, to respond to your experience of humiliation, lack of belonging, and desire for acceptance: welcome my son!

Unfortunately being actually equipped with a penis and occasionally—and often inappropriately—a phallus, does not mitigate these feelings. Your experience is very much a part of being a man. One always seems to have a sense of the phantasmagorical conditions of acceptance into the fraternity and the commensurate difficulty in realizing this fantasy. Perhaps even realizing the difficulty in recognizing that maleness *is* a fantasy.

Introducing the concept of maleness as a limit also arrives with the implication that it has a fragmented relationship with some form of utopian state. Hence the correlations between hyper-masculinity and fragility. These contrive—at their limit—to perpetually undermine each other. Yet the biological inevitable of an engendered state does little more than indicate a direction toward a "normative" code toward which a boy/girl is encouraged to dress and behave. The process of socialization encourages this orientation towards binaries of male/female dress in children and, particularly, young adults. Many at this point choose to contest this pre-received notion of oriented conformity as the first principle of rebellion. It is also worth noting that these forms of rebellion against gender codes are quite distinct and separate from emerging senses of sexual orientation, although they may correlate.

But men fluctuate in our sense of gender orientation, and we know we do. We know the rate of exchange too. We constantly calibrate our gender topography. Your experience at Meron Mountain only made you realize your limit as a man *because you were at it.* Most men are too wary to push themselves that far for fear of an exposure, a rejection by other (pseudo-imaginary) super-male constructs: the classic locker-room humiliation being the feared and anticipated result. Much homoerotic culture is predicated on the excitement generated by the raised stakes at this edge of the gender map.

Your desire kept you there, *at it,* for several hours, you write. This is nothing short of an astonishing display of virility: you should be very proud of that.

The visit to a sacred, men-only, ritual symbolizes the dichotomies of the male/female binary. On Meron Mountain suggestions of gender ambivalence (undermining) might have resulted in some form of heavy punishment if you were found out. But you "took" away an experience. At the other opposite stands the suggestion of "giving" that emerges from "Say Cheese,"*** where you invited audience members to join you on a bed in a bedroom and permitted them to ask you to "do anything" with them.

The bedroom ritual inaugurates a female space, representing a womb or a vagina perhaps, and as it is also an art-space it also inaugurates Nietzsche's observation that "one ought not to demand of the artist, who gives, that he should become a woman." This is "ought-not art," and here Marcus is engaged, as a man, with the (according to Nietzsche) art-act of "giving" in the most literal sense: a responsiveness and receptivity to the requests of an audience, a giving of his time and of himself. This undermines traditional masculine codes, which, as you are aware are *also* undermined by Oreet Ashery's perceptions of the feminine resonance of the Orthodox Jew. All this, in turn, is undermined further by the suggestion (articulated clearly during the performance) that Marcus is *not a real man.*

So not only did you reach your limit as a man but also pushed toward a boundary as a woman. Meron Mountain has become figuratively turned inside-out on itself and has become a vagina-bedroom in "Say Cheese" (with all the implications of the breaking of patriarchal law, and subverting of phallic symbolism, taken into consideration). Then you consecrated this engendered space as sacred by your procession from chest-of-drawers to bed with a prosthetic phallus, having been asked to show your cock by a male participant audience member. The return to the bed, holding the prosthesis, recalled ancient fertility rites: a person of ambiguous gender carrying a symbol of the male fertility organs. Richard Payne Knight describes such processions in *A Discourse on the Worship of Priapus* (1865, p. 28) as having their origins in worship of Osiris: but the imagery is more familiar today because of the Christian church's expropriation of the early T symbol (representing the male generative organs) to make a crucifix (with the subsequent addition of a symbolic head). The procession itself, of course, symbolizes the nomadism of ancient peoples, a performance that has been mimicked by your nomadic gender identity.

Ancient notions of the sacred are by no means irrelevant here and are particularly complicated by your insistence on wearing traditional Orthodox dress. There is a strong sense of invocation marbling the flesh of both the bedroom performance and the experiences you encountered on Meron Mountain. I was reminded by your film *Dancing with Men* of the Islamic scholar Peter Lamborn Wilson's recounting of Hasan-i-Sabah's proclamation of the Great Resurrection (*Qiyamat*), where his followers—also on a mountain (Alamut in then Persia)—experienced immanent realization and demonstrated this by breaking fast (this occurred during Ramadan, in 1164 Western calendar) and drinking wine. Perhaps your invocations (and their underminings) are the erections of orthodoxies by which manner heretical behavior can be encouraged to occur? As P. L. Wilson also writes, "'heresies' are often the means for transfer of ideas and art-forms from one culture to another" (*Scandal: Essays in Islamic Heresy*, 1988, p. 13). Yet immanent realization (apparently akin to an ecstatic epiphany) also abolishes binaries, and so, although Marcus fluctuates between limits of male and female identities, there is also a sense that you exist permanently in a real immutable condition of paradox.

At this point I suppose that we can identify a mode of address, of the voice of Marcus-the-art-concept. This voice communicates across cultures via the medium of heresy, and this voice is paradoxical.

Where there is heresy, there is transgression, and transgression needs limits or, as you wrote in your last letter, border-crossing possibilities. I think in our correspondence so far that we have, quite deliberately, established limits, established these borders. We also know that these limits are, to a certain extent, themselves compromised, unattainable and fluid: moreover that certain constructs exist at both limits simultaneously although sometimes only in part. Marcus. (Mr. Cunt.) The Orthodox. Jewish. Exilic. Male.

Nonetheless, this should not alter the essence of the limits' existence. I believe that you encountered this as such at Meron. Perhaps, as a nonconventionally equipped man, you encountered *both* limits at the same time. In other words you had a male experience that was not available to the *other men*. Perhaps you had a secular experience, and they a sacred one; possibly the reverse was true (and let us not ignore that priapism has its own routes to the divine).

So at which point does your transgression occur?

Thinking through the establishment of a mode-of-address as a voice, and searching for a visual shape that represents gender in a more useful way, I find myself imagining a diaphragm, something similar to the tympanic membrane within the ear. The tympanic membrane oscillates when it "hears," both intruding into the body, and extruding to the outer world, or the "direction" of the sound. The loudness of the sound causes the oscillations to increase in both directions *until a limit is reached in each*: a degree of maximum elasticity.

Imagining this metaphor permits us to place our gender binaries at the limits of maximum oscillation. Masculine and feminine are both represented, both equal. Our behavior regarding gender oscillates between the limits as does a physical sound wave. There are perceptions of simultaneity. (When we hear we cannot detect whether the membrane is in, or out; it happens too fast.) This seems to equate to the paradoxes of gender exhibited by your work.

The analogy also encourages the potential to change gender: the greater physical potential to return to a state of rest exhibited in a fully stretched elastic. This state of rest that occurs when the membrane returns to its flat position is the condition of hearing absolute silence. It is equilibrium. But it could also be construed metaphorically as some central(ish) border between the genders, a threshold over which a person passes in the transfer of gender.

In transgender discourse "passing" is a common enough terminology. But what if we make it into the border crossing of transgression? Perhaps it makes sense to suggest a *third* limit: one placed at a point between male and female binaries. Thinking it in this way repositions Michel Foucault's "A Preface to Transgression." (From *Language, Counter-memory Practice*, 1977)

> Transgression is an action which involves the limit, that narrow zone of a line where it displays the flash of its passage, but perhaps also its entire trajectory, even its origin; it is likely that transgression has its entire space in the line it crosses. The play of limits and transgression seems to be regulated by a simple obstinacy: transgression incessantly crosses and re-crosses a line which closes up behind it in a wave of extremely short duration, and thus it is made to return once more right to the horizon of the uncrossable. (pp. 33–34)

Placing a borderline between limits renders it as super-permeable: "incessant." Yet far from making this border irrelevant "transgression would be pointless if it merely crossed a limit composed of illusions and shadows" (Foucault, p. 34). I think placing a "passing point" between masculine and feminine, a point that is incessantly transgressed by your work, makes transgression not pointless but cancels a requirement for transgression itself. There becomes through incessant transgression a revocation of the silence of gender: the movement *through the normative* gives gender a voice. A *proper* articulation.

The bidirectional oscillations of gender fluctuation pass over, vibrate through, and continue onwards to explore the limits in both directions. I believe you illustrate this fulsomely with your work; you generate a sound, make a noise ... can we be poetic and assign to this sound a vocality? It seems to fit in with the need to recognize a human body buried in the rubble of gender; yes, I think this is where you, Marcus, fit in (to answer the question you asked me in your last letter ... finally!).

There is a boldness and directness about your body in much of your performance work that belies the "fallen bodies" of (Christian) sin in Foucault's essay. Far from invisible, I recall photographs of you, Marcus, with your B cup hanging out from under your jacket. (Your lecture stated that a typical audience reaction was to imagine that your breast was a prosthetic.) Similarly the matter-of-fact retrieval of the latex phallus for the satisfaction of the participants' curiosity in the bedroom. Your dick was in your drawers. No problem.

The body that contains this voice, particularly the engendered body, carries a strong emphasis in your work. There is a simple (frightening?) reclamation of a "plastic" all-gender embodiment occurring there that perhaps has deeper roots in Jewish culture than one might suspect. Was not the Golem—the original prosthetic yid—an incarnation of flesh from clay that carried more than an attempt to *make visible* the ghetto Jew his claymation masculinity an historical parallel with your own version of prostheticized gender?

Any racially motivated slur is a pronounced abuse of a language. In recent times there has been a movement to "reclaim" the language of the abuser/oppressor back for the people/race that has endured the abuse. This trajectory has been viewed as particularly controversial, not least because, in turn, it requires the division of the human along racial grounds in order to ascertain who is permitted to use the reappropriated term of abuse and who is not.

Thus the reappropriated term "yid" remains compromised, always dangerous, and tainted. This is how it should be.

In my view the creation of the Golem was an equally compromised horror-Jew-made-flesh. Although the Golem made the Ghetto-dweller visible, it was the terror of the Jewish other that was embodied, via a superstitious medium (magic amulet in this case). So he was both a defender of the Jewish ghetto AND an embodiment of gentile fear. I think the term Yid is appropriate in this case.

A similar negotiation occurs in your work, where you embody gender variation via prosthesis in a process of making visible. It is both a defense of sexual difference and, inevitably, a threat at the same time. It's a process that has come to be associated with "queer" bio-politics. But where the Golem made the Jew visible, the Golem was silent. Your more complex aesthetic articulations make the engendered Jew *more audible.*

Applying the phrase "Yid" MUST carry an implicit level of threat and offence. (Like "cunt"?)

The term "prosthetic yid" (which I use with great reservation) makes a direct textual connection to your "prosthetic voice" ... effectively raising that voice, via the mechanisms of shock and transgression (which are not inappropriate to your work themselves) to an audible level: moreover that audible level is made loud enough that it can now be heard resonating through the last century.

Your version of embodied gender has a prosthetic voice: whether this voice yet has a language I am unsure.

I think that this largely ties in with your question about "a redemptive lack of object-hood." Is the choice of the Orthodox a suitable vessel for a redemptive strategy?[64]

Much depends on your interpretation and that of your audience (and that of those that read this). I'm not sure that a language is a particular necessity to communicate either. A voice might be enough.

Yours in fraternity,

Barney

---

[64] Georges Bataille (1988) writes a little cynically about the relative proclivities toward redemptive desires of various religions in his book *Inner Experience*. He isolates the Catholic and the Hindu as being redemptionists ... is the Jew to join them?

Dear Barney,

I feel that your observation that "although Marcus (I) fluctuates between limits of male and female binaries, there is also a sense that you exist in a real immutable condition of paradox" is key to my idiosyncratic sense of existence: that which is between orthodoxy and heresy, between female and male, between Israeli and Jewish, between art and life, whereby the actual motion of transgression is in fact fixed in the impossible paradox. I am very interested in the notion of transgression you mention as a form, or an act, that defines the actual border line *and* trajectory between gender binaries and hence extends the limits or thresholds of both feminine and masculine spaces in the act of the crossing over. In organized religions, heresy or blasphemy act at this threshold of transgression, whereby the transgression can only accrue within the limits of the rules and regulation of the particular belief system. Step outside the belief system and the agency of transgression no longer exists .... As with gender-crossing and with heresy, transgression can only take place from within the structure. The transgressive impulse hence mobilizes the existing structure rather than stepping outside of it altogether. So then, both in heresy and in "gender-bending" activities, the border-crossing act is also an act of confirmation, a confirmation of the limits crossed, of thresholds straddled, almost a naïve call for a change from within. Of course, I am differentiating between a forced or a compulsive transgression, whereby a person's life can be threatened by, for example, oppressive familial, cultural, and political oppressive regimes, and one of a philosophical position, where there is a choice to be made, yet the choice is to transgress rather than to abandon. In the case of a "willed" transgression, I do believe that a sense of invested loyalty or belonging to the gendered or religious structure is actually firmly imbedded.

In this context, I am aware of Ashery's current research into enigmatic historical Jewish male figures who have crossed over to the Islamic faith. Sarmad the Saint, also called the Jewish Saint of India, was a 17th century Jewish traveler (some say Armenian) who arrived in Delhi and increasingly attracted followers with his poems and translations. Sarmad questioned the structures of organized religion and religious philosophy and, although mainly known as a Sufi, he moved freely and critically to "pick and mix" between Judaism to Islam, Sufism, and Hinduism. One of Sarmad's poems says

True, I am an idol-worshipper;
I am not of the faithful flock.
I go to the mosque,
But I am not a Muslim.
(Ezekiel, Sarmad Jewish Saint of India, p. 35).

I feel something of the flavor of the intervention *Dancing with Men* in this poem—something of a desire to belong by performing certain communal rituals, yet only critically and on one's own terms. Sarmad was living openly with an Indian man he loved, named Habichand, despite pressure from family and the Mughal court to separate. In more than one way, he stood by his critical and transgressive impulses, which led him to his traumatic end. When he was asked by Aurangzeb, the last Mughal ruler in India, to declare the Muslim affirmation that "there is no Allah (god) but Allah (god)," Sarmad proceeded only to affirm that "there is no god."

Then he fell silent ....

Having been convicted of religious heresy for the incident described above, as well as additional accusations of wine drinking and marijuana smoking, Sarmad was sentenced to death. His head was cut off.

Another historical case of the performance of religious heresy alongside psychosexual transgression is Shabtai Zvi, an influential and controversial prophet, known as the "false" Messiah. Shabtai Zvi, who today we might recognize as a manic-depressive, performed many blasphemous acts, including saying the name of God, which shall not be spoken, declaring that the three main Jewish holidays would take place all in one day, and demanding that women should have access to the cabbala and should be permitted to touch and hold the Torah in the synagogue: something that by tradition only men do according to Jewish law. He was known for his external beauty, and he was also described as a cross-dresser, or at least a serious dandy, and he engaged in homosexual acts.

It seems that intuitively Oreet has been acting out through me her notion of a transgressive Jewishness and that these impulsive performative acts are both recalling and anticipating other "fictional" characters based on "actual" historical cases of both religious and gender transgressions. I can see myself sacrificed in favor of new characters articulating this particular Jewish canon of transgression. I think that Oreet's investigation into Jewish masculinities reveals men who are not quite men, and hence could be women, and who are not altogether Jewish either. Feeling just as impossible to articulate these paradoxes as I was before this conversation, and feeling still outside articulation myself, I feel I must be satisfied to simply embody a performative prosthetic vocality that is more powerful as a producer of sound than an articulator of a language.

Yours,

Marcus, but probably not for much longer

**Marcus Fisher's Wake* (2000) is a mock documentary video charting the fictional life of Marcus Fisher from childhood through adulthood to a presumed death. The footage includes home videos of Oreet Ashery's family as well as documentations of interventions Marcus did in Soho, London, a Turkish men's café in Berlin, and a beach in Tel Aviv. The video was used later in a performance called "Marcus Fisher's Wake," celebrating Marcus's putative death.

** *Dancing with Men* (2003), an intervention and a video documentation.

*** "Say Cheese" (2001–2003) a one-to-one interaction that took place over seven cities worldwide in curators' bedrooms, constructed bedrooms, and hotel bedrooms. For more detailed information on "Say Cheese," see http://www.7actsoflove.org/archive/saycheese/index.html.

III
Emasculation and Its Discontents

9

TROUBLE ON MAX NORDAU STREET: MICHAEL CHABON REWRITES JEWISH MASCULINITY

WARREN ROSENBERG

Jewish-American writers of the mid-20th century—primarily male and almost all first generation children of East European immigrants, such as Saul Bellow, Bernard Malamud, E.L. Doctorow, and (most characteristically) Norman Mailer and Philip Roth—are caught between two contradictory definitions of manhood. On the one hand, their identities were shaped by Diasporic rabbinic Judaism, by a culture that valorized scholarship, worship, sacrifice for family and community, and nonviolence—a culture of *Yiddishkeit*. On the other hand, in Europe and America, they were also shaped by ideals of manhood that emphasized the physical over the mental, the individual over the family or group, that held up the warrior as the ultimate male. From this perspective, as Sander Gilman and George Mosse represent the history, the Jewish male was perceived as feminized, as not fully male, by the dominant culture. Yet Biblical heroes like King David and Samson, who gained God's favor and succeeded by using violence, also influenced these writers as part of their cultural heritage. When linked to the values of American masculinity, Mailer and his contemporaries developed an ethos of toughness that collided with the values and realities of Diasporic life they also absorbed in their homes and synagogues. This collision added complexity and anxiety to Jewish male identity,[65] leading to gender confusion and a resultant suppressed rage evident in a wide range of texts by Jewish-American writers and filmmakers.

Mark Helprin, David Mamet, Barry Levinson, and Steven Spielberg, all Jewish baby boomers, are caught, like their predecessors, in an overcompensatory view of masculinity, which in some cases "out-Mailer's" Mailer. These artists are, to varying extents, participants in a process Jeffords (1989) labeled "remasculinization," a culture-wide attempt by American patriarchy in the 1970s, 1980s, and 1990s, and some would argue still occurring, to regain its mythical male hegemony after the defeat in Vietnam and in light of the "threat" of black and female gains. One only has to read Helprin's first novel, *Refiner's Fire* (1977) or see Mamet's film *Homicide* (1991) to grasp how these men reify a particularly macho, although not uninflected, response to the legacy of Jewish masculinity. An initial countermovement to this remasculin-

[65] In my book *Legacy of Rage: Jewish Masculinity, Violence, and Culture* (Rosenberg, 2001), I follow the groundbreaking work of Paul Breines, David Biale, Sander Gilman, Howard Eilberg-Schwartz, Daniel Boyarin, and Harry Brod in taking a critical look at the historical construction of the Jewish male. While in my study, like Biale and Eilberg-Schwartz, I look at the Hebrew Scriptures and, like Gilman and Boyarin, consider the Diasporic role in that construction, my primary focus is the representation of the Jewish male in 20th century American culture.

ization can be seen in the work of Cynthia Ozick and Tony Kushner, a woman and a gay man, who seek to resist the traditional romantic macho script. In her novel *The Puttermesser Papers* (1997), Ozick rewrites the golem legend from a feminist perspective and thereby transforms its theme of retribution through violence. In *Angels in America* (1993), Kushner takes on the critique of Jewish men as being less masculine by offering gay Jewish male characters who refuse to accept societal norms of masculinity, and in this he joins Boyarin's (1997) attempt in *Unheroic Conduct* to "conceive of the structure of Jewish gender as being differently configured" (p. 354), as rejecting, specifically, the imperative of being heterosexual and violent.

In this context it would be natural to wonder how Jewish writers of the current generation have responded to what I have called this "legacy of rage" (Rosenberg, 2001), and, in the work of Michael Chabon, born in 1963, there is one compelling answer. Chabon's novels reveal a full awareness of the historical construction of Jewish masculinity, European and American. His increasingly accomplished writing moves from the coming-of-age struggles of his first novel, *The Mysteries of Pittsburgh* (1988), to the more distanced but still self-referential exploration of writing, academe, and manhood in *Wonder Boys* (1995), to the grand scope of his Pulitzer Prize winning *The Amazing Adventures of Kavalier & Clay* (2000). More recently, Chabon has gone even further in deconstructing and rewriting the image of Jewish masculinity in *The Yiddish Policemen's Union* (2007a), *Gentlemen of the Road* (2007b), and in a collection of essays entitled *Manhood for Amateurs* (2009).[66]

It would be useful to sketch, briefly, the origins of this new hero in Chabon's first two novels (1988, 1995) before considering their fuller embodiment in his subsequent work. Art Bechstein, the protagonist of *The Mysteries of Pittsburgh* (1988), is home after graduating college. His father, an organized crime figure, had revealed his true profession to Art on the day of his bar mitzvah, connecting the realities of violence to the coming of age of a Jewish male. His father, however, insists that Art not romanticize a profession, one that apparently led to the death of Art's mother, of which he himself is ashamed. Thus, even as Art ceremonially becomes an adult Jewish male, he is separated from a full engagement with his father's past, and this explains the chapter title, "A Free Atom." Art seems free in America to shape himself.

Art's violent friend Cleveland, though, embodies the Mailer/Roth masculine roving id, the need to confront the big father, the gangster as well as God. This character's uncommon name is, I believe, Chabon's (1988) homage to the creation of Superman, whom Cleveland, with his mysterious background and masculine powers, resembles.[67] He is indeed Superman to Art's Clark Kent; both are needed to con-

---

[66] While I do not have the space here to discuss the novel *Gentlemen of the Road* (Chabon, 2007), it clearly shares the themes of Jewish male transformation explored in this essay, although the book is set in Khazar, a supposedly Jewish Empire, during the 10th century. I will refer briefly to *Manhood for Amateurs* (2009) at the end of this essay.

[67] See Brod's (1996) essay on the creation of Superman by two Jewish teenagers in Cleveland, Ohio, in the 1930s.

struct the contemporary American Jewish male. At the conclusion of the novel, Art's father, in a rage over his son's drawing too close to the violent Cleveland, indirectly arranges for the friend's death. Art, though, has already set out on his own quest for manhood. With a Swiss Army knife and "three thousand ancient, inviolate bar mitzvah dollars" (Chabon, p. 295), he leaves Pittsburgh, never to see his father again. In his first novel, then, Chabon directly confronts the historical forces shaping Jewish masculinity and at least imagines viable alternatives. His protagonist makes the very American final assertion that "one can learn, for instance, to father oneself" (Chabon, p. 295).

That this may be a naïve understanding of how one comes of age is illustrated in *Wonder Boys* (Chabon, 1995), where male-male interaction is centrally represented. While the narrator and protagonist of *Wonder Boys*, college professor Grady Tripp, is not Jewish, there is a Jewish leitmotif in the novel, as Judaism becomes integral to Grady's character development. Grady's father-in-law, Irv, is Jewish, and is the most positive older male figure in the novel. I would argue that a Passover Seder at Irv's house, which makes up a major portion of the novel, plays a critical role in Grady's transformation. Initially, Grady is almost constantly stoned on pot, is cheating on his wife with his college dean, who is now pregnant with his child, and can't finish the novel he has been working on for years. Yet to Chabon, he is clearly a mensch.

By the novel's end (Chabon, 1995), Grady marries the dean, gives up daily pot smoking, and settles down to be a model father and husband who can now finish his novel. Passover, the defining libratory holiday of the Jews, parallels Grady's peripatetic moral life, as he seems to wander aimlessly in search of his true self. The time devoted to talking about the different rituals surrounding the meal and of the reading of the Hagaddah provides something solid in the middle of this postmodern novel and in the middle of Grady's decentered life. After the Seder, he uses the body of the family's pet snake to ward off an attacker, comparing himself to Aaron, "the silver-tongued shadow of Moses" (Chabon, p. 319). The blow knocks the gun out of the attacker's hand, and, in this comically violent scene, one senses that the wonder boys of the title combine comic book and biblical heroes. At the end of the novel, Grady assumes the father role to his depressed student James, a process that leads to Grady finding his adult self as well.

The themes of fathers and sons, violence, and the search for Jewish male identity that permeate Chabon's earlier novels emerge against a much broader historical backdrop in *The Amazing Adventures of Kavalier & Clay* (Chabon, 2000), a sweeping imaginative recreation of the history of comic books in America as related to the Holocaust and American life in the 1940s and 1950s. While Solotaroff (1996) predicted that the wave of Jewish-American writing in the late 1990s, one he labels "post-acculturated" (p. xv), would have to make Israel a central motif to keep the Jewish past and Jewish difference a central theme, Chabon clearly chose, in this novel and his next, not to do so. He is more interested in looking at the Diaspora and Americanization, focusing on the central role Jews have played in defining America in this century, mostly through popular culture, and the effect American life has had on the

Jews. As 17-year-old, Brooklyn-born Sam Clay (Klayman) says on the first page of the novel, "To me, Clark Kent in a phone booth and Houdini in a packing crate, they were one and the same thing" (Chabon, p. 3). They both represented escape and transformation and were thus heroes to "little men, city boys, and Jews" (Chabon, p. 3) like Clay.

Superman, however, turns out not to be the ideal Jewish male, because violence is not, ultimately, a positive Jewish value for Chabon. Here is where he most significantly rewrites the legacy of Jewish masculine rage, a legacy his characters fully embody. The key to his ability to make this radical change is art, specifically comic book art, for which the novel (Chabon, 2000) makes an eloquent case. Chabon grew up in the 1960s, obsessed with comics, a narrative pictorial form that offered free reign to fantasy. And, while the consumers of comics knew no ethnic or class boundaries, the creators, interestingly, were primarily Jewish.[68] This mode, so linked with the complex heritage of Jewish masculinity outlined above, yet created by men who felt the security and freedom derived from being acculturated Americans, gave Chabon the artistic means to escape what appeared to be a cultural imperative toward violence.

Kavalier & Clay (Chabon, 2000) uses comic book violence to comment on and replace real violence by alternating and frequently blurring the lines between the two. At times a chapter will begin, without warning, within the comic book world, thus disorienting the reader. That Chabon can actually pull this off—that Josef (Joe) Kavalier, the novel's hero, can move in and out of real and imaginary worlds—is the novel's triumph, and critics who have argued that Joe is too good and too "large" to be true do not appreciate that this is exactly Chabon's intention.[69] Joe isn't perfect, but he is Chabon's representation of the ideal Jewish male, a unity of European and American masculinity at its best. One might even argue that Chabon's naming his protagonist Josef is intended to evoke the most Yiddishkeit biblical hero. As Lefkovitz (1988) writes, the biblical Joseph's "strength is not physical: it is vision, calculated management and prudence, rather than brawn, that are his saving features" (p. 28).

How Josef escapes from Europe illustrates these traits and constitutes a critical transformative element, because Chabon (2000) takes the oft-used golem legend and defuses its violent content. In a spare but beautiful evocation of 1939 Jewish life in Prague, Chabon introduces us to the Kavalier family. Only Josef, because of his being born in a neutral country, has any chance of officially getting out, and, when that falls through due to heightened Nazi restrictions, Chabon turns to a more creative

[68] Jewish comic book writers dominated the genre and included Jerry Siegel and Joe Shuster, the creators of Superman, Bob Kane (Batman), and Will Eisner (The Spirit), who, according to Buhle (2004) broke new ground in integrating a cinematic perspective into the comic form (p. 108).

[69] In an otherwise brilliant laudatory review of Chabon's work, Deresiewicz (2007) reveals a preference for a kind of novelistic realism that, to me, does not adequately characterize the writer's project.

and surreal solution. Josef is smuggled out in a coffin with the golem. This is a significant revision because, of course, the golem's legendary fame is based on its huge size, strength, and capacity for violence. Modern redactions, including the Superman character itself, are also based on these traits. The sad reality, of course, is that even the golem cannot stand up to the Nazis, and Prague's Jewish elders decide to smuggle the body to a neutral country to save it for a possible future fight.

The key figure in all of this for Josef is his former magic teacher, Bernard Kornblum, a "dutiful Jew" (Chabon, 2000, p. 15), who is perhaps the greatest living practitioner of the escapist arts. He trains Josef to pick any lock and escape from any confinement—vital skills for a Jew who wishes to survive in 1939 Europe. Kornblum also arouses in the assimilated Josef a renewed interest in his own Jewishness. Combined with these escapist skills, Josef possesses a toughness that is, ironically, derived from a love of American gangster films. From the same films he acquires a sense of panache that serves him throughout the novel. While a number of neo-masculine Jewish characters try to affect a Hemingway-esque grace under pressure, Josef Kavalier really achieves it. It is Kornblum, however, the quintessential Eastern European Jew, who literally saves Josef and his brother from drowning when, at 14, Josef tries a dangerous escape for which he is not yet ready.

The entire trope of escapism is a fascinating compromise between the violent versus passive potentialities of the body. The Jewish body through history, as Gilman (1986) and Biale (1992) have analyzed it, alternated between violent resistance (the biblical, American, and Israeli ideal) and a kind of self-abnegating acceptance (the Diasporic ideal). According to Chabon (2000), one reason Jewish boys became escape artists was to escape the feeling of being "imprisoned by invisible chains" (p. 37) that the world put on them as Jewish men. But Kornblum tries to convince Josef that it is more important to "reserve your anxieties for what you are escaping 'to' not 'from,' so the emphasis is on future transformation (Chabon, p. 37). Yet what Josef cannot escape, and Chabon believes he should not, are his father's Diasporic values of "stubbornness, persistence, orderliness, patience, and calm" (p. 58).

The literal escape is presented in a tone of black humor, as Josef and Kornblum make up the golem to look like a dead gentile giant. Josef crams himself into the bottom of the coffin as it is transported hundreds of miles and almost suffocates. That he survives leads not only to future escapes but to his remaking himself in America, culminating in his transformation of the golem legend into a comic book. Immersing himself in Jewish studies, reading "thick reference volumes and tractates" (Chabon, 2000, p. 541), Josef creates a masterwork that fuses Jewish tradition with a modern American popular form, one itself a fusion of high and low culture. It is clear that Josef successfully heals himself from the grief of losing his European family through this creative act, and it sets the stage for his assuming his role in his new American family when the war is over.

In a very real sense, Joe and his Brooklyn-born cousin Sam Clay are redrawing the golem when, in 1939, they create an immensely successful comic book hero, the Escapist. He is first imagined as they walked the streets of New York City constantly talking. As Chabon (2000) writes, "Every golem in the history of the world," from Rabbi Loew's to Dr.Frankenstein's, "was literally talked into life" (p. 119). Sam's father had been a circus performer, a tiny man with enormous strength who billed himself as the World's Strongest Jew. But Sammy describes him to Joe as "all muscle. No heart. He was like Superman without the Clark Kent" (p. 120), who walked out on Sammy and his mother. Joe's father was a doctor, a good man but decidedly not the strongest Jew in the world. What Sam suddenly realizes is that they need a "super-Kornblum" in Europe to help all the Jews escape, and then Joe comes up with the new hero—"Armed with superb physical and mental training, a crack team of assistants, and ancient wisdom, he roams the globe, performing amazing feats and coming to the aid of those who languish in tyranny's chains!" (Chabon, p. 121). The Escapist, like Joe himself, is a "lithe, acrobatic man" (Chabon, p. 121) with more dexterity, intelligence, and endurance than strength.

But can a comic book character save the Jews from Hitler? As Germany's militarism increases, Joe pours all of his growing rage into the Escapist's battles, hoping but not fully believing that his wildly popular comics will have the propaganda effect of bringing America into a war that might save his family. Part of him knows, however, that these are empty hopes, and the level of impotent frustration leads him to wandering the streets of New York seeking fights with Germans. The reality is, however, that he always gets badly beaten, because Joe is not a fighter, although he can clearly take a great deal of abuse. One day he wanders into the office of the Aryan-American League, where he realizes that its sole operative, the pathetic Carl Ebling, is a fan of the Escapist, even as he attacks the "Jew cartoonist" (Chabon, p. 202) creators as threats to Germany. Joe and Ebling get into a fight, and Joe wins, but instead of feeling good about this, he feels ashamed, wondering if, in creating comic book heroes, he and Sam were "indulging their own worst impulses and assuring the creation of another generation of men who revered only strength and domination" (Chabon, p. 204). It is an extraordinary insight for a refugee otherwise enraged by the constant thought of his family's persecution in Europe.

As a result of besting Ebling, and under the influence of his American Jewish girlfriend Rosa, a wonderfully vivid character, Joe changes. His masochistic desire to confront and be beaten up by German-Americans disappears, and he begins to pour his creativity into a female comic hero named Luna Moth. At this point, however, he learns that a German U-boat has sunk a children's refugee ship, The Ark of Miriam, and his beloved younger brother Thomas was on that boat. The news of their deaths overwhelms him, and, the day Pearl Harbor is attacked, he runs away from New York without even saying goodbye to Rosa. It is a regression, although perhaps an understandable one, in Chabon's (2000) rewriting of the violence script. As Rosa tells Sam, "He wants to go kill them ... I don't think anything I tell him"—even that she is pregnant with Joe's child—"could stop him now" (Chabon, p. 421).

The final and most compelling evidence that Chabon (2000) is consciously rewriting Jewish masculinity occurs in Antarctica, where Joe is frustratingly stationed. He, of course, wanted to be sent to Europe to fight the Nazis directly, but Chabon has other plans. A faulty heating system in the remote listening station has left only Joe, one other sailor, a pilot, and one sled dog alive. They must wait out the long winter, barely holding on to their sanity. In the process, Joe becomes the radioman and picks up the signal of a German outpost more than 1,000 miles across the ice. It is manned by a single geologist, and Joe directs all of his pent-up rage at this one "Nazi," even though he is aware that he is not a soldier and would only be involved in "the most tangential, metaphysical ways" (Chabon, p. 455) with the deaths of his family. Yet while he longs for face-to-face retribution, listening to the "haughty-sounding" (Chabon, p. 447) voice of the geologist, hour after hour, Joe identifies with him and even feels "an odd reluctance" to betray him, "as if in doing so he would betray himself" (Chabon, p. 447).

Joe finally decides to travel more than 1,000 miles across Antarctica to take revenge on the German, his powers of endurance and ingenuity demonstrated by the fact that he makes it, despite the pilot's dying of a burst appendix half way there. Joe never flew a plane before, but manages to get to the German station. What will he do when he confronts the German? Getting the plane flight ready involved the macabre use of the skins of the dead sled dogs to cover the wings. He is haunted by dreams of having had to sacrifice the last surviving dog that he has become close to, so the reader is clear about the extent of Joe's need for revenge yet is left wondering how a man so sensitive to life will be able to take one.

When Joe finally arrives at the German station, the question is answered in a scene that dramatizes just how much he abhors violence. The narrative point of view shifts to the German's as he watches Joe's plane descend and fearfully grips a pistol he had never fired. Chabon (2000) describes him as "a peaceful and scholarly man who had always deplored violence" (p. 464). However, in his fear he fires, hitting Joe in the shoulder, then erratically empties the gun with his eyes closed until Joe walks right up to him. Joe calmly greets him and reaches into his own parka for his gun, but, before the German realizes that Joe intends to throw the gun away, he hurls himself at Joe and is accidentally shot as they struggle. Joe has the following extraordinary realization as he drags the German inside to try to save him:

> The shock and fragrance of life, steaming red life, given off by the trail of the German's blood in the snow was a reproach to Joe, the reproach of something beautiful and inestimable, like innocence, which he had been lured by the Ice [capitalized by Chabon] into betraying. In seeking revenge, he had allied himself with the Ice, with the interminable white topography, with the sawteeth and crevasses of death. Nothing that had ever happened to him, not the shooting of Oyster [the sled dog], ... or the death of his father, or internment of his mother and grandfather, not even the drowning of his beloved brother, had ever broken his heart quite as terribly as the realization, when he was halfway to the rimed zinc hatch of the German station, that he was hauling a corpse behind him. (p. 465)

Not the death of his father? Not the drowning of his brother, which led him to attempt suicide? Chabon (2000) is making the strongest and clearest possible statement here. Joe, the ideal Jewish male, is tremendously gifted and physically capable, but he is not emotionally or morally able to take another person's life. This, I believe, for Chabon, constitutes the Jewishness of the Jew. It is what distinguishes him from the Nazi—not from the meek German geologist. In itself, of course, this definition is not new. Isaac Bashevis Singer makes it in his story "Gimpel the Fool;" Roth gives it lip service but doesn't really believe it (1991, p. 159). Boyarin (1997) sees it as the rabbinic ideal. The Talmud in fact asserts it. But Chabon makes the refusal to kill heroic, larger than life.

With this experience behind Joe, Chabon (2000) can end the book with a return to the golem newly interpreted—no longer a violent figure out of human control. By retelling the story through the art of the comic book, the "shaping of a golem, to him, [becomes] a gesture of hope. It was the expression of a yearning that a few magic words and an artful hand might produce something—one poor, dumb, powerful thing—exempt from the crushing strictures, from the ills, cruelties, and inevitable failures of the greater Creation" (Chabon, p. 582).

In Chabon's next novel, it can be seen that art and the retelling of stories once again become the means for Jewish male transformation. By placing much of the action of *The Yiddish Policemen's Union* (Chabon, 2007a) on the imaginary Max Nordau street in Sitka, Alaska, Chabon again reveals his concern with the historical and cultural context of Jewish masculinity. The conceit of the novel follows a path that history might have taken in 1938, but didn't, to transport Eastern European Jews to Alaska, both to save them from the Nazis and help create a larger economic buffer between the United States and the Soviet Union.[70] Chabon imagines this plan being carried out (while the new State of Israel fails), and in the process establishes the Diaspora and Yiddishkeit culture as winning out over Zionism—at least until the book's climax. Having his protagonist, Detective Meyer Landsman, live on a street named for Nordau, an early Zionist and proponent of "Muscle Judaism," the movement to reshape Diaspora Jews into the kind of tough Jews who deserved and could defend their own homeland, suggests a subtle critique of this particular iteration of Zionism.[71] Is Landsman a tough Jew? Does the *sholem* (gun) he carries make him like Mamet's violent and angry detective Bobby Gold in the film *Homicide*, or is he a Jew of another sort?

Chabon (2007a) turns to another popular art form, the detective novel, not only to shape his narrative but to interrogate the tough-guy image itself. Like the Coen brothers (two other Jewish masters of contemporary American art) in their film *The Big Lebowski*, Chabon rewrites the hardboiled detective character, making Landsman and his half-Jewish, half-Tlingit partner a distinctly Jewish creation.[72] This,

[70] This plan was proposed by Secretary of Interior Harold Ickes and a bill was written, but it never came up for a Congressional vote, partly due to administration concerns about the excessive number of anticipated immigrants.

[71] See Biale (1992, p. 178) where he explains that for Nordau "to create a new image of the Jewish body became a symbol for creating a new Jewish nation."

[72] Interestingly, the Coen brothers are planning to film Chabon's (2007a) novel.

however, doesn't mean Landsman is a bad detective or not "a tough guy, in his way, given to the taking of wild chances" (Chabon, p. 10). As the narrator tells us, he "has faced down shtarkers and psychopaths, has been shot at, beaten, frozen, burned" (Chabon, p. 10). In fact, he "is the most decorated shammes in the District," one who has solved difficult murder cases and who "has the memory of a convict, the balls of a fireman, and the eyesight of a housebreaker" (Chabon, p. 2), a man who has a "love affair ... with violence" (Chabon, p. 137). But when not on a case, Landsman is a depressed, lonely alcoholic, lacking faith in anything. His wife and soon to be boss, Bima, left him after Landsman had decided to abort their unborn son because of a chromosomal problem that might, or might not, have caused abnormalities. Yet he is the moral center of the novel, the consciousness through which his own angst is observed as well as all of the tsuris facing the Jews of Sitka at a time when they face expulsion from their Alaskan home and forced assimilation into American society. The resurrection of his life and of his masculine identity follow the arc of a murder case he has been ordered *not* to investigate but which he of course must.

The victim of that murder is also a new kind of Jewish male or, in a sense, an amalgam of old and new, and Landsman's obsessive quest to solve the crime leads him to an understanding of this man—initially a John Doe heroin addict found shot in the head—that will be transformative. What Landsman and the reader discover is that the victim is Mendel Shpilman, the son of Reb Heskel Shpilman, the head of the Verbover Chassidic sect, which in Sitka is the equivalent of an organized crime family. The victim was a language and chess prodigy as a child, who not only grew up with the expectation that he would follow his father as head of the Verbovers, but also faced the general belief that he "might be the Tzaddik Ha-Dor" (Chabon 2007a, p. 168), the Messiah. But it is a role that Mendel, for a variety of reasons, rejects. In an interview with Wiener (2007), Chabon describes him as "a superman who has refused the cape" (online).

Mendel becomes a son in a long line of Chabon sons who are deeply ambivalent about their fathers and the expectations those fathers impose on them. In addition to the grotesquely fat and scheming Reb Heskel, who appears to be a serious suspect in his son's death, there is Landsman's own father, who damaged him by pushing him as child to be a great and aggressive chess player, like himself, and then commited suicide. Landsman's cousin and partner Berko's father is a hostile and violent European Jew who turns out to have been partly responsible for the death of his American Indian wife, Berko's mother. Perhaps the worst father figure is the interestingly named Alter Litvak, another aged immigrant who is the brains and muscle behind a plot to retake Jerusalem from the Arabs by blowing up their holiest mosque. In giving us these characters, Chabon (2007a) is clearly *not* nostalgically invoking *Yiddishkeit*; these Jews, who narrowly escaped the Holocaust, are brilliant, aggressive, and full of rage. Their sons inherited that rage and brilliance, but, in the environment of Alaska, the sons struggle to shape themselves into something new.

Perhaps Chabon's (2007a) most imaginative example of this new-world amalgam is Landsman's partner, Berko, who, according to strict Jewish law, would not be Jewish because of his Tlingit mother However, he chooses to be an Orthodox Jew in a misguided attempt to win his father's favor. At one point, Landsman and Berko, huge and almost golem-like, confront some very tough, well-armed Verbovers or "black hats," intent on keeping these cops out of their enclosed community. When threatened, and against all reason, Landsman responds to a gun-carrying "blond bruiser" who had ordered him back into his car with "how about you come over here and make me?" (Chabon, p. 103) Berko steps out of the car displaying "his ancestral bear bulk" (Chabon, p. 103). He also pulls out his homemade, hand-painted war club, "the uncanniest hammer any Jew or gentile is ever likely to see" (Chabon, p. 103), with a 35-pound piece of meteorite iron head attached to a large baseball bat. Berko has learned to play up his savage side, and, when he "goes Indian" (Chabon, p. 104), fear is inevitably aroused in every Yid's heart. But when they see his yarmulke, they relax. Berko has never needed to actually use his club, and this is Chabon's point. When he recognizes one of the Verbovers, greeting him with "A sweet Sabbath to you, Sussman" (Chabon, p. 104), the entire potentially violent situation is diffused. The message is a deeply multicultural one and is certainly meant to evoke the Israeli-Palestinian conflict, to which parallels are made throughout the novel. Like the Escapist in *Kavalier & Clay* (Chabon, 2000), Berko has a kind of fluid, creative identity that grows and survives by taking strength from a variety of sources—Native and Jewish, European and American.

Landsman, the hero, is so interesting because he is in the process of creating such a self as he pursues this case. Ironically, it is the victim's father, the Verbover rebbe (a representation, of course, of the Reverend Lubavitcher Reb Menachem Schneerson), who intuits Landsman's troubled condition. The Jewish father, and especially a Chasid, part of a group exposed to centuries of external hostility, understands Landsman's "love affair ... with violence" (Chabon, 2007a, p. 137). But in Chabon's representation of the tradition, these fathers have become so hardened and bent on survival at all costs that they are not capable of accepting the new Messiah—the Reb's son—in their midst. They only wish to use him. While the Reb recognizes that there is a special "fire" in his son and that he "gave off light and warmth" (Chabon, p. 141), he excommunicates him and refuses to see him for 23 years because he is gay and thus could not take his place as the next rebbe. As the narrator tells us, "every generation loses the messiah it has failed to deserve" (Chabon, p. 196).

Chabon (2007a) uses Mendel, the son, and Naomi, Landsman's sister, to represent alternative masculinities in the Boyarin (1997) mode of questioning traditional gender lines. Naomi, a pilot, decides to save Mendel from being used by the Jewish extremists, led by Alter Litvak, and, as Landsman slowly realizes, her death in a plane crash is not accidental. As the narrator tells us, "Naomi was a tough kid, so much tougher than Landsman ever needed to be.... She was boyish as a girl and mannish as a woman" (Chabon, p. 238). Conversely, Mendel secretly visits his mother dressed as a woman, and, at other times, his gentle, feminine manner contributes to the feeling others have that he might indeed be the Messiah.

This working against gender type is seen most dramatically in Mendel's meeting with Litvak, as noted, the quintessential tough Jew. As he grasps Litvak's hand, Mendel plays the role of "tough and masculine in a way that mock[s] toughness and masculinity and his own relative lack of both qualities" (Chabon, 2007a, p. 351). Litvak, against his impulses, is horrified to feel affected by the unmistakable charisma of this gentle man, but he initially believes that he can still use him for his plot to reclaim Jerusalem for the Jews. However, after he hears Mendel say, "I left my cape at home," and observes his almost magical awareness of things as revealed in his "strange mosaic eyes," Litvak feels "the blood-red broth of his own anger" and strikes out violently at Mendel to fight off the weakening of "the fist of his heart"—"[he's] not ready" (Chabon, pp. 353–355), he realizes, to accept this Messiah and to change. Here Chabon brilliantly reveals the contradiction inherent in forcing a redemptive return to the Holy Land through the use of violence. Traditional biblical masculinity was forged by a God the Father who commanded his sons to take the Promised Land by force of arms. By questioning that legacy, and the understandable but flawed desire of Zionism to reenact it, Chabon must, in essence, rewrite patriarchy itself.

But that momentous change must be wrought from within, not imposed from without, and Landsman is the seemingly incongruous Jewish male created to enact it. In order to make the reader see his protagonist's very ambivalent and problematic masculine self, Chabon (2007a) stages a scene that echoes, but does not duplicate, Josef's accidental shooting of the German geologist in *Kavalier & Clay* (Chabon, 2000). On the Sabbath, no less, Landsman, ignoring his wife's direct orders (she is his police superior), goes alone to a deserted neighborhood to arrest the suspect in another unsolved murder case, a clear attempt to reestablish his traditional masculine self-image. While approaching an abandoned grocery store named the "The Big Macher" (ironic Yiddish for Landsman trying to be a big shot?), bullets come at him, one grazing the back of his head, and he is struck by "a paralysis of regret" as he realizes he has "no plan at all" and no backup (Chabon, 2007a, p.180). Hearing footsteps coming in the snow, he raises his weapon and fires—and a woman cries out in pain, wishing, appropriately, "cancer upon Landsman's testicles" (Chabon, p. 180). When the suspect jumps on him, trying to grab the gun out of Landsman's hand, Landsman's regrets disappear as he is caught up in a struggle for survival. He lets go of the gun, sending the suspect flying in a similarly awkward, Keystone Cops version of Joseph and the German's struggle (Chabon, 2000), then jumps on top of him, grabs his gun back, and "without a thought in his head" shoots the suspect dead (Chabon, 2007a, p. 181).

The narrator uses an interesting phrase to describe the shooting—"the world pulls the trigger on all its guns" (Chabon, 2007a, p. 181)—not that Landsman pulls the trigger. Here Chabon reinforces the idea that Landsman is but part of a larger violent script over which he appears to have very little control. He had killed two people, not planning to, and the reality of "gore on his coat" and "tatters of brain" make him throw up: "Doubts begin to crowd in around the knowledge of the mess he has made" (Chabon, p. 181). He passes out in the snow, and Chabon says he dies but only to wake up the next day in his cousin Berko's apartment to the cries of what he thinks is his dead son but is really Berko's. In the bosom of this multicultural Orthodox Jewish family, Landsman wakes up to the potential of a new, yet somehow old, life.

The fact that Landsman had killed two murderers (the woman turns out to be a nurse who killed one of her patients) is quite beside the point. The shootings are only superficially justifiable as self-defense, since he stupidly put himself in harms way, and as cases to be cleared (these people are never proven guilty). The killings can only be made redeemable in the novel's moral economy if they positively affect our protagonist, and the incident is, in fact, the beginning of his desire to care and change. Here Chabon (2007a) is of course following the detective genre, as the Sam Spades, who begin coolly professional and world-weary eventually become involved. But Chabon, as always, has more at stake than reworking a genre that uses violence as its stock-in-trade. He is going up against one of the oldest violent plots in human history: the biblical story of the Jews and their taking possession of a particular piece of land, supposedly promised to them, through the use of genocidal war.

Here it must be said that Chabon is not unsympathetic to historical anti-Semitism and the plight of the Jews. He clearly believes they should have a place where they can live safely as Jews, be it their own nation or as members of various nations. The anxiety over what is called "the Reversion" (Chabon, 2007a, p. 76) in the novel, the 60 year limit of their stay in Alaska, is palpable. Yet the bad guys are clearly those who would use violence to secure a Jewish state, raising red heifers to return to the prescribed ritual sacrifice that would be required for the establishment of a third temple in Jerusalem and for the coming of the Messiah. These bad guys include the Reb, Mendel's father, Alter Litvak, and several other Yiddish men of the older generation. Landsman's uncle Hertz, Berko's father, is also a problematic figure, but one might say he is redeemed by his role in Mendel's death, which turns out not to be the clear-cut murder that everyone assumed.

Landsman's ultimate transformation, however, occurs not in response to his Jewish legacy but to the historical discourse of Christianity. The real bad guys at the end of the novel turn out to be Christian Americans, government agents who play a central role in the extremist plot to destroy the Dome of the Rock Mosque. One of these agents, blatantly named Cashdollar, interrogates Landsman and talks about the "end of times coming" (Chabon, 2007a, p. 366). In order for the messiah, Jesus, to return, Jerusalem must belong to the Jews, and, "sadly, there is no way to do that without some bloodshed, unfortunately ... that's just what is written" (Chabon, p. 366). He offers to get Landsman's gun and badge back (taken after the Big Macher shooting) and hints that, even with the Reversion, Landsman just might be allowed to keep his job—if he keeps his mouth shut about the plot he has discovered. Landsman also notices the gun that he suspects Cashdollar is itching to use to keep him permanently silent, but, as he thinks about what he does have to lose, mostly images of Diasporic life and a picture of Mendel, the "dead messiah" (Chabon, p. 368), he finally lets it all go in the climactic, liberating speech of the novel:

> "Fuck what is written," Landsman says. "You know what?" All at once he feels weary of ganefs and prophets, guns and sacrifices and the infinite gangster weight of God. He's tired of hearing about the promised land and inevitable bloodshed required for its redemption. "I don't care what is written. I don't care what supposedly got promised to some sandal-wearing idiot whose claim to fame is that he was ready to cut his own son's throat for the sake of a hare-brained idea. I don't care about red heifers and patriarchs and locust. A bunch of old bones in the sand. My homeland is in my hat. It's in my ex-wife's tote bag.'" (p. 368)

Calling Abraham a sandal-wearing idiot sounds like heresy, but here Landsman, and Chabon, cut their ties to a certain strain of Judeo-Christian history and to a story that is no longer inevitable. Like Joseph revising the golem story at the end of *Kavalier & Clay* (Chabon, 2000), biblical stories about the Promised Land can be changed. Landsman decides that his homeland is where he, as a Jew, is and where those he loves are.

At the end of the novel (Chabon, 2007a), Mendel's murder is solved and Landsman has changed; he has found a kind of faith, but it is in his wife Bima and the promise of new children and in himself. He apologizes to Bima "for his craziness, his erratic behavior" (Chabon, p. 409) but realizes that he missed his chance at any redemption a messiah could have provided in not having been blessed by Mendel. Now, while he knows only a "flood [could] wash his wickedness [his violence] from the face of the earth" (Chabon, p. 409), he might save himself by again trying to have a child and by reneging on the promise he made to the Christian government agent not to tell the true story of the Jerusalem plot. In deciding to do both, he is looking toward the future and not the past, "striking at the membrane that separates the legacy of the yids who made him from that of the yids whose errors, griefs, hopes, and calamities" made Bima (Chabon, p. 407).

As in the conclusion of *Kavalier & Clay* (Chabon, 2000), the fate and the future of the Jewish man, Chabon concludes, is "on the tip of the tongue" (Chabon, 2007a, p. 411) in his ability to create and recreate himself through procreation but also through language, story, and art. This is, perhaps, a postmodern insight but one that can be traced back to the creators of the Hebrew scriptures and to the Talmud, who first spoke Judaism into life.

And one can see Chabon continuing this tradition, recreating his Jewish masculine self through both procreation and writing, in his wonderful book of essays *Manhood for Amateurs: The Pleasures and Regrets of a Husband, Father, and Son* (Chabon, 2009). While he begins this book with a dark meditation on circumcision, echoing Landsman's view of the Hebrew God as an "arbitrary and capricious ... asshole" (Chabon, 2007a, p. 22), he ends it with the bat mitzvah of his daughter, seeing in the timeless ceremony of her reading the Torah the irrelevance of generational and gender difference, the triumph of just experiencing "our life happening" (Chabon, 2009, p. 306) over the supposed inevitability of violence and death.

References

Biale, D. (1992). *Eros and the Jews: From biblical Israel to contemporary America.* New York: Basic Books.
Boyarin, D. (1997). *Unheroic conduct: The rise of heterosexuality and the invention of the Jewish man.* Berkeley: University of California Press.
Breines, P. (1990). *Tough Jews: Political fantasies and the moral dilemma of American Jewry.* New York: Basic Books.
Brod, H. (1996). Of mice and supermen: Images of Jewish masculinity. In S.B. Boyd, W.M. Longwood, & M.W. Muesse (Eds.), *Redeeming men: Religion and masculinities* (pp. 145–155). Westminster: John Knox Press.
Buhle, P (2004). *From the Lower East Side to Hollywood: Jews in American popular culture.* New York and London: Verso.
Chabon, M. (1988). *The mysteries of Pittsburgh.* New York: Harper Collins.
Chabon, M. (1995). *Wonder boys.* New York: Picador.
Chabon, M. (2000). *The amazing adventures of Kavalier & Clay.* New York: Picador.
Chabon, M. (2007a). *The Yiddish policemen's union.* New York: Harper Collins.
Chabon, M. (2007b). *Gentlemen of the road.* New York: Ballantine Books.
Chabon, M. (2009). *Manhood for amateurs: The pleasures and regrets of a husband, father, and son.* New York: HarperCollins.
Deresiewicz, W (2007, May 28). The imaginary Jew. *The Nation*, 44–48.
Gilman, S. (1986). *Jewish self-hatred: Anti-Semitism and the hidden language of the Jews.* Baltimore: Johns Hopkins University Press.
Helprin, M. (1977). *Refiner's fire.* New York: Knopf.
Kushner, T. (1993). *Angels in America. Part One: Millennium approaches.* New York: Theatre Communications Group.
Jeffords, S. (1989). *The remasculinization of America: Gender and the Vietnam War.* Bloomington: Indiana University Press.
Lefkovitz, L. (1988). Coats and tales: Joseph stories & myths of Jewish masculinity. In H. Brod (Ed.), *A mensch among men: Explorations in Jewish masculinity* (pp. 19–29). Freedom, CA: The Crossing Press.
Mosse, G. (1985). *Nationalism and sexuality: Respectability and abnormal sexuality in modern Europe.* New York: Howard Fertig.
Ozick, C. (1998). *The Puttermesser papers.* New York: Vintage.
Rosenberg, W. (2001). *Legacy of rage: Jewish masculinity, violence, and culture.* Amherst: University of Massachusetts Press.
Roth, P. (1991). *Patrimony: A true story.* New York: Somon & Schuster.
Solotaroff, T. (1996). The open community. In T. Solotaroff & N. Rapoport (Eds.), *The Schocken book of contemporary Jewish fiction.* New York: Schocken Books.
Wiener, J. (2007, spring). Arctic Jews: An interview with Michael Chabon. *Dissent*, April 14, 2007. http://www.dissentmagazine.org/online.php?id=10

10

The New Queer Jew: Jewishness, Masculinity, and Contemporary Film

Michele Aaron

There is a long and often ugly history attending the interaction of queerness and Jewishness. Fundamental to it, and best known, is anti-Semitism's feminization of the Jew (and by Jew was meant the Jewish man, a conflation that I will be sticking to for the time being). In this chapter I want to consider how cinema continues to break with, replicate, or refashion this figuring of Jewish masculinity. In doing so, I will address the various connections between the depiction of Jewishness and gender, connections that were forged by anti-Semitic discourse, disseminated within popular culture, and reevaluated by queer theory. The last decade's embrace of *queer* as a politically, critically, and sometimes socially productive position, often shrugs off its difficult history, a history that used it to both define and denigrate sexual and racial difference. While it would seem to have ceased to function in this way, its current use and usefulness must still undergo scrutiny: as long as homophobia and anti-Semitism exist, queer's offensive past will haunt its present.

Two key questions underlie this essay: How dependent on queerness is the representation of Jewishness in cinema? What is the meaning and value of queerness as it comes to describe contemporary representations of Jewishness? In order to address these questions, more basic questions need to be answered: What is the relationship between queerness and Jewishness? How is this relationship articulated by cinema? Is the Jew still queered? Is the queer still Jewed? What's new about all this?

The Old Queer Jew

The connection between gender and Jewishness was taken up by Jewish cultural studies in their attention to the discourses of sexual and racial difference emanating from late 19th, early 20th century Europe (see Gilman 1991, 1993). Of primary interest was the period's anti-Semitic concept of the "Jew as woman." This concept encapsulated the popular belief in the Jew's (i.e., the male Jew's) effeminacy and inferiority and coalesced in Weininger's (1906/2009) book, *Sex and Character*. In it the former Jew, Weininger—he had converted to Protestantism—identified women as both physically and mentally inferior to the Germanic/gentile male and identified Jews as like women. His thesis brought long-standing myths concerning the feminization of the Jewish male to the aid of the late-19th century's intensifying project of differentiating gentile and Jew along the plane of masculinity (see Gilman, 1991, p. 133; Trachtenberg, 1943/1983, p. 50). In being like a woman, the Jew was not only feminized but homosexualized. The Jew, and with it signatory Jewishness (its depiction within cultural representations), defied the natural borders of gender and sexuality: he was innately queer.

The collection of essays, *Queer Theory and the Jewish Question*, takes up the discussion of the exchange between Jewishness and gender and places it center stage in what the editors call the "newly queered Jewish Studies" (Boyarin, Itzkovitz, & Pelegrini, 2003, p. 3). The book's aim, they suggest, is to show how "the emergence of the modern Jew [and] the emergence of the modern homosexual ... is more than historical coincidence" (Boyarin et al., p. 3). Instead, the two must be seen as mutually dependent. So it is not just that the social construction of Jewishness required reference to sexual deviance, to what one might call the "old queer," but that the social construction of queerness required reference to the discourse of anti-Semitism, to what one might call the "old Jew." This two-way street is the subject of Paul Franklin's chapter in Boyarin et al. (pp. 121–148), which addresses the coverage of the Leopold and Loeb murder trial in the 1920s in Chicago. In the chapter, Franklin demonstrates how the depiction and analysis of the two men's pathology depended not only on their status both as sexually deviant and as Jewish but also on how one fed into the other: so that the Jew was queered, and the queer was Jewed. Not only did anti-Semitism build on the queering of Jewishness, but homophobia leaned on the racialization of queerness.

The latter formulation, the racialization of queerness, has been the less explored area within queer theory and yet remains in constant play. By emphasizing its currency, I mean to privilege the point that queerness is not only about gender and sexuality but also their intersection with other aspects of identity. So that queer necessitates, as Mercer (1991) declared, an apprehension of "the complexity of what actually happens 'between' the contingent spaces where each variable [race, class, gender] intersects with the others" (p. 193). I also mean to note the prominence of Jews in the formation of queer thinking and queer being: Judith Butler, Eve Kosofsky Sedgwick, Marjorie Garber, Leslie Feinberg, Kate Bornstein, etc., even if I won't account for it here.[73] But my main aim is to explore how Jewishness remains a potent site for the expression of the new queer, even as queerness might cease to be the potent site for expressing the new Jew.

I will now turn to cinema and its role in the association of queerness and Jewishness. A pivotal text in this discussion is Marjorie Garber's (1997) reading of Barbra Streisand's (1983) film *Yentl*, which neatly unfolded the queer undoing of "category" itself through the film's interweaving of gender and religious identity. At the same time, Garber delineated the two crucial contexts for understanding the queer figure in the film: on one side, the anti-Semitic properties of queering Jewishness, and on

[73] Assorted reasons for this statement center on Jews' special relationship to study. A fascinating point is made by Brook (2003), after Naomi Seidman, who sees these academics as donning "gayface" in order to establish "their multicultural credentials" (p. 157). However, Brook misses the point that these academics are identifying as queer rather than simply over-identifying with gay men as feminists.

the other its recuperative potential (which, like the discussion above, opposes queer's old and new capacities). In my reading of the film, however, *Yentl* is also located within a historical shift in cinema's queering of the Jew, thereby showing how the sway of anti-Semitism has effected a transition in the cultural representation of Jewishness (Aaron, 2000). Streisand's film is found to re-create an earlier cross-dressing comedy—*Yidl Mitn Fidl*, Joseph Green's (Green & Nowina-Przybylski, 1936) classic of Yiddish cinema—and, in so doing, to reiterate characteristics of the queer Jew.

Both *Yentl* and *Yidl Mitn Fidl* are *Yiddisher* cross-dressing musicals that share the same basic plot, the *shtetl* setting, and several scenes. The striking resemblance of their gamine, black-suited heroines (Yentl/Anshel and Yidl) is, perhaps, inevitable but confirms that the films' commonalities are, as I have argued elsewhere, not coincidental: "Indeed, Norman Jewison once described *Yidl* as 'fifty years ahead of its time.' *Yentl*, some forty seven years later, is that future, queerer, incarnation" (Aaron, 2004, p. 98).

In *Yidl* the queerness of the little Jew is explicitly used to recover Jewish masculinity from the slur of anti-Semitism. The tough Jew, Froim, who Yidl falls for, is everything that Yidl is not, everything, in fact, that Jews were not: gentlemanly, handsome, strong, and practical. The little Jew (the literal translation of Yidl) as a woman is used to recover the real Jew in terms of an idealized masculinity. Queerness in the film is finally distanced and dismissed. In *Yentl*, however, queerness is most certainly indulged, since the film depends on the charm, comedy, and, often, essentialism of its inevitable gay and homoerotic setups in which the cross-dressed Yentl/Anshel pursues "another" man or is pursued by another woman. Ultimately, queerness is contained—Yentl leaves the country, and the other man and woman marry—heteronormativity restored all around by the film's end.

Yidl distinguished and idealized the tough Jew by exploiting both the old queer and the old Jew—the offensive stereotypes of the discourses of anti-Semitism and homophobia. *Yentl*, however, indulges the anti-Semitic stereotype with its weak bookish hero but avoids blatant homophobia (which is hardly surprising given Streisand's significant gay fan base). The old Jew in *Yentl* is tempered by the absence of the old queer.

There is a further link in this trajectory of films, or continuum of representation, and one that appears to dismiss both of these "old" phobias. Indeed, "nowhere is Jewishness more queer, or queerness more Jewish (or my argument so always-already) than in Jean-Jacques Zilbermann's [film] *Man Is a Woman* (1998), which opens with a man walking through a gay sauna cruising to the strains of klezmer" (Aaron, 2004, pp. 98–99). The film's narrative follows Jewish musician Simon, who, through financial necessity, pretends to be straight. He marries a woman, discloses his sexuality but realizes, too late, that he is in love with her. The film is not about passing as the opposite sex but as the opposite sexuality; it is about crossing more than cross-dressing. Its links to the earlier films are explicit: it re-creates the *shtetl* in the woman's ultra religious family, offers another false but *frum* wedding, and is punctuated by music despite not being a musical. It also directly references its predecessors: it incorporates a scene from *Yentl* and, has, Rosalie, the woman, sing "Yidl Mitn Fidl."

As well as consecrating *Yidl* and *Yentl* as the seminal if not canonical texts for cinema's queer Jews, *Man Is a Woman* indicates a further transition in the association of queerness and Jewishness in cinema. This transition is from the old queer Jew to the new queer Jew: from the implicitly and problematically feminine Jewish man, the Jewish man as woman, embodied by both Yidl and Anshel/Yentl, to the sexy and pseudo-sexually-free queer man embodied by Simon. Where *Yidl* uses queerness to disprove anti-Semitism and to recover the Jewish male, *Yentl* indulges queerness temporarily to enhance its comedy and heterosexual romance narrative. It is only *Man Is a Woman* that celebrates queerness, denying the rigidity of sexual preference and universalizing the flexibility of gender identity in its abiding sentiment that man is a woman. But why, one cannot help ask again, does Jewishness lend itself so readily to this queer project? Why does the Jew continue to be defined or framed by reference to sexuality?

The New Queer Jew?

The anti-Semitic equation of sexual and racial deviance was readily licensed by the resonance of the key signifier of Jewish masculinity: the circumcised penis. Both gender and Jewish identity coincided at the site of sexuality. Signatory Jewishness necessarily referenced sexual characteristics, therefore, and, through circumcision, unnatural ones at that. The queer Jew represents not only the legacy of the Jew as woman, which clearly connects circumcision to castration, but always also the Jew as, in some way, sexually peculiar.

Looking more broadly at contemporary mainstream cinema, that is, away from cross-dressing comedies where gender play is a genre requirement, there remains a telling repetition of these old associations. It seems that cinema in constructing Jewish masculinity cannot help but allude to the Jew's genital organ in both extreme and less extreme ways. Take the most infamous scenes of masturbation in Hollywood history—*Portnoy's Complaint* (Ernest Lehman's 1972 film) and *American Pie* (Paul Weitz's 1999 film). In both, it is only the distinctly Jewish character in the film who performs such excesses. Alternatively, the British comedy, *Leon the Pig Farmer* (Vadim Jean and Gary Sinyor's 1993 film), provides a less explicit but nevertheless consistent representation of this point in a plot that revolves around the dramatic and, often insurmountable, differences between Jew and non-Jew.

On a date at a restaurant, a sweating (and familiarly neurotic Jew) Leon has accidentally ordered lobster. This is a mistake not only because he keeps kosher but because he hasn't told his gentile would-be girlfriend yet and suspects this might ruin his prospects. The dish is brought up the stairs to their table: before the lobster itself is spotted, the frame centers on the grossly exaggerated shadow of its pincers. Leon's declaration of his identity as Jew is premised not, as narratively stressed, by dietary difference but, as the anatomical snipping that the pincers necessarily imply, by genital difference. Similarly, the excessive squeals of the lobster foreshadow the pain of the suggested snip rather than summon sympathy for the lobster. Jewish difference is sexually grounded again: located within the circumcision-castration combo.

Even within the supposedly new queer culture and the liberalisms of cinema, both in terms of politics and permissiveness, since the "naughty nineties," the queer Jew remains haunted by old tales. This is evident in television too, especially in the out-Jewish fare of *The O.C* (Bartis et al., 2003-2007), where dialogue is punctuated by *oys*, and bagel-eating characters are disturbed mid-*shmeer*. Its central character, Seth Cohen, is charmingly geeky, a self-declared nerd, and his ineptness is intimately tied to his romantic failure. For his ex-girlfriend, such traits define him to such an extent that his oh-so-Jewish name is rendered a verb: to act inanely, inappropriately, is to Cohen. But nowhere is the "haunting" more apparent than in the recent Hollywood hit, *Meet the Fockers* (Jay Roach's 2004 film). One doesn't have to be Jewish or even so-so versed in the history of anti-Semitism to notice how the family's ethnic identity informs every aspect of their kooky characters and that the film's smorgasbord of silly jokes rests on it. In fact it does more than this, it repeats the fundamentals of the queer Jew that have preoccupied this essay. In its central character, Greg (Gaylord Focker) the nurse (Ben Stiller), not only is the Jew still a woman, as Jack (Robert De Niro) keeps reminding everyone, but he is, in the words of one of the film's favorite jokes, really Gay (short for Gaylord). As for his nymphomaniac parents, Ros (the sex therapist) and Bernie (the former lawyer-cum-full-time-mom and otherwise dancing Floridian), could they be any more sexually inappropriate (which reads perverse in the lexicon of our more liberal times)?

In some ways this seems too heavy a reading of a genre rooted in the irreverent joys of social offensiveness and of a narrative anyway full of hyphenated Americans, curvaceous Cubana included. But why are only the Jewish Fockers played by Jewish actors (Stiller, Streisand, Hoffman), where the other actors can "cross-code," as if the essentialism of their identity prevents imposture, or, alternatively, requires Jewish stars to somehow license any potential offence?

But this isn't the end of the story, even if it provides the next notch on the queer Jew trajectory of cinema history. The feminized Jew had been considered only one of two dominant cultural stereotypes of Jewish masculinity. According to Brienes (1990), in opposition to this soft Jew exists the tough Jew who arose in response to him and to the Zionist project.[74] The discussion of Jewish masculinity within Jewish cultural studies and men's studies has increasingly eroded the polarization of these two stereotypes, the tough and the soft, and especially of their positive versus negative implications. For some this means recovering a legacy of Jewish aggressiveness predating Zionism; for others the soft Jew has been recuperated as a source of cele-

[74] These two stereotypes could be recast as the European model of the Jew and a secular model of Jewishness embodied by both Zionist settlers and the assimilated American. The two resonate, also, within Brook's (2003) "too Jewish"/"not Jewish enough" delineation of Jewish characters on television.

bration (see Rosenberg, 2001). Boyarin (1997), for example, has noted "that traditionally Jewish men identified *themselves* as fem(m)inized ... and understood fem(m)inization as a positive aspect of their cultural identity" (p. 307). For him, this positive feminization represents the capacity of Jews to embody an alternative masculinity.

In the final part of this essay, I want to take up this emerging potential for Jewish masculinity to pose an alternative to mainstream masculinity within popular visual culture, one that similarly bridges the two extremes. Desser (2001) has placed this idea of an alternative masculinity into the realm of heteronormative life and actively, and gladly, de-queers it. He distinguishes an important turn in contemporary popular culture, a counterimage of masculinity offered by the Jew, and welcomes this image in its accomplishment of male heterosexual ideals that depend on rather than denigrate Jewish characteristics. For Desser, then, this "image of the Jewish man"

> ... has not necessarily significantly shifted from the traditional portrayal of the Jew as urban, weak, frail, and intellectual, but rather has itself, to some extent, been transformed and transposed into one of desirability.... Even more simply: Jewish men are sexy precisely when they exhibit the very cultural traits ascribed to Jews.... Playing off the most notorious antisemitic imagery of all—that the Jewish man is the despoiler of the Aryan woman—contemporary images find the Jewish man as a desirable partner for non-Jewish women. (p. 271)

In this way, the Jew, although unable to shake off his old queer signs, becomes the embodiment of the new man. Woody Allen emerged as a prototypical example: his tireless and stereotypical Jewishness is his charm, but his desirability is certainly self-authored and therefore, less authentic. For Desser, the more striking examples of these new Jews, and their counter-masculinity, are provided by the highly popular Jewish wits of 1990s television who live in the "archetypal locale" for Jews (large cities like New York) and have archetypal occupations in "show business, medicine, publishing, and so on" (p. 276). These "overtly Jewish characters, [are] sometimes portrayed, in fact, by Jewish stars, such as Paul Reiser, Jerry Seinfeld, and Jerry Orbach" (Desser, p. 276). Gay Focker and the *O.C*'s Cohen similarly stand out as not only irreverently queered but as highly, and heterosexually, appealing: *Meet the Parents* and *Meet the Fockers* are premised on Gay getting the girl (oh-so-gentile at that), and Cohen is one of the program's main teenage heartthrobs.

It is precisely this combination—of old style traits and new style charisma—that is exploited and enjoyed in the recent film *The Pianist*. The protagonist, played by Adrien Brody, is excessively and familiarly Jewish. According to film critic J. Hoberman (2002), Brody has "refined looks and thin, beaky elegance. He's blasé, foppish, almost a dandy." In other words he possesses the physical attributes and associations of the traditional Jew. He also possesses his social characteristics: he is refined, artistic, a pianist. But, crucially, as with his small-screen counterparts, he is also heterosexually self-possessed and clearly sexually appealing. Indeed, it is hard to recall a more emphatic display of sexual charisma, especially given the subdued and traumatic circumstances of Nazi-occupied Poland in which it is embedded. In the scene in which he asks the gentile woman out, Brody's eyebrows rise jauntily, his dimples flash, and there is an almost distinguishable twinkle in his eye.

Brody is the perfect image to end on. He is clearly defined in the film by the queer markers of the Jew: anti-macho, lithe, educated, artistically talented. At the same time, he sports the developmental analogies to the penis, he is big-nosed, long-limbed, indeed, long-digited (Gilman, 1998, p. 84). But his character also manages to celebrate the new queer Jew as an image of a counter-masculinity, which renders these markers sexually appealing. That Brody, despite his many Jewish roles, does not identify as a Jewish actor reinforces this as a cultural rather than essentialist formation. Most importantly, following his success in this film, he became the poster boy for the Italian fashion designer, Ermenegildo Zegna. Despite the covert presence of the attractiveness of Jewish masculinity within the annals of Hollywood history and the legacy of its stars—Burt Lancaster, Kirk Douglas, Paul Newman—never before has the aesthetics of Jewish masculinity been so explicitly acknowledged, appreciated, or publicized.

To end by attributing queerness, a radical potential, to this new-style Jewish masculinity seems more than a tad generous. Brody, Seinfeld, or even the *O.C*'s Cohen offer oppositional representations only in so much as they are compellingly heterosexual. These new men, such as those in *Meet the Fockers*, provide prominent, popular, and even defiant representations of Jewish masculinity, but they do so through a "normativizing" of anti-Semitism's cultural rhetoric. As long as Jewish masculinity, indeed any kind of identity, is redeemed through heterosexuality, it remains in the oppressive service of ideology. As such, despite the successes and certain charm of its new spin, it will be destined to tell the same old story.

I want to wind down instead by pointing to a post-Fockers swathe of comedies that involve out Jewish characters—films such as *Prime* (Ben Younger, 2005), *I Now Pronounce You Chuck and Larry* (Dennis Dugan, 2007), and *Knocked Up* (Judd Apatow, 2007)—but a larger group would include most of Adam Sandler's comic roles. These films could be seen to represent a new phase in mainstream cinema's relationship to Jewishness. In 1995, Rebecca Ascher-Walsch wrote of Hollywood's Jewish problem, of executives' ambivalence toward Jewishness that led to it being written out of scripts and to films being cast or recast so that they did not appear too Jewish (p. 28). What is striking about these recent comedies is their absolute lack of ambivalence about their Jewish characters. Indeed there is not only a lack of ambivalence but a lack of angst. The heroes of *I Now Pronounce You Chuck and Larry* and *Knocked Up* couldn't be further from the savvy urban wits of 1990s TV in their appearance or in their occupations. Seth (Ben Stone) in *Knocked Up* is a slacker; Chuck (Adam Sandler) in *I Now Pronounce You Chuck and Larry* is a firefighter and as such is the embodiment of the tough man and, in post 9/11 New York, of the tough American. At the same time, however, the characters sustain the familiar old-new mix: Seth is the geek who gets the gentile (here epitomized by Katherine Heigl and in *Prime* by Uma

Thurman), and Chuck provides an excessive reformulation of the queer Jew: he pretends to be gay in order to gain domestic partner benefits. Of course, Adam Sandler's star-persona is very much tied up in this old-new mix. Like Ben Stiller, his comic roles often blend his sexual appeal with his sexual oddity.

In their easy expression of, even delight in, the Jew, do these recent films suggest a new comfort level for executives or for directors or even audiences? And at what point will this ease impact on the depiction of Jewish women? I want to end with a brief look at Tim Story's 2005 blockbuster *Fantastic Four*, which neatly illustrates these closing sentiments on Jewishness and gender in contemporary U.S. film.

Fantastic Four is interesting for several reasons beyond its Jewish heritage as a Stan Lee creation or the fact that one of its members, the Thing, was the first comic character to come out as Jewish (see Weinstein, 2006). The film stars Iaon Gruffudd who, like Adrien Brody, had come into the public eye through playing a Jewish man—in this case in the Paul Morrison 1999 film *Solomon and Gaenor*—and thus had a potential Jewishness encoded into his star persona. Like his fantastic colleagues, Reed Richards, Gruffudd's character, is zapped by radiation while they are in outer space and gains special powers. For Reed, this means becoming a kind of Mr. Stretchy, or elasticized. His body parts can elongate to enormous lengths, and several jokes are made by his male friends about this capacity. In many ways, Gruffudd/Reed fulfils the classic traits of the Jewish coded character. He is a scientist, an egghead. Indeed, in Tim Story's 2007 sequel *The Rise of the Silver Surfer*, there is even a dramatic moment of Reed's self-declaration as a geek. In the emphasis on his bodily extensions, Reed is undoubtedly sexually peculiar. But of course he is also a superhero, Mr. Fantastic, who wins the beautiful blonde. The geek triumphs again and gets the gentile girl. Or does he? At the moment when Reed and Sue Storm, the invisible woman, resolve their differences and Reed asks her to marry him, Sue is shown wearing a Star of David. Although this is something that the film's producers deny (see Sanders, 2005), its presence seems indisputable (and the impossible visibility of the Jewish woman resonates further). It is at this point, in fact, that Sue, involuntarily, disappears. At the moment of romantic union between the sexually freakish Jew and the blonde beauty, the frame of Jewishness is finally made explicit, but only briefly, only, ever, in passing.

References

Aaron, M. (2000). The queer Jew: From *Yidl* to *Yentl* and back again. *Jewish History and Culture, 3*(1), 23–44.

Aaron, M. (2004). Cinema's queer Jews: Masculinity and Yiddish cinema. In P. Powrie, B. Babbington, & A. Davies (Eds.), *The trouble with men: Masculinities in European and Hollywood cinema* (pp. 90–99). London: Wallflower Press.

Ascher-Walsch, R. (1995, August 18th). Does Hollywood have a Jewish problem? *Entertainment Weekly*, http://www.ew.com/ew/article/0,,298356,00.html

Bartis, D., et al. (Producers). (2003-2007). *The O.C.* [Television series]. New York: Fox Network.

Boyarin, D., Itzkovitz, D., & Pelegrini, A., (Eds). (2003). *Queer theory and the Jewish question*. New York: Columbia University Press.

Boyarin, D. (1997). Masada or Yavneh? Gender and the arts of Jewish resistance. In D. Boyarin & J. Boyarin (Eds.), *Jews and other differences* (pp. 306–329). Minneapolis, MN: University of Minnesota Press.

Breines, P. (1990). *Tough Jews*. New York: Basic Books.

Brook, V. (2003). *Something ain't kosher here: The rise of the Jewish sitcom*. Rutgers, NJ: Rutgers University Press.

Desser, D. (2001). Jew in space: The "ordeal of masculinity" in contemporary American film and television. In M. Pomerance (Ed.), *Ladies and gentlemen, boys and girls: Gender in film at the end of the twentieth century* (pp. 267–282). Albany: SUNY Press.

Garber, M. (1997). *Vested interests: Cross-dressing and cultural anxiety*. New York: Routledge.

Gilman, S. (1991). *The Jew's body*. London: Routledge.

Gilman, S. (1993). *Freud, race and gender*. Princeton; NJ: Princeton University Press.

Gilman, S. (1998). Creating beauty to cure the soul: Race and psychology in the shaping of aesthetic surgery. Durham, NC: Duke University Press.

Green, J., & Nowina-Przybylski, J. (1936). *Yidl mitn fidl* [Motion picture]. United States: Green-Film.

Hoberman, J. (2002, December). Portraits of the artist. *Village Voice*, 25–31. Retrieved July 11, 2003, from source (http://www.villagevoice.com/issues/0252/hoberman.php).

Jean, V., & Sinyor, G. (Producers/Directors). (1993). *Leon the pig farmer* [Motion picture]. United Kingdom: Fox Lorber.

Lehman, E. (Director). (1972). *Portnoy's complaint* [Motion picture]. United States: Chenauall Pictures.

Mercer, K. (1991). Skin head sex thing. In *Bad Object Choices* (Ed.), *How do I look?* (pp. 169–211). Seattle: Bay Press.

Morrison, P. (Director). (1999). *Solomon and Gaenor* [Motion picture]. United Kingdom: APT Films.

Roach, J. (Director). (2004). *Meet the Fockers* [Motion picture]. United States: Universal Studios.

Rosenberg, W. (2001). *Legacy of rage: Jewish masculinity, violence, and culture*. Amherst, MA: University of Massachusetts Press.

Sanders, G. (2005). Invisible? Yes. Fantastic, yes. But a member of the tribe? *The Jewish Daily Forward*, 19. http://www.forward.com/articles/2588/ (accessed 10 Jan, 2007)

Steisand, B. (Director). (1983). *Yentl* [Motion picture]. United State: United Artists.

Story, T. (Director). (2005). *Fantastic four* [Motion picture]. United States: 20th Century Fox.

Story, T. (Director). (2007). *The rise of the silver surfer* [Motion picture]. United States: 20th Century Fox.

Trachtenberg, J. (1983). *The devil and the Jews: The medieval conception of the Jew and its relation to modern antisemitism*. New Haven, CT: Yale University Press. (Original work published 1943)

Weininger, O. (2009). *Sex and character*. Charleston, SC: BiblioLife. (Original work published 1906)

Weinstein, S. (2006). *Up, up, and oy vey!: How Jewish history, culture, and values shaped the comic book superhero*. Baltimore, MD: Leviathan Press.

Weitz, P. (Director). (1999). *American pie* [Motion picture]. United States: Universal Pictures.

11

Mendoza Forever

Sylvia Paskin

> I think I have the right to call myself the father of the science (of boxing) for it is well known that prize fighting lay dormant for several years. It was Humphries and myself who revived it in our three contests for supremacy and the science of pugilism has been patronized ever since. (Mendoza, 1816)

> Those were the days when Ben the Big and Johnson fought of old,
> Mendoza, Humphries, Bristol Pearce and both the Belchers bold
> That was, I mention it with pride, Pancratia's age of gold,
> When men who fought to Prize Ring Rules were neither bought nor sold,
> But shone true British pugilists
> Men of the olden time. (An Old Song)

> Come along: pull out your purses, and vat do you do vid your fish-hooks in my box?
> If you don't take them out again, I shall give you a Mendoza and lay you all along so flat as if you vas a flounder, my dear.
> (The Jew-Pedlar by Charles Dibdin, Universal Songster, Vol. 2 [1825])

The position of Jews was not a happy one in late 18th century England—the Regency period. In 1753 there was an attempt to pass a Jewish Naturalization Bill but there was a popular outcry and the bill was rescinded. The so-called Jew Bill controversy erupted in response to Parliament's legislation. There was a panic amongst the populace that the Jews were going to take over. At a time when there was much discussion of the idea of national idenity, the idea that the Jews could become cohesive in any way was viewed with deep suspicion. There was a widely circulated belief for example that everyone would have to be circumcised. The Jews were accused of being regicides—killers of Christ the King. Pork banquets were held in mockery, and the cry went up, "No Jews, no wooden shoes. "Wooden shoes" was either a term for the French Hugenots, another despised minority or it could refer to the fact that many of the Sephardi Jews living in London had arrived there via Holland. The reality was that only a small group of rich Jews would have been able to apply for naturalization. They would not have had to take the sacrament or take a Christian oath at law, but certain professions and the ownership of land would have continued to be denied them.

There were 15,000 to 20,000 Jews residing in London at this time. Their position was not helped by the Chelsea Murders of 1771 when four Jews were accused of stealing and killing a man in the course of a burglary. The four Jews were found guilty and hung. Further riots followed the case. It is apparent from contemporary caricatures and comments that the Jews were viewed in a very negative light. A visitor from Germany, Karl Moritz (1782) wrote in *Travels in England in 1782*, "I have seen many Jews hooted, hunted, cuffed, pulled by the beard, spat upon and so barbarously assaulted in the streets without any protection from the passers-by or the police."

If they were poor, then in ballads and visual material they were uniformly represented as dishonest, cunning, and conniving pedlars with side locks and sporting long, grey beards. Allegedly they had crooked noses and spoke in a strange dialect. As many jobs were denied them, many Jews were secondhand clothes dealers and pedlars, and it is probably true that they stole things to sell them on. If Jews were rich, and very few of them were, they were thought of as parvenus and arrivistes, trying through their wealth to claw their way up the social ladder. In plate 2 of Hogarth's famous painting series, *The Harlot's Progress*, the heroine is the mistress of a wealthy, old, besotted Jew. But she is seen sneaking a young and handsome Gentile lover out of the backdoor.

Songs and ballads routinely referred to Jews as usurious embezzlers, clandestine and hypocritical eaters of roast pork as well as being small and physically repellent.

> Friend Ham, our Rabbi said
> Don't look at pork, t'is sinning
> But were hot pork for dinner
> What can a poor Jew do?
> But eat like a wretched sinner
> (The Catastrophe of a Pork-Chop Dinner, Universal Songster, Vol. 2, [1825])

It is into this narrow and prescribed world that Daniel Mendoza was born in Aldgate, east London in 1764. His was a Sephardi-Jewish family. When he was born on July 5, his mother would have been praised for spinning gold (spinning wool was the expression when a daughter was born). Mendoza had a Jewish education at the local Gates of Hope School. He had a loving, supportive and large family who had immigrated to England from either Spain or Portugal to avoid the bonfires of the Inquisition or indeed having to become conversos or Marranos. Traditionally Jews were advised to avoid violence. The rabbis of the period did not encourage a preoccupation with the body, whether for sensual purposes or physical force. Commerce and religion were considered appropriate as was an intellectual education. Mendoza called his family "middling" in his *Memoirs of The Life of Daniel Mendoza* in terms of their worldly possessions, but they were in fact poor. His parents did their best to bring up their progeny with an awareness of their duty and heritage.

However, one reads about the seeds of rebellion in Mendoza (1816) in his *Memoirs*. He got into street fights at an early age, usually to protect others from insult. Mendoza recounts the many occasions he returned home with yet another black eye. One can only assume he had a naturally fearless and pugnacious nature. He wrote with regard to his father, "If he found I had acted only from self-defense or from any justifiable motive, he would freely forgive me ... being well aware that courage is not only useful but almost indispensably necessary to carry us through life."

At the start of his career as a fighter Mendoza saw himself as a battler against prejudice and everyday anti-Semitic insults, but as he gained in status, he made the journey from personal and community identity to being a national British figure. His name is still known today amongst both the Jewish community and the boxing fraternity. His was a remarkable and unique trajectory with lasting consequences.

At 13, Mendoza was apprenticed to a glass cutter, but this was the first of many kinds of short-lived employment. He lost the job when he gave his employer's son a thrashing for attempting to bully him. The next job was with a Jewish fruiterer, but he had numerous fights protecting his employer, a woman, from anti-Semitic insults.

Mendoza quickly developed a hunger for fighting. In his *Memoirs* (1816), he recounts how in just one day he got into three separate fights—one with a loud-mouthed carter, another with a pack of riotous butchers, and the third with a group of youths who ill-advisedly mocked his way of riding a horse.

Another time he and a friend had work delivering Passover bakery in Northamptonshire. Someone had the temerity to suggest to the two young Jewish travelers that they be sent back to Jerusalem. Mendoza fought him for an hour and a half, after which his opponent could no longer walk or stand.

At 16, he was working for a tea dealer, and a stout porter picked a fight with him. The bout that followed lasted an hour, and, though the porter was larger and stronger than Mendoza, Mendoza bested him. This fight was witnessed by a group of cheering onlookers—after all what draws a crowd more than a street fight? Amongst them by the intervention of fortune was a master pugilist of the time, Richard Humphries, the epitome of blonde English elegance as a man and a fine fighter. Struck by Mendoza's courage and stamina, Humphries offered to become Mendoza's mentor and teacher. In a short space of time Mendoza had become a professional prizefighter with Humphries as his second.

One might imagine that Mendoza was tall and imposing—an obvious look and build for a puglist—but he was in fact small, only 5 feet 7 inches in height, and he weighed a mere 160 lb, a middleweight by today's standards. Nevertheless, he was well-built, courageous, and indefatigable. Blessed with a barrel chest and fast, fancy footwork, Mendoza was deft, observant, and, in the language of the day, scientific in his approach. Given that there was no discrimination in weight, Mendoza quickly realized that he was no match for a bigger opponent (i.e., a heavyweight), if they both just stood there slugging it out.

There needs to be no misapprehension as to what being a bare-knuckle boxer/pugilist would have meant in this late 18th century period: The Marquess of Queensbury rules were not formulated until 1867. Boxing has had a long and tumultuous history; it was known in ancient Greece. Boxing matches with prizes are mentioned in both the *Iliad* and the *Aeniad*. It is depicted in all its exuberant, combatative spirit on various artifacts of the period. There are Minoan frescos on the Greek island of Santorini that depict two youths boxing. In Rome the gladiators undertook bare-knuckle fighting, but their fists were supported by a caestus, a kind of leather cover full of iron spikes. One can only imagine the damage these would cause to an opponent's flesh.

Thankfully, the 18th century fighters were not armed in this way, but the bouts were extremely arduous and violent. The first London Prize Ring rules, such as they, were had been organized by Jack Broughton in the earlier part of the century. He was known as the "Professor." His goal was to create a profession for the fighters and introduce some humanity and rigor. He knew that, if he moderated the encounters sufficiently, the upper classes could observe and even eventually partake without fear or abhorrence. The term *pugilism* had been popular until this time and was still used after Broughton's rules were made, but the term *boxing* to indicate a change of attitude to the sport became widely used as well.

Broughton's rules included the following. There would be a particular area cordoned off by ropes and in the centre of this was the *scratch*, a chalk-drawn square yard. Each boxer was permitted just 30 seconds to recover between bouts/rounds—he then had to return to the scratch. If he failed to come up to the scratch, he lost the match. The rules prohibited blows below the waist but not above. Two gentleman umpires ensured fair play. They were nominated by each fighter. There was a third umpire who would adjudicate when they disagreed.

These fights were in reality a mixture of boxing and wrestling. There was no limit to the length of a fight and it was not unheard of for there to be a hundred of them. These were bloody, brutal, and sometimes ill-matched encounters, since bigger men would fight smaller ones and there was no concept of heavy-, middle- or lightweight fighters. A fighter was not supposed to hit or kick a man when he was down, but he could pull his hair or ears, hold him and hit him, and even gouge his eyes with his knuckles. An additional favorite tactic was to throw an opponent in a hip lock or trip him over and then "accidently" fall on him, smashing a knee or elbow into his face or rib. Gloves, or mufflers as they were called then, were only used for sparring. Fighting with bare fists occasions much more damage than wearing gloves. One could inflict terrible facial injuries on the other fighter as well as running the risk of fracturing a fist.

The fighters did have seconds—men who held their bottles of refreshment and on whose knees they sat for their brief respite between the rounds. The bottles held not only water but brandy. The seconds also had a sponge to wipe the contestants' brows. Thus, when a fighter lost a match, he was deemed to have "thrown in the sponge." So heightened was the atmosphere at these fights that men patrolled the edges of the fighting area with whips to keep it clear and the spectators at bay. There was a constant danger that spectators would enter the ring and join the fray.

Bare-knuckle fighting draws a lot of blood, and bets were placed as to who would bleed first and how much. Many boxers were grievously or fatally injured. However extreme this form of fighting sounds, one has to remember that bull- and bear-baiting as well as cock and dog fighting were common then. There were different standards at that time, so, like his fellow fighters, Mendoza had to have had tremendous personal courage and self-belief to be a pugilist when so little protection was offered.

Broughton knew his game. He associated with the aristocracy. Men of wealth and rank began to patronize the sport, and so a degree of financial stability and respectability began to filter through. These men bet on the fights, and soon other gentlemen, trainers, writers, and politicians (Sir Robert Walpole, Dr. Johnson, Jonathan Swift, Henry Fielding, and Alexander Pope among them) joined in the pleasure of the spectacle. This large, informal troupe of enthusiasts became known as the Fancy. But bare-knuckle fighting was not simply the province of pleasure for the gentry, it was also beloved by the populace. It was the respectable middle classes, the authorities and clergy, who feared it. They saw it as a danger to public order, a waste of time and money.

Broughton was also an entrepreneur. He opened an academy of boxing and offered to teach wealthy young men the sport. In his advertisement for students he wrote, "Britons then who boast themselves Inheritors of the Greek and Roman virtues should follow their example, and by encouraging conflicts of this magnanimous Kind, endeavour to eradicate that foreign effeminacy which has so fatally insinuated itself amongst us and almost destroyed that glorious spirit of British Championism." The word champion implied fighting for a just cause rather like knights in medieval times. It also brings out the British ideal of fair play. Broughton made the point. Boxing was a truly British art.

Thus, the prize ring that Mendoza entered was a reflection of a complex mixture of ideas and ideals. Underlying Broughton's advertisement is an emphasis on national pride and identity, generosity in defeat, physical prowess, honor, and a notion of masculinity born of Olympian tenets.

The spectators at a match were fully dressed, but the fighters were bare chested with tight-fitting knee-length "drawers." They wore soft black shoes for ease of movement. There was every opportunity to marvel at their muscles and beautifully formed bodies that recalled the athletes of Greece and Rome. This masculinity—on display—was a potent antidote to the frills, frock coats, and furbelows of the Fancy and the young bucks or the rough clothes of the working men (and sometimes women) who attended the fights.

Allied to this ideal of British sportsmanship were (at least to the authorities) less agreeable aspects. Gambling not only on blood shed but the winners was a large part of the popularity of prizefighting. Enormous sums were placed as bets. When Broughton lost a match in 1759, his patron, the Duke of Cumberland, forfeited his £10,000 stake. In revenge the Duke of Cumberland encouraged the law against pugilism. Broughton's Amphitheater closed; prizefighting was outlawed and entered a period of obscurity. The situation changed in the 1780s, and this coincided with Mendoza's life span.

The situation changed not the least because the Prince Regent, the future George IV, and his brothers all loved and encouraged the sport, and, where they led, others followed. It became as much of an obsession in Britain as football is today. People gathered in great numbers, tens of thousands to see a match, often travelling over huge distances. The authorities were against prizefighting—the chaos and unruly nature of the crowds perturbed them. This was, after all, an age of revolution in America and France and soon to be a time of war. Hence, the matches were often threatened with closure by the magistrates and the military. They were held outside London and the location kept a secret until the last minute. Thus, the authorities would hopefully arrive too late to stop the proceedings. This was not always the case, and many fighters were fined and imprisoned though not, of course, their backers.

Thus the fights and attendant furore were given a transgressive, carnivalesque air. The fighters' earnings came from both the generosity of the patrons as well as coins placed in a cap and circulated amongst the spectators. This may be the origin of the expression "to throw your hat in the ring." The presence of the aristocracy, sometimes royalty, and the Fancy kept the sport going and the authorities at bay.

Mendoza's claim to fame was that he introduced a new art and craft to this sport aka "the sweet science." He did not fight simply offensively, though he was capable of this, but defensively. He adopted swift, dancing movements, sidestepping, and guarding that eventually wore his opponents down and gave him the advantage of surprise. This novelty was criticized at first and perceived as unmanly—the action of a coward, especially when he danced backwards. Was this another example of what a cunning little Jew was capable of? But people began to understand and accept and finally imitate. Mendoza introduced finesse and technique to boxing. He is also credited with perfecting the straight left.

In his work *The Art of Boxing* (1789), Mendoza recommended hitting opponents "on the eyebrows, on the bridge of the nose, on the temple arteries, beneath the left ear, under the short ribs or in the kidneys." This "deprives the person struck of his breath, occasions an instant discharge of urine, puts him in the greatest torture and renders him for some time a cripple" The manual is full of close and detailed observations on fighting. The young man being taught is referred to as the Scholar and his teacher is the Master. Mendoza elevates boxing at one stroke with these terms.

Under Humphries' tutelage Mendoza became a gifted boxer. What is notable is that he always fought as Mendoza the Jew, The Star of the East, and The Light of Israel. His first recorded professional fight (i.e., no longer in the street) was a win over Harry the Coal-Heaver. He then fought a man called Tyne and fought and won against the Bath Butcher, Sam Martin, in 1787. By this time his fame and fortune were secure. The money poured in, and he was lauded at every level of society. He was able to marry his cousin Esther with whom he had 11 children. His wife did not like his fighting, fearing injury or death, so Mendoza, like Broughton, opened a boxing academy in Capel Court. It was known as the Mendoza or Jewish school of boxing. A newspaper, *The Daily Register*, noted that that was consistent "with his character as a Jew" because his school was "near the Bank!". In the academy he encouraged, in particular, many young Jewish fighters, such as Isaac Bitton, "Dutch" Sam Elias, the Belasco brothers, Israel, and Abraham, who all went on to become champions.

However, this arc of success did not meet with the approval of his mentor Humphries, who was jealous of his younger protégé. Humphries had also defeated the Bath Butcher in 1786 in front of Prince George, his brother the Duke of York, and the Duc d'Orleans. There was nothing left but for them to fight each other. An opportunity presented itself as the two men quarreled, though it is not quite clear why. It may have been an argument over stake money for a match or Humphries' disapproval over Mendoza training for a fight with a Bermondsey man called Nelson Worth.

It was agreed they would meet for a 400 Guinea stake in Odiham in Hampshire on January 9, 1788. It was noted that Humphries' fighting dress for this fight comprised a "pair of fine flannel drawers, white silk stockings, clocks, pumps and black shoe ribbons." The fight was watched by 60,000 spectators as well as the Prince of Wales, who sat wrapped in furs in his open carriage in the rain, rather fat and increasingly grumpy, especially as he had backed Mendoza, who lost the fight. The Prince of Wales was an avid fan, so much so that, when he finally became king after a very long wait of 30 plus years, he had a group of boxers, including one Black boxer, Bill Richmond to keep order at his coronation. Mendoza had met the Prince Regent the year before his fight with Humphries and later met his father, George III. Indeed Mendoza was the first Jew that the king had ever met or spoken to. Mendoza (1816) wrote in his *Memoirs*, "I had a long conversation with His Majesty, who made many ingenious remarks on the pugilistic art." Mendoza also recorded that he was disappointed not to be given money by the king at this meeting.

In the first of these three legendary fights with Humphries, Mendoza slipped in the 28th minute and sprained his ankle. He was forced to concede the contest. The Jewish population had bet heavily on their hero. It had been arranged most theatrically that, if Mendoza won, a white pigeon would be released to fly back to London, but in this instance it was a black pigeon that made its way home, signifying defeat. A song of the time recorded:

> When the combat was over the pigeons they flew
> With bad news to Duke's Place to dishearten the Jews
> The Fate of Mendoza disturbed their minds,
> Worse than all the bad shillings or counterfeit coin

Humphries penned a note to a patron: "Sir, I have done the Jew and am in good health. Richard Humphries." It was a controversial match, however. Humphries' second, Johnson, deflected one of Mendoza's blows, giving Humphries an unfair advantage and time to recover.

There were two more fights in this series. The one in 1789 (won by Mendoza) was considered so important that an account of it appeared on the front page of every newspaper in the land and the news of the French Revolution was relegated to the back page. Mendoza defeated Humphries soundly in the last (third) match in 1790 and became Champion of England—the highest accolade imaginable. It secured

Mendoza a place in the nation's affection and respect. At the same time it elevated the status of Jews because here was one who embodied every masculine virtue—self-discipline, persistence, courage, honor, and personal integrity.

At this point Mendoza was carried shoulder-high by the cheering onlookers who sang "Hail the Conquering Hero Comes" and shouted all the way back to London, "Mendoza Forever." Mendoza consolidated his position after this defeat of Humphries by beating Bill Ward in 1792.

Mendoza was by now a national hero, and as such he toured not only England but Scotland and Ireland, demonstrating his exceptional talent in exhibition fights as part of Astley's Circus. When he was in Ireland, he thrashed a certain Squire Fitzgerald for making anti-Semitic remarks.

Mendoza held his title for five years until 1795 when he fought Gentleman John Jackson. Jackson was five years younger, six feet tall, a sprinter, and an athlete. He was 42 lb heavier. Johnson won the match by seizing hold of Mendoza's long hair and pummeling him into submission in 10 minutes. Even in those times when rules were very lax, this was considered a foul. In spite of Mendoza's remonstrating with the umpire, he said there was no rule against it and he allowed it. At the time, it was fashionable for the boxers to have long hair, but since then boxers have always worn their hair short. Maybe it was a partisan crowd or maybe the tide was turning, and the Jewish champion was not to be allowed to win every time.

The partisan nature of a crowd was seen again in 1810 when there was a famous fight between the Englishman, Tom Cribb, and Tom Molineaux, a Black American ex-slave. It was the first international bout, and Cribb seems to have been given extra time to recover. He then won the match against Molineaux, when in reality he had lost it, since he had not come up to the scratch in time. The entire crowd was on Cribb's side, and Molineaux did not stand a chance when he protested,

Mendoza's name was on everyone's lips when he was champion. Jugs and vases, ballad sheets and chapbooks, and song sheets all bore his image—often the scene was of his winning fight against Humphries. He became a character in pantomimes and plays. In an age when not everyone could read, prints, portraits, engravings, broadsheets, and caricatures all spread his fame.

Mendoza fought his way through prejudice and oppression to be an acknowledged expert and celebrity. Fighting was the only way open to him to gain respect for himself and his brethren, who were ridiculed and despised for their religion, customs, appearance, and manners. This fighting through to fame and fortune was one he shared not only with fellow Jews but the Irish and Black fighters who also competed at this time. Mendoza set up a tradition for Jewish boxers, which has endured. In the 20th century, there was a great revival of boxing around the time of World War I and II. There were several well-known Jewish boxers who came out of the East End of London—Ted "Kid" Lewis, Jack "Kid" Berg, Harry Mizler, and Jack Bloomfield as well as boxers from the Irish and Black communities. Their example encouraged others when Oswald Moseley held his Fascist rallies with his Blackshirts in the East End.

The Jews came together to offer fighting resistance, spurred on by their heroes and their example. Mendoza and all he achieved lived on.

But there is another source of information about Mendoza that confirms the regard in which he was held. Much is owed to the Irish journalist, Pierce Egan, the first great sporting journalist. Other newspapers and magazines reported blow-by-blow accounts of the fights, but no one did it quite like "Glorious Pierce." He wrote his multi-volume *Boxiana*. This was a series of racy, idiosyncratic press reports of the matches he witnessed. Egan was a bold, quirky, and ubiquitous writer. Like Broughton he emphasized the nationhood of boxing. He celebrated England as a country where the use of the stiletto was not deployed as on the continent. Swords, pistols, and knives were for foreigners. Men got killed in duels—boxing might give them a bloody nose or black eye or a broken limb. Men would fight, but afterwards there would be "reconciliation with their antagonist, faults mutually acknowledged and perhaps [becoming] inseparable friends ever afterwards"

Egan admired and celebrated the boxers as descendents of the Greek athletes. He was very fair minded in his comments and made no racist comments about Black or Jewish boxers. He celebrated them for their merits. This may be due to his own Irish ancestry, another beleaguered minority at that time. He may have been more sympathetic to the notion of the other. Egan in *Boxiana* referred to Mendoza as a "complete artist" and a "star of the first brilliancy" .

Egan wrote with considerable verve and many of his boxing terms permeated the language of the time. This too underlines the importance and prevalence of fighting in popular culture. Some of his slang includes such words as "claret" (blood), "bottom" (a boxer has courage and endurance), "milling" (fighting), the "bread-basket" (stomach), "smeller and ogles" (nose and eyes), "to be in twig" (be on form), and "fibbing a nob is a most excellent gig" (getting a quick succession of blows to the head is great fun).

The trajectory of fighters can be tragic. Many boxers at that time and since have been badly injured or become alcoholics. Mendoza escaped this fate. He was an accomplished self-publicist, writing (or dictating) his *Memoirs* (1816) and a self-help manual *The Art of Boxing* (1789). But Mendoza was not a business man. He was very often in debt and hounded by creditors. He spent time in prison when he could not pay his bills. Later on in his life, he attempted many forms of employment to support his large family. He opened a candle and lighting oil shop, printed his own money, became a recruiting sergeant and a sheriff's officer, and was reasonably successful as landlord of two pubs—the Admiral Nelson and later The Royal Oak, both located in the East End in Whitechapel.

He fought 35 times, but like all boxers he moved inexorably to the last fight. His nemesis was Tom Owens, whom he fought at Banstead Downs in July 1820. He lost in 12 rounds. He died in 1836 in penury but with his reputation intact and ineradicable.

Boxing is a sport that divides people as no other, but there is much to admire in Mendoza. In an age with power through words and images to diminish and ridicule the Jews, he took control of his own image. When he was denied the means to charge entry to his fights, he sold reproduction portraits of himself. Those who bought the miniatures could then gain free entry to the match. Prior to his second and third matches with Humphries, he made sure their acrimonious interchange was printed in the newspapers. This was both to show himself in an honorable light and to excite interest even more in the fights. He was thus very skilled at self-promotion.

Mendoza made boxing more skillful and less brutal. He introduced new moves and stimulated new attitudes to the sport. He raised the social and cultural status of Jews and made it far more unlikely they were abused in the street. By becoming a national figure, he demonstrated that Jews were part of British society and not outsiders. He helped accelerate the position of Jews in Britain. In the 19th century Jews made their way into the higher ranks of society. Rufus Isaacs, first Marquis of Reading and Lord Chief Justice, was a descendent of Mendoza.

Mendoza fought as a Jew and won as a Jew. Mendoza, forever, indeed.

References

Mendoza, D. (1789). *The art of boxing.*

Mendoza, D (1816). *Memoirs of the life of Daniel Mendoza.*

Egan, P. (1812, 1829, 1829, 1824). *Boxiania: Or sketches of ancient and modern puglisim* (Vols. 1-4).

IV
Hearts and Souls

12

The Odyssey (of a Jewish Man)

Rabbi Mordechai Liebling

I was born in Brooklyn in 1948, the first child of two Holocaust survivors who were each the sole survivors of their immediate families. I was conceived in hope—I was to redeem both the past and future—and marinated in fear, growing inside the body of a woman who had just emerged from years of terror and now faced an uncertain future.

My inborn fear of physical violence was reinforced by living in a violent and decaying neighborhood, Brownsville, until I was 10 and then as the only Jewish family on a working-class Catholic block of East Flatbush, with its attendant anti-Semitism. Hope and promise were reinforced by my parents, who gave me the constant message that I could succeed to any heights.

I was held up for the first time at the age of five or six, in my first and last attempt to sell lemonade at the corner. I only felt safe walking in a fairly circumscribed area of a few blocks. I felt physically unable to protect myself (a pale replay of my parents' experience) and sought power by joining the school's Guard Force, the student police force, eventually becoming the head of it. When we moved, and I entered Junior High, I again joined the Guard Force. This time it resulted in the opposite. Out of my sense of justice or fairness, I reported a school bully for some infractions. He stalked me, and for the next 2 years I walked the streets in fear, constantly on the lookout for him. This was the era of John Wayne movies, where being a man was defined by physical prowess and courage. I think I unconsciously embraced courage in the absence of physical toughness. I was well acquainted with fear; perhaps that made courage a little easier, and I certainly did not feel manly.

My dad was a very emotional, heart-centered man. He openly expressed his feelings of love, joy, sadness, or anger. He could just as easily dance with joy, cry at a movie, or be in a rage. He had been a dentist in Poland before the war, when dental school was more like a trade school than a college. My mom was a world literature major in her second year of college when the Russians occupied her part of Poland, and she graduated the day the Nazis attacked Poland. She was an intellectual and much more reserved in her feelings. In some ways their gender roles were reversed, and they were, to an extent, that caricature of a Jewish couple with a dominant woman and submissive male. I identified more with her, and he didn't fit the model of the "American man."

There was, however, a very significant counterpoint: My dad had saved her life. In 1943 in their town of Czortkow, they were in a *lager*—a labor camp. They were recently engaged. Many of the town's Jews had already been murdered. One morning all of the remaining Jews were laid out in front of machine guns. The lager *führer* (camp commander) called out some men whose work was still valuable—my father among them for he worked as a dentist. My father saw that everyone else was about to be killed—among them his fiancée, her sister, and his own sister. Risking his own life, he walked up to the lager führer and asked that his wife's life be saved. The lager führer responded that this was a quick marriage but motioned to my mother to come forward. My parents then witnessed their sisters being murdered.

I heard this story as a boy through the lens of my father's guilt at not saving his sister. The story as was told did not celebrate his courage for risking his life to save his beloved, but the pain of his choice and inability to save others. It was not till I was in my 40s, after he had died, that I was able to reframe it and see him for the heroic man he was.

Flash forward to 1969, my senior year in college, the height of the draft and the war in Vietnam. I was at Cornell University, a hot bed of antiwar activity, and a member of Students for a Democratic Society (SDS), a radical group. It was inevitable that I would be drafted soon after graduation. By this time the New York City draft boards were wise to every form of trying to beat the draft through medical or other means. I saw my options as go to jail (which one of my friends did), leave the country, or get into an Army Reserve unit—they were not sent overseas at the time, and it meant only 6 months of active duty. I was unresolved.

Naturally, it was very difficult to get into the Reserves without a connection. However, one day my father read about a Reserve unit opening up on a first-come basis. He begged, pleaded, and cajoled me into signing up—I did it more to appease him, thinking I would not go when called. I began standing in line in the middle of the night and made it onto the list. The rule was that, once on the list, one would be called and had three chances to say yes; if one turned the offer down a third time, the name was removed from the list. The first two times my name came up, I turned it down, and my dad accepted it without an argument since going then would have delayed my graduation.

My last semester of college was tumultuous. My best friend, Jimmy, had a psychotic break and then two other friends did as well. African-American students with rifles occupied the student union. I was part of a group of White students who were protecting the occupiers from being attacked by other White students. I remember how frightened I was, standing there in the cold morning waiting for what in my mind were the Cossacks coming for a pogrom. They arrived, big, blond, and wielding baseball bats; we held them off in a confrontation about which the campus police were clearly ambivalent.

Soon after, I got my third call from the Reserves; the moment of truth had arrived. My dad pulled out all the stops, ending with his ultimate line, "I didn't survive the Nazis to have my son killed in a war."

I had just been accepted to graduate school and finally had a sense of what I wanted to do after college. Jimmy was in a psychiatric institution, and I was shaken up. I relented and signed up. Was this courage, cowardice, or survival? It has taken me years to work that through.

Two months after graduation I was in basic training at Fort Dix, New Jersey. Army Reserves undergo basic training along with the regular army. In my platoon of 50, there were about 4 or 5 Reservists, all of us college graduates. Most of the others were younger, many were high school dropouts, and more than a few had been given the choice by a judge to join the army or go to jail. Most importantly they were all destined for combat in Vietnam, and we weren't. I was the only Jew.

My friend Jimmy committed suicide my second week in the Army. I sat under a tree and sobbed for a long time. A corporal asked what was going on; I told him, and nobody said a word to me about it. Grief for a dead friend was acceptable.

Physically, basic training was challenging. I was unrepentant in my antiwar views and refused to be a gung-ho recruit. This did not endear me to my platoon. The combination of my relative privilege, anti-Semitism, and opposition to the war was the trifecta; my platoon wanted to throw a blanket party for me: At a blanket party the guest of honor is wrapped in a blanket while asleep in the middle of the night and is dragged outside where everyone kicks and pummels him. The injuries are usually serious. Luckily, a few of the older guys who had befriended me intervened as it was about to take place.

Soon after, a sympathetic doctor excused me from the last couple of weeks of basic training exercises. I spent my days painting combat helmets and surreptitiously painted peace signs on the inside of them. My male self-image would have been burnished by completing basic training, but I hated it.

The second half of the training was as a clerk. I was off every day at 5:00 p.m. and was allowed to go off post into Wrightstown. One of the innovations of the antiwar movement was G.I. coffee houses. Outside of posts around the country, coffee houses were set up to give soldiers going to and returning from Vietnam a chance to speak and to learn about the war from the antiwar perspective. I heard firsthand from returning vets about the horrors of this war. This was October 1969, and the largest antiwar demonstration to date was being organized in Washington, DC. The prize for the organizers would be soldiers marching in uniform against the war. The Army, naturally, forbade this. A bus was arranged from our Ft. Dix coffee house, and I decided to march in uniform along with a number of the soldiers just back from Vietnam. We were at the head of a million people marching against the war; rarely have I felt so proud—albeit with a hint of pretentiousness. Men opposing war was becoming a new way of expressing manliness.

In January 1970 Linda, my college girlfriend, and I moved to Somerville, Massachusetts. I was in graduate school, and we were deeply involved in the antiwar, urban hippy counterculture and most of all in the women's movement. Given my deep respect and love for my mother and having my father's very open emotional nature, I was a strong supporter and ally. That is not to say that I didn't have to go through many struggles around my own sexism and education about feminist values. I was the only male in a feminist street theatre group, understood that it was male privilege to take my shirt off in public, and knew that holding hands with my partner in public was a heterosexual privilege. At the very same time, we were involved in violent street protests against the war. Our feminism did not lead to a critique of violence.

Throughout the 1970s I was involved in radical political activism. Physical intimidation and street culture were a part of my life, alongside feminism and a growing spirituality. The urban counterculture of the 1970s was an interesting mix. For two years I was the only Jew and only Anglo man in a 10-person collective that organized and ran the Jamaica Plain-Roxbury food cooperative, the mission of which was to combat racism in our mixed race neighborhood. This was during the time of the Boston busing crisis, a period of very high racial tension. The other men in the collective were African-American or Latino and deeply immersed in street culture. We had weekly daylong staff meetings that were essentially encounter groups with no facilitator and fueled by drugs and alcohol. Nothing was off the table.

One incident from those years: We came to an agreement that men could not hit their partners on co-op property or at co-op functions. One afternoon, one of the men struck his partner in the parking lot. I saw it, went outside, and intervened. He was furious, saw it as an insult to his masculinity, and threatened to kill me. The incident ended, and I left. I was then told that he had a gun and was looking for me. I hid out for several days until other members of the co-op were able to negotiate a truce. At the moment I intervened, I was very scared and knew what I had to do—doing the right thing, interrupting an act of violence. I think it was how I was defining being a man.

Dropping my English name, Marvin, and assuming my Hebrew name, Mordechai was a pivotal act. I was in one of the earliest children of survivor consciousness-raising groups and able to process that experience for the first time. At the same time I was active in Re-evaluation Counseling and focusing on issues of internalized Jewish oppression. In our co-op, collective talking about fascism was commonplace. The truth was that my grandparents, aunts, uncles, and cousins were murdered by fascists. I was learning to celebrate Jewish resistance to the Holocaust, and Mordecai Anielwicz had been the prime organizer of the Warsaw Ghetto uprising. This all came together, and on July 4, 1976, on a bus from Boston to Philadelphia to attend the People's Bicentennial, I announced to my collective that I was taking my Hebrew name.

The immediate reaction was that taking on a Hebrew name was explicit support for the Zionist Colonialist Imperialists. That began my journey of over 30 years as a Middle East peace activist, advocating for a two-state solution. Most importantly, I was explicitly claiming that I was a Jewish man. The collective had to deal with me in that identity. In that context, being a man still meant to be willing to fight to prove it, and I saw clearly how that was a culture of using violence to mask pain and insecurity.

I left the co-op collective after a series of internal thefts and additional violence. I decided to learn carpentry, to have a productive skill. Very few of the Jewish men I knew could work with their hands or manipulate the physical world in that way. It was, also, part of the counterculture survival—do-it-yourself ethic. I even learned how to change the brakes on my car. In time I became a shingle roofer. I clearly remember climbing off a roof, feeling strong, with a tool belt around my waist and a hammer at my side, and feeling like here I was a man in this culture.

Another strand of my development in those years was beginning to explore spirituality. I taught myself yoga and had a regular practice. In my counterculture world I dabbled in a variety of New Age spiritual practices. I knew that there was something that deeply connected all life and was a fount of meaning. With taking on my Jewish identity, I began celebrating Jewish holidays and reading more about Judaism. Slowly I began putting together the various aspects of my life. I began to understand that my commitment to be an activist for peace and justice was rooted in the historical experience of the Jewish people—including my own family—the values of Judaism, and the intuitive spiritual knowing of the connectedness of all life.

However, I did not see Judaism as that spiritual path; the idea of an omnipotent, omniscious, supernatural God made no sense to me in light of the Holocaust and other suffering. One day I felt too sick to work and decided to stay home and read. I picked up a book about Jewish thought that I had borrowed from my sister (Noveck, ed., 1963). There was an essay by a man named Mordecai Kaplan, whom I had never heard of, and I decided to read it simply because we had the same name. Reading that essay changed my life. Kaplan was the founder of Reconstructionism, the movement that rejects supernaturalism, choseness, and patriarchy while affirming equality, democracy, social justice, and the in-dwelling of God in all life. I had found a Judaism, the theology and world view of which affirmed and deepened everything I believed in. Reading the Kaplan essay was a Eureka moment.

In my political life I had come to believe that I would be most effective as an agent for social change, working in the Jewish community. I also realized that to be successful I would need a credential and to know more. I wasn't sure what I was going to do. After reading the Kaplan essay, I called the rabbi of my parents' congregation (we had both been in the same class at Cornell) to find out more about Kaplan and Reconstructionism. He told me about the Reconstructionist Rabbinical College (RRC) in Philadelphia.

At the same time, in my New Age spiritual life, I met Rabbi Zalman Schachter at our local Sufi house. Reb Zalman was the embodiment of Hassidic Jewish spirituality, with New Age sensibilities. He made living a Jewish life look exciting and fulfilling. And he lived in Philadelphia and taught at RRC.

I decided that becoming a rabbi would give me the credential to be an effective social change agent, that the education would make my work deeper, and that it would be a fulfilling spiritual path. One year later I was a student at RRC. Later, they told me that I had been an experiment, the first older student they accepted who had been estranged from Judaism.

Flash forward to Philadelphia 1994. I was a Reconstructionist rabbi and the executive director of the Jewish Reconstructionist Federation (JRF). I was successful and had a high profile national role. I was, also, the husband of a Reconstructionist rabbi, Devora Bartnoff, and the father of four children: Anna, 2, Lior, 4, Yoni, 7, and Reena,

10. Lior has Down syndrome. I struggled with the tension of work and family. Work was demanding, and I traveled a lot. I was committed to an equalitarian relationship and supported Devora in the work choices that she made. She functioned as the primary parent; however, with four kids, I did spend a lot of time parenting. For me my success and contribution to the world was defined far more by my work than by parenting. In October Devora was diagnosed with stage 4 breast cancer.

In my wife's 2½ year struggle with breast cancer, my role as a parent changed. Devora's treatment included a bone marrow transplant, which entailed nearly a month of isolation in the hospital, and, for the last 1½ years, monthly trips to Seattle for 10 days of acupuncture treatment. While still running a national organization, I became the primary parent to four children, who were coping with having a severely ill mother. In April 1997 Devora died.

I hired a live-in nanny to be able to keep working; she lasted about 6 months. I wanted to work; so much of my self-worth, understanding of being a man and of being productive, was tied up with work. My father came to the United States with no proof of education; he never had a satisfying job here, and he never had a meaningful day of work. I was determined to have meaningful work.

I slowly came to the realization that I was giving neither my family nor the Reconstructionist movement what they needed or deserved. One morning I was waiting for Lior's school bus, and the bus was late. I was running in and out of the house, calling the bus company, getting other kids ready to leave the house, and being anxious about getting to my first meeting. In that moment I realized I had to resign.

The board of the JRF was very understanding; they allowed me to stay on as a half-time consultant. I could devote my primary energies to being a father.

About six months after Devora died, I was ready to go out. Lynne Iser was a woman in our community who I was attracted to, and in fact Devora had once pointed her out to my daughter Reena as someone I ought to go out with. I was still wearing my wedding ring, and it didn't feel right to see another woman while wearing it. I decided to call together some of my men friends for a ritual.

One of the things that got me through the whole period of Devora's struggle with cancer was a weekly *mikvah* (bath) with my male friends. Every Friday afternoon for that whole time, we met at Cy Swartz's house to hang out in the hot tub. There was a core of men who always came and others who showed up on occasion. The agenda was to give me support. It was the place that I could complain and talk about my feelings and what was bothering me. As the son of Holocaust survivors, I was well accustomed to taking care of the feelings of others and treating my feelings as less important or less legitimate than the feelings of others. As I child any hurt that I had paled in the face of my parents' suffering, and, as the husband of a cancer patient fighting for her life, my feelings felt secondary. This weekly mikvah was the place that I could allow my feelings to emerge.

Convening my men friends for a ritual to begin dating was the natural step for me. About eight men came together, and I realized that what I needed to do was give a eulogy for my marriage. This was different than a eulogy for Devora; this was for our marriage that had died with her. I was able to talk honestly about both the good and the bad while crying for what might have been. After talking for quite awhile, I felt ready to take off my wedding ring, the symbol of our marriage. Someone had thoughtfully brought a small pouch. I took off the ring, passed it around the circle, and then dropped it in the pouch; the sound reminded me of the thud of the first shovel full of dirt hitting the coffin. I wept. I was ready to begin being with another woman. Lynne and I married about a year later.

I stayed at JRF for two years and then began working part-time for the Shefa Fund, positions with no executive responsibilities, allowing me to focus on caring for my children and building a new marriage. I had made a clear decision that family took precedence over work. I knew it was right in my heart and in my head, but feelings of being unimportant, wasting my talents, and being unfulfilled persisted. Men are raised with the expectation that achievement—which is equated with fulfillment—comes primarily through work. With so much injustice in the world, how could I spend so much time on my family?

Thankfully, Lynne and other women in my life have repeatedly taught me that raising loving children with good values is as important a form of *tikkun olam* (repairing the world) as anything else. This is a hard lesson for a man to learn and still flies in the face of current social norms. Equally important is the commitment to building my relationship with Lynne. Creating and nurturing a loving life partnership is another aspect to bringing about a better world. By loving each other, we create/make/bring love into the world.

I have learned to bring loving, caring energy into the world of political activism. Happily, I am on the staff of Jewish Funds for Justice,[75] which is helping to develop a new paradigm for political change and organizing, one that combines a focus on results with a concern for the quality of relationships. The Jewish Fund tries to embody the teaching by Martin Luther King that for me reconciles tensions that I have lived, "What is needed is a realization that power without love is reckless and abusive, and love without power is sentimental and anemic. Power at its best is love implementing the demands of justice, and justice at its best is power correcting everything that stands against love."[76]

Reference

Noveck, S. (Ed.). (1963). *Great Jewish thinkers of the twentieth century*. Washington, DC: B'nai Brith.

[75] Since writing this, I am now Director of the Social Justice Organizing Program at the Reconstructioist Rabbinical College.

[76] Quote taken from Martin Luther King Jr.'s "Where Do We Go From Here: Chaos or Community" address to the Southern Christian Leadership Conference, Atlanta, GA. August 8, 1967.

13

Telling Our Stories: Liberation Work for Jewish Men

Billy Yalowitz[77]

Jewish men have had a busy few generations here in North America. As many of us have made considerable contributions to society and attained degrees of material comfort relative to the immigrant generation, some of us have begun to take a look around to try to get an accurate picture of what has happened to our relationships with each other along the way. In previous generations, Jewish men were central in each other's lives. In the work that I have been doing with a group of primarily North American Ashkenazi Jewish men in our 20s through 60s, as part of the Re-evaluation Counseling[78] communities, we have begun to tell our stories, to recover from the effects of living in the U.S. gentile, capitalist culture, and to rebuild a sense of group among us. We start with the stories of our grandfathers.

As we tell these stories, it becomes clear that, in the immigrant generation and to some extent among the first generation in the United States, the communal values of Jewish life allowed and encouraged closeness, solidarity, cooperation, and interdependence among Jewish men. Our fathers, grandfathers, and great-grandfathers built their relationships within structures growing out of these values, including trade unions, cooperative housing developments, mutual aid societies, radical political movements, and economic cooperatives. In religious life, Jewish boys and men built close relationships in *yeshivot* (study centers) through *chevruta* (spiritual study dyads) and group relationships through *minyanim* (traditionally fellowship circles of 10 men or more) in synagogues. As we have been telling stories about our fathers and grandfathers and their relationships with other Jewish men, we are struck by the

---

[77] Thanks to my coworkers in doing this work, including, but not limited to, Dan Alter, Michael Saxe-Taller, David Weingarten, Dave Cook, Yonah Diamond, Jeremy Bloch, Steven Kleinman, Jay Raymond, Isaac Zones, Albert Fields, Joe Silverman, and Alan Epstein, and to mentors Cherie Brown, Diane Balser, Tim Jackins, and Rudy Nickens.

[78] Re-evaluation Counseling is a process in which people exchange listening to heal the emotional damage done to all of us by the oppressive societies we live in, helping participants to recover from hurts caused by racism, sexism, anti-Semitism, class oppression, etc., even while they seek to empower people to fight against these injustices. Activists and organizers from dozens of countries have found the tools of Re-evaluation Counseling to be useful in supporting themselves and the people with whom they work. These tools help people reclaim their full intelligence, power, and effectiveness as social change activists. Re-Evaluation Counseling has also been used by many people to find greater joy in their lives as they work to create a just and sustainable world free from oppression of any kind. To learn more about it, go to www.rc.org.

depth of their connections, love, and commitment to one another, which were sometimes literally lifesaving.

Remembering and appreciating the solidarity among Jewish men of previous generations helps us to gain perspective on the kinds of relationships we want to reclaim and build on. Some of us also had experiences of closeness and connection with the Jewish boys with whom we grew up—often within Jewish communal structures, such as youth groups and summer camps. In order to reimagine and rebuild deeply connected and committed relationships with Jewish men in the present, it has been important for us to understand the commonality of our experiences growing up in the United States, to reclaim and build on what has been good, and to understand and change what has been damaging.

> My grandfather was a first generation Russian Jew, born in Canada, as were his five brothers. They all moved together to Philadelphia to find wives and to "start their lives." They had a plan to work and to save money, which they pooled and gave to my grandfather to start a business. When his business, a small corner grocery store, turned a profit, he gave them each seed-money to start their own businesses. The demands of their being self-employed made it hard for them to hang out like they had and eventually competition among them made their relationships hard. Compared to my grandfather, my dad grew up very isolated. He lives alone now and has no real friends. (Evans, personal communication, Feb. 16, 2008)

In the last three generations in the United States, the traditional closeness of Jewish males has been eroded by the forces of upward mobility, assimilation, and individualism. The breakdown of extended families was hastened by geographic mobility—dispersion, really, of the kinds of close working-class Jewish neighborhoods that many of our ancestors lived in. There is a strong message that success beckons from somewhere out in the American landscape, far from our families and communities. As we sought to learn the ropes of being American men, we strove to be accepted in the mainstream white, U.S. Gentile male culture. The distance and isolation of this culture are foreign to traditional Jewish male culture. But the social norms of U.S. maleness have become the air we breathe; it has been difficult for us to perceive what we are up against and the ways that these norms are counter to the Jewish male culture of our ancestors. We begin to notice the distance that has opened among us, and we undertake to reconnect with one another as Jewish men on our own terms.

A Jewish Men's Space

In our groups and workshops, then, part of what goes on is a reestablishment of Jewish male space. This is an alive, warm environment, with lots of *kibitzing* (playful joking and ribbing). Many of us are relatively at ease with physical touch with one another, a capacity for closeness which some of our fathers held onto and passed along to us. The group tone becomes more and more relaxed, with more playful interaction. We are in the process of reclaiming ways of being which got temporarily buried by assimilation. We have begun to fight through where we have lost contact with each other and where it has been difficult to hold onto our voices and ways of being with each other.

At first it can feel quite harsh to be together with other Jewish men, as we come in from the cold of U.S. male culture where we've each tried to function on our own and to pass; Jewishness has seemed to be a liability in the quest to be accepted on Gentile male terms. The capitalist society has us believing that we are competing for scarce resources in order to survive and succeed, each on a separate, individual track. We are set up to see other Jewish men as rivals—who among us will excel and pass enough to be accepted by and succeed among the non-Jews? This sense of solo struggle becomes attached in our minds to the kinds of survival fears that many of us inherited from previous generations, survivors themselves of pogroms, expulsions, and the Holocaust.

But in our groups, the competition and harshness tend to dissipate more quickly than expected as we tell our stories fully, notice the closeness among us, and begin to redefine our ways of being for ourselves. We rediscover some of what we knew about closeness as boys; our gatherings are marked by singing, playful wrestling and roughhousing, basketball, joke-telling, physical closeness. As the groups progress, we feel a regrowing sense of belonging to a group of Jewish males. As a leader in this work, I can feel the group being more and more able to back my leadership instead of resenting or competing with me. The "I" of having lived individualistically begins to dissolve into the "we" of being a part of a group of Jewish males again.

Apologizing for Our Existence No More

And we become able to face one of the core emotional patterns that we carry as Jewish men: apologizing for our existence. Given the history of anti-Semitism and being in the minority as we have tried to enter U.S. male culture, we have inherited a constant sense of asking for permission to be allowed to exist. This is a key element of the internalized oppression among Jews, where we turn in on ourselves the negative and destructive lies about who we are and our place in the world that result from anti-Semitism. As we tell our stories of growing up as Jewish boys, we see more clearly the contents of this internalized oppression: deeply held feelings that we are less-than-fully male, worthy of ridicule, an embarrassment to others. Unchallenged, internalized oppression tends to have us perpetuate and agree to our own oppression—we try to talk or look or act Gentile so that we may be tolerated and allowed to scavenge around on some outer rim of a group, if only grudgingly. We are left hoping that an exception might be made for us if we approach things just right, but that this limited inclusion could be revoked at any moment. This is where the residues of anti-Semitism live in each of us, in which a temporary invitation was made to Jews in different historical periods for limited periods of time, to be followed unpredictably by an expulsion or attempted genocide (*Ruah Hadashah*, 2000, pp. 6-8). We are learning to be able to express and release the painful emotions we carry from this unaware habit of apologizing for our existence. We are becoming able to remember and to heal from the battles that we faced as Jewish boys in our neighborhoods and schools, often alone and under attack from groups of non-Jewish boys.

For me, growing up in a working-class neighborhood in New York City, I was hard at work trying to be included in the local gang, dominated by the tough sons of Irish-Catholic longshoremen of the Hudson River piers.

In 4th grade, I wanted to emulate the older 6th graders who I so admired, Richie Buckley and Jimmy Barnes, brassy, out there. In my neighborhood, they ruled the streets and playgrounds and dominated the coming-of-age rituals of urban life—street games, parties, making trouble.

At the height of the war in Vietnam, my brothers and I with our left-wing background refused to stand at school assemblies during the Pledge of Allegiance. Afterwards, in the schoolyard on 26th Street, Buckley held my brother down with a brick over his head— "Say the Pledge of Allegiance, you goddam commie Jew."

I knew that brick was being held over my head as well, but, rather than surrendering, I determined that I would do what I had to in order to make it out there on the street. The unstated agreement for my being allowed to run with this gang was to stay silent, not to fight back, to swallow the humiliation and go on, trying to belong.

The specific stories vary depending on our different generations, class backgrounds, and geographical regions, but what seems to be common among many of us is having been singled out and humiliated as Jewish males. Some of us fought back and landed some punches, but for many of us there was a sense of having our hands tied behind our backs in these sometimes violent encounters with non-Jewish males during our boyhoods. If we were told by our parents that we were better than those who attacked us by foreswearing violence in response, it didn't help—we came away feeling ashamed and that it wasn't possible to really stand up for ourselves. And some of us react to our early experiences of anti-Semitism at the hands of non-Jewish males by jumping to the oppressor role: since we didn't get to fight back fully, and because of the victimization of Jews historically and especially during the Holocaust, we may be prone to take rigid positions that never being victimized again means becoming the aggressor. (In the absence of a sustained opportunity to heal from the early hurts of being targeted for oppression as Jewish boys, we are vulnerable to manipulation into oppressor roles. In much of Israeli policy dealing with the Palestinians, I see these unhealed wounds in action. Likewise, jumping from a subordinate role, as Jewish boys in relation to Gentile males, to role of oppressor as adults, is a key dynamic in the socialization of males into the dominant role towards females in sexism.)

Now, among a group of Jewish men, we are able to travel back to these memories and begin to heal from the rage and terror that have accumulated below the chronic survival habit of apologizing for our existence. With the group behind us, many of us are able to feel and recover from our experiences of being targeted by the gangs of Gentile boys in our neighborhoods. When one of us can tell these stories and release the painful emotion he carries, it palpably moves the whole group forward, helping to restore our sense of solidarity and pride.

Upward Mobility and Assimilation

As we tell the stories of our Jewish boyhoods, we have chances to reflect on our places in the class narratives of our families. As the sons, grandsons, and great-grandsons of the immigrant and first generations in North America, many of our families' class positions shifted from poor and working class to the middle and owning classes in one or two generations. Without romanticizing the struggles of our ancestors in their first decades in the United States, we notice the losses in our relationships with other Jewish men that have accompanied upward economic mobility. Many of our poor and working-class fathers and grandfathers moved from the more collective economic relations of their extended families and close-knit working-class Jewish communities to more individualized careers as they moved into the middle class. In their new middle-class lives, Jewish men had to learn to function largely on their own as workers and in their nuclear families. In the generations when Jewish entry into many jobs and colleges was restricted, there was a tremendous pressure toward assimilation and away from identification with one's Jewish background. (My own uncle changed his name from Yalowitz to Yale in order to increase his chances of getting a job in the 1940s.) Following is an excerpt from a short story called "Getting On" (Goldberg, 1926) written by my maternal grandmother, Sarah Goldberg Cantor, describing the assimilation of a young working-class Jewish man from New York City as he tried to make his way up at a Midwestern college in the 1920s.

> From the day Charles Cogan became old enough to understand the poverty of his parents and the hopelessness of their lives, Charles had begun to plan and dream of "getting on," a term he had heard his uncle, the lawyer who lived on Riverside Drive, use.
>
> ... And Charles had gotten on. Though at fourteen he was already working in a factory, nine hours a day for a wage of four dollars a week, here he was at eighteen, a freshman in the university, having all the hopes of becoming a doctor as successful and as rich as his uncle ... who had delivered a long lecture to Charles, that the great necessity was Americanization, the discarding of the Russian East Side behavior and psychology. The change, the metamorphosis rather, was going to take place at the western university where he was to keep away from the Jewish students and associate with and behave like the Gentiles. (p. 2)

When he arrived at the university, the Charles Cogan character had changed his name from Cohen and started attending Presbyterian Church with the Protestant students there.

> As he was hurrying from the library to his room, he met a little clique of fourteen Jewish students of New York, heard their loud voices, unrestrained laughter, and peculiar, characteristic accent, and saw the free movements of their hands. He was not like them. He was getting on … he was succeeding and would continue to succeed. And he would return to New York, as Americanized, as fine mannered, as perfect as his immaculate, well groomed uncle.
>
> As Charles began to absorb the ways and attitudes of the Gentile students who were his friends, he was happy. The more he observed the Jewish students on the campus, the more contented and proud he felt. He was getting on. He was learning while they were not. It had not been easy to win the confidence and companionship of the Gentile students in his boarding house and class rooms. For no matter how polite and friendly they were to him they, nevertheless, seemed to resent his persistent attempts to gain their friendship. Patiently and diplomatically, Charles had laid his plans. And so at last they had nearly accepted him as one of them. (p. 2)

Assimilating, however, seemed to be an ongoing challenge for Charles.

> Just when he had gotten to feel that he was considered an American and was really like one, he had been cruelly disillusioned. Once as he was walking on the campus, a student who was decidedly Jewish, stopped him with a delighted nod and said: "At last, it is good to see a Jew here. I have been looking for one all day. I just arrived and would like to find Jewish family with whom I could board." Charles was crestfallen, and asked whether he really looked like a Jew. Most people did not take him for one. "Of course you do. The East Side and the whole map of Jerusalem is written on your face," smilingly answered Mandell, the newcomer…. Charles quickly hurried the new student through side streets to Greenberg's boarding house … and avoided becoming friends with him. (p. 2)

The story continues with "Cogan" alternately steeling himself against the anti-Semitism he faced, ingratiating himself by tutoring his Gentile classmate in physics, and longing for his community.

> There were times when Charles felt he was a traitor, and then the blood rushed to his face, and he felt humiliated and uncertain. There were times when his new Gentile friends assembled in his room, and ridiculed and imitated the Jewish students of their classes. Once the red-haired fellow who worked together with him in the cafeteria winked at the other boys and asked Charles whether he was willing to eat bacon and ham…. There were times when Charles felt lonely and out of place in the presence of his Gentile friends, when he longed for the friendship and companionship of those foreign Jewish students. But those moments were rare. And when he saw how sneeringly his friends stared at and spoke of those foreign students from New York, he felt more certain of his aim and principle. (p. 2)

The result of this kind of intensive assimilation for many Jewish men who have come of age after the first generation here in the United States was to live in a wholly unfamiliar social world, where the interdependence, warmth, mutual aid, and communal institutions of Jewish culture were suddenly gone. My grandmother ends her story:

> In bed, listening to the peaceful breathing of his roommate Paul Kennedy, Charles was still thinking ... wondering whether it was all really worthwhile; wondering whether he was really getting on. (p. 3)

Written more than 80 years ago, this story still echoes loudly in many of our lives today as Jewish men. Each subsequent generation has struggled with different and changing versions of anti-Semitism, the confusions of internalized oppression, the allure of getting on in the mainstream culture, and the loneliness, self-repudiation, and isolation that come with assimilation. In the Jewish men's liberation work, we are working to become aware of and to challenge the internalized messages regarding the superiority and standards of the mainstream U.S. Gentile culture of maleness, especially as that culture has led to our distancing ourselves from our families and communities, from our Jewish selves, and from each other.

As we get our own voices back and rebuild strong group relationships, standing on the shoulders of our male ancestors with new awareness, we begin to be able to ask questions about creating the kinds of lives we want: What does loyalty among Jewish men look like, without sexism? How can we play equal roles with women in building liberated Jewish communities? How do we want to parent? What kinds of work lives will fulfill our desire to be part of more collaborative efforts, rather than working in isolation? What kinds of family and parenting arrangements and economic relations do we want in our communities, beyond the individualistic models of capitalism?

The Role of Allies, and Rooting Out Sexism

Jewish men's liberation work is not undertaken in a vacuum. Within the Re-evaluation Counseling Communities,[79] we are closely allied with groups of Jewish women and with men from other backgrounds who are doing this kind of personal and group healing work, challenging their own internalized oppressions and building lives and communities based on a reclaimed sense of their own power, value, and worth. Along the way, we have been mentored and backed particularly by Jewish women who have blazed their own paths in reclaiming deep and trusting relationships with one another, challenging the mainstream culture's ideals of femaleness and developing their leadership in the women's liberation movement more broadly

[79] An international network of local groups that are involved with the ongoing process of Re-evaluation Counseling.

in the work to end sexism. In fact, in doing this work to develop closeness and pride among Jewish men, it has been important for us to learn to include as a central tenet the rooting out of the sexism that we have also inherited from previous generations in both the Jewish world and society in general. We have begun to learn to support the leadership of Jewish women in their own work as well as in the larger joint project of Jewish liberation.[80] We have also begun to build mutual alliances with men of African, Asian, Indigenous and Latino heritages, who are doing their own work to define maleness on their own terms and to recover from the emotional hurts of internalized racism. Our work on Jewish men's liberation cannot be separated from these allied efforts.

We are still learning many things in Jewish men's liberation as more young adult, gay, queer, Sephardi and Mizrachi men, and Jewish men from other countries, including England and Israel, begin to participate and bring their own stories. I love doing this work. Having a home base of Jewish men has made new things possible for me and for many of us. I think our grandfathers and great-grandfathers would be proud.

References

Brown, C., Jackins, H., et al. (2000). Jewish liberation policy statement #5. *Ruah Hadashah #10,* 4-15.

Goldberg, S. (1926, August 20). Getting on. *The Jewish Tribune*, 2-3.

[80] Jewish liberation is the permanent freeing of all Jewish from oppression, in both its internalized and external forms, as a part of ending all oppression. See Jewish Liberation Policy Statement #5, *Ruah Hadashah #10*, pp. 4–5.

14

Why Men Gather: The Jewish Men's Retreat Journey

Allen Spivack and Yosaif August

Jewish men gather—to pray, share stories, solve a vexing problem, to complain, and even to worry a bit. Yes, generations of Jewish men have found their ways of connecting and through a variety of affiliations have found unique opportunities to connect as men and as Jews. The typical synagogue not so many years ago depended on men to bring their skills to ensure that the "shul" remained a vibrant, thriving institution. They hired and fired, raised money, established rules of governance and mentored leadership. Such was also the case in their lives as businessmen where the community of Jewish men developed a unique kind of relating (not unlike men of other ethnic groups) that established a special kind of trust and privilege. Perhaps no other group characterized this gathering of men as the synagogue's brotherhood—a way of enticing a broader network of men to participate in synagogue life. Just remember those savory Sunday brotherhood breakfasts where men cooked, served and cleaned. There were other venues for men to gather too—the Bnai Brith lodges, charity golf tournaments, friendly poker games, Jewish-only country clubs, and the Jewish Community Center sports teams.

Why did these men—our fathers, uncles, family friends, brothers—participate in these groups and activities? And what did they hope to get out of them? Seen from our perspective of today, these affiliations gave men opportunities to connect in an informal way since, for most, more natural opportunities (such as child-rearing and school-based activities through children) rarely existed for them in their lives. In my view, men were coaxed into these groups and then found something that they longed for—special and valued companionship through back slaps, humor, cooperation and teamwork that was generally unavailable in their worlds of work.

While these times of connection were often fleeting, many men used their Jewishness as the glue to build and sustain meaningful relationships.

My father is a classic example of this kind of affiliation. Nathan Spivack owned a pharmacy and usually worked seven days a week, often twelve hours a day. He had little relief from the daily grind of work. Fortunately, we lived in an apartment above the store, and so I was often entrusted to bring him lunch and dinner. I spent a lot of time with him in the store—talking, learning the business (as an eight year old!), even helping to stock shelves and wait on customers. He had so little time for anything other than his work. But there was one thing he always made time for no matter how fatigued he might be, his twice monthly poker games, rotated from house to house among the ten men who were part of the group. All Jewish, he had met these men either through business connections, the husbands of my mother's friends or from activities he attended from time to time at the local conservative synagogue.

These games seemed to brush away the tiredness of his day. When the game was at our house, the men would gather, smoke, have a few drinks and eat some delicacies my mother prepared. Nat (as my father was called), allowed me to come and sit on his lap before bedtime. The men joked and chatted and exuded a sense of comradeship and devotion for each other. Now I appreciate how much they all relished their time together. When my father died suddenly, many of these men extended themselves to my family offering us comfort and support.

As I became a married man myself and young father, I wondered how I would find my connections to other men. Like many men my age, life revolved around two activities—work and time with my wife and two sons. We had an active social network, but personally, I had few men with whom I could be in relationship. We always seemed to be with couples, and there were few opportunities available to establish my own time and space.

Like my father, I found many of my significant opportunities through Jewish connections, but unlike him, I found an alternative to the more casual relationship-building that went on with many of the men of my father's generation. It was the 1970s and the world was awash in gender politics. Not only did we as men reexamine our attitudes and relationships with women but with men as well. I intentionally sought out other men who, like me, wanted relationships with men that were based on openness and intimacy. I hoped that by consciously cultivating supportive relationships with other men, I would discover new connections that would help me to find my voice, to understand power issues in my relationships, to nurture my sense of caring, to master a new vocabulary of relating, and to accept that men can love each other in profound ways.

As it happened, several men, all members of our spiritual community (an egalitarian, lay-led *Minyan*), discussed forming a father's group. The group's primary focus would be on our role as fathers. Inevitably, such discussions led to conversations about our relationship with partners and then to our relationship with parents, especially our fathers. And so it went. The six of us remained together for nearly 16 years, meeting every three weeks. As Jewish men, we each owned a unique upbringing around Jewish learning and practice. Our politics differed widely, especially about Israel. Several of the group had spent years in the Jewish education system. Many of us struggled from time to time with our practice and ritual observance or had different expectations about ritual practice than our spouses. Yet it was our Jewish core that served as a unifying theme for us—whether to send children to the Jewish day schools or to take them out, how to understand the life cycle events we celebrated, and our dilemma when our children dated non-Jewish men or women.

We worked at building our connections with each other and defining how we as a group needed to evolve to sustain ourselves. These years of sharing and connecting really manifested itself for me during the High Holidays. I liked to stand in the sanctuary before our services began and search out each of my men. I could feel the wonderful strength and power of our collective history. It was nothing less than the power of love. This experience of connecting to my brothers made it possible for me to acknowledge that the traditional ways of being in relationship with other men in my life wasn't working. The six of us had spent years breaking through barriers and building up connections, and now this new paradigm needed to be "the" model for my future relations with other men.

Our meetings were powerful reminders of this emerging new consciousness. We met every three weeks, and usually there was plenty to discuss about events in our lives. There was no agenda per se other than the agenda of listening. We evolved a set of simple, unspoken rules: no facilitators and no topics; check-in and listen; ask questions; offer support when requested; don't get angry; don't discuss sex. We would check-in about the past weeks-work, spouse, children, parents, ourselves, Israel, our spiritual community, the group rules. Frequently, someone would request time to discuss a contentious issue with a recalcitrant adolescent or a troublesome issue with an aging parent or a spouse who was unsupportive. We were a group of men, all now married, several divorced, with hundreds of years of cumulative relationship experience and we talked and shared and gave advice. We did this for 16 years, until it was time to move on.

The sinews that held us together all those years still keep us connected even though our group no longer exists. We share a love that only comes when men like us choose to sit together and open ourselves in honest and thoughtful ways. Our years together built trust and deep interconnections that allowed me to expose some of those painful personal stories that often remain hidden and haunting. One such tale began when, as an 11 year old, my father suddenly died at age 53. Our family was devastated, and I can remember feeling abandoned, lost, drifting and alone. My mother, in her desperation to help me cope, sent me to a local psychiatrist whom my father had helped out on a number of occasions. As I entered his office for the first visit, I saw two enormous German Sheppard dogs approaching me, snarling and then barking. I was terrified. Dr. Cass was close by and gave a command. They quickly quieted down and retreated. He led me to his office and we talked-about what I can't recall. All I did was think about those dogs.

I continued to see Dr. Cass, and each time it was the same—the dogs, the barking, the fear. We talked about learning to deal with tragedy and moving on and finding ways to survive even when many obstacles stood in my way. He befriended me and kept repeating this theme of surviving and enduring. One Sunday, he took me on a trip to visit his two teenage sons who were living that summer at a camp on land Dr. Cass owned. He had built a simple dwelling for them and a few outbuildings, and his goal was to have them learn to manage on their own, to survive. When we arrived, they were glad to see him, but he kept his distance. They went to the car with him and brought back their supplies for the next two weeks. As they showed me around, there was a corral for several farm animals. Dr. Cass told me to pull the wires apart and go in, but when I touched the wires, I got a jolt of electricity that stunned me. He looked at me and said, "Don't always do what people tell you to do." All I thought about were the dogs.

On the drive home, Dr. Cass told me about his experiences in World War II—being a soldier in the Army, being captured in the Pacific and being a prisoner of war for several years. How he had endured death marches and deprivation and other horrors. How he wanted to make sure his sons knew how to survive and take care of themselves no matter the situation. Now I started to understand the dogs. The irony was that this bizarre, sick man taught me how to survive and endure through many difficulties in my life. He taught me resolve and resiliency and being watchful. He even had my mother send me to an Outward Bound School so I would know "how to survive on my own."

The father's group offered us all the opportunity to bear witness and to embrace a new vision of what was possible. This group of men helped me to become a man like my father, a man I deeply loved and admired, to learn ways to nurture and support, to kiss a man out of love, to relish the unique physical contact that men can share with each other. This group taught me how we could use one another to rehearse the new selves we wanted to become. It also opened the other possibilities for my own growth, if I was willing to be adventurous, daring and take some risks. I soon found this opportunity for my adventurous spirit when I heard about a Jewish Men's Retreat (JMR) at a place called Elat Chayyim in the Catskills. My way to the JMR was both circuitous and fortuitous.

After leaving my full-time fundraising work with the local Jewish federation and spending two years staying at home caring for my two sons when my wife went back to work, I began to spend some of those free hours doing handyman jobs here and there. I always had some facility for manual work and learned as I went. People always needed a little of this and a little of that done, and soon enough I had a real business! I started getting busy. The handyman work became a home renovation business with employees and partners and lots of tools and equipment.

I used to call myself the "other Jewish carpenter" and many of my clients were people in the Jewish community. Many thought it odd to have a Jew doing this kind of work. I still juggled caring for my sons and work, dropping them off at school, running to the lumber yard, strapping on the toolbelt, working, supervising, meeting with my business partners, and then picking up the boys and heading to after-school activities. Evenings were filled with dinner and then looking at potential jobs and doing estimates. As the business grew, I needed another carpenter and hired Steve, another Jewish carpenter! We worked well together and talked about everything from framing to family life, from nail guns to finding our way in this new world as men. Who would have ever suspected that my entry point into this lifelong work—helping men to find healing and strength—would come from banging nails? This is certainly one of the great ironies of my life—a true re-visioning of my masculine identity in that most masculine of male bastions—the building trades.

One day Steve told me about a Jewish men's retreat he attended the previous year, and how it had opened him up to so many new possibilities in his relationship with other men and with his wife. I asked him, "What's so different about this retreat? I mean I'm already in a father's group." But there was something in his voice that intrigued me about this event.

He talked about the singing, the conversation at meals, the davenning and spirited praying and even dancing, the small group meetings that helped each man to search deeply. Steve said that Torah stories came alive and took on a whole, new meaning.

Steve encouraged me to attend the third Jewish Men's Retreat (JMR) in the fall 1994 with him, and we made the drive from Boston to a place called Elat Chayyim, then in Accord, New York. As we entered the main building, I noticed that there were lots of drums scattered about. Men embraced. What was this Jewish Renewal everyone was talking about? I remember feeling anxious and uneasy and wondered if I had done the right thing agreeing to attend. Yet as the weekend progressed, I recall how profoundly I was moved by so many things—the intensity of the *davennen*, the spirited singing and dancing, the willingness of many men to reveal the pain in their lives, the risk-taking and sharing and sense of self-discovery that exploded around me. I was captivated and paralyzed simultaneously.

This is how I found my way to the JMR, an event unlike anything I have ever experienced before, or since, in my adult life. Men come together for a weekend and weave themselves into a community of brothers. Men let go of pretense, posturing, and their armor as each steps delicately into a world of new expectations where openness, softness and caring are the norm. Men move beyond the masks of their normal lives—as the breadwinner, husband, father, son, sexual purveyor, competitor, stoic—and venture out on new turf where suddenly the rules of engagement are different. It has been a painstaking journey—embracing those new personal masks that strengthen, support and enrich me and discarding those that restrict, limit and subvert who I believe I want and need to be.

For example, I chose to be a full-time partner and a full-time father. I chose to find an emotional core for myself by discarding those stereotyped beliefs about how men need to be. I chose to find humor and lots of laughter in life. I tore off that mask of indestructibility and invulnerability and chose instead to love hugging men and finding new ways of building intimacy and doing work that I cared about. I gave up the mask of a stodgy, uninspired Jewish practice for the exuberance of Jewish Renewal. I rejected the security of playing it safe and making sure everyone was happy and painted a mask that let me take more risks and accept more failures. I ask "what would I love to be doing?" rather than "what should I be doing?" While Steve never came back, I never stopped attending.

Mine is a familiar story for those many men who have participated in this remarkable event. Each man is an accretion of personal stories and experiences—some more dramatic and challenging, others more pained and tragic—but events that shaped each person's journey toward manhood and beyond. Some men attend once and disappear while others return, year after year, building a strong, loyal corps of *mensches* who reserve one special weekend in October for the JMR. We return year after year to celebrate our companionship, exuberance, acceptance, spirit and sense of renewal.

The vision and sensitivity of a new generation of Jewish "patriarch" tapped into the emerging needs of Jewish men that gave birth to the JMR. Yosaif August, one of the founders of the JMR, has told me many times that the retreat was a natural outgrowth of the need of Jewish men to find unique and meaningful ways of connecting with each other. In 2008, Yosaif shared the evolution of the retreat with me as part of the preparation for this article, stating:

> We began convening spontaneous ad hoc gatherings at renewal retreats, *kallot*, etc. These gatherings were simply circles of men getting together to share and support each other. These venues gave us a natural way of creating sacred space together, including the agreements of confidentiality and mutual respect. Usually we would chant a *niggun* (melody) for a while and then do a go-around, sometimes using a talking stick, followed by conversations about whatever seemed to hold sway or have some energy for the group. What I particularly remember about these early informal gatherings was how ripe and primed all of us were to dive right into the "stuff" of our lives. I also remember these meetings as occasions to begin a healing process between gay and straight men.

Reb Shawn Zevit, one of the original planning team members and recently, rabbinic leadership for the JMR, remembered his first connection to this emerging movement of Jewish men's work:

> At the 1993 Jewish Renewal Aleph Kallah in San Francisco, I was the only man to sign-up for the first day of a workshop for Jewish men that was being facilitated by Yosaif August, an organizer of the first Jewish men's gathering at the 1988 Aleph Kallah. Yosaif and I wondered why only the two of us were at this men's only session given the hundreds of people gathered at the event in the hills of Berkeley, and the large attendance by both men and women at courses that emphasized women's rituals and issues. We realized that it was not safe to assume that Jewish men, who sought a renewed connection with their Judaism, would necessarily see the unique aspects of their male identity and spiritual expression as something they needed to pay attention to. Making this an important item on the progressive Jewish agenda would take patience, authentic soul-searching and a willingness to break through the barriers that existed to intimacy, trust and connection that many Jewish men carry like a heavy backpack on their life's journey.
>
> By the next day a few more men attended the program, and we ended our week of drasho-drama on Jacob and Esau, in which we gave each other blessings that we wished our own fathers had given us. In the inspirational bubble of this unique time together, Yosaif, myself and a group of other committed Jewish men gathered together with the support of Rabbi Jeff Roth, to begin an annual Jewish Men's Retreat in the fall of 1992 at Elat Chayyim, near Woodstock, New York. The JMR met there until 2005, when Elat Chayyim relocated to the Isabella Freedman Retreat Center in Connecticut.

Some of the earliest work by Jewish men explored new ways of living as Jewish men and identifying powerful new rituals of spiritual engagement. In discussing the early roots of Jewish Menswork, Yosaif recalled that in the late 1980s and early 1990s, many Jewish men started raising the bar for their work of self-exploration and masculine renewal and began developing programs that were presented at various kallot and other gatherings:

> One example of this was an innovative program presented by Marc Kronisch and Rabbi Moshe Halfon entitled "Re-creating Jewish Men's Rites of Passage" that combined Jungian archetypes, kabbalah and developmental psychology. Also, Mitchell Flaum and I led a week-long class exploring the implications for men of the story of Joseph. Reb Zalman Schachter-Shalomi led a couple of creative and dynamic men's gatherings at kallot. One was a gathering in the men's locker room at the kallah at Bryn Mawr College in Pennsylvania. He led another one that involved a walking meditation focused on the stages of our lives as men. Rabbi Arthur Waskow and I taught a class at Elat Chayyim about "Becoming Brothers, Becoming Brotherkeepers" in which we focused on several brother-pairs; Cain-Abel, Jacob-Esau, Isaac-Ishmael, Moshe-Aaron. We also included David and Jonathan, because their relationship illustrates the full range of possibilities of love, trust and faithfulness between men. As we planned and organized these sessions in a variety of venues, it became quite clear to all of us that there was a growing desire to move beyond these larger venues and gather ourselves exclusively as men to go deeper into this work of self-discovery.

From these sessions and workshops emerged the idea for a weekend retreat that would be lay-led and offer men the opportunity to become part of a community of men, one that would sustain itself from year to year and build itself on the strength of community, profound and supportive relationships and acts of loving-kindness. The first retreat was entitled "Our Fathers, Our Selves" and used the structure of the Sabbath to create a vessel where men could experiment with various ways of creating sacred space to promote intimacy and trust. Yosaif recalled how the planning group brought innovative, cutting edge programming ideas into the mix, an ongoing hallmark of the JMR planning process:

> One thing we did was build a sweat lodge. We played a healing and non-competitive game of ultimate frisbee. I remember being in tears as I gazed into the eyes of my brothers during our closing circle—actually two concentric circles in which we faced each other—while chanting "May the blessings of Yah rest upon you, may Yah's peace abide with you, may Yah's presence illuminate your heart, now and forever more."
>
> The second retreat, "The Mild One Meets the Wild One," focused on the story of Jacob and Esau, inspired by Rabbi Rami Shapiro's *Embracing Esau: Reclaiming the Deep Masculine in Judaism*. It marked our journey into fully em-

bracing our entire Jewish legacy—our stories, rituals, language, humor—as a means toward our awakening and becoming whole. Out went the sweat lodge; in came the *mikveh*. Ironically, there are many Jewish young men whose only *mikveh* experience has been the "hot tubs" during our men's retreats. They consider the hot tub the "real thing" —and for us, it is! Out went Grimm's fairy tales and Robert Bly; in came our authentic Jewish mytho-poetic treasure trove, those delicious and rich Torah stories of inspiring characters, deeply flawed ones, dysfunctional families, moments of revelation and more. Out went "Ho" and in came the affirmations: "*Hineni!*" (I am here) "*Dibarti*" (I have spoken); and "*Shamati*" (I hear you). In came the inspiring *tisch*—a time to gather, tell stories, learn, laugh and sing- along with "*Shlivivitz*" time and later, after *Shabbos*, scotch and cigars (maybe this isn't exactly Jewish, but maybe it's another link to the generation of our fathers!).

I have such vivid memories of that second retreat. During the Torah service each man wrestled with his twin brother and was then "born" as either Jacob or Esau. At that moment, the Jacobs were given blue bandanas and the Esaus were given red ones, which everyone wore for the rest of the retreat. Each man's task was to work on issues related to healing with his twin. I was "born" an Esau. My twin was Reb Shawn Zevit. The dramatic point of the journey was a dawn encounter with our twin. The night before, we spent preparing for this encounter. Since it was raining, in lieu of the intended campfires we used candles, and at daybreak all of the Jacobs marched up a large hill playing their tambourines. The fierce drumbeats of the Esaus could be heard in the distance. Then came the encounters—the wrestling, the pantomiming, the yelling, the crying, the hugging, the loving and especially the healing.

One ritual we initiated that year was the "brotherkeeper" button, which I created as a powerful symbol to encourage men to support each other. A "brotherkeeper" is a man who challenges and supports other men to be their most magnificent self. That's what the twin Jacob-Esau pairs were doing at the retreat. At the conclusion of the retreat, all men who were attending for the first time were invited into the center of the circle. Those men who had previously attended the retreat not only pinned a green "brotherkeeper" button on them but gave each of the first-timers two other buttons to give out to other men in their lives—men they knew who embodied brotherkeeper qualities or would be encouraged to move in that direction. The ritual is simple, but it's the *kavanah* (intention) that gives it its power. Over these 18 years, over three hundred men have received the buttons and then reached out to other men in their lives. It's hard to ever know the ripple effects of these things, but I can only imagine that there are so many good stories out there waiting to be told about this.

Reb Shawn Zevit recalled that the second retreat explored what it meant to be a Jewish man by entering into a narrative between Jacob and Esau, and then becoming these archetypes through study and ritual, exploring each person's personal identity.

> This experience remains forever etched in my soul as an evolutionary step for me in integrating my awareness of the constructs of masculinity and of male and Jewish identity. I have taken these profound lessons into my teaching, my rabbinate and now my mentoring of a younger generation of Jewish men and women.

Each retreat has had its own special character that reflects the chosen theme, the unique style of that year's new leadership team, and the inevitable spontaneity and happenstance of the men who chose to attend in any particular year. JMR retreats are entirely lay-led. In some years, professional rabbinic leadership has enhanced the ritual aspects of the retreat. However, JMR assiduously avoids having a headliner to attract attendees. Men have learned about the JMR because a friend invites a friend, or a man brings his son or father, or a group decides this would be a great way to enhance their work together. Many men have found the JMR when they are in need of personal healing, when a man wants to explore alternatives to his current lifestyle, when men seek some renewed commitment to Judaism. The JMR has always offered a new framework for how men can lovingly interact and support each other. The JMR suspends the normal rules of engagement that most men face day in and day out, and men leave the retreat having learned a new paradigm and strategy for connecting with the significant men in their lives.

At the end of each retreat, the current leadership issues an open invitation for men to step forward and declare their intention to become part of the leadership circle for the next year's retreat. This is a very exciting and poignant moment. With full hearts from this intense, intimate and joyful experience, men face each other in a closing circle, knowing that many of us will be back together the next year, full of the JMR's unique brand of enthusiasm and creativity.

The leadership group develops the theme and the program, generally but not always, drawing on the thematic material contained in that week's *parasha* (Torah portion). Over the years, the leadership has developed a natural way to mentor men to assume these leadership roles. Virtually all leadership roles have a double, a man who shares the role and is supported in stepping up to doing it himself the next time. Another recent innovation has been the water ritual. Each man brings some water from a place sacred to him. Each contribution is announced, and then the water offerings are mixed in a large bowl. Each man receives a vial of our combined special waters. Men have brought water from the Nile River, the Jordan River, the Dead Sea and places throughout the United States. This is yet another example of the JMR's work-creating new rituals and unique programming that speak to men in very personal ways.

One of the most exciting aspects of the JMR is the way many Jewish men have experienced their first joyful reconnection to Judaism and a Jewish community. So many men of all ages have had significant wounding and alienating experiences related to Judaism earlier in their lives. Many men come to the retreat seeking connection with other men; the Jewish dynamic may have no immediate attraction to them. The inclusive nature of the JMR makes for a safe space where men can dip their toes into the pool of Jewish practice and feel comforted and supported for doing that—whether it be impassioned singing during the Shabbat services, putting on *tefillin* or experiencing the beauty of the *Havdalah* service. Another aspect is the intergenerational healing that goes on when sons bring their fathers, fathers bring their sons and brothers bring brothers. Observing this process of men working on their relationships with fathers, brothers and sons often helps some of the other men at the JMR begin the process of repair and reconciliation with their own families when they return home.

The JMR process has identified new paths of self-discovery and exploration and created new definitions and road maps for a healthy, vibrant and alive masculinity. Yosaif has thought deeply about this process and has often talked about the impact of this work on the world of Jewish manhood.

> I believe we have appropriately begun this process by examining our own lives and our relationships with those closest to us. We are moving through barriers between us, as Jewish men, and other men, doing the work of healing—especially between gay and straight men. This has opened up ever widening opportunities for us to cultivate richly textured relationships with each other. The annual JMR has been one means of doing that. It's like a *mikveh* for us. By dipping into these waters of trust, love, caring, truth, we establish joyful connections, thereby break down the artificial barriers that separate us and ultimately dilute our true goodness and capacity to care for each other.
>
> We now need to have the audacity to widen the circle of healing—to tap into our passion, fierceness, and power to become agents of *tikkun olam* (the process of repairing and restoring the world). Part of *tikkun olam* involves men getting our act together—both as individual men and as brethren. At the same time, I believe that there is so much broken-ness in this world—on both the global and local levels. We have an opportunity, as Jewish men, to find ways to make a difference—for peace, for justice and for planetary sustainability. There's a robust and inspiring history of women's movements for peace and justice. Let men take a page from these inspiring and courageous women and find our own ways of co-creating a healthier world. Imagine the kinds of dialogues we might create—talking dialogues and maybe working dialogues, such Habitat for Humanity—with our African American brothers, our Muslim brothers, and our Christian brothers, as we are all sons of Abraham. Perhaps a focus on immigration issues, the growing economic disparity in the United States and the world, global warming, or water conservation.
>
> I can imagine the JMR creating an intergroup retreat to begin to explore this process or a father-son retreat. For example, Jewish and Muslim men and boys—all children of Abraham-Ibrahim—can study our common stories, which despite significant differences, can provide rich material for dialogue. For example, in the Torah portion about the binding of Isaac (*Akedah*), Isaac is identified as the son to be sacrificed and the Koran refers to the "favorite son," which

Muslim tradition identifies as Ishmael. Both Isaac and Ishmael, wounded by their common father, ultimately meet to mourn over Abraham's-Ibrahim's grave.

At one JMR, which focused on the themes of the Akedah, we did a drasho-drama that reenacted this scene. How much richer might it be to do that with our Muslim brothers! I can even imagine, some day, dancing in a dance troupe consisting of Jewish Israeli and Palestinian men focusing on peace and social justice. Or just simply dancing—that would be *tikkun* in and of itself.

I don't yet know what unique wisdom, insights, and perspectives we, as Jewish men, may bring to this work. But I believe that, together, we can begin to create a vision and let our wisdom move us forward. And the time to do that is now! The fact that Reb Shawn Zevit is co-producing this book with Harry Brod and Allen Spivack is writing his personal account of the JMR are affirmations of the positive direction of this men's movement.

When Reb Shawn showed up at the "Torah and the Deep Masculine" session at the 1993 Kallah, he was about to enter rabbinical school. He enthusiastically helped to co-create the exciting beginnings of our JMR work. Over these years, during which he graduated, was ordained and assumed a leadership role in the Reconstructionist movement, he helped bring bibliodrama to our men's work as he has brought his own creative contributions to a much wider scope of work in the larger Jewish world. Along the way, he has mentored other men including two beautiful step-sons. He embodies an emerging model of masculine leadership as he continues to contribute to the deepening of our JMR work, especially our vision of *tikkun olam*. I want to also *kvel* (take joyful pride) about his musical performance style—full of vitality and spirit—which I feel embodies the qualities of the renewed masculinity we are aiming at.

When Allen first attended the JMR in 1994, he was doing home renovation work that he described in his recollections. Over these years he changed his work—got a degree in social work and, helped to bring a renewed masculine perspective to that work —especially working with men who commit domestic abuse. He is a role model "brotherkeeper" in mentoring so many men—many of whom he has brought to the JMR. He has also co-led a number of the retreats. He brought his own sons, one of whom, Lev Natan, has grown into a mature and wise leader and mentor in his own right. Allen is indeed a *mensch*—a *mensch* among men!

It's a *machaya* (deep pleasure) to have deepening relationships with both of these men—and many others—over the years. It's one of the gifts of doing this work together. We've been able to continually include new men in our gatherings—at least a third of each year's attendees are new—while we have created this potent and poignant shared history together. For me, this shared history actually began during the Berkeley Kallah that Reb Shawn described above. As we offered each other blessings that we had wished our fathers had given us, Rabbi Phil Labowitz offered me an additional one. Conjuring up my father's spirit, he blessed me for continuing to take care of my mother. I was stunned, since most of us in the group hadn't known each other before the *kallah*. But, as it happens, Rabbi Phil had been a friend and also the hospice rabbi where my father Max (Mordechai Chaim) spent his final days. He gave the eulogy at my father's funeral

> and gave our family precious support and love. All I can say is that bringing his blessings into our men's work was a *machaya*! This shared history makes our JMR community more like a family and these men more like brothers!

The JMR offers men a new paradigm for both relating and relationships. The insufferable distance that men often feel between one another, toward their connections to Judaism, to Jewish practices or their pasts can begin to melt away as men discover new ways of seeing and believing and listening. There is a beautiful vignette that, for me, so poignantly captures the transforming and transformative quality of the JMR.

I remember it was a late Saturday afternoon at a JMR, and our *mishpacha* group (small discussion group) decided to meet in the hot tub at Elat Chayyim. We had just gotten to know each other at our first session on Friday night and here we were naked together in this hot tub! I noticed that one man was uncircumcised. The heat of the water relaxed me. We all sat quietly together for a few moments as we hummed a sweet *niggun* and clasped each others' hands. The conversation turned to our sexual identity and preferences, and I realized no one has ever asked me about this before nor had I discussed this with other men.

One man revealed that he is married but no longer had sex with his wife because he now knew he was gay. Another disclosed that he was a gay man and joked about finding someone to "hook up with" at the retreat. We soaked in this hot water and told stories to each other of our sexual discovery, pain and awakenings, from men who were gay, straight, bi-sexual, and celibate. We listened to each other and offered blessings for healing, joy and resolution because, in the end, that's all any of us really wanted for each other. The hot tub washed away, for me, a thousand generations of men who equated male intimacy with sexual passion. Some part of me accepted this belief too. But these men, my brothers, showed me how to escape from beliefs that kept all of us imprisoned in a narrow, stifling room.

Many men's lives have been transformed as they have entered the sacred space of the JMR on a Friday night and then emerged refreshed and renewed on Sunday afternoon. Men enter the retreat still drenched in the detritus of the past week and are reborn as men reshaped by new insights, new friends and profound love. For the first time, many men take risks and disclose painful life experiences that have remained hidden. Or they rise up and dance, perhaps awkwardly, as the *davenning* swirls around them. Or the man sitting nearby says a kind word of concern, "I understand what you're going through" and that brings tears to your eyes. As I've discovered, profound and inspirational moments often come at the most unexpected times.

15

Men and Dreams: Embracing Esau

Rabbi Rami Shapiro

Torah is, technically speaking, the Five Books of Moses, but saying this says so very little. It is only when we internalize it, that we experience the delights it contains. We internalize Torah when we understand Torah not as history, revelation, ritual law, or moral code (though it contains all of these), but as dream: a map of inner awakening projected outward as a vast family drama of a people moving from homelessness to home, and from slavery to freedom.

If Torah is simply a family history, it has little relevance to any other than the Jews. But if it is a historical fiction, that is if it uses the past to speak of the timeless, and if it uses the Jews as a paradigm for all humanity, then it is a book for all time and all peoples. I believe it is this and more.

I believe that Torah is a timeless archetypal drama not only of outward events but inner ones, not only of peoples in search of home and freedom, but of every person in search of the same. I believe that the stories Torah contains are contained in each human being. They are the mythic forms our lives follow; the timeless frames that help us grapple with meaning and purpose. And to understand them we have to eat them, internalize them, personalize them. Jacob and Esau, Isaac and Rebecca, Laban, Leah, Rachel, and the Angel of God, to single out the characters in the story that shall occupy us here, are not merely fictional characters or even historical persons, they are aspects of ourselves. And because they are aspects of us I speak of Torah as dream.

Reading Torah is like recalling a dream. In a dream there are protagonists and antagonists, ordinary events and magical ones, timeless truths and transient noise—and all of it is the reader, the dreamer. I read Torah as a dream, my dream. All the characters are me; all the places are me; all the holy and all the horror is me, aspects of myself (and yourself) that when read correctly can reveal the path to spiritual maturity, the path to the awareness of God in, with, and as all reality, and the capacity to live in a godly manner rooted in justice, compassion, and humility.

When I read the Torah as my dream and when I seek to see in Torah a map to my own spiritual unfolding, I cannot help but read Torah as a man. My masculinity is part of my conditioning, one of the most profound lenses through which I see the world. I cannot meet the world as a generic human but only as a man conditioned to understand myself and the world through the eyes of my father, grandfathers, and thousands of years of patriarchal rule. I see only what I am allowed to see by the lenses I wear. And so I am blind as well.

No two sets of lenses are ground exactly alike. No one sees exactly what another sees, and no one is blind exactly as another is blind. By sharing my sight and my blindness, I begin to grasp what is hidden from me. When I want to understand the nature of my spiritual life, I find myself returning again and again to the story cycle, the dream cycle, of Jacob and Esau and to the promise of being *Yisrael*, which in this context I take to be the fully realized male uniting masculine and feminine energies to manifest God's qualities of strength, compassion, and nurturing.

And that is what I intend to do with this essay: to share the dream of Jacob and Esau as I see it unfolding in me, as me. I do this not because this is the one true reading but in order to add to the seeing and push back the blindness. If the reader sees a bit more in this story, I am blessed. If readers see a bit more of themselves, I am doubly so.

A dream is never emptied of meaning. One works with a dream like an archeologist works a tell, slowly pealing away layer after layer of insight only to discover more layers underneath. Dreamers are never done with a dream until that dream is done with them. The dream of Jacob/Esau/Yisrael is not done with me yet. I don't pretend to offer the definitive interpretation of the story, nor do I claim to have uncovered all the nuances the story contains. All I can do is share what I find in this story at this point in my life. As with all great dreams, the insights deepen as the dreamer does. And, because Torah is a dream—my dream—my take on the story need not match that of anyone else's. My hope in sharing this dream and my understanding of it is not to convince readers of the rightness of my interpretation but to invite readers to find their own. Dream is the "gateway to heaven" (Genesis 28:17). It is through dream that one taps perennial truths filtered through (and often distorted by) the archetypes of the collective unconscious and the network of conscious associations attached to them. I take dreams seriously, though rarely literally. I read in my dreams as revelations from Wisdom, bubbling up into my waking mind and pointing me toward spiritual maturation. I read Torah the same way.

Torah, for me, is the dream of my people. The wisdom of Torah is not Jewish but human—not tribal but universal—but this wisdom needs a language in order to be articulated and shared. There are as many such languages as there are people to create them. Torah is one of them. Her stories and teachings are particular expressions of universal insight. The dreams of a people belong to that people; the wisdom of those dreams belongs to the world.

Because I am a Jew, Torah is my dream as well as that of my people. As a Jew I dream Torah, and only when I am willing to take my dream personally can it speak to me personally. As a dream Torah is mine to interpret, and, when I do interpret it, what I discover are truths about my life and myself.

I am not much interested in the historicity of Bible stories, or in the applicability of biblical ethics or mores to modern times. Still less am I inclined to see Torah's Bronze Age worldview as a viable alternative to modern science or the wisdom of the Enlightenment. The primary value of Torah for me—the reason I study it, teach it, and return to it over and over again—is that Torah's great narratives hold some of the deepest truths about human nature—my nature—and how best to work with it. This is nowhere more true than in the dream cycle of Jacob and Esau.

Jacob and Esau represent two sides of my psyche. Esau, the red, hairy, hunter-warrior beloved by the father, is my masculine side. Jacob, the smooth skinned, tent dweller beloved by the mother, is my feminine side. Jacob and Esau are both males for I am male, and I make no claim that they are universal archetypes of masculine and feminine energies. Esau is how the masculine develops in a male. Jacob is how the feminine develops in a male. Each is in need of the other—the masculine must embrace the feminine, and the feminine must embrace the masculine—but even in this unity of opposites there is differentiation: Jacob never becomes Esau, and Esau never becomes Jacob.

Both Esau and Jacob are capable of maturation, each becoming more like the other, but only Jacob has the capacity to become something new—*Yisrael*, the "God-wrestler"—which is why this dream cycle focuses on Jacob.

Here is what I remember of my first dream in this dream cycle:

> Rebecca, daughter of Bethuel the Aramean and sister of Leban the Aramean, is pregnant with twin boys. The twins battle within her womb, and she suffers greatly. She turns to God for an explanation, and God says, "Two nations are in your womb, two regimes from your insides shall be separated; the might shall pass from one regime to the other, and the elder shall serve the younger." (Genesis 25:23)

If Esau and Jacob are the two sides of my psyche, Rebecca is the feminine force that not only births me but also directs me toward becoming Yisrael. Throughout this dream cycle it is the power of the feminine (first as Rebecca, then as her brother Laban, and then as her niece Rachel) that moves me toward to becoming Yisrael and embracing Esau. The feminine is the active power in my maturation. While it may be God with whom I ultimately wrestle, it is the goddess who trains me for the fight.

Whether this is true for the reader or not, I cannot say. But for me the power of the feminine, both as my actual mother and more importantly as the *Shekhinah*, the presence of God, is the active spiritual force in my life. It is she who guides me, protects me, and pushes me to become what I can only dimly imagine.

As I said, the warring boys are the two sides of my male psyche. Esau, the older and more primitive, is the warrior male driven by hunger, greed, and desire, who longs only for the love of his father. Jacob, the younger and more cultivated, is the somewhat acculturated ego, who journeys from passive pawn to active trickster to a new kind of warrior, Yisrael, who reveals a fully realized male spirituality that no longer yearns to be loved but to love.

When Rebecca gives birth, the first to emerge is Esau. He is a wild man, filled with power but lacking discernment and direction. He is red—because he is driven by blood, passion, and strength—and hairy because his way in the world is through power and strength. Esau is the elder power, a more primitive aspect of myself. He is to be honored but not followed. He is, to loosely borrow from Sigmund Freud, my id and must be given direction by Jacob, my ego.

Jacob is so named because he emerges grasping the heel (*ekev*) of his brother. Jacob comes into the world, not by his own strength but by clinging to that of his brother. This will be their relationship for decades. Esau has power but lacks direction; Jacob has direction but lacks power. The two need one another, but before they can embrace one another each must find something of the other in himself. The masculine Esau must discover his feminine energy just as the feminine Jacob must develop his masculine energy. Each will do so in his own way, and, when they do, they can embrace and move beyond their warring rivalry.

As the boys grow up they could not be more different. Esau is a hunter, "a man of the field," while Jacob dwells in tents with the women, where he learns to cooks rather than hunt. The first values autonomy, freedom, and the wilderness of the forest and the field. The second values relationship, cooperation, and the community of the tent and the family. Their father Isaac prefers Esau, their mother Rebecca prefers Jacob, and in so doing reveal their dream natures to the readers. If Esau is the active masculine, Isaac is the passive masculine. If Jacob is the passive feminine, Rebecca is the active feminine.

Isaac does little in the Bible. He is a near victim of his father's homicidal faith. He uses his wife as a substitute for his mother (Genesis 24:67). He is easily tricked by his wife into blessing the wrong son. He has neither power nor direction. He is a man without inner reserves who latches on to Esau to feed him, just as Jacob clings to Esau to help birth him. The difference is that both Esau and Jacob will mature, while Isaac never does.

Isaac, I suspect, is the false masculine aspect of myself that must die before the greater journey toward spiritual maturity can begin. He is the pseudo-masculine who has the title of leadership but none of the power or skill to actually lead. Isaac is the good boy many fathers want their sons to be—the obedient son, obedient unto death, that will extend the father's power rather than challenge or usurp it. This is an unhealthy image of what a man can become. Isaac must die, but not just yet, and when he does die he must do so in a way that furthers the dream's unfolding.

Rebecca is the active feminine side of myself. She, like Isaac, operates in my unconscious. She is not the face I present to the world but the power that makes that face possible. Rebecca is a decision maker, a visionary, who dares to turn the status quo upside down in service to the greater maturation of Jacob into Yisrael. Yet she too must disappear from my dream. Jacob cannot mature under her tutelage. She can only move him forward; eventually he must act on his own.

I dreamed again.

> Many years have passed and the warring twins are now competing young men. One day Esau returns empty handed and exhausted from the hunt. He passes Jacob's tent and smells a stew his brother is preparing. He enters his brother's tent demanding, "Pour into me now some of that very red stew, for I am exhausted!" (Genesis 25:30). Notice he doesn't ask Jacob to provide him with food but demands that Jacob "pour it into him." While it was Esau's power that

> carried Jacob into the world, it is Jacob's power that sustains Esau in the world. Jacob must pour sustenance into his brother for Esau has not the strength to pour it in to himself.

Esau is outer-directed. His inner life is barren. Jacob is inner-directed and, as far as the dream tells us, has no life outside the tent. One might think that Esau could just brush his brother aside and take what he wants, but this is not his lot. Jacob's stew has to be purchased. The masculine cannot simply demand sustenance from the feminine. He must purchase it, and the price is his future dominance.

Jacob demands that his brother sell him his birthright. That is to say, the feminine Jacob, cook and tent dweller, says to the masculine Esau, "I will sustain you, but you must promise to cede dominance to me." The feminine does not ask the masculine to give up his power but only the possibility that, because of his power, he will play the dominant role between them. In other words, Jacob is saying: "You may live because of me but only in order to serve me."

It is important to note that Jacob makes this demand on his own. Just as I am surprised that Esau is so powerless in this dream, so I am surprised that Jacob is so powerful. That is why this dream is important. Esau realizes his limitations, and Jacob realizes a bit of his potential.

Because Esau has no interior insight, he sees no value in the birthright: "Look I am going to die, so of what use to me is a birthright?" (Genesis 25:32). The dream is silly on its face. Esau is home. He could walk into his own tent and find something to eat. He is not going to die from hunger. But Esau is driven by immediacy and prone to exaggeration. He wants what he wants, and he wants it now and cannot wait. The future is meaningless to him, and so the birthright passes to Jacob.

Jacob can make no use of the birthright in the moment, however. If it is useless to a starving Esau, it is of no more use to his brother. In fact, the birthright is of no value to either brother as long as their father Isaac lives. It pertains only to who will inherit once the father is gone. Torah is talking about my development as a man over time. While it would seem natural that the masculine side of the male would dominate, Torah is saying that nature must surrender to nurture, and the more thoughtful, cultivated, and feminine side of me must eventually triumph if I am to achieve the status of Yisrael, the spiritually integrated man.

Throughout my youth I tried to be Esau. I only wanted to please my father in the fields my father valued: work and sports. I failed at both. I had no talent for the family business and no skill at the family sports: baseball, football, and golf. I could not bring my father the game he loved. But, like Jacob, I excelled at women's work, at the work of the tent, especially learning and writing. My strength was shallow but my emotions ran deep, and I could talk. I felt more comfortable among the women than the men. And still do.

I dreamed again.

> Years have passed and Isaac is on his deathbed. The birthright is no longer Esau's, and Jacob will inherit his father's wealth, but Esau can still walk away

> with his father's blessing that all may know that the spirit of Isaac rests not with the feminine Jacob but with the masculine Esau. The blessing speaks a deeper truth than the birthright. The blessing speaks to interiority, while the birthright speaks to exteriority.
>
> Isaac summons Esau and commands him to take to the hunt and return with game for his father. "Then make me delicacies such as I love and bring them to me and I will eat, so that my soul may bless you before I die" (Genesis 27:4). Isaac's words are important because, through them, it is learned that Esau, too, has become a cook. He is to hunt *and* prepare the game for this father. Esau has matured and has begun the process of marrying masculine to feminine.
>
> Isaac, however, hasn't matured at all. Indeed he is something of a caricature of the younger Esau. Where the younger Esau came home empty handed from the hunt, Isaac is powerless to leave his tent and secure his food. Whereas the starving Esau demanded food from his brother, the power-starved Isaac demands it of his son. Where the shortsighted Esau was willing to barter his birthright for a bite of stew, the dim-sighted Isaac is willing to give his final blessing for the fleeting joy of a last meal. If Esau is the masculine cut off from the feminine and Jacob is the feminine cut off from the masculine, Isaac is the shell of a man cut off from both. While in time Jacob and Esau will learn to reconcile, Isaac is going to die as powerless on his bed as he almost died powerless on the altar of his father.
>
> Like Isaac and unlike Esau, Jacob also seems not to have grown. It is his mother who overhears Isaac's plan and spins the scheme to rob her eldest son of his rightful blessing, and it is his mother who calms his fears when he objects. Rebecca says to Jacob, "Go now to the flock and fetch me two choice young kids of the goats, and I will make of them delicacies for your father, as he loves" (Genesis 27:9).
>
> Here Jacob seems to have lost the ability to cook. Esau cooks, his mother cooks, but Jacob is reduced to fetching (not hunting) from the domesticated (not wild) animals his mother will turn into his father's special meal. Jacob is, if anything, less powerful now than when he extorted the birthright from his brother.

What might be made of this? If this is my dream—and it is—Torah is telling me that as Jacob I am only a puppet. If I do not leave the protective tent of my mother, I will lose even the skills I do have. I will become like Isaac. Rebecca knows this as well, and that is why she works behind the scenes, beneath the surface, pushing me—Jacob—toward my destiny: "Rebecca then took her older son Esau's clean garments, which were with her in the house, and clothed Jacob her young son. With the skins of the goat-kids, she covered his arms and his smooth-skinned neck" (Genesis 27:15–16).

The fact that Rebecca has access to Esau's clothes and that these clothes are kept in her house suggests that Esau too has a connection to the feminine. This may be why Rebecca is the real actor here. It is she who knows what is best for the clan and the future of the family. She knows Esau is a mighty warrior who can learn to soften himself, but she also knows that his clothing, his presence in the world, will always be that of a hunter/warrior and never that of a nurturer. He must be made to serve his brother but only if his brother can grow worthy of Esau's loyalty.

Jacob brings his mother's cooking to his father, and there follows the humorous scene in which Isaac recognizes the voice of Jacob but allows himself to be fooled by the smell of Esau. Why? I can only guess. Since this is my dream, my guess is this: Despite Esau's ability to grace his masculine energies with feminine ones, Isaac also knows that Esau cannot achieve the true harmony of masculine and feminine energies that is necessary to become the servant-leader (the future Yisrael) the people need. So he goes along with Jacob's trickery, hoping that someday he will not have to pretend to masculine strength but will have matured in that strength on his own.

In other words, Jacob, while as yet unproven and showing no sign of opening to the masculine energies so powerfully represented in his brother, is both Isaac's and Rebecca's choice for the future. They see in him what he cannot see in himself, the potential to become Yisrael, the divine androgyne, a fully integrated and individuated human being. So Isaac accepts the masquerade and blesses the second son as if he were the first.

When Esau returns to his father with his meal, he discovers the blessing has been given and his future is sealed. He must serve his brother. But the murderous rage that is to shortly overtake Esau does not just now come forth. Instead, this mighty hunter collapses in sobs of grief. His birthright is gone and so, too, his blessing. He has nothing of his father to sustain him when the old man dies.

Again it is Esau, red and hairy, who shows emotion. He cries, and he will cry again. He is not raw masculine energy only. Something has happened to him over his life that has allowed him to soften a little. At this point he is the more balanced of the brothers, and yet he is the one cut off from both father and mother.

It is important to note that what Esau wants above all else is the love of his father. Isaac never got Abraham's love and was perhaps incapable of giving love to either of his sons. He loved Esau, not for who he was or could become, but because of the food he could give him. It is what Esau could do for him that Isaac loved, not who Esau is in and of himself.

I suspect Esau knows this. That may be why the birthright is less important to him than this fatherly blessing. The birthright went to the firstborn simply because he was firstborn. It said nothing about his character or worth. The blessing was something else. While it was given to the firstborn, the content of what was given was up to the father. Isaac could have blessed Esau any way he saw fit, so that in that blessing Esau would at last know if his father's love was for him or only for what services he rendered.

The blessing was more than a sign of status in the community, it was a bond between father and son that would transcend the father's death. This is why Esau is crushed rather than angered by the loss of the blessing. This is why he begs his father for some blessing, even if it can not be the one he intended. "It doesn't matter that Jacob stole that blessing," Esau seems to be saying. "I don't care about that formality. I care about you and whether you love me. Show me that love, Father! Bless me, too!"

And at last, and perhaps for the first time in his life, Isaac acts on his own. He blesses his son from the heart saying, "Behold, the fatness of the earth shall be your dwelling and of the dew of the heavens from above. By your sword you shall live, but your brother you shall serve; yet it shall be that when you are aggrieved, you may cast off his yoke from upon your neck" (Genesis 27:39–40).

Esau is blessed with "the fatness of the earth." He will never go hungry even if the hunt goes poorly. The dew of the heavens will slack his thirst and make the earth fecund. With this, his father is healing the original wound Esau suffered at Jacob's hand when he lost his birthright because the hunt had gone poorly and he was hungry. Moreover, it links Esau to the feminine. The fatness of the earth is her fecundity. The dew is the milk of the Mother's breast. Esau is linked to the life-giving power of Mother Earth but only as a taker. The Mother will feed him always (just as he fed his father), but Esau will, unlike his brother Jacob, never come to be a feeder himself. This is as close as this masculine archetype will come to a divine union of masculine and feminine. He will take but have nothing to give.

Esau, Isaac tells him, will live by the sword, as a warlord, but it is living that is promised nonetheless. Isaac does not say "you will die by the sword," but "you will live by the sword." Just as heaven and earth will sustain you, your sword will protect you. Life, not death, is at the heart of Isaac's blessing of Esau. But this living by the sword is not really life sustaining.

Isaac's blessing assures Esau life and power. What it denies him is peace and love. Isaac is saying to Esau, "I cannot make you master of your brother, but I can protect you from becoming his slave. Serve him if what he asks of you is just, but free yourself from him if what he asks is unjust." In this blessing Isaac's love for Esau is clear. He has blessed him with sustenance and success and has promised him freedom if ever his self-esteem demands it. Esau now knows that his father does indeed love him.

I dreamed again.

> Now Esau harbored hatred toward Jacob because of the blessing with which his father had blessed him. (Genesis 27:41)

But why? If what Esau desired from his father was a clear expression of love, why did his receiving of it breed hatred toward Jacob?

The answer, perhaps, is this: Esau is not yet a mature male, integrating masculine and feminine energies and becoming the divine androgyne. He is moving in the direction of integration but has not achieved it. Even as he softens under his father's blessing he hardens against his brother's deception. He is learning to be loved, but he has not yet learned to love.

Rebecca hears from her servants that Esau is plotting to murder Jacob after Isaac dies, and again she takes action to save her youngest by sending Jacob to her brother Laban.

This is a crucial turning point in the unfolding of this dream-cycle. Jacob is powerless to act in the world. He must learn to live outside his mother's protection, but, as the feminine aspect of the male, he cannot enter directly into the masculine world. He needs a transitional world in which to grow into his masculine energies. This is why Rebecca sends Jacob to her brother, his maternal uncle.

Laban, whose name means *white* in contrast to Esau's *red*, is the fresh slate on which Jacob is to reinvent himself. As the maternal uncle Laban represents both mother and father, both the feminine and the masculine (if Laban has a wife she is absent from the story, making Laban's dual status all the more clear). Laban is powerful and wealthy in the ways of men, but he is Jacob's maternal uncle. And it is through Laban that Jacob learns to partner with the feminine by marrying Rachel and Leah rather than being dominated by it as he is by his mother.

I dreamed again.

> Jacob journeys to Haran. He walks from Beersheba toward Haran, from his mother's tent to his mother's brother's tent, from the feminine only to the first blending of feminine and masculine. This is the first time he is seen outside the tent and protection of his mother. It is an intermediate journey from the mother, the maternal-feminine, to the uncle, the maternal-masculine. One night he goes to sleep and dreams of a ladder linking earth and heaven. Angels are ascending and descending upon it.
>
> And the LORD stood beside him and said, "I am the LORD, the God of Abraham your father and the God of Isaac.... Know that I am with you and will keep you wherever you go, and will bring you back to this land; for I will not leave you until I have done what I have promised you." Then Jacob woke from his sleep and said, "Surely the LORD is in this place—and I did not know it!" And he was afraid, and said, "How awesome is this place! This is none other than the house of God, and this is the gate of heaven." (Genesis 28:13–17)

The ladder unites heaven and earth just as Laban unites masculine and feminine and foreshadows the unification of human and divine energies in the transformation of Jacob into Yisrael. God promises to protect Jacob, but Jacob is still afraid. Why? Because, thus far, it is his mother who has protected him. Can he trust this God? Indeed God's protection appears to be conditional for God says he will stay with Jacob only until he is finished with him. Then what? Is Jacob a pawn in God's plan as Jacob seems to be in his mother's? Jacob is afraid, but he journeys on.

What can be made of God's conditional promise? God is the fully integrated masculine/feminine reality out of which I come that I might realize that integration in myself and thus become the divine androgyne. God is an outer projection of my inner promise. Thus, God's concern with me is temporary and situational.

God is concerned with me only until God has finished with me, only until God has brought about what God wills in and through me. What does God will?—that I become the divine androgyne, Yisrael, one who wrestles with God and human and survives. Once Jacob can hold his own against God, he no longer has need of God. He will have become the vehicle for godliness that God desires.

Knowing none of this, however, Jacob finds no comfort in God's promise, yet he does not abandon his journey. This is Jacob's first act of heroism. He has not defeated fear, but he has not succumbed to it either.

The dreaming continues.

> Jacob journeys on to Haran where he meets his cousin Rachel watering her flocks. This is the first time in the story that the work of a woman is seen outside the tent, and the work she does is distinctly masculine since all the other shepherds in this story are men. Just as his maternal uncle Laban brings the feminine into the masculine, so Rachel brings the masculine into the feminine. Jacob is at last coming into the world of integrated, if not yet fully realized, human beings.

In this dream Jacob is me, and in Rachel I see a female version of myself or what I might become if I can learn, as she as learned, to be true to my masculinity (as she is true to her femininity) and yet cultivate my feminine energies as she has cultivated her masculine energies. This is why Jacob falls in love with Rachel at first sight. Falling in love with her as other is a first step to discovering her within himself.

Jacob asks Laban for Rachel's hand in marriage. Jacob is negotiating with his transitional mother for a new relationship with his feminine energy. Laban cannot, however, simply give Rachel to Jacob. Jacob must work for her, that is, he must earn her by developing his masculine skills and energies under Laban's tutelage. This parallels the price Esau had to pay for the stew Jacob was cooking. What is desired always carries a price.

So Jacob agrees to work for his uncle for seven years in exchange for Rachel. At the end of his labors he is married, but when he wakes in the morning following his wedding night he finds it is Rachel's sister, Leah, that he has married and with whom he has had sex.

Laban's tricking of Jacob mirrors Rebecca's tricking of Isaac. Jacob was a pawn in each drama, and it is important to note that the same side of Jacob's family plays out both tricks: his mother and his mother's brother. Rebecca and Laban, sister and brother, play the important role of trickster: through their actions they overturn the natural order of things. Isaac expected to bless Esau; Jacob expected to marry Rachel. By turning things upside down, the trickster initiates a deepening of the dream that symbolizes a new stage in the story of the hero's development.

To begin to understand this new stage of the dreaming, one has to understand the role of Leah, and to do that the following must be recalled: First, Rebecca has two sons, and her brother has two daughters (his sons are not named and play no role in the story). Second, Leah is the older of the two daughters of Laban just as Esau is the older of the two sons of Rebecca. In the world of Rebecca and her brother Laban, the older son rules and the older daughter marries first. In Torah's dream the trickster siblings, Rebecca and Laban, overturn the first rule and stop Jacob from overturning the second. Third, Rachel is the barren sister, while Leah is the fecund sister.

So who is Leah? Leah is the female version of Esau. Where Esau is all masculine, the great producer of meat for Isaac, Leah is all feminine, the great producer of sons for Jacob. Leah, not Rachel, brings forth the masculine from within Jacob. Yet Jacob loves Rachel and not Leah. That is to say Leah is not the feminine energy Jacob needs to move him toward becoming Yisrael. While he must become a nurturer, he cannot become a mother.

What we see in the dream of the two sisters is a recapitulation of the earlier dream of the twin brothers. The sisters vie for Jacob's affection, just as Jacob and Esau vied for the affection of their father. There is even a story mirroring Esau's demand for stew: Leah's son Reuben is out in the field gathering *dudaim*, a fruit thought to induce fertility. The fact that the son brings this home to his mother is meaningful. Reuben is gathering rather than hunting; he is doing the work of the female rather than the male; he is Jacob-like in this scene representing the masculine power of Leah in the world.

When Rachel sees that her sister has the dudaim, she demands one just as Esau demanded stew from Jacob. Leah refuses, saying that Rachel has Jacob's love and that is enough. But Rachel offers to pay Leah by allowing her to sleep with Jacob that night, though it is her night to be with him. The deal is struck, and, when Jacob comes in from the field, Leah instructs him that he is hers for the night, and Jacob goes to her bed. Again Leah takes Rachel's place in Jacob's bed, but this time he is aware of the bargain. Leah sells her fecundity to her sister, just as Esau sold his birthright to his brother.

Jacob is still passive, however. His maternal uncle manipulates him, and his wives sell him one to the other. And yet something is happening within him, because Jacob is laboring in the field, tending the sheep, and making a fortune for Laban. He is, under the guidance of the maternal masculine, slowing learning what it is to be a man.

I dreamed again.

> After years of barrenness, Rachel at last conceives and gives birth to a son, Joseph. This signals a huge change in Jacob. He has had many sons with Leah by this time, but it is the birth of Joseph that triggers a new stage in his maturation. Joseph is the product of Jacob's union with Rachel, the union of his masculine side with his desired feminine side. Jacob has already learned to be creative with Leah, and, now that he done so with Rachel as well, he has achieved a new level of integration and is ready to move out from under the protection and control of the feminine altogether. He has internalized both aspects of the feminine and no longer needs the male carrier of the feminine that Laban symbolizes. Jacob can carry the feminine for himself, within himself, as a vital and creative part of himself.
>
> Thus it is that as soon as Joseph is born Jacob demands his freedom from Laban "that I may go to my place and my land" (Genesis 30:25). This is the first

time that Jacob speaks of belonging anywhere. Hitherto, he is simply moved from place to place by his mother and his mother's brother. But now that he has made a child with Rachel, he discovers his own sense of self and place. (The meaning, I hope, is clear: Jacob is coming into his own.)

Then follows a dream of great magic in which Jacob grows a great flock of sheep for himself, and steals away with his wealth and his wives and children without saying anything to Laban. This mirrors his flight to Haran from Beer-sheba to escape from Esau. (In other words, while Jacob has now fully developed his feminine side he has yet to completely cultivate his masculine. He cannot confront Laban just as he could not confront Esau.)

Laban races after Jacob and, when he catches up with Jacob, he demands, among other things, the return of his gods that he claims Jacob has stolen. Laban's gods represent his potency, and the fact that he worships them as objects outside himself reveals that he himself is not fully matured. Unbeknownst to both uncle and nephew, Rachel, not Jacob, has stolen the gods. She hides them by sitting on them and pretending to be menstruating. This is an act of ultimate disrespect. Rachel is declaring the death of god as fetish and idol. She, perhaps more than any other figure in the Torah, frees herself from worship of the other, showing utter disrespect for the gods by trumping her real capacity to create life over their false claims to do so.

If Rachel represents my active feminine side, she is saying this: Free yourself from false gods and take ownership of your own creative energies. Until you do this you are not yet ready to confront the true God.

Laban brings about the reconciliation with Jacob in this dream. Laban knows that running away is not going to bring Jacob the maturity he needs. He must confront his uncle and make a treaty with him, that is, he must confront his mother (in the form of his maternal uncle) and negotiate a deal that honors her even as it allows him to move on without her. The fact that Laban is a maternal uncle allows him to function as a father figure as well, so this treaty makes peace with both Jacob's active mother and passive father. Jacob is leaving these unbalanced forces behind and moving into greater and greater circles of wholeness. This, coupled with the death of the gods at the hand of Rachel, removes all external forces from Jacob with one exception: Esau. Jacob has not yet developed his raw, red masculinity, so Esau is still an external concern to him and a threat to the safety of all he loves.

When Laban departs, Jacob sends messengers ahead of his caravan to find his brother Esau and to buy his favor with gifts of flocks and slaves. In other words, Jacob has learned the power of bargaining and treaty making and imagines that his new-found skill will set his world aright. Would that it were that simple.

I dreamed again.

Esau has become a mighty warlord and marches toward Jacob at the head of 400 soldiers. He wants nothing from Jacob and rejects all that Jacob offers him. He wants nothing but Jacob himself.

> Jacob fears for his life and the lives of his family and household. He sends more gifts to Esau. For the first time in his life, he puts the concerns of others in front of his own. He also prays to God for salvation, but God remains silent. This is important. God had promised to protect Jacob until He was through with him, and now God is silent. Could it be that God is through with Jacob?

By not responding to Jacob's plea for protection the dream is telling me that there is nothing more God need do with Jacob. Jacob has achieved a new status and no longer needs the protection or guidance of an externalized deity. He is ready to draw on the God within that emerges when the male has integrated his masculine and feminine energies. Jacob has done this, and the birth of Joseph and then Benjamin symbolizes it. He just doesn't realize it.

> To protect his household Jacob sends his family and possessions across Jabbok's Ford that he might confront his brother alone—no running away here—no tricks or treaties. Jacob must face his twin. That night "a man wrestled with him until the break of dawn" (Genesis 32:24). This man, who is God or an angel of God, is the complex of inner masculine forces that Jacob must wrestle and subdue. It is his final test.

Jacob hold's his own against the man. He doesn't defeat him, nor is he defeated by him. In other words he has achieved a dynamic balance. The man dislocates Jacob's hip but cannot get free of Jacob's grip. Just as Jacob held to the heel of Esau, he now holds to the angel of God. And just as Esau pulled Jacob out of his mother, so this man pulls him out of his old clinging self. As dawn comes the man begs to be released, but Jacob demands a blessing first.

Jacob has earned this blessing, just as he earned his marriage to Rachel and his wealth from Laban. This is not the Jacob who exploited his brother's weakness for a birthright or his father's blindness for a blessing. Gone are the deceiver and the trickster. Jacob is now a new man, one who has integrated his masculine and feminine energies to become something new. But he has not consciously realized this new status. He needs the man to point it out to him.

The fact that the man cannot survive the light of day suggests that he dwells in the night realm of Jacob's unconscious. This man is Jacob's spiritual twin, just as Esau is his physical twin (as is made plain when Jacob says that seeing Esau's face is like seeing God's face!).

Instead of blessing Jacob, the angel asks Jacob to reveal his name. A name represents one's sense of self, and Jacob responds, "Jacob," still not realizing he has changed. The man doesn't change Jacob's name but announces that it has been changed. Jacob is no longer the person he was. He is someone new. He is no longer the powerless heel-clinger but Yisrael, one who struggles with God and human and survives (Genesis 32:28).

With the announcement of Jacob's new name and status, the man departs, and Jacob/Yisrael raises his eyes to see Esau charging toward him at the head of 400 warriors.

God and human are the ultimate opposites. Each represents a world unlike the other. Jacob/Yisrael has learned to survive in both. It is of note that he does not defeat the man, nor does the name Yisrael carry with it a victor's role. Yisrael is one who struggles with God, not one who defeats God. There is no need to defeat God, all one need do is not surrender to God.

"Esau ran toward him, embraced him, fell upon his neck, and kissed him; then they wept" (Genesis 33:4). Esau initiates the action at dawn just as the man initiated the action during the night. Why? Because Jacob, the ego of the dream, cannot control unconscious events but only respond to them courageously. The man and Esau are to the masculine side of Jacob/Yisrael what Rachel and Leah are to his feminine side: projections he has learned to embrace as part of himself. Esau runs to his brother and hugs him. He falls on Jacob's neck with unabashed love. And then, and only then, do the twins weep. As Jacob has matured from the powerless heel-clinger to the powerful Godwrestler, Esau has moved from the red, devouring masculine to the weeping, protective masculine. The two have found balance within themselves and now can find love between themselves.

But the dream does not end here.

> Esau says to Jacob that he will travel beside him, as brothers should, that they might make their way home together. On the surface this makes sense: Esau is a warlord with 400 warriors at his command. He can protect his brother who travels without armed escort, easy prey to caravan raiders. Yet Jacob/Yisrael refuses. He no longer needs protecting, either from Esau or from God.

What is crucial to the conclusion of this dream is not simply Jacob/Yisrael's capacity to defend himself but the reason he gives his brother for not wishing to walk with him side by side: "My lord knows that the children are tender, and the nursing flocks and cattle are upon me; if they will be driven hard for a single day, then all the flock will die. Let my lord go ahead of his servant; I will make my way at the slow pace according the gait of the drove before me and the gait of the children, until I come to my lord at Seir" (Genesis 33:13–14).

Jacob, the pawn of his mother, has now become a mother-like figure himself: guarding the well-being of the nursing children and calves. Jacob the powerless has now become Yisrael the Godwrestler, who walks not at the pace of the swift and strong but at the gait of the slow and weak. Esau marches; Yisrael limps. In the world of Esau, such a limp is a mark of weakness, but, in the world of Yisrael, it is a mark of strength.

Esau has achieved a level of balance, but he is still the red warrior. He travels with men, and no mention is made of his wives, children, or flocks. He moves hard and fast and is a force to be feared. Yisrael limps. He chooses the slow pace of the nursing calves and babies to the military cadence of the warrior. Yisrael is not the feminized man but the fully integrated androgyne. He has achieved the marriage of masculine and feminine, human and divine. He has become the divine *anthropos*, the fully realized human. He displays his power, not by leading but by serving, not by walking ahead but by walking among and perhaps even behind.

Yisrael's internalized ideal of servant leadership is represented outwardly by Jacob's limp. Jacob is the wounded warrior. He is imperfect. His way in the world, his walk, is hampered by his wound. One would expect him to be healed in the end, to achieve the standard of perfection expected of men, but this is not Torah's message.

Torah is saying that the fully realized human being is not perfect in the sense of being without imperfection but whole in the sense of including imperfection. Jacob/Yisrael's compassion for the nursing ones doesn't come from outer strength (represented by Esau and his soldiers) but from outer weakness, his wound. Esau has no wound and cannot relate to the weak. Jacob earned his wound by wrestling with the strongest of the strong, that he might walk at the pace of the weakest of the weak. This is his final unification, his final integration.

Yisrael is the archetype of the fully realized male. He is a warrior who can hold his own against angels and God in the spirit world and a limping servant of the children and cattle who nurtures life in the material world.

I have devoted a lot of time to this dream because it nurtures me. It is for me the ultimate map to my own spiritual maturation.

If I am to embrace Esau, and tap into the pure red energy of the masculine without becoming a warlord myself, I must learn to marry Rachel and Leah within myself. I must learn to make an honest peace with Laban. I must learn not simply to be mothered but to become a mother/father myself. For unless and until I can do this, no man will appear, no wrestling will occur, and no transformation will be realized and lived.

I yearn to achieve my potential as Yisrael, but it must be earned. I have tried to coerce it, to steal it, to trick others into giving it to me, but in the end I will have to wrestle with God alone to earn it—or die trying.

To embrace Esau is the final stage of male spiritual growth, not the first. It is the culmination of much inner work and not the catalyst for it. Seeking to imitate Esau with pseudo-rituals of red masculinity without first embracing the mother and marrying the feminine within is a cheap grace that leaves one sweaty but unchanged. I worry that much of what passes for male spirituality is only Jacob dressing up as Esau to fool the father. It is easy, and fun, and one can blame the mother (women) if things go wrong, but it isn't transformative.

What men need is a deep and challenging path to Yisrael, the fully realized and integrated male. Men need to leave home and marry the active feminine. They need to make a treaty with the inner energies of mother and father in all their guises. Men need to face the red warlord who they think comes to slay them. Men need to call out to God, the final source of external protection, and find only silence. They need to stand alone and face their demons and meet the man who, if they are strong enough to hold on, tells them they are not who they were but at last who they could come to be. And then men need to embrace their brothers, to love their red and hairy sides, and yet to put them in their places, that they might take up their own places at their own paces and nurture those who need their love and protection.

So now the question is "How?" How does one meet these needs? I wish I could offer a neat package: Twelve Steps to an Integrated Male, or some such thing. But the truth is there is no path to be packaged and purchased, and pretending there is robs one of the true masculine quality of this process.

Jacob didn't leave home because it was good for him. He wasn't seeking wholeness or integration. He was fleeing for his life. He may not have been fully cognizant of the danger he was in, but his mother knew. Esau, the wild side was going to murder the greater potential and, in so doing, kill all hope for its own transformation as well. Men will only move toward wholeness when the lack of wholeness threatens to kill them.

Some men have been there. I have been there. I remember specific moments of such intense anger (really self-loathing projected on and directed at loved ones), where I did real violence to another person. I remember anger that excused and perpetuated such violence; violence that broke walls and hearts. I was out of control. Esau was tearing me apart and hurting those I loved—those he loved as well, though he was too wild with hate to notice. This is the first step out of the madness—experiencing the madness.

I was so appalled at who I was and what I had done that I had to run away to save my life. I needed distance from Esau (yes, he was/is inside of me, but psychological distance is possible). I turned to therapists, to friends, to loved ones. I began to see that there was more to me than him. That is the second step—seeing, glimpsing the something more. This is Jacob dreaming the greater unity of earth and heaven.

Then one has to travel. One has to fall in love with feminine. The danger here is mistaking She Who Is Within for a woman who is without. Some run into the arms of a lover or a mother thinking that this external woman will save them from themselves. But this doesn't work. They will only project their feminine onto someone else and never discover it in and as themselves. So, one wanders in search of the feminine. Perhaps one takes up some skill associated with the feminine: painting, for example, or dance or pottery—something centering. In my case it was chanting the names of God.

At first I did this by using the names I knew, masculine names. I found the chanting itself to somehow open me to something other. In time new names came to me, feminine names, and I found myself in dialogue with the divine mother, God manifest as the feminine within me as well as around me. This is the third step—calling to the feminine within and without.

And then comes the wrestling—wrestling with the other or wrestling with names or the lack of names or the new names. All one can do here is hold on. When one encounters the divine feminine, one is not in control. One has no idea where this will lead. One can fight her and fight her, but, in the end, the wrestling just goes on until one is ready to change, to become Yisrael. This is not one's choice but her's. This is not a matter of one's own will but of her fierce grace. She wrenches one's thigh; she leaves one limping, broken, wounded, and more alive than ever before. But this is not a step. This is not something one does. This is not a process one can package or a seminar one can attend or a drum circle one can join. This is true spiritual chaos. One is no longer who one was. There is a moment, and one that can last years, when one knows the old name doesn't fit but has not yet heard the new name. One limps, nameless, for however long it takes to be stripped of the last vestige of the old. And then one changes. Or, rather, one is changed.

The change is marked with tears, reconciliation, and forgiveness. One finds oneself filled with compassion for the old self and all selves. One finds oneself drawn to the nursing infants and calves, not to protect them only but to nurse them oneself. Now one embraces Esau and channels his power in service to the powerless. Now one is whole, though one cannot point to the moment one became whole. Now one knows the name; one is Yisrael.

16

FINDING THE LIGHT— *KIDDUSH LEVANAH*: A RITUAL OF RENEWAL FOR JEWISH MEN

RABBI KERRY M. OLITZKY

Introduction: A Ritual for Men

Borrowing from the traditional ritual of *Kiddush Levanah* (consecrating the moon), this article is designed to provide a context for men to get together that includes the regular celebration of an unusual and engaging ritual. While public rituals have been part of the core of Jewish life and living, few have been identified as decidedly for men only, although feminist critics will argue rightfully that that was the main message of classical Jewish tradition for many generations. Through making this guide available and providing easy access to the ritual of *Kiddush Levanah,* my goal is to provide a means through which men can begin to reclaim their places in the Jewish community without eclipsing the progress made on behalf of women during the course of the last 50 years.

For some communities of men, the celebration of *Kiddush Levanah* will provide them with a reason to get together each month. For others, it will help to extend what has come to be the common fare in synagogue men's clubs and brotherhoods. Bagels and breakfast are no longer enough to build bridges among men. Like women, men look for rituals of meaning to anchor their lives. By reclaiming this ritual, men can join together for transcendent moments that they thought were never before possible!

What are some of the social-religious implications of the new ritual?

It is clear to me that this is a leadership ritual, emerging out of a time when men were the sole leaders of the Jewish community, even if a few women could be named as leaders. As a result of male leadership, women claimed *Rosh Chodesh* as their own. But times have changed. The makeup of leadership in the Jewish community has changed. Now, the roles have nearly reversed. Women, particularly in the liberal community, have emerged as significant Jewish leaders, nearly eclipsing the role of men entirely. Thus, *Kiddush Levanah* has the potential to now function for men as *Rosh Chodesh* groups once functioned for women, providing them with a specific role in the community and affirming the importance of the men who participate in it.

Why Have Some Jewish Men's Groups Adopted This Ritual?

For many years women have gotten together to celebrate *Rosh Chodesh.* Many say that the marking of *Rosh Chodesh* allows them to express themselves in ways that other aspects of Jewish tradition cannot. They have found that getting together regularly within the framework of a monthly Jewish ritual helps them to bond together as women with women. Men want to get together to share their common needs and striving as well. In recent years, the nascent Jewish men's movement has taken *Kiddush Levanah* as its rallying point. A growing number of men's groups have adopted this ritual, because they desire to engage in a monthly ritual of personal renewal that connects them to a community of other Jewish men and that does not bring them into conflict with Jewish women who seek such an expression in the celebration of *Rosh Chodesh*. In *Kiddush Levanah* they find a complementary celebration.

Many among the current generation of Jewish men in our synagogues do not resonate with the familiar programs undertaken by men's groups and synagogue brotherhoods. This is particularly true for men who have begun to find an avenue for their spiritual yearnings in private but have not yet found a path for it in Jewish communal living. For men, the *Kiddush Levanah* ritual helps to provide a nexus for the private life of the spirit and its public counterpart to meet.

It's true that men do not make rituals easily. Unlike what is evident in the women's movement, there has not been a groundswell of activity among men in the form of creating rituals to mark those passages that are unique to men. Some will incorrectly argue that most of Jewish ritual does that, and, therefore, there is not a need to do so. While it is true that most of Jewish ritual evolved through a male prism, little of it can be described as indigenous male activity. The renewal of the *Kiddush Levanah* ritual provides one of the first answers to this dilemma and hopefully will lead the way to others.

How to Use This Ritual Guide

For those who may be unfamiliar with *Kiddush Levanah* or are accustomed to working with a *moreh derekh* (guide) in the form of a rabbi or teacher to direct them through the intricacies of Jewish life, the ritual of *Kiddush Levanah* may seem difficult and somewhat cumbersome. It is true that some Jewish ritual is difficult and takes time to learn. But this ritual has the inherent potential to speak individually from the very first time each person experiences it. Nevertheless, its depth of meaning will increase over time as individuals become more comfortable with it.

Whether participants choose to do the ritual in Hebrew or English (or a combination, which I suggest), they should be familiar with the text and its context, particularly if they are responsible for leading the group. The leader may want to prepare an index card that highlights the elements of the ritual until he becomes more fully familiar with them. Or he may want to invite different individuals to take responsibility for one or more of the 15 individual steps, as I have outlined. One should feel free to use the material as written or to augment the ritual with other elements that are personally meaningful to Jewish men. If one chooses to invite others to participate in the ceremony, the individual assignments should vary from month to month. This would allow all of the men in the community to become familiar with all of the aspects of the ritual. If it is possible, the group leader (an assignment that should probably also change each month) may want to meet with each individual prior to the evening's program to help him prepare the assigned section so that each section leader knows how the whole ritual fits together.

As an alternative, as the group makes its way through the ritual, they may choose to focus on one of the elements in the ritual (probably in successive order) each month. This will allow the group to move through the steps in the ritual so an individual element can be highlighted. By using this method, after a little over a year, the group will have focused on each of the steps in the ritual in depth.

There are twelve lunar months in the Jewish calendar. Each of them has either 29 or 30 days. Since the lunar year thus totals 354 days, while the solar year amounts to 365, it is necessary to periodically add an extra month in order to reconcile them. Approximately once every three years, a 13th month (called *Adar* II) is added following *Adar* I. With this addition of *Adar* II, the year is designated as a leap year. That will mean that some of the program years will include 13 opportunities for *Kiddush Levanah*, rather than only 12.

A Ritual of Renewal

What is *Kiddush Levanah*?

Like their ancestors before them, many people are enchanted with the mysterious. The moon glows in the sky and casts its glow on them. It may even beckon them to dance in its light. The ritual of *Kiddush Levanah* (alternatively called *Birkat Levanah,* blessing of the moon, among Sephardic Jews) is performed when the moon is clearly visible in the sky. Throughout its history, the Jewish community has maintained a fascination with the moon. Some have even suggested that Jewish destiny can be measured by the constant changes in the moon. According to Jewish tradition, *Kiddush Levanah* reflects and is a manifestation of the longing for redemption and for an intimate relationship with God. It is where one of the religious myths of Judaism finds concrete expression. It is not moon worship. Rather, it is a recognition that, just as the moon reflects the light of the sun, one can potentially reflect the light of the Divine. More than anything else, people want to believe that, wherever Divine light shines, evil cannot exist. So they affirm the moon's regular appearance in their lives as a sign that goodness exists, that it and they along with it have the potential to overcome evil. The moon provides the foundation for the entire Jewish calendar. The Jewish calendar's months are fixed by the cycle of the moon, while the years are fixed by the earth's revolution around the sun. This coordination of lunar and solar phenomena ensures that the Jewish holidays will occur in their proper seasons as specified in the Bible (i.e., *Sukkot* in the fall, *Pesach* in the spring), even though their dates in the secular civil calendar, which is based solely on the earth's movement around the sun, differ each year. As a result, just by looking up in the sky, one can get a rough idea of a particular day in the lunar month.

According to the *Talmud*, any person who witnesses an important natural object or event—such as seeing a lofty mountain, great desert, vast ocean, falling star, rainbow, blossoming tree, or bolt of lightning—is required to say a blessing (Babylonian *Talmud*, Berakhot 54a). But it is not enough to silently acknowledge such things, to emphatically say "wow," or even to recite the traditional formula for blessing (and filling in the appropriate subject matter). The appearance of the new moon provides people with an individual and spiritually disciplined opportunity to offer praise to the Creator. But the ritual also provides the Jewish people with a symbol of its capacity to regenerate itself much in the same way as the moon seems to do each month. It allows people to witness and affirm the reliability and constancy of nature and make a personal connection with it. Because the moon wanes and grows fuller, it gives a sense of the continuing process of creation. It reminds people that God is still at work in the world. So they are encouraged to join in the partnership.

The mystics, who relate every aspect of the natural world to an emanation of the Divine, associate the moon with the *Shekhinah*, God's indwelling presence. The *Shekhinah* is part of the lowest and most accessible of the *sefirot* (the Jewish mystical system of the metaphysical emanations of the Divine). It is this aspect of God that is welcomed again with this ritual.

Performing This Ritual of Renewal

How

Before people put their own creative spin on *Kiddush Levanah*, they should understand the traditional approach to its observance. Such an approach provides them with an entry point for the ritual. The ritual, specifically the recitation of the blessing of praise, which is its main feature, should be performed while standing: people are welcoming God's presence in the form of the *Shekhinah*, and such a posture reflects the stance to be taken when one is greeting a sovereign ruler. Since it is a community celebration as much as it is a celebration of community, people are encouraged to say the blessing in the context of a *minyan*, but it may be done with as few as three people. Party clothes should be also worn. Those who say it following *Tishah b'Av* should remember to put their leather-soled shoes back on (if they were taken off for the observance of the holiday). Even the traditional requirements are flexible: one may still fulfill the *mitzvah* of *Kiddush Levanah* even if these specific requirements cannot be met.

When

The blessing should be recited at night following the evening service, when one benefits most from the light of the moon. This is also in keeping with the general principle of Jewish ritual that suggests that one recite a more common blessing before reciting a less common one. However, one should recite *Kiddush Levanah* before midnight. Otherwise, one might be tempted to fall asleep having completely forgotten to perform the ritual! If one can participate in a *minyan* for *Kiddush Levanah* prior to the evening service but fears that the *minyan* will quickly disperse immediately after the evening service, or if it looks like the moon will be covered by clouds by the end of the evening service, then one is encouraged to say the blessing before the start of the evening service. One can see how flexible the *halakhic* requirements are for this ceremony.

The blessing of the moon usually takes place between the 7th and 15th days of the Hebrew month, while it is waxing and not waning. However, authorities differ as to the earliest or latest day in the month when it may be said. Maimonides ruled that *Kiddush Levanah* is permitted as early as 24 hours after the moon has first been seen. (The first appearance of the moon is called the *molad.*) As a result, it is customary in Israel to say it immediately after the appearance of the moon. The only firm principles are that the ritual must take place after the molad and only as the moon is increasing in the sky. Thus, it should not take place during the second half of the month, when the moon appears to be growing smaller.

Authorities also disagree as to the impact of *Shabbat* and holidays on the performance of the ritual. Some people like to recite *Kiddush Levanah* on *Motza'ei Shabbat* (Saturday night) or *Motza'ei Yom Tov* (evening immediately following a holiday) while still in a celebratory mood and dressed for the occasion. Even if one says the blessing during the middle of week, however, one is encouraged to put on dress clothes to welcome the *Shekhinah* into our midst. But if 10 days have already passed in the month, then one should not wait until the evening after *Shabbat* or a holiday. However, the blessing should not be said on *Layl Shabbat* (the evening of *Shabbat*) or *Layl Yom Tov* (the evening of a holiday) so that one does not mix the joy of two occasions, another standing principle of ritual. Some explain that this restriction is imposed because one has already greeted God with *kiddush* (over wine). Others explain that it is because supplications such as those of *Kiddush Levanah* are not permitted on *Shabbat* or *Yom Tov*. Some suggest that saying *Kiddush Levanah* on *Shabbat* or *Yom Tov* might force a person to walk beyond the traditional limits of *Shabbat* or holiday walking. For all these reasons, it is strongly discouraged. Nevertheless, these same authorities suggest that if *Layl Shabbat* or *Yom Tov* is the only opportunity that one has to say the blessing, it is permitted. For different reasons, one should not recite it before *Tishah b'Av*. Some extend this by suggesting that one should also not recite *Kiddush Levanah* following a fast day. Others do not recite it any time in *Tishrei* before *Yom Kippur*, because they are uneasy during those days in anticipation of the impending judgment. But there are individuals in some communities who intentionally recite it at that time in order to gain an extra mitzvah before standing before God on *Yom Kippur*. There is much flexibility and room for the creative interpretation and application of the ritual.

Where

Just as one would not remain inside but rather go out to greet a sovereign ruler, one should go out of doors to recite *Kiddush Levanah*, facing east toward Jerusalem. According to Judah Halevy, the medieval Jewish poet, whenever one prays, if one is unable to determine the direction of Jerusalem, then one should direct one's heart to the holy city. For many, Jerusalem is always in the center of the world. The blessing should be said in an open area in order to fully benefit from the moon's light. The ritual is performed outside as a way of reclaiming the connection to nature that is sometimes lost to city dwellers. If it is not possible to go outside, then it should be recited at a window or near an open door so that the moon can be seen and its light can be enjoyed. One should not recite the blessing under a roof. Rather one should stand under the heavens, because one is receiving the *Shekhinah*. However, according to rabbinic authorities, one should not go outside if the place is unsavory, if one does not feel well enough to do so, or if one lives in a neighborhood where it would be unseemly or dangerous to do so. Perhaps this is a challenge that the tradition makes for people. If the neighborhoods are dirty, then they should join together to clean them up. If the neighborhoods are dangerous, then they have to work to make them free of crime. And if they are uncomfortable with their neighbors of other religious and ethnic backgrounds, then they have to extend a hand of friendship to them.

If the moon is covered by clouds or any other obstruction that completely obscures its light, one should not recite the blessing. Instead, one should wait until the moon can be seen. However, if there is enough light available to discern objects usually distinguishable by moonlight, one may recite the blessing. One should not begin reciting the blessing unless one feels that the moon will remain in sight for the duration of the ritual. But if one starts the blessing while the moon is visible and it then becomes covered, one may continue to recite the blessing until its conclusion.

Often the moon is visible during the day, particularly at twilight. However, *Kiddush Levanah* may not be recited unless the sun has fully set.

Special Cases

Those in mourning are generally exempt from the ritual, unless there is no other time than shiva (seven days of mourning) for them to say it. Visually impaired individuals are not exempted from reciting the blessing, because they benefit from the moon by being assisted by people who make use of its light to see.

The Basic Ritual

Kiddush Levanah should be recited outside (or near a window) at night when the moon is fully visible during the first half of the Hebrew month. The leader should make sure that participant observers understand that they are not praying to the moon. Rather, they are praying to the Source of all creation.

Before the month began, we prayed,

May it be Your will, *Adonai* our God and God of our ancestors, to renew our lives in the coming month. Grant us a long life, a peaceful life with goodness and blessing, sustenance and physical vitality, a life informed by purity and piety, a life free from shame and reproach, a life of abundance and honor, a life embracing piety and love of *Torah*, a life in which our heart's desires for goodness will be fulfilled. Amen.

May the One who wrought miracles for our ancestors, redeeming them from slavery to freedom, redeem us soon and gather our dispersed from the four corners of the earth in the fellowship of the entire people Israel. And let us say: Amen.

May the Holy One bless the new month for us and for all our people, the House of Israel, with life and peace, joy and gladness, deliverance and consolation. And let us say: Amen.

As the month unfolds, with these hopeful prayers in people's hearts, they look at themselves and confront the month in which they find themselves.

1. Making the Transition

As people are gathering and getting comfortable, the transition into sacred time and sacred space is made by singing a *niggun* (wordless chant).

2. Contextualizing

The material from the section called the calendar and this ritual of renewal should be reviewed for this particular month in order to frame the context for this month's ritual. The following phrase is used: *We have come together to celebrate our lives in the month of* ________________.

3. Forming Community/Checking in

Each participant shares one thing that has happened to that person, good or bad, over the course of the previous month that is desired to be shared. Before each individual speaks, the community welcomes the individual into the group by saying *Shalom aleikhem, peace to you*! At the conclusion of each individual statement, the individual responds, *Aleikhem shalom*, [and] *peace to you*![81]

4. Study

As part of the celebration of the moon and its seasons, participants study a short selection that emerges from the theme of the month. Participants should feel free to choose their own text or to use one that follows the section entitled "the calendar" and this ritual of renewal. (The leader may want to initiate the study with the blessing by using the traditional blessing beginning, ending with *la'asok b'divrei Torah* and concluding with *Kaddish d'Rabbanan*—the prayer of the Sages.)

[81] As a symbol of community, some groups shake hands following the exchange of greetings, nod in acknowledgment to one another, or embrace.

5. A Blessing

The blessing is as follows:

> Praised are You, *Adonai* our God, Sovereign of the Universe, who created the heavens by your command and all their array by your mere word. You have subjected them to fixed laws and time, so that they might not deviate from their set function. They are happy to do the will of their Creator, the true Author, whose achievement is truth. You ordered the moon to renew itself as a glorious crown over those You sustained from birth, who likewise will be regenerated in the future, and will worship their Creator for Your majestic glory. Praised are You, *Adonai*, who renews the months.[82]

6. Dancing

Before repeating the statement below three times while rising up on their toes (or actually jumping up) and while reciting the first three words of the statement—*Kishem sh-ani roked*—participants should share with others in the group their heartfelt desires, what they have been struggling to change in their lives. Others in the group should be invited to respond with words of affirmation and encouragement or even suggestions for self-improvement.

As I raise myself up to you [or attempt to leap, literally dance toward you], I recognize my limits and the power we have harnessed to actually reach the moon in our day. I pray to recognize my small part in creation and the enormous power I have to affect the world at the same time.[83]

> Repeat the following three times:
> Long live David, King of Israel!

---

[82] By using the traditional words of blessing, the dialogue is initiated with God and a relationship with the Divine is entered into. This text helps participants to realize that the creation of the moon (and the rest of the world, including them) is not by mere chance. Some like to interpret the text through the numerology of *gematria*. They argue that the last word in this psalm (*ya'avor*) has the same numerical value as the number of sparks that were created in an early *midrash* that describes the moon's dispute with God over the size of the sun. According to the *midrash*, the sun and moon were initially the same size. When the moon complained, God reduced the size of the moon. After complaining some more, God relented and told the moon that although its light was less than that of the sun, the moon alone would light the world-to-come and provide illumination for people's passage from this world to the next. Thus, by using a *kabbalistic* lens on the text, the ceremony is used as a means of collecting these sparks and repairing the brokenness of the world.

[83] This is a custom, initiated by Rabbi Isaac Luria, known as the ARI. The traditional text stated, "I reach for you but cannot touch you, so may it be for my enemies." Rabbi Arthur Waskow suggested the change based on the precarious use of nuclear and other energies and the extending human impact into space itself.

"Now participants say as follows:"

As I raise myself up to you [or attempt to leap, literally dance toward you] but cannot reach you, so may those who attempt to injure us, be unable to reach us.[84]

7. The Future

The following should be repeated three times—once to the person on either side of the participant and then to the group:

May we and all Israel have fulfillment and good fortune! Amen.

8. A Final Psalm-Song (Psalm 150)

The following is then recited:

Halleluyah! Praise God in the sanctuary. Praise God in the glorious heaven.
Praise God for mighty deeds. Praise God for abundant greatness.
Praise God with the blast of the horn. Praise God with the harp and the lyre.
Praise God with drum and dance. Praise God with strings and flute.
Praise God with resounding cymbals. Praise God with clanging cymbals.
Kol haneshama tehallel Yah! Let everything that breathes praise Adonai. *Halleluyah*![85]

9. A Word of Blessing

As an option, each individual is invited to offer words of blessing to the person sitting on the right. Participants may want to use the traditional priestly benediction (as follows) or words of their own.[86]

May God bless you and keep you
May God shine light upon you
May God's Presence rest upon you and bring you peace

Each member of the community exchanges these greetings with one another:

---

[84] While this may seem awkward or even artificial at first, this heavenly dance is a way of expressing an attempt to reach and understand God, things that one ultimately cannot fully do.

[85] The inclusion of Psalm 150 recognizes the times when one has no fitting words of praise or is simply unable to say them. There are many contemporary melodies for the psalm that provide a powerful ending for the ritual. Some may want to use Psalm 150 as guidance for expressing praise with the help of instruments and dance. Others may want to focus on the breathing suggested by the line *Kol haneshama tehallel Yah!*

[86] This section of the ritual is used as a means of checking in. Each person should share with the others the challenges and celebrations in his life. And, after each individual shares, someone may want to offer a blessing in recognition of what has been shared.

Shalom aleikhem, peace to you!
Aleikhem shalom, [and] peace to you![87]

The Calendar and This Ritual of Renewal

The Hebrew calendar year has two beginnings, one in the spring with *Nisan*, when the Jewish people begin their journey from slavery to freedom, on their way from Egypt to the land of Israel, and the other in *Tishrei* with the fall holidays. Each month has its own character, reflecting the emotions that emerge from various calendar markings that take place during that month: holidays, seasonal changes, Torah readings, and historical events. Thus, participants can enhance *Kiddush Levanah* by adding a different theme that emerges from each Hebrew month. In this way, they can capture the spiritual essence of the ritual by allowing it to reflect the rhythm of the month in which it is celebrated. Leaders should use the context that emerges from the thematic elements of the particular month to provide them with program direction for their groups. The ritual makes room for the inclusion of these themes that are driven by the calendar. However, there are other themes (listed below) that may be used in their place.

Tishrei

This month, in the tradition of the New Year for kings, is thus known for its regal character, and the first of this month is called *Rosh Hashanah*, the New Year. This month is introduced by the *aseret yamei teshuvah*, the ten days of repentance, as preparation for standing in judgment before God at their end on *Yom Kippur*. Following a month of introspection, participants are ready to enter the synagogue and themselves. Then as soon as the gates of *neilah* close on *Yom Kippur*, after a full day in exhausting communion with God, participants rush out to begin the building of a temporary shelter, the *sukkah*, which reminds them of their fragility in the universe. The month will end with a celebration of dedication (*Shemini Atzeret*) and rededication to *Torah* (*Simchat Torah*). But in the midst of the building of the community *sukkah* and the annual attempt to embrace nature, time should be taken out to recite *Kiddush Levanah*.

(Mar) Cheshvan

The rabbis add the word *mar* (bitter) to the name of this month, claiming that it is a bitter month because there are no holidays in it following a month that is brim-

[87] According to the Maharsha (in his comment to Sanhedrin 42a), *Long live David, King of Israel* is repeated three times in order to achieve the numerical equivalent of *Rosh Chodesh*. Thus, this connects the ritual to the messianic hope of Israel. Once Rabbi Judah haNasi instructed Rabbi Hiyya to go to *Ein Tov*, a place in Judea where the *Bet Din* met. He was supposed to instruct them to sanctify *Rosh Chodesh* on the 30th and notify Rabbi Judah haNasi that it was done by sending him this secret password message: "David, King of Israel, lives and endures" (Babylonian Talmud, *Rosh Hashanah* 25).

ming with them. Perhaps it is the bitterness that remains in the soul, knowing that the cleansing of the fall holidays remains incomplete. So the light of the moon is used to see what remains and the opportunity is taken once again to remove the barriers that keep people from their brothers and friends. Regardless of where people live or what they do, this month helps them make the transition into the fall and the rest of the year. Following the ritual, each should be invited to share remains burdening his soul after the fall holidays. His brothers should be invited to help him develop ways to relieve the burden.

Kislev

It is in the midst of this month that winter turns blackest, even before the weather is potentially at its worst. It is in these darkest days of winter that the miracle of light is celebrated. In the celebration of *Hanukkah*, participants are able to share their gifts with others and celebrate the modest contributions of those around them. When their world seems darkened, the light of the moon and then the lights of *Hanukkah* and an acknowledgment of its Creator and theirs will carry them through even the worst of times. The moon will shine and warm their hearts.

While *Hanukkah* is celebrated toward the end of the month and the ritual of *Kiddush Levanah* must be performed during the first half of the month, a great deal of time is used to prepare and plan for the festival. Following the performance of the ritual this month, a few men should be invited to lead the discussion on preparing for this year's rededication (*Hanukkah*) in your home.

Tevet

This month represents for many the turning point into the harsh days of winter. It begins with the last days of *Hanukkah*. It is the hopeful light of anticipation of the end of the darkness that is carried into the month ahead. The holy city of Jerusalem runs cold with mud as a result of Israel's unrelenting winter rains, but the golden glow of Jerusalem is never dimmed. So participants are taken to the cold outside for a short time in order to acknowledge the Source of all Creation, to affirm the belief in the cycles of life and their endless variety.

Since it can be cold for many homeless people during the winter, this month's ritual should be planned so that the community of men can volunteer to spend the night working with other men in a homeless shelter following the performance of the ritual.

Shevat

When it is hard to believe and the northeast weather seems unforgiving, the sap begins to flow in the trees. And in Israel, the almond trees are blossoming. These first signs of spring are acknowledged on *Tu Bishevat*. It is a further affirmation of God's promise to continually redeem the world. It is known that spring will come, that the trees will flower once again. But one has to do one's part too. And so in the midst of one's *tikkun olam* work, through the celebration of this ritual, one needs to pause to celebrate the light that he helps to bring into the lives of others.

Adar

Centered on *Purim* and its silly celebrations, this is most frivolous of months, when everything seems reversed. But there is much depth to one's rejoicing. People have survived when others much stronger than them have not. This month's celebration of Kiddush *Levanah* should be lighthearted and worry free: One is here. So the evening that surrounds this ritual should be used to be a social get-together for the men of the community without any agenda in mind.

Nisan

In preparation for *Pesach*, participants do a thorough spring cleaning. They scrub their homes and themselves. Everything reflects the warm glow of renewal. They know that they have cleaned their homes of leavened bread. They have sold what they did not give away, and they have burned the few crumbs that might have remained. But there is more work to be done. So they use the light of the moon to ensure that they will bring no *chametz* of the spirit, no souring of self, into the weeks that follow.

The *Kiddush Levanah* should mark the beginning of one's spring cleaning in the synagogue in preparation for *Pesach*. One should rid oneself of the *chametz* that puffs up his soul as he endeavors to make his home leaven-free.

Iyar

The celebration of Israel's independence is scarred by the recognition of the *Shoah* and the many lives that contributed to the defense of the homeland (first through the observance of *Yom Hashoah u'Gevurah* and then one week later by *Yom Hazikaron)*. But it is also a recognition of one's own independence, freed from the male stereotypes forced on him by an aggressive western society, and open to the options presented to him by his tradition. Hillel said it best: In a place where there are no *menschen*, strive to be a decent human being (*Pirke Avot* 2:5). So after the land is celebrated, participants join together as a community to celebrate the human beings they have become. Instead of lighting a candle, they illuminate the sky with the prayers of the *Kiddush Levanah* ritual and, afterwards, celebrate Israel.

Sivan

This is the month for which participants have all been waiting. For seven weeks, they have counted the days on the calendar and marked the path of their journeys. And, at the end of the trip, they offer the first fruits of their labors. This month focuses on *Shavuot*, which celebrates the spring harvest and also marks the time the *Torah* was given to the Jewish people. As they gather together, they imagine the way the light shone on that mountain! The time this evening should be used to study in preparation for the nightlong study on *Shavuot*.

Tammuz

This month is characterized by the summer solstice: from then on the light of day slowly decreases as people make their way through the summer heat. From their history, they recall the breach of Jerusalem's walls by Nebuchadnezzar and later by Titus during this month. They are in the straits, as the three weeks prior to *Tishah b'Av* are called. This disposition threatens to consume them and color the remainder of the year. So they huddle together and ask for support from one another as they face this challenge of the past and the days yet to come.

Av

During the summer, most people take life a little less seriously. They vacation, leave work a little early, even dress more casually. In the face of freedom, they can enjoy life more fully. The Hebrew calendar reminds them that it was not always so easy to do so. It was not always so good for the Jewish people. They refrain from celebrating during the early part of the month, until the ninth day of *Av* marks the destruction of the ancient Temples and their people's exile from the land. At the same time, the daily increase in the size of the moon reminds them of God's promise of redemption to their people throughout their history. Most of the month falls in the period of time in which God consoles the people over the destruction they have experienced in their history. So they offer a blessing as a way of reminding themselves and keeping that promise ever-present in their collective memories. Following the ritual, they study the book of Lamentations with the rest of the men in the group.

Elul

Throughout the year, participants spend a great deal of time in preparation and anticipation. Each week, they begin planning for *Shabbat*, then they hesitate to let it go. Throughout the year, they are always getting ready for one holiday or another. It seems that they are unable to make the transition simply from one time to another. They separate out the sacred from the profane and try to bring the blessings of one into the other. Following the reciting of the ritual during *Elul*, they recite Psalm 27, as the tradition suggests that they do each day, and they use it as a lens for their *teshuvah* work. They want to make sure that they will be ready for the arrival of *Rosh Hashanah* and *Yom Kippur*. This month, they use the light of the moon to help them see the process more clearly. They let its gentle glow help to illumine their paths in the world.

Texts to Study

Some men's groups like to incorporate study as their marking of the new moon. The texts for these studies are all sacred, but they come from a variety of sources, including the classic sacred literature of their people. There is room in the ritual for such text study as part of the performance of the ritual itself. Following are some text study possibilities.

Ellen Umansky, *A Midrash on Genesis 22*

It was morning. Sarah had just awakened and reached over to touch her husband, Abraham, to caress him, but Abraham wasn't there. Neither, she discovered, was Isaac, her only son, Isaac, whom she loved more than anyone or anything in the world. She quickly dressed and went outside, hoping they'd be nearby. But they were gone, and so was Abraham's ass and his two young servants. It wasn't unusual for Abraham to take Isaac somewhere, but never this early and never without saying good-bye. And so she waited and wept and screamed.

Hours passed. It was hot, and Sarah thought about going inside to escape the heat of the sun. *But what if I miss them,* she thought. *I want to make sure that I catch the first glimpse of them, even if they're far away.* And so she stood and waited ... and waited ... and waited. She felt anxious, nervous, upset. Where could they be? Where has Abraham taken my son? The sun began to set. She started to shiver, partly from the cold, mostly from fear. Again she cried and wailed and moaned. Isaac had been God's gift to her, a sign of His love and a continuing bond between them. She had laughed when God told her she was pregnant. She was old and no longer able to bear a child. But God had given her Isaac and filled her breasts with milk, and for the first time in her life Sarah was happy.

She looked around her and saw the fields, now empty, and in the distance saw the mountains, sloping upwards into the sky. And then she saw them ... Abraham walking with his ass and his servants and Isaac far behind, walking slowly, his head turning from side to side, his hands oddly moving as though they were trying to make sense of something, and Sarah knew in that instant where Abraham and Isaac had been and why they had gone. Though she could barely make out the features of Isaac's face, she could tell from his movements and his gestures that he was angry, that he wanted nothing to do with his father who had tried to kill him. Abraham was almost down the mountain by now and soon would be home. He'd try to explain, to make her understand *his* side of the story. But Sarah wanted no part of it. She was tired of hearing Abraham's excuses and even more tired of hearing what *he* thought God demanded. And so Sarah turned and went inside and prayed that, if only for one night, Abraham would leave her alone.

Rabbi Abraham Joshua Heschel, *Man's Quest for God*

To attain a degree of spiritual security one cannot rely upon one's own resources. One needs an atmosphere, where the concern for the spirit is shared by a community. One is in need of students and scholars, masters and specialists. But one needs also the company of witnesses, of human beings who are engaged in worship, who for a moment sense the truth that life is meaningless without attachment to God.

One often discovers that a human being is driven by alien pressures, by false fears. Living becomes drifting, aimless moving. To pray is to stand still, to rise above enforced digression, and to await signs of direction. Tearing off inner masks, imposed makeup, delusions, conditionings, conceits, a spark breaks through all thoughts: what is worth being thirsty for?

Psalm 30, A Psalm of David. A Song for the Rededication of the Temple

I celebrate You, *Adonai*,
for it is You who has lifted me up
and not let my adversaries triumph over me.
Adonai, my God,
I cried out to You,
and You healed me.
You brought me up from *Sheol*,
preserved me from going down into the pits.
You who are faithful to God, sing to God,
praise God's well-deserved reputation.
For God is angry only momentarily
there is life when God is pleased.
Weeping may delay the [end of the] night,
but at dawn there are shouts of joy.

When I was free of trouble,
I thought that nothing could shake me up
for when You, *Adonai*, were pleased [with me]
You made me as sturdy as a mighty mountain.

When You hid Your face
I was panic-stricken.
I called out to You, *Adonai*,
to my God I appealed.
What is to be gained from my death,
were I to descend to the Pit?
Could I as dust praise You?
Would I be able to declare my faith in You?
Hear me now, *Adonai*, have mercy on me;
Adonai, help me!
You turned my lament into dancing,
You unfastened my sackcloth and clothed me with joy,
so that I could sing endless praises to You with my entire being;

Adonai, my God, I will praise You forever.

Babylonian Talmud, *Ta'anit* 23a

A rabbi was passing through a field when he noticed an elderly man who was planting an acorn. "Why are you planting that acorn?" he asked. "You surely do not expect to live long enough to see it grow into an oak tree." The man replied, "My grandfather planted seeds so that I might enjoy the shade and the fruit trees. Now I do similarly for my grandchildren and those who come after me."

Psalm 27 (read each day during Elul as a prism for doing *teshuvah*)

A Psalm of David
Adonai is my light and my help, whom shall I fear?
Adonai is the strength of my life, of whom shall I be afraid?
When my enemies try to hurt me, they will stumble and fall.
Even if an army stands against me, my heart will feel no fear;
One thing I ask of *Adonai*, for this I plead:
To live in *Adonai*'s House all the days of my life;
In order to see God's beauty and to visit God's Temple.
God will shelter me in a safe *sukkah* on an evil day,
Hide me in God's Tent, lift me high on a rock, out of danger's reach.
Now I can raise my head high above my enemies around me.
I can worship in God's Tent with happy shofar sounds.
In times of danger and fear, God is my trusted shield,
Even if my father and mother left me, God would take me in.
I never stopped believing that I would see
Adonai's goodness in the land of the living.
Hope in *Adonai*. Be strong and let your heart be brave.
Hope in *Adonai*.

Additional List of Agenda Topics

In addition to the themes that emerge from the calendar and are described above and for which a place has been reserved in the ritual itself, one may want to consider the following themes, by month, as discussion topics for the monthly get-together.[88]

Tishrei: How one relates to God as defined by Judaism,
Cheshvan: How one creates a new men's midrash,
Kislev: How one understands what it means to be a Jewish leader,
Tevet: How one forges and understands cross-cultural connections,
Shevat: How to rediscover a prayer life,
Adar: How one may internalize anti-Semitism and act the part of the "Jewish prince" or the "good Jewish boy,"

[88] This list and the one that comes after it is significantly informed by the work of Rabbi Shawn Israel Zevit as described in his introduction to my book, *From Your Father's House: Reflections for Modern Jewish Men*, which may serve as a resource for men's gatherings.

Nisan: How to lead others in a search for the sacred,
Iyar: How one responds to Israeli male identities,
Sivan: How one uses and renews traditional rituals,
Tammuz: How one finds a way in: how to engage the sacred text,
Av: How one reconnects with what came before him in Jewish tradition, and
Elul: How to inherit the father and carry his name forward.

Here are some additional themes one may want to consider:

- raising sons to be *mentschen*,
- understanding our sexual selves,
- gratefully aging and facing death,
- handling intimacy,
- responding to the challenges of feminism,
- raising and relating to our children,
- having regard for our bodies and taking care of them,
- competing and socializing with other men,
- creating and maintaining our families ands friendships,
- succumbing to addictions,
- reacting to violence,
- experiencing our work lives, and
- creating legacies to leave behind.

Notes to Facilitator

For some of the men assembled, the notion of a male ritual may be awkward. The facilitator should try to set their minds at ease by acknowledging the awkwardness. He should allow them to define the group's agenda as he goes along, even though he will use the framework of this chapter to guide him. He should be as familiar as possible with the ritual contained in the chapter. The facilitator should try working through the ritual and its marginal notes. (He can invite the rabbi to help with the more difficult parts of it.) By nature, men do not share intimacies with one another (especially outside the locker room). Thus, it will be the facilitator's obligation to shape a supportive and confidential environment. He should make sure that the space used is relatively private and comfortable in order to ensure both.

While the traditional format for *Kiddush Levanah* is merely a recitation of the ritual following evening prayers and then men return home to their regular routines, the ritual contained in this chapter contains many other elements in it so that the ritual can be transformed into a program. The first meeting of the group may require some introductions, and the format for the evening should be rather loose. However, the men should come to expect and depend on a particular ritualized routine. The facilitator begins by suggesting that what is exchanged in this sacred space should remain among the men who share it. Then he invites each person to tell the others his name and earliest Jewish male memory. As an alternative, he may want to share a portrait of the most significant Jewish man in his life and why that man has had such great impact on his life.

Because of the nature of the ritual, meetings should take place in the evening. As a means of continual group building, the ritual will give everyone an opportunity to check in. However, the first time the group gets together, the facilitator may want to separate some of these things out from the ritual itself and use them as a way to warm up to the ritual. He invites the men to respond to the following: *What happened during the month that passed since we were together? What good news do you have to share? What challenges have you faced at work or at home?* The facilitator should invite others to comment or offer support, consolation, and advice. Following the ritual, he should leave people some time to luxuriate in its afterglow and to reflect personally before returning inside. He should invite members of the group to comment on the experience as an "I" statement. He should avoid criticism: this is only the time for feelings not actions. Then he should turn to one of the themes for the evening. Then at the end of the evening, he should invite each individual to turn to his neighbor and either shake his hand or give a hug and wish him "*shavuah tov*—a good week" for the days ahead. The ritual provides an opportunity for doing so, as well.

Acknowledgments

I would like to thank the Synagogue 2000 (now Synagogue 3000) teams who encouraged the development of this project and helped to field-test it in their congregations, as well as the students at the New York Kollel who shared their reactions and offered numerous suggestions during a *Tikkun Layl Shavuot*, when this material was presented in a draft form. I would also like to thank the staff at Synagogue 2000 for helping to shape this project and renew the ritual along with me. In particular, I acknowledge the enthusiastic insight of Adrienne Bank and the assistance of Karen Lustig. Similarly, I thank former colleagues Drs. Larry Hoffman and Ron Wolfson for bringing the dream of a new synagogue closer to reality. In no small measure, it represents the culmination of their lives' work. I must also thank the following colleagues who reviewed the material and made helpful suggestions from the perspective of their own work in the Jewish community: Rabbis Norman J. Cohen, Leon Morris, and Shawn Israel Zevit. The sensitive pen of Rabbi Jennifer Krause, former rabbinic intern at Synagogue 2000 must also be noted with abiding appreciation. Further, I want to make mention of the pioneering work of Rabbi Avram (Ramie) Arian, whose rabbinic thesis at Hebrew Union College-Jewish Institute of Religion many years ago served as an indispensable resource for developing this ritual resource booklet.

Reference

Olitzky, K.M. (1999). *From your father's house: Reflections for modern Jewish men.* Philadelphia: Jewish Publication Society of America.

17

When the Stories Stop...

Doug Barden

> My *zeyde* [grandfather] came to the synagogue because he was a Jew. His grandchildren, if they come at all, come to become Jews. But the synagogue will fail them if it thinks that it can be a surrogate for family and home. The rabbi is not father or mother, the lectern is not the table, the temple is not preparation for Jewish living at home.... The synagogue must focus its energies upon the family and help parents recover their roles as singers of songs and tellers of tales, reclaim their generative power to create memories and to answer questions. (Rabbi Harold Shulweiss, undated Union for Reformed Judaism document, "Why are we talking about synagogue transformation?")

Because I have been working side by side with hundreds, if not thousands, of Jewish men for the past 15 years and have sadly witnessed firsthand the increased disengagement of many of their contemporaries from Jewish communal life, I would modify Rabbi Schulweiss' comment and give it a deliberate gender slant, rephrasing it to read: "The synagogue must focus its energies upon the family and help *men* recover their roles as singers of songs and tellers of tales, help *men* reclaim their generative power to create memories and to answer questions." For if in the Hasidic storytelling-tradition stories and the storytellers themselves are often venerated, in the early part of the 21st century, these are fair questions they must ask themselves: What happens when there are no longer male storytellers to tell their tales to a new generation? What happens when the tale itself is no longer told? What then happens for the future and continuity of the Jewish people? What is their legacy?

In January 2006, I wrote a monograph entitled: *Wrestling with Jacob and Esau, Fighting the Flight of Men. A Modern Day Crisis in the Reform Movement* (Barden, 2006). The approach I brought to the controversial and politically sensitive issue of male flight was a reflection of my own unique background. My advanced degrees in social and cultural anthropology and a business degree (MBA) in organizational development are combined with over 25 years as a Jewish professional, working extensively with volunteers, both Jewish men and Jewish women. I began my professional career as the executive director of District II (New York State) of Women's American ORT—as a 25-year-old male working with dozens of highly motivated and dedicated female volunteer leaders—and was subsequently brought into the national headquarters as the first national organization department director. In 1994, I assumed the position of executive director of the North American Federation of Temple Brotherhoods (NFTB), now the Men of Reform Judaism (MRJ), historically the men's service arm of the Union for Reform Judaism (URJ). Working with a knowledgeable and committed corps of regional and national male lay leaders, my job is to provide needed assistance, guidance, and direction to the hundreds of affiliated men's clubs or brotherhoods throughout North America. Thus, I wrote the monograph as someone who has been, and continues to be, in the trenches (i.e., working daily in the Jewish communal field). My days (and many nights) are filled with meeting and working with many of the men of the Reform Movement who remain active and have found fellowship and a sense of community within their local synagogues and local brotherhoods—men who have remained involved and choose to give their time, energy, and skills to leading their local brotherhoods and many of whom go on to provide manpower and leadership to their temples' committees and boards. Their continued presence gives me hope.

As a trained social anthropologist, I look at entire systems, the gestalt (i.e., the actions and interactions of cultural values, attitudes, and beliefs and how these values and beliefs are expressed behaviorally in outward, public, cultural settings). Classical social anthropologists do their best not to disturb the culture and group dynamics being observed, ideally having no significant impact and certainly not consciously seeking to effect change. I do not have that ivory tower, academic perspective or professional option. Also trained in organizational development, I have a goal not only to actively identify the key components of a social and cultural system that are in transition but to attempt to accelerate, reverse, or maintain these cultural changes. Specifically, as the key professional of MRJ, I have had the responsibility and challenge to work with a national lay leadership to revisit the traditional service role and purpose of a local brotherhood within a given local Reform synagogue and urge their adoption of an expanded programmatic agenda (i.e., an agenda that explicitly focuses on a now underserved population of the congregation: the adult men themselves).

My monograph demonstrated that the disengagement of men from religious institutions is a real cultural phenomenon—one that has not only impacted one of the most liberal arms of Judaism, the Reform Movement, but nearly every religious institution in American society, be it conservative or liberal. And while this disengagement is not necessarily new, since there is documented evidence from some religious denominations that this disengagement of men is at least 40, almost 50 years old (i.e., what cannot be disputed is that there has been a marked increase in the rate of disengagement of men from religious institutions in the past 20 to 30 years).

While my monograph was one of the first attempts to comprehensively approach the male disengagement topic within the Reform Movement and place it in its proper larger sociological and cultural context, I was certainly not the first to recognize the loss of men's involvement in synagogue life. Over a decade ago, Rabbi Sheldon Zimmerman, then head of Hebrew Union College-Jewish Institute of Religion, wrote the following:

> The reality is that there has been a flight of Jewish men from synagogue involvement. There has been a flight of men from the structuring process of the synagogues and communities in which we work and that there are fewer and

fewer Jewish men giving of their time, their energy, and their lives to the ongoing creative survival of the Jewish people. If you look at the major activity generating, energy driven parts of our synagogue and religious lives, if you look carefully at the most hands-on people who are running Jewish institutional life today, you are going to see fewer and fewer men. I'm not suggesting that our egalitarianism and inclusiveness is not important. They are important. That's who we *are ... and ta*lking about the volunteer ranks where we [still] will see many, many men involved in synagogues on Board of Trustees. But if you look at the committee structure, if you look at who comes to synagogue services, particularly on holidays, not only Rosh Hashanah and Yom Kippur and the other festivals, you will note fewer and fewer men taking organized Jewish life and organized Jewish prayer very seriously. (NFTB archive, speech presented at 1997 NFTB Biennial Convention)

On this theme, Rabbi Jeff Salkin (1998a) wrote as follows:

Let's face it. The great, unspoken crisis facing modern Judaism is the disengagement of its men. While no one mourns the exclusive male minyan, men increasingly see Judaism as being the province of women. Men are distancing themselves in ever growing numbers from synagogue life—as worshipers, as students of Torah, and as trustees and committee members.... On any given festival morning, 90% of the worshipers in my synagogue will be women over the age of 70 ... about 60 to 70% of the participants in the Union for American Hebrew Congregations' (now the Union for Reform Judaism) summer kallot (study and spirituality retreats) are women; the men who do come are usually accompanying their wives. Men constitute only a tiny percentage of converts to Judaism. In sixteen years in the rabbinate, I have converted hundreds of women but no more than five men. And every rabbi can testify to the frequent apathy of Jewish men when they join their partners at Introduction to Judaism classes as a prelude to conversion. Temple youth groups are increasingly filled with young Jewish women craning their necks and wondering, in the words of one Long Island teen, "Where are all the guys?" (p. 5)

The reality is, however, that in the past 10 years there were few public articulations of this disengagement issue and even fewer suggestions on how to rectify the situation. The crisis fell on collective deaf ears. I contend that this trend of men's disengagement has been obscured for, and by, various cultural, linguistic, and political reasons, including a profound misreading of progressive feminist ideology. This misreading has led to an all out press to eliminate not only gender stratification but also all signs of gender differentiation. Within the Reform Movement, for example, the leadership, lay and professional, to its individual and collective credit, has appropriately sought to eliminate gender stratification, that is, the uneven distribution of positions of power, leadership, involvement, and recognition. No longer does gender determine who sits where, who serves as temple president, and who leads the congregation in prayer and song. For this the gender-egalitarian-based religious institutions are to be applauded. Unfortunately, too many professional and lay leaders, men and women alike, have also mistakenly sought to eliminate all signs of gender differences. This is a mistake. Whether what is defined as masculine traits or feminine traits is a function of biological hardwiring and/or social constructs, the nature/nurture controversy is a distraction for this discussion. To deny that gender differences—whatever their origins—affect how adult men and women express themselves as individuals and as Jews or to deny that gender is one—not the only one, but one—of the key variables that shape an individual's gestalt is to deny human reality and is, in fact, anathema to the goals of genuine feminism. Rabbi Michael Holzman (2004) wrote:

> Yes, we have heard feminism's call for equal access, but some of us have failed to completely heed a central part of the feminist message: gender matters. It affects the way we see the world, relate to community and connect with God. Gender influences our self awareness, our personal relationships, and our intimacies. For most of our community, this message falls on deaf ears. When a segment of our community does apprehend and perceive the power of gender, women dominate that segment. These women create Rosh Hodesh groups, women's liturgy, new women's life cycle ceremonies or even a women's tikkun olam committee to focus on issues like Breast Cancer. But men continue to largely ignore the spiritual significance of gender. Reform Men certainly have sensitively heard the message of equal access and respect, and despite their courageous dedication to equal opportunity, most men still fail to recognize that feminism contains a powerful lesson for Jewish men as well. We do not argue here that men deserve greater inclusion or equal rights. This is not a "pendulum-has-swung-too-far" argument. Instead, men need to hear more of the feminist message and go beyond the women's rights piece of the communal puzzle. Gender matters, feminists have taught us, but rarely do we consider how significantly masculinity affects the way we live our Jewish lives. (p. 8)

I concur with Rabbi Holzman, and a primary goal of *Wrestling with Jacob and Esau* (Barden, 2006) was for my professional and lay colleagues to recognize the error of their ways and reconsider the impact of their past attitudes and behavior. Current key gatekeepers operate in a cultural system they inherited and, often unintentionally, maintain. As the Reform Movement's cultural history has shown in the past four decades, however, cultural systems are never static. Cultural systems can be changed through proper internal and external intervention, sometimes dramatically and profoundly. While there is always a great deal of system inertia and a resistance to change, cultural systems can and will change when the proper energies and efforts are directed at the key components of the social system. Changing the attitudes and beliefs of individual gatekeepers will, in time, therefore, change the Reform Movement's collective behavior and change the movement's existing culture.

My monograph's success will be measured in time by how many of my colleagues, lay and professional, men and women, come to understand and then actively support, if not direct, the efforts to reverse the flight of men (Barden, 2006). In calling for this change effort, the goal is not to turn the egalitarian clock back 30 years; it is not to reverse women's gains or to return to an imbalance of gender stratification. Rather, it is to establish a new equilibrium, an updated, truly profound balance of gender differentiation. The goal is to create and maintain a cultural climate within the congregational community that fully respects and integrates the different spiritual and religious needs and wants of Jewish women and men. And, while the message was written for a very specific audience—the Reform Movement's leadership—its implications for the leadership of any religious denomination currently suffering a parallel phenomenon are apparent.

What accounts for this disengagement phenomenon? If the goal is to reverse men's disengagement from the religious institutions, it certainly helps to review what might be prompting their disengagement in the first place. However, in favoring any given cause as the definitive explanation, I urge caution. This complex cultural phenomenon cannot be explained away by saying "it's all the fault of feminism" or "it's because men just aren't as spiritual as women." For example, a case can certainly be made that the disengagement by some men is primarily the result of their traditional positions of status and power, based solely on their gender, having been legitimately eliminated in the Reform Movement's egalitarian (or some would say post-egalitarian) climate. From this perspective, men's inability to "get with the program" and their failure to adapt to the new, power-sharing requirements rests heavily on their own shoulders. An alternative argument can be made that the male flight phenomenon is not so much about the loss of status and power but primarily the result of men perceiving their spiritual and social needs as being ignored. From this perspective, much of the blame must then be directed at the current leadership of the institutions in failing to properly respond. I would suggest that it is probably a combination of both—neither cause can be ignored—but what cannot be dismissed is the resultant mass phenomenon itself. So I urge anyone truly interested in addressing the issue to acknowledge and appreciate the interrelationships and complexities of the issue.

The disengagement of men from religious institutions as a major cultural phenomenon is a manifestation of a significant and complex number of economic, societal, and cultural macro changes that have combined to accelerate already weakened support for religious institutions by American men of many denominations. It is also a product of the specific micro cultural changes within the most liberal of our religious institutions, specifically, in the name of gender equality and inclusiveness, the adoption of a cultural climate that is increasingly perceived by many men as favoring the needs and interests of women, a culture that, in the extreme case, is perceived as ignoring, if not demeaning entirely, men's spiritual needs and interests.

The Reform, Conservative, Reconstructionist, and Renewal movements, to their credit, for nearly three decades have sought to meet the needs of women on a variety of liturgical, programmatic, and leadership opportunity fronts. Whether Jewish male needs were intentionally or unintentionally ignored is problematic. What cannot be denied is that many men have increasingly perceived their temples as more welcoming of women than men. Increasingly—by the language, the programs, and the actions of the congregations and its leadership—many Jewish men increasingly feel underappreciated, and in the extreme, therefore, unwelcome. Rabbi Eyse M. Goldstein (2004) wrote:

> The synagogue is no longer a proving ground for masculinity. Because of that it has also suffered. Many have noticed the "flight" of men from egalitarian synagogues as more and more women take leadership roles. What is this flight about? Is it about the last male bastion being stormed, or about the feeling of not being "needed" anymore, or about a male devaluation of something as soon as it becomes open to women, or about a genuine frustration with the "feminization" of today's Judaism? These are questions that must be answered by the men who take their Judaism seriously and who wish the next generation of boys to do so as well.

Perceiving themselves as unimportant, as invalid, many men have responded with varying degrees of passivity, a form of disengagement. Some only show up during the High Holidays or life cycle events of close family members; some are dues-paying members only; in the extreme case, they are not even part of the temple membership.

Again, the issue of not feeling valued any longer is not unique to Reform Judaism. When Reverend Kathleen Rolenz (2004), a Universal Unitarian minister, asked a group of men why they don't participate in religious life, one responded: "If men are, in fact, vanishing from church life (or other voluntary associations), it's because we feel that what we have to offer is not considered important or valid" (p. 12).

However, if the only focus is on the increased feminization of religious institutions, other vital factors are being ignored. For example, traditional societal values make it clear that a man's first priority is to economically provide for his family, and if this means sacrificing other personal needs, such as finding spiritual or religious fulfillment, so be it. While men are often no longer the only family member with a career or job outside the home, they generally remain the primary breadwinner. Unlike their fathers and grandfathers before them—who certainly worked long hours, five, even six, days a week—men no longer have a clear demarcation of when work begins and when it ends. Too many contemporary men are always working! It is not uncommon to find men working 40, 50, or even 60 hours a week. They are working while commuting to the offices, and they are working when they are commuting home. They even bring their laptops with them on vacations. Worse, for all their increased efforts, men know they are no longer guaranteed the gold watch upon retirement from the same company after 30 years. They are constantly, legitimately, worried that they will lose their jobs. For all their efforts men recognize they are not in full control of their own economic fortunes and may very well lose their jobs. With loss of job comes a phenomenal loss of self-esteem and self-identity. They fear they will be perceived as a failure in the eyes of their spouses, family members, friends, and former colleagues. Unfortunately, I know firsthand that their perception is accurate: too often when a man loses his job, he finds he has also lost many so-called friends, who treat his unemployment as a contagious disease.

On the other hand, I have never encountered a situation where a man was thought less of because he failed to actively pursue his spiritual or religious needs. This is not surprising since it supports another simplistic explanation for men's disengagement—the popular belief that men are simply less spiritual than women.

While dozens of books and daily articles confirm that Americans, both men and women, Christians and Jews, are constantly engaged in "spiritual searching," (see especially Roof, 1993). It is a widespread belief in America that women are more spiritual and men are—well—less spiritual. Cohen and Eisen's (2000) comment below, while directed specifically within the Jewish community, certainly typifies the broader society's perception:

> The relatively new interest in spirituality in Judaism is a concern to which women are generally more open than men. Conversations about and experiences of transcendence come more easily to women than to men, if our interviews are a reliable indicator. And the visibility of women rabbis, lay leaders, and communal professionals has galvanized and legitimated re-interpretation of the tradition and re-direction of institutions, both of which in turn attract women who might otherwise have remained aloof. We suspect that the very language of search and quest presumes a hesitancy with which the men we met were often uncomfortable. (p. 206)

Countering the widespread belief that spiritual searching speaks primarily, if not exclusively, to women, a number of authors have explored and written about male or masculine spirituality. Oddly, the terms are rarely used within the admittedly small body of contemporary Jewish Men's Movement literature. This is surprising, since the notion of balancing masculine and feminine energy is not new to Judaism. Such language is found throughout one of the major historic streams of Judaism, the study of Kabbalah (Matt, 1994), especially the *Zohar*. In the *Zohar*, the *Hesed* and the *Gevurah,* two of the 10 *sefirot* components, are often presented as the opposing feminine-masculine forces or poles that need to be brought into equilibrium, into balance.

For an explicit discussion on male spirituality, one can turn instead to the works of Christian colleagues (McGrath, 2004).

> There's something about healthy masculine energy, just as there is about healthy feminine energy that is necessary to our wholeness as a society.... Any organization needs both masculine and feminine energy to be whole. There's been an admirable amount of creative work being done on feminine energy and what it offers society. For the good of society, men need to disengage from their roles in the current structure, become "outsiders" for a time, and discover what positive masculine energy can offer. And just as feminine energy is not limited to females, neither is masculine energy limited to males. (p. 12)

Or as Father Richard Rohr (1988) has stated:

> Masculine spirituality is not just for men, although it is men who are most likely going to have to rediscover and exemplify it. Strangely, it is an approach that many women are more in touch with today than men. Women have been encouraged and even forced to work on their inner [lives] more than men in our culture. In general, they are far ahead of men in integrating the masculine and feminine parts of themselves. Their inner journeys have left many of us men in the dust. Our sisters' pursuit of the authentic feminine has made the brothers aware that there is also an authentic masculine. But what is it? Quite simply it is the other side of the feminine energy. It is the other pole, the contrary, the balance. (p. 7)

How does men's spirituality differ from women's spirituality? Are the religious beliefs significantly different? Are the religious behaviors significantly expressed differently? Do Jewish men's spiritual journeys take parallel, convergent, or divergent paths from that of their Christian or Muslim neighbors? Are men's differences from women in terms of religious belief and/or religious behavior truly a function of gender, a function of maleness, or based more on cultural tradition? To date, I don't believe there are good answers to many of these questions, but they are questions worth posing and exploring.

In trying to explain not necessarily why men are disengaged from religious institutions, per se, as much as why the rate of disengagement has risen so much within the past 20 years, it is also appropriate to consider the possible impact of men's beliefs and behavior from a generational perspective. As Putnam (2000) conclusively documented, the younger generations (i.e., the baby boomers, the Generation Xers, the millennium generation) all show less interest in civic institution, including participating in religious institutions, than did an earlier generation, such as the Depression/World War II era generation, what Putnam called the Civic-Engaged or Civic Building Generation. Whether in fact people would totally agree with Putnam that there is a direct correlation between increased civic and religious disengagement and the extraordinary increase in the number of hours that people watch TV (or nearly a decade later, Putnam, I think, would add Internet surfing) is not important. If people are serious about reversing men's flight, then generational differences also will need to be appreciated.

Clearly, some of the critical factors for male absence within the Reform Movement have nothing to do with gender-related distinctions, nor are they necessarily identical to those factors within Christian denominations. There may be factors that are distinctly Reform Movement issues. For example, the Reform Movement has revisited the role of traditional observance and has placed new emphasis on Hebrew study and prayer. Numerous prayer books, employing more Hebrew as well as being gender sensitive if not outright gender neutral, have been widely disseminated within the past 20 years. And, inevitably, new tunes in Hebrew have also been introduced to prevent monotony. Unfortunately, for a generation of classically Reform-educated members who were raised in an English-only environment, the discomfort level has increased. There is widespread ignorance of traditions, rituals, and prayers by both men and women of this generation, and men especially are not going to openly display their ignorance by participating at public, congregational events. Their absence avoids potential personal embarrassment.

Finally, the religious institutions may be viewed, fairly or unfairly, as primarily pediatric institutions, focusing more on the interests of children than adults—men or women. It is not necessarily a gender issue but a perception that a younger generation of congregational members receives more attention than another. However, while there is increased discussion and in some cases actual implementation of equal sharing between spouses, when it comes to home and its extensions (e.g., the children's schools), the primary responsibility and active participation in children's education, be it public or religious, still falls more often to women.

> To a remarkable degree, the "action" where Jewish activity among the moderately affiliated is concerned now rests with women, who undertake such activity either with or without the assistance of male partners. Given the centrality of ritual to our subjects, and the fact that so much of Jewish ritual takes place in the home and involves children, the predominance of women in undertaking Jewish practice is not surprising. Women retain primary responsibility for child-rearing, even in two-career families. Home remains their domain, recognized as such by men and women alike. (Cohen & Eisen, 2000, p. 206)

Not Just a Boy Crisis

The Reform Movement's and, for that matter, Jewish community's greater interest in meeting the needs of young people rather than that of their parents was brought into sharper focus for me recently. There has been a series of articles in the Jewish and general press acknowledging the reality of the male-flight phenomenon. The primary focus of these articles, however, is not on the decreasing enrollment of men at Hebrew Union College-Jewish Institute of Religion as rabbis, cantors, or educators nor on the decreasing attendance and participation of adult men in numerous venues of temple life; rather, the focus has been on the boy crisis—young teenage males, especially post-Bar Mitzvah age. Now, the cause for concern is genuine: in 2006, the Reform Movement's national leadership examined numerous venues where one would expect the relatively equal participation of young male and female teens and unfortunately found that there was not one venue where young male teens predominated. Whether at the Union for Reform Judaism's summer camps, local or regional youth groups, or national Youth Leadership venues, post-thirteen-year-old young women were more than in the majority; in some cases the ratio was disproportionately closer to 75% female, 25% male.

And, at one workshop that I recently facilitated, I was sadly informed by one, well-intentioned rabbi: "Well, we have already lost one generation of adults. Let's make sure we focus all our attentions on the young male teens!" I fear such statements and beliefs are too common.

To focus only on young male teens is for me, obviously, too shortsighted. This is a multigenerational problem, and any effective remedies are going to have to address the problem at its roots, and address what I call the "Missing-in-Action Father Syndrome." As stated earlier, there are too many fathers who are spending so many hours at their careers that they are missing too many important events in the lives of their children. These are the Jewish fathers who pass the phone call from the rabbi to their wives, and who leave the Hebrew school education of their children to their wives, just as they leave the public school education of their children to their wives. The Missing-in-Action Jewish Father may start off Sunday morning by doing his share of caring for his children by driving them to Hebrew school but then declines the temple brotherhood's offer to join them for a program inside the temple walls. Why? Because it competes with his standing date with the tennis pro at the health club or his opportunity to get in a few holes at the nearest golf course. Yes, with little discretionary time, adult men are entitled to some time to themselves, but they shouldn't think for a moment that the kids, especially young male teens, aren't getting the message as to what is really important to their fathers!

It is all about role modeling, and too many Jewish men are setting a poor example for the next generation. So, though the Jewish press may choose to focus on the young male teen issue, the boy crisis cannot be separated from the father crisis. The next generation of Jews needs to observe and interact with both female and male role models, both lay and professional. Young men will follow by example. For them to see Judaism as an important aspect of their lives, they must continue to see their fathers, grandfathers, uncles, and older brothers taking it seriously.

Making Room for Men's-Only Space

I am a Jewish male feminist. I seek equal respect and opportunity for both men and women within liberal Jewish life. That said, if I truly want a stronger and healthier Jewish community, then it is fair to ask the question: Are Jewish men today fully receiving the assistance they need to define their new roles and seek opportunities within their faith community? If I want a young generation of male teens to see their fathers taking their Judaism seriously, then I must ask: What is it going to take for their fathers to find the time to explore their spiritual and social needs within their local temples? What is it going to take for men to overcome the many obstacles that they have articulated earlier? And, if they are prepared to find the time to explore their needs, will they be welcomed and find value in their decisions? What is the synagogue currently offering them and is it sufficient? The most difficult question here is whether the synagogue, or any religious institution for that matter, is prepared to give men the opportunity, the room, to do more than just talk about who is likely to win the next Superbowl or next local or national election. Will it give men the opportunity to do more than usher or raise funds on behalf of the temple? Are our religious institutions prepared to give men the opportunity to do the kind of spiritual searching and men's work that true feminists, men and women alike, were calling for nearly 30 years ago but that rarely came to fruition?

What is this men's work I am talking about? In much of the literature in the men's movement for the past 30 years, there is a great deal of discussion about how men are hurting, how they are angry and lonely. Too many men ensure they are always in tight emotional control and don't explore the full range of their inner feelings and emotions, afraid of what they might (or might not) find. As a result, their relationships with their loved ones, be it their mothers or fathers, their brothers or sisters, their spouses, their sons or daughters, or their fellow community members, are filled too often with unfulfilled promises and frustrations. Too many men today are on autopilot and never take the time to work through the difficult relationship questions, too often saying they will get to them someday. Harry Chapin's song "Cat in the Cradle," a father's recounting of missing all the important events in his son's life until, at the end, he is a grandfather and now his son has no time to see him and the father realizes "his son grew up and became just like [him], [his] son is just like [him]" sadly resonates with too many men, too well. Someday is always too late.

In the spring of 2005, I attended a North American Federation of Temple Youth (NFTY) leadership convention with 1,300 young people. It was both exhilarating and, quite frankly, a frustrating experience for me because over 75% of the attendees were young women. Bobby Harris, URJ director of Camp Coleman, ran a workshop specifically geared for the male teens. Because of Harris's patience and facilitation skills, I observed 30 young men opening up and talking about their relationships with their fathers. The first young men to speak indicated that they had good relations with their fathers, that their fathers were their friends. However, as more young men spoke out, deeper, more negative feelings emerged. I began to hear: "My father doesn't have a clue as to what is going on in my life," "my father spends more time at his computer than he does with me," "my father is a rabbi, and sometimes I feel he cares more about the congregation than he does about me," and "I wish my father would sit down and talk with me about what's going on in his life."

More than one young man was teary-eyed by the end, and, when the session concluded, several of them came up to Harris to thank him for giving them the opportunity to talk and open up. Many of them expressed that it was the first time that they had had an opportunity like this to just be in a room with other Jewish teenage males and talk about such issues. It didn't happen in public school settings and it certainly didn't happen in their temple youth group activities.

I was sorry that so many of the young men felt that they could not approach their fathers and express these feelings. I was sorry that so many of them felt that the initiative to have a heart-to-heart talk had to come from their fathers. I looked around the room and thought: These boys are going to grow up and become just like their fathers—and be as lonely as them! And I was sorry that more of the men I work with, the fathers of these boys, could not have been flies on the wall in order to hear what contemporaries of their own sons were feeling and articulating.

Men need to acknowledge their hurt, their anger, and their loneliness and engage in men's work to resolve these issues. I often find, however, that the directions for this men's work can be described in two related, but nonetheless distinct, ways. First, for many feminists (both male and female), men's work is synonymous with men getting in closer touch with their feminine side, which usually translates into getting in touch with their feelings, their nurturing modes, their underdeveloped listening skills, etc. Second, for a different group of authors, especially those who identify with a major wing of the general men's movement—the mythopoetic movement—men's work is associated more with men exploring their shadows—their darker, unresolved issues—which may or may not include feminine-associated issues or relationships with the women in their lives. Authors, such as Robert Bly, Michael Mead, the Jesuit Patrick Arnold, and Richard Rohr , employ Jungian archetypes as paradigms for men to probe their inner shadows. Archetypes, such as men as warrior, men as wildman, men as magician, and men as king, are common. I know Jewish men who have no difficulty with using these archetypes and have found them a valuable tool to do their work.

More often than not, men's work for this second group centers around confronting issues related to the absent father, the verbally abusive father, and even the physically violent father. By digging deep and exploring their shadows—those dark parts of themselves that men don't readily admit to—and then working through these unresolved aspects of themselves, men learn to control these darker impulses or urges and to redirect them in more positive, constructive ways. They come to integrate them but not necessarily eliminate them.

Clearly, in the feminist and men-as-warrior camps, there is some overlap as to what is meant by men's work, but it is not identical. For many feminists in the first camp, the sooner that men eliminate their more aggressive nature entirely, the better; for the men-as-warrior followers, men become whole by integrating their Jacob/Esau impulses, not by eliminating one at the expense of the other.

The overemphasis on making men more feminine has its critics. In attempting to reduce a legitimately perceived negative trait, men's tendency to be overly aggressive and revert to violent behavior, a positive masculine attribute has also been lost. A sense of fierceness, the ability to commit and even to be passionate have also been lost. Has there been created a whole generation of soft males?

In the 1960s men and women both went through a major shift in perceptions of gender identity. Women were finding their voice and their power, and men were discovering their "feminine side." While this movement has, on the whole, been a welcome development for one and all, the process produced a generation of what observers like Bly and Rohr call the "soft male." These men are characterized by a gentle attitude and a receptivity and openness most likely not found in their fathers and grandfathers. "But many of these men are not happy," says Bly. "They are life-preserving, but not exactly life-giving. What they miss is fierceness, a resoluteness that is needed if a relationship is to flourish. They lack an ability to commit with passion to a course of action based on deep values. Turning their back on masculine energy has left them without vital energy. American society produces many young men who extend young adulthood well into their 30s and 40s—unattached, uncommitted, playing at life. The culture also produces many young men who form an alternative gang society, mimicking in a twisted way what they needed and failed to receive from the larger society. Workaholics and deadbeat dads abound. And if you look closely, you'll surely see a whole host of men who vaguely sense there's something more to life and who go about living out their commitments, wondering what that something more is." (McGrath, 2004, p. 5)

Jewish men are no exception. I can certainly attest to having observed this first-hand among many men, having spent hundreds of hours conversing and working with such men. But I am not a trained social worker and thus am not qualified to suggest therapeutic solutions. Nor do I believe every male needs therapy. And I certainly have had the opportunity to work with Jewish men who are not angry, who are not lonely, and who are not confused.

Is there such a thing as *Jewish* men's work, something that is unique because of Jewish men's Judaism? In some cases, yes—in others, no. The Jewish Men's Movement literature, starting with Harry Brod's (1988) *A Mensch Among Men* recognized that Jewish men were historically part of a counterculture that made Jewish males distinct from their Christian male neighbors. For centuries, American Jews prided themselves on functioning often within a countercultural subset of the larger gentile American society. As a result, their definitions of masculinity, their relationships with their mothers, fathers, and community, and, in a sense, their total world, gestalt view were at times significantly different from the mainstream gentile culture (Salkin, 1998b).

> "Real" Jews have a different way of praying, learning, studying, and seeing the world. For generations, Jewish men have found their "macho" in mastery of Torah, in heartfelt worship, and in feats of loving-kindness and charity. Jewish men have typically rejected the culture of "sowing wild oats" and "boys will be boys." Jewish men feel the need to talk about the masculine models in Jewish terms. (p. 7)

As Jewish men pursue their men's work, I sincerely hope they will continue this counterculture tradition. Exploring masculine models in Jewish terms is as legitimate a pursuit within the temple community as Jewish men pursuing ritual observance, engaging in prayer, taking trips to Israel, providing service to the congregation, or performing acts of *tikkun olam* in the temple and the broader community. They are all vital components of Jewish men's work. They are all vital parts of a Jewish man's spiritual journey, and his religious institutions should help him on his journey.

When I talk about the importance of men doing important work, or when I talk about the importance of role modeling, I encounter little disagreement. However, when I propose that the temple community actually creates as many opportunities as it can and suggest that this may require creating exclusive gender space, then the balking and disagreement begin. For years, women's programs have been encouraging mothers to bring their daughters to various events, but when I suggest a father-son-only outing sponsored by the local temple, eyebrows get raised and heads begin shaking.

If one accepts the notion that men are different from women—that they have been impacted by feminist ideology, but differently than women and that their children need male Jewish role models—then there is the need to move beyond talking and begin to program in gender terms, including creating the appropriate men's space within synagogues. If the community wants men to move beyond superficiality, if it wants them to dig deeper, then it needs to create safe, nonthreatening havens. There needs to be a place where, on a Sunday morning, men talk about who is going to win the next Superbowl but also engage in an intense, therapeutic, psychodynamic Rolfing session; there should be room within the temple community for men as fathers, as sons, and as brothers to do their work. And for those who concur, theoretically, that such men's work is important but, in practical terms, that it does not require men to have their own exclusive space, I emphatically disagree.

Was the conversation better because it was a boys-only session at the NFTY workshop cited above? No, but I sincerely believe that the teenage males felt the environment was safer to express themselves, more conducive to opening up sooner, and that macho-fronts could be let down easier; there was less worry about having to impress since girls were not in the room. No, the conversation was not necessarily better, but it was different, and heartfelt, and that is a sufficient reason to create more of these opportunities. Young male teens in our Movement shouldn't have to travel 2,000 miles to be given such an experience!

Would the young men at the NFTY Convention have benefited from engaging in a similar session talking about their mothers or about their parents in general? Of course. Would the young men have benefited from engaging in a co-ed session on similar topics? Of course. In emphasizing the need for creating specific gender-only space or creating intergenerational, gender-only space, I am not proposing it become a replacement for co-ed opportunities, rather that it be added to the legitimate arsenal of temple programming, an appropriate venue within a changed temple egalitarian culture.

I certainly believe that most of the time it is appropriate for men and women to come together and pray, study, and interact as a single community. But for the spiritual needs of some men and women to be sufficiently met, the synagogue must also at times create gender-exclusive space—both women's space and men's space. The Reform Movement has readily in the past four decades recognized and supported the need for women's space; however, many in the Movement find the suggestion of a men's-only space to be threatening and problematic. A men's-only space is not the only place where all men will do their work, but, for many, it is a minimum, nonnegotiable requirement. The community needs to make room for that exploration within its congregations.

If men are properly approached and appreciated, I believe they men are still prepared to seek answers to their spiritual searching within the congregations. This will require, however, that it be recognized that men's spiritual energy comes in many different forms and has both masculine and feminine components. A number of suggestions for congregation leadership to begin this sensitive but vital journey are listed below.

1. Be prepared to talk about gender in board rooms, in committee meetings, in temple bulletins, and from the pulpit.
2. Acknowledge that there are gender-related subjects that are worthy of exploration. The question is not whether men and women are different with regard to religious beliefs and religious behavior. The two related and more important questions are "How are they different?" and, if so, "are the differences significant enough to require the congregational leadership at times offering alternative programming, study, and even prayer venues for men and women?"
3. Create men's-only space. Explore opportunities in study, prayer, and social community, where men can explore and celebrate being contemporary Jewish men in the company of only other men.
4. Review and evaluate existing adult programs. What other programs might have greater appeal to adult men? Consider both the content and the style of the program. Yes, the following are stereotyping, but are often true:

   Men like to either observe or participate in sports activities; it is a good way to bring men together, especially those who are new to the community or group. Fellowship is a great foundation for men to come together later to explore more personal and difficult relationship issues. Men often prefer doing to talking. It has been noted that when women talk to each other they often face each other. Men's conversation style tends to be more directed and more sideways (i.e., they talk to their colleagues while they are doing something together). Projects should be found that give men an opportunity to do more than sit and talk.

   Men like to focus, and they need to have a sense of accomplishment on a project. Remember, they bring their work mode with them into the temple and are looking for a clear sense of what has to be done. It should be given it to them.

   Men have less discretionary time than ever. They should not be expected to sign up for and commit to long-term endeavors. They should not be expected to attend multiple adult education study programs. They should first be asked to commit to a one-time program.

   Men will have gone through Hebrew school and bar mitzvah, but it should not be assumed that they have even a rudimentary grasp of Jewish history, rituals, or liturgy. In many cases, over two decades have passed since they were in a formal (or even informal) education setting. They should not be put in potentially publicly embarrassing situations. Tjose leading will not get a second chance.

   Men are competitive. This should be turned into a positive, not a negative. They should be challenged! They should be helped to gain entry into synagogue life, not have obstacles put in their way!

5. Go beyond a simple men's-only sporting activity. A Torah study that discusses gender perspectives should be considered. A men's-only Seder event should be

conducted; one hour during *Shavuot* should be used to focus on a topic of special concern to men. A pre-ushering High Holiday event should be held to turn ushering into more of a meaningful welcoming event than merely a monotonically handing out of prayer books. All of the cultural dynamics operating within congregational life should be more deeply explored.

6. Develop venues for men to explore their familial roles, especially their roles as fathers. While I have stressed so far the importance of temple leadership appreciating and recognizing gender differences and the need to create programs that speak to men, I need to caution that the actual promotion and marking of such programs will not necessarily benefit by promoting them as men's programs per se. Unlike promoting programs for women, who, through the Women's Movement, perceive themselves often as a collective group with reason to come together with their sisters, there is little in our society that encourages men to come together with other men just for the sake of being with other men, to come together with their brothers. Thus, promoting the gender card will not be sufficient to get men to show up. Instead, I strongly suggest a slight change in language: when promoting programs for men, promote the events in familial relationship terms, not gender terms. Rather than focusing on men as brothers, I believe there will be more success in focusing on men as fathers. And while I appreciate that not all men are fathers, the majority of adult male temple members are, and it is therefore appropriate to offer programs that meet this important segment of the temple community.
7. Develop programs that help men increase their competency. If the community wants fathers to be appropriate role models for the next generation, the men need to perceive themselves as having the appropriate competency. I believe that men want to be positive role models for their children, but they must be offered safe havens and encouraged to learn, and if necessary relearn, what their faith tradition has to offer them.
8. Develop programs that help men increase their religious competency, and then develop intergenerational programs. Develop intergenerational activities that will give adult men an opportunity to interact with their sons, and, yes, develop intergenerational activities that will give men an opportunity to interact with their daughters. Whether organizing an intergenerational softball game or a weekend retreat, give men the opportunity to spend more time with the next generation. Young men must see their fathers engaged in temple work!
9. Revisit life-cycle events, holidays, and rituals from a gender differentiation perspective. Suggesting the promotion of male-only, ritual-related activity within a gender egalitarian community borders, for some, on the blasphemous! Yet it is exactly in the worship and ritual areas that the community must be prepared to explore the gender issues. Why? It is because men don't specifically need their temple or church to engage in a father-son sports activity or to go hiking together. Men don't need the temple or church to get together with a group of other men. They certainly don't need the temple or church setting to go bowling with their sons! If the community wants their men to be more than role models and if they want them to be competent and religiously in-

spired role models, then the children need to see their fathers performing an active role in the *Beit T'fillah* (prayer venues) and the *Beit Midrash* (study venues) of the temple or church, not just serving on the finance committee!

10. Recognize the diversity of the target audience! One model will not fit all. Be realistic in expectations. Men will find the time to participate in those activities that they feel are important to them. Men will find the time to participate in those activities in which they feel needed. While they want to be good male role models, how they will choose to explore and express those roles will be varied and diverse. Men's spiritual paths are multidimensional. Those paths will be expressed through worship, ritual, education, meditation, prayer, social action, service, and any combination thereof. A brotherhood/congregation that offers men a variety of venues to express their search for meaning has the best chance of succeeding.

The challenge is to reverse the disengagement of men without setting the egalitarian clock back 30 years. As women must search out ways to access and celebrate their feminine spiritual energy, men too must search out ways to celebrate their unique masculine spiritual energy and role. Communities must find ways to reengage men, not to disenfranchise women.

I work with men, Jewish men. I am not prepared to give up on them. This group is fighting major societal, economic, and cultural trends that have pulled men away from the religious institutions. The community is fighting to regain their attention. It is fighting to overcome their passivity and regain their involvement. It will have to fight to regain their confidence that the synagogues have something to say to them, that it can make a difference in their lives as Jewish men, as Jewish fathers, sons, and brothers. If not now, when?

The community must find ways to honor and to make places for both the feminine and masculine spirits in the religious life of the people. It is not a zero-sum game. Rather, the challenge is to find new win-win paradigms for both men and women interested in ensuring a strong religious community in the 21st century. The differences must be celebrated and cherished, not ignored!

Yes, both men and women must recover their roles as singers of songs and tellers of tales, but it is time to recognize that men and women have different songs to sing and different stories to tell. Men's voices are not better than women's; women's voices are not better than men's. Men's stories are not better than women's; women's stories are not better than men's. They are different. And a vibrant, liberal Jewish community will benefit when both men and women tell their tales, when there is a loud chorus of both men and women singing.

The community should begin. Together now: *Hinei Ma Tov Uma Na-im Shevet Achim Gam Yahad*, How good it is for brothers to come together!

References

Barden, D. (2006). *Wrestling with Jacob and Esau—Fighting the flight of men: A modern day crisis in the Reform Movement.* New York: North American Federation of Temple Brotherhoods.
Brod, H. (1988). *A mensch among men.* Freedom, CA: Crossroads.
Cohen, S., & Eisen, A. (2000). *The Jew within, self, family and community in America.*
Goldstein, E.M. (2004). Where do we go from here? One woman's perspective. *Achim Magazine*, p. 6.
Holzman, M. (2004). Male gender awareness. *Achim Magazine*, p. 8.
Matt, D. (1994). *The essential Kaballah.* New York: Harper.
McGrath, T. (2004). Is men's spirituality out of the woods? http://www.uscatholic.org/2002/04/cov0204.htm
Putnam, R. (2000). *Bowling alone.* New York: Simon & Schuster.
Rohr, R. (1988, September-October). Masculine spirituality. *National Catholic Reporter.*
Rolenz, K. (2004). The vanishing male. *Achim Magazine*, p. 12.
Roof, W. (1993). *Generation of seekers: The spiritual journeys of the baby boom generation.* New York: HarperCollins.
Salkin, J. (1998a). Real aches. *Achim Magazine*, p. 5.
Salkin, J. (1998b). Jewish macho. *Reform Judaism Magazine*, p. 5.

18

Poems for the Postmodern Man

Ties
Rabbi Ed Stafman

He came to me
and said, Dad,
Can you tie my tie?
At eighteen,
he was looking smart
Beaming with the ripeness of his age.
Yet a childish part remained,
he had still to learn to tie a tie.
Sitting on my chair
I replied,
Of course, son, kneel
with your back to me
and he complied.
My arms moved over his shoulders
over territory
ordinarily forbidden to me.

He felt like my baby as I slowly
Worked the knot, folding
my arms around him, folding
until the knot moved up
tightly under his collar.
Turn around, I said, and my hands
took one last permitted touch of his shoulders
I wondered when I'd get another.

So full of life he looked as he headed off
To his graduation party.

A week or so later,
Son, he said to me
Can you tie my tie?
He had no dexterity left,
his limbs and his mind barely functioned.
Of course, dad, I said
And as he sat on the bed's edge,
I climbed up behind him.

I reached across his shoulders
Touching places
I had not touched in decades.
My hands passed over his aged
and tattered skin.
As I reached over his shoulders to tie
the knot, folding
my arms around him, folding
until the knot moved up
tightly under his collar.
I came around to the front of him,
and my hands took one last permitted
touch.
He smiled blithely
as he headed off,
headed off.

OPEN HEART SURGERY
Jacob J. Staub

At forty, I raced to the airport, hoping
to reach you and kiss your leaky valve.

But you, you feisty thing, you barged
out of intensive care, blockages
ballooned away, before we could reserve
a private nurse. Holiday sunset approached,
whisking your daughters back to the blintzes,
their families. It fell to me to nurse you
for a single eight-hour *tikkun*,
to see you broken-ribbed and moaning,
and to love you, reduced.

Ice chips, washcloths,
more blankets, fewer. Helpless, you
were commanding. The room was an icebox,
the mattress, an inquisitor's rack. I held you,
reminding you to sip. I promised
it would be all right. I kissed
your clammy forehead. I mothered you.
When they switched the mattresses,
you grumbled that the new one was worse,
but in your kvetch, you seemed
grateful that I had tried, at least.

Five years later, there were no hurried
flights, no stolen kisses. You were in
your own bed. Your heart gave out
while you slept.

At fifty-five,
you hold me like you never did before.
Though you rarely offered me a kind word
face-to-face, you knew your daughters
would relay your *kvelling*. You did the best
you could, mothering by indirection.

As I light the candle, you look at me
directly.

Facing You Facing Me*
Jacob J. Staub

Moses misunderstood in the cleft of the rock.
He was trapped in the essentialist fallacy.
Up on the mountain, on top of the world,
after forty days suspended over the clear, crisp desert vistas,
of leaning into Your muscular arms, penetrated by Your words,
imbibing the call to sacred leadership,
he yearned, like every lover, for all-consuming union.

Having surrendered to You,
he asked You to reciprocate,
and when he beheld You, still inconsumable,
he thought You were holding back. You weren't.

Like every lover, every human being,
who self-discloses through an endless stream of masks,
You, too, reign in garbs majestic and humble,
strong and broken, compassionate and judgmental.
He had already seen Your face, Your infinite faces.
You had kissed him with the kisses of Your mouth,
caressed him, transported him on Your wings.
He had seen what could be seen.
He heard You saying that he could not live,
when what You meant was that in this life,
there are only manifestations
of that which is ever changing.

Wherever You are described as majestic, the rabbis taught,
You are also described as humble
because you are neither.
This is the ultimate Purim Torah.
Elijah on that same mountaintop,
saw you in the raging gales and quaking earth
and in the deafening silence that pierced his heart
opening him to that which can't be seen or touched.
You face us when You turn aside.
You face us when You fill us up to overflowing.
You face us when You contract to be filled by us.

This is the ultimate Purim Torah—
that we mask ourselves to disclose what is hidden, just like You.
We cannot see Your face, as we cannot see the face of any other.
Neither You nor we have a single face to see.

* This poem won an Honorable Mention in the 2005 *Presence* Poetry Contest.

From a Father to a Son
In Honor of Yigdal Raphael's Bar Mitzvah
Simcha Paull Raphael

Baby boy birthed into the world
First-born son of mother and father
Destined to become
A full-standing member of the Jewish people
Inheritor of the ancient religion of Judaism
Creator of the community of twenty-first century Jews

Slowly, day-by-day
Baby boy grows up
Learns to walk
Learns to talk
Meandering the halls of Germantown Jewish Centre
Discovering the rhythms of Jewish life
Holy days, Shabbat
Celebrations of the sacred seasons of Jewish time

Slowly, week-by-week
Boy child grows up
Learns to read, to write
To sing and pray
In the language of the ancestors
Hebrew, holy hebrew, Lashon Ha-Kodesh.

Yigdal—he shall grow mighty
Once a four pound, four ounce preemie
Yigdal, grows mighty
A good student
athlete
friend
son
brother
Year-by-year
Yigdal, grows mighty
And approaches the vestibule of puberty
Preparing to pass through the mysterious portal
Into the sacred realms of Jewish life
Slowly, methodically
But very definitely
Boy morphing into man
Embarks upon the mythical trek
To become

A Bar Mitzvah!
A—what?
A Bar Mitzvah?
What exactly is that?
Son of the Commandments
A man of Mitzvot
A *mensch* among Jewish men
Like his father, grandfathers
Great-grandfathers before him
Thirteen years old
Able to be counted in a *minyan*

But what is a Bar Mitzvah?
What is this holy event?
This sacred tribal gathering
We are here to celebrate?
Is this only the final culmination of
A dizzying carousel of
Logistics beyond logical expectations
Parties and planning
Invitations and menus
Guest lists and to do lists?
Is Bar Mitzvah any more than the
Serendipitous or perhaps fortunate result of

Parents planning into the wee small hours of the night
As the young man sharpens his voice
Agonizes over music and melodies
Speeches and the far reaches of understanding
Torah and tradition in our time?

Then..... finally.....
The day has arrived!
Here comes the shul
Here comes the Bar Mitzvah boy
Today I am a party favor
Today I am a monogrammed blue kippah!
Today I am a man!
Is that all there is to a Bar Mitzvah?

What does it mean to become a man?
A woman can change an embryo to a boy
But what changes a boy to a man?
Answer: walking the sacred pilgrimage
Towards becoming a Bar Mitzvah!
Bar Mitzvah—a time to read Torah

To study, to learn, to give a speech
To daven, to serve as a leader of prayer
To participate in the community of Jewish men
To participate in the community of Jewish men and women
Bar Mitzvah—a time of deepening
A time of learning and growing
And knowing and showing
Of praying and staying the course
Of course.

Bar Mitzvah is not only the end of boyhood
Talking to girls, not only boys
Giving away your old toys
Bequeathing outgrown beanie babies to your sister
Growing to an extra large size
Or maybe a man's small?
Is he really that tall?
Clearly, right before our eyes
The boy-child is dying off
The little boy is no longer
A young man is being resurrected
A second birth, he grows mighty minute by minute
Watch out, here comes another growth spurt!

As a Bar Mitzvah, you have begun
The journey of a lifetime
To become who you truly are
A rite of passage to a fuller you
An adventure in search of full self.
A voyage to strange new worlds
To discover who exactly is Yigdal
Who is your God?
Who are your people?

But wait!
None of the great Jews of antiquity had Bar Mitzvahs
Not Abraham or Moses
Not Solomon, David or Jonathan
Not Rabbi Akiva
So what is this journey?
How can this rite of passage
Birth the soul of a Jewish boy?
Abraham journeyed through the desert
Called to be father of a nation
Moses journeyed in the wilderness
Called to be a leader

The Israelite tribes
Journeyed from slavery to freedom
Called to become a holy nation
And a kingdom of priests.

And you, Yigdal
Bar Mitzvah boy
You now begin your journey
To grow into the mighty person
You are called to be.

At thirteen, the Rabbis taught
The *yetzer ha-tov* enters a person
The desire to act from beneficence is born
And you are now given the opportunity
To nourish and grow your *yetzer ha-tov*
Your sense of what is right for the world in which we live today

At thirteen, Bezalel, the sacred architect
Designed the Holy *Mishkan*
And you, Bar Mitzvah boy, are called to journey
Towards the fullness of your creativity.

At thirteen, Avraham smashed
The idols of his father Terah
And you, Bar Mitzvah boy, are called to find
What is your own truth
Your own God.

At thirteen, Esav and Yaakov
Each went their ways
One into idolatry
One into service of God.
And you, ben Simcha v'Geela Rayzel
Are now called into your tribal community
To live a life of Torah, *Avodah* and *Gemillut Hasadim*
However you understand that to be
To learn and study the ancient
Wisdom lineage of the past
And to make it your own
To find your own ways of wrestling with God.
However you understand God to be
To find your ways of serving this world
A world at war
A world in which there is richness and poverty
A world where there are haves and have-nots

And you—Bar Mitzvah boy
Have begun the journey of self-discovery
To find your own voice
your own song
your own spirit
To take your place
In the community of Jews
In this wonder-filled community of Mount Airy
In this nation, at this time in history
And in the world community which desperately cries out for healing
And today, on this sacred day in your life
Your parents
Your grandparents—in this world and the world beyond
Your aunts and uncles
Your cousins and friends welcome you
Into our sacred tribal gathering
Blessing you with our love
Proud of how you have grown
These past thirteen years
And knowing
Wherever you go
Whatever you do
Wherever you travel
Whomever you love
We will love you
We will always welcome you
As a member of this ever-changing
Family of tribes
Gathered around the holy of holies
Gathered together in God's Name.

Happy Bar Mitzvah!
The journey awaits my son
Travel wisely, gently
Courageously, faithfully
Thanks for giving all of us the opportunity
To stand together with you
And welcome you into our family of tribes united as one.
Baruch Atta Adonai Eloheinu RuakhHa-Olam
Shecheyanu v'kiyemanu, v'higiyanu la'zman ha'zeh.
Blessed be the Holy One who has brought us all
To this most auspicious and sacred moment.

The Last Kaddish
In Honor of Harold Paull
Simcha Paull Raphael

As I did every other time
I said Kaddish for you
In a public venue
I stood up
Closed my eyes
Attuned to your soul
And to the pain in my heart
As I did every other time
I said the words of Kaddish
Aspiring for thoughtful, heartfelt connection
I made this sacred time
A moment for our brief visit
With each other
And then
Reciting the last phrases of the Kaddish
Thoughtfully
Mindfully
Lovingly
I paused
Breathed in one last
Tear-choked sigh
And breathed out
Relief
Perhaps an end to grief
At least a stopping point
A transition
In this journey of
Life, death and transformation
Nothing more
Nothing less
I made it to this moment
And while its obvious
Your life has ended
For me, the rest of my life
The next chapters
Of a totally unknown story
Are just about to begin
Fasten your seat belt
The adventure is just about to begin.

Afterword

A Midrash for the Post-Modern Man

Inspired by the Biblical book, "Kohelet" (Ecclesiastes)

Rabbi Shawn Israel Zevit

On men and the quest for the Divine-

Utter change! says the Seeker-
Utter change! All is in flux!
Yet there is real value for a man
In all he quests beneath the sun

One generation of experience and inquiry goes,
And another comes.
Identities rise, others shift-
And what is in vogue comes 'round again.
No one can ever fully express the
Turns that every season holds.
And, my sons and daughters,
There are so many opinions and
Expectations of who you are to be
And so many roads that your ancestors
Have traveled beneath the sun
To these days of utter change.

So, I said to myself, "Here I am a man of my time,
Seeking to be the change I desire in the days of change,
Seeing my own role, desires, expectations and responsibilities
Being challenged and changed in my lifetime.
Let me set my inquiry
To what I as a Jewish man have become,
So that I may leave you
With the questions I am living into
As generations unfold beneath the sun."

And I learned-
That for all I have prided myself in becoming –
A man of equity and justice,
Of love and compassion,
Of feminist and male-affirmative consciousness-
A man of GOD-
I learned, there is still much change needed ahead
So that the breakthroughs of one generation
Would not become the exit door
For a whole generation to come.

I learned that I hold the generations within me
Even as I strive towards
A different tomorrow.
If I pretend otherwise
Then I will relegate both the richness and the shadow-side
Of my tradition, cultural and gender inheritance
To the realm of the nonintegrated and unseen.
There may be nothing new under the sun
Yet an enlightened life is still a soul's unending quest.

I set myself to look at our tradition
And the journey of men before me.
I discovered that the reverberations
From the "lech lecha"
Of God's calling to Avram
To journey into the unknown
Still echoes for us today.
The quest to meet the yearning of the soul-
Where the desires of our heart
Intersect with the needs of
The world in which we live,
Has not diminished with time.

As I opened my eyes and ears to the voices of my brothers around me, they spoke of gender roles in flux, expectations and hopes shifting and stretching. They spoke of challenges to understand where they are, even as they try to figure out where they are headed. Their connections to, and definition of what is Jewish and masculine, and what lies beyond the construct of "masculinity," are also buffeted by winds of change. They talked of the ancient call to chart their unique path, connect to loved ones, and find their place in community and the world at large. Many struggled to understand the world of their fathers, let alone find their purpose in a now unfamiliar landscape.

Some men had been handed the richness of faith, with its customs, rituals and insights and so could add their life stories to the ancient ones. However, for many tradition was not a given. What they had received from their parents no longer resonated in their own hearts. Some spoke of experiences in general men's groups or social, political and environmental movements, but they felt out of touch with their Jewish identity.

Others were well grounded in their Jewish expression, but had never explored being in a group of men. Many expressed sadness at having few or surface relationships with other men. Initially I found few resources to help my brothers deal with these concerns, yet an intense need to address their questions and longing. Our sisters were generally encouraging of this search, knowing their liberation alone would not free us from a *mitzrayim* of historic social, political, economic, cultural and political structures that were limiting and destructive, or aid us in reconstructing these roles and constructs in light of emerging paradigms and reality maps.

I was deeply moved, even as I heard my brothers speak of their alienation and pride, that there does exist the rich legacy of what it has meant to be a Jewish man. There has been encouragement and resource to make a profound contribution to our families, our people, our world. There is a legacy of great creativity, of GOD-hunger, a Soul-wrestling, and the commitment to live principled lives, to stand for justice, compassion, and our people. There have been eras of great learning and insight, of enormous contribution to human endeavor supported by unending energy and passion, despite barriers and brutality met along the way. There has been a limitless range of diverse expressions of Holiness and Wholeness, brush stroked as a canvas on the Soul of the world.

There is also growing attention to exploring our relationship to God, traditional and creative ritual, sexuality and intimacy, internalized and external anti-Semitism, women's contributions, partnering, raising and relating to children, physical health, competition and isolation, homophobia, cross-cultural connections, understanding Jewish leadership, gender and men's studies, friendship, addictions, violence, work and money, creating and sustaining men's groups. All part of the legacies we have inherited and may wish to leave behind in part or whole (or not) to our sons, daughters and communities.

I also turned the light of inquiry toward the shadowed corners of our legacy as Jewish men and discovered other truths. There were voices of pain, grief and loss linked to great expectations relentlessly pursued. There were internalizations of the need to be saviors and the expectation in many generations that maybe "this boy child" would be the messiah—a tall order to fill. There were many Jewish brothers feeling compelled to save humanity and save the remnants of their people, or perhaps excel at their professions and obtain positions of power to ensure security and influence- often at the expense of their own unfulfilled dreams or well-being. I met men who were bent or broken under the weight of trying too long to be the redeemer, to be perfect, to get it right at all costs- men who bore the scars and had inflicted the scars of hand-me-down abuse and addiction- the silent conversation of previous generations. The drive to be the best, change the world, earn more than- be more than- have more than- had crushed some before they blossomed.

Some men paid no attention to their physical lives, having retreated to the mind and left the body over many centuries when the world became unsafe for them as Jewish men.

Others reinforced their physical prowess so as to counter historical passive images internalized through prejudicial projections from other cultures and faith traditions of asexuality, sexual disinterest and physical weakness and found militaristic, highly sexualized, aggressive religious or anti-religious uniforms from which to fight back. A distancing and stereotyping of Jewish women, and a counter-stereotyping by Jewish women also entered the lexicon of Western world Jewish relationship dynamics as Jewish men (and women) made a dash for mainstream societies in the age of mass immigration.

Faced with so many pressures, many of their hearts grew into thick forests of rigid practice and identity, or opaque wisps of "assimilationist" distance fleeing the synagogue or Jewish community that had been a previous generations' heritage, even as their female counterparts entered Jewish ritual and communal life in unprecedented numbers. New opportunities in the greater Western world and Israel meant a Jewish identity menu of multiple options, including partnering Jewishly or non-Jewishly (though many discovered their partners' curiosity about Jewish life and the arrival of children challenged their own wounds or alienation, as opposed to allowing for a haven away from questions of religion, culture and Jewish male identity).

> So, I was left to ask myself,
> "What could and indeed, has begun,
> to draw my Jewish brothers together again
> in healing, balanced ways?
> What of the future?"

For some men it is the opportunity, structured and informal, for sharing with other men and deepening their connection to their Judaism. Some have sought to address the desire for a re-connection to longstanding Jewish traditions, renewed in a dance of tradition and innovation to speak to us today. Some spoke of gathering for Kiddush Levanah, a monthly celebration of the new moon and month. They began with study and sharing, followed by a trip outside to a nearby park for recitation of the liturgy for sanctifying the new moon and to exchange blessings or mark transitions such as fatherhood, bar mitzvah, and marriage, or offer healing prayers for ill friends and family. Some men created support groups to deal with issues of concern to them as Jewish men. The previous generation's gathering places of brotherhoods and men's clubs have begun to restructure themselves and develop programs to address issues of concern to contemporary Jewish men.

I discovered an array of groups, workshops, courses and publications, retreats, newly emerging egalitarian and male-affirming prayer groups, klezmer-jazz-hiphop-world-music-fusion groups, social justice and tzedakah collectives; programs held at synagogues, Jewish Community Centers, campuses, bookstores and homes dealing with gender and Jewish men lives.

I found men re-engaging with traditional and post-modern/midrashic Torah study, mikveh, reclaiming, transforming, and with men who were exploring male role models in Jewish history and new rituals that spoke to their unfolding, unsettling and liberating life experiences. My own time became more focused on existing and new relationships with Jewish men- Israeli men, heterosexual, gay, bisexual and trans-gendered identified men- in fact, with men who were asking about and challenging the very constructs of masculinity itself. I built deep connections with men interested in re-examining their life at work and at home, health issues, *tikkun olam,* economic, social, political, environmental and spiritual sustainability, globalization and the male and Jewish contributions, roles and impact on current state of affairs in the world.

My work helped me break down my own male fears and self-image, turned my heart and mind to my own father and a new journey of meaningful relationship. I broke the intimacy barrier and partnered, bringing about new challenges to concepts I held intellectually but had not embodied about who I was as a Jewish man in ideal and who I saw myself revealed in action. Like the heroes I had inherited, I saw my own self-image crumble and reconstruct in the light of love. Partnering twice brought about parenting young Jewish men- and age and life experience added mentoring and helping support a new generation of seekers and sojourners.

In this all I have seen the gulf between beliefs and "becomings," thought and action, masculinities and actualities. I have seen myself and my holy brothers rise to new awareness that transcend self-limitation and larger world expectation and constraint. I have seen the bearers of the sacred vestments and leadership titles fall into valleys of shadows and destructive behavior that shattered those they inspired. And yet as the path I set myself to explore, and the horizon line still unfurling its banner before me brings me back to the beginning I say-

Utter change! All is in flux!
Yet there is real value for a man
In all he quests beneath the sun

Through the cracks in our hearts,
Sacred light has begun
To pour into new vessels.

And so I say to you,
Appreciate your journey as it unfolds,
Do not give in and say,
"This inquiry is of no concern to me!"
If you leave the inquiry only to our sisters,
Or passively appreciate the holy brothers
Leading the inquiry
Or satisfy yourself
Only in the attractions of the greater culture,
The foundations of your spirit
Will become shaky.

Build trust between yourselves
And learn how to relate to each other as men
Beyond the avenues previously afforded.
This will allow you the opportunity
To see beyond and behind competition,
Insecurities and fears.
You will be able to
Forge compassionate,
Relevant and authentic spiritual lives.

You will be able to deepen your souls,
So that your renewed Jewish expression
Enhances and supports the
Journey of men and women
In an age of rapidly changing roles and expectations.
Guilt, feelings of shame,
Inadequacy and blaming others
Is the surest way to keep the baggage
We drag along
Stuck in place.
The emergence of a new Jewish male identity
Must neither be dominating and abusive
Nor so passive and apologetic
That it leads to a total flattening
Of behavior that de-energizes and immobilizes.

If we seek to deepen our connection to each other,
To women,
To our and the world's children
To people of all faiths and backgrounds
To the planet of which we are an expression
We will need to realign relationships in community
In such a way that values
What is rich and meaningful in the past,
And allows us to work together
And support each other
In creative, compassionate and insightful ways
Towards a healthy future.

So, I say to you in summary,
When all the books have been read,
All the seminars, committees and retreats attended,
The prayers and sacred texts spoken,
Honor the potential in your own soul
And the Divine spark in all life,
Do not despair on the journey,
Nor give in to simple solutions.
For this applies to all men and women of all times
That in the end we will be held accountable
For our choices in life
And the extent to which we truly became
The blessing we were meant to be
In the short time we were here.

Contributors

Michele Aaron is a senior lecturer in film and American studies at the University of Birmingham. She is author of *Spectatorship: The Power of Looking On* (2007) and editor of *New Queer Cinema: A Critical Reader* (2004) and *The Body's Perilous Pleasures: Dangerous Desires and Contemporary Culture* (1999). She has published widely on contemporary film culture, queer cinema and theory, and Jewishness and gender, and is currently completing a book entitled *Death and the Moving Image: Ideology, Iconography and I.*

Barnaby Adams is a writer, artist, and cultural theorist. He is particularly interested in the areas of sound and voice. He is also a full-time father and lives in North London.

Oreet Ashery is a London-based visual artist, working in performance, digital media, and objects. Her work tends to be complex and relational but, at the same time, humorous and accessible to a wide variety of audiences and communities. She has an ongoing interest in the intersections among Jewishness, race, and gender and the Arab and Muslim worlds. Frequently, Ashery will produce work as a male character. Her characters include a rabbit, a black man, a Norwegian postman, a fat farmer, and an Arab man, among others. Marcus Fisher, an orthodox Jewish man, is Ashery's most consistent character and alter ego. Ashery's work has been shown extensively in the United Kingdon and internationally in art spaces, cinemas, and site-specific locations. Most recently it has been shown in Brooklyn Museum (New York), Pompidou Centre (Paris), Tate Modern (London), Institute of Contemporary Arts (London), OK Centre for Contemporary Art (Linz), Bodhi Gallery (New York City), Arnolfini (Bristol), Whitstable Biennale (United Kingdom), Kapelica Gallery (Ljubljana), Kontejair (Zagreb), Herzliya Museum (Israel), EDS Gallery (Mexico City), ZKM (Germany). Ashery's work has been reviewed in numerous prominent books and art publications in many languages.

Yosaif August organized the first Jewish Men's Retreat and has been involved with every retreat since that time, mentoring and supporting each year's retreat leadership. As a retreat participant he feels especially blessed to have personally experienced the rich development of this work that each year's leadership has brought to this work. He has taught men's classes and workshops at Aleph kallot and at Elat Chayyim. He co-wrote an article with Lawrence Bush entitled "Brotherkeeping: Jewish Scripture and the Reconstruction of Masculinity" that was published in the *Fifty Eighth Century: A Jewish Renewal Sourcebook* (Aronson, 1996), a tribute to Rabbi Zalman Schacter-Shalomi. For several years Yosaif's work has focused on improving the healthcare experiences of patients and families, especially improving bedside environments in hospitals and nursing homes. He invented and markets Bedscapes®, a system that helps patients to relax while in the hospital. He co-authored *Help Me to Heal* (Hay House 2003) with Dr. Bernie Siegel, and is now providing life coaching to people around the U.S. who are dealing with medical and health issues. He is married to Rabbi Tsurah August, a hospice rabbi and chaplain. He loves music, especially singable Jewish music and has written several niggunim and chants that are used in Shabbat services. He has a son and daughter and two gorgeous grandchildren.

Doug Barden has spent over 25 years as a Jewish professional. Earning an MA degree in social anthropology (SUNY, Binghamton) and subsequently an MBA in organization development (New York University), he began his professional career as the first executive director of District II (New York State) for Women's American ORT (WAORT). Five years later he was promoted to become WAORT's first national organization department director. In 1994 he became executive director for the National Federation of Temple Brotherhoods (NFTB), now known as the Men of Reform Judaism (MRJ), the men's arm of the Reform Movement. In 2005 Barden authored *Wrestling with Jacob and Esau: Fighting the Flight of Men* and in 2007 served as consulting editor for *The Gender Gap: Beginning the Conversation About Men's Involvement in Synagogue Life*, and *The Still Small Voice,* both URJ Press publications. In 2008 Barden authored *Making Time for Sacred Fellowship: A Men's Workbook and Facilitator's Guide* (MRJ Press).

Israel Bartal is Avraham Haramn Chairperson in Jewish History and Dean of the Faculty of Humanities at The Hebrew University of Jerusalem. He is the Chairperson of the Historical Society of Israel. Among his books are *Poles and Jews: A Failed Brotherhood* (with Magdalena Opalski) and *The Jews of Eastern Europe, 1772–1881.*

Harry Brod is a child of Holocaust survivors and a child of the 1960s. Both heritages shape his commitments to justice, much of which he has expressed in over 20 years of teaching, writing, and activism in the academic study of masculinities (where he is recognized as one of the founding figures of the field) and the profeminist men's movement (for which he has been a leading spokesperson). His most recent book is *White Men Challenging Racism: 35 Personal Stories,* coauthored with Cooper Thompson and Emmett Schaefer, and his next will be *Superman is Jewish?: How Comic Book Superheroes Came to Serve Truth, Justice and the Jewish-American Way.* He is the editor of *The Making of Masculinities: The New Men's Studies* and *A Mensch Among Men: Explorations in Jewish Masculinity,* coeditor (with Michael Kaufman) of *Theorizing Masculinities* and *The Legacy of the Holocaust: Children and the Holocaust,* and author of *Hegel's Philosophy of Politics: Idealism, Identity and Modernity.* He has served as director of the Iowa Regent Universities Men's Gender Violence Prevention Institute and on the Humanities Iowa Board of Directors, Iowa Governor's Task Force for Responsible Fatherhood, and American Philosophical Association's Committee on Public Philosophy. He received the Harry Cannon Award for Exemplary and Sustained Contributions to the Field of Men's Studies from the American College Personnel Association's Standing Committee for Men, was the first scholar-in-residence for the Men's Center for Leadership and Service at Saint John's University in Minnesota, and held a fellowship in law and philosophy at Harvard Law School. A DVD of his lecture "Asking For It: The Ethics and Erotics of Sexual Consent" is distributed by Media Education Foundation. He is Professor of Philosophy and Humanities at the University of Northern Iowa and the father of two children.

Lawrence Bush edits *Jewish Currents* magazine. He is the author, most recently, of *Waiting for God: The Spiritual Explorations of a Reluctant Atheist* (Ben Yehuda Press). His essays and fiction have appeared in the *New York Times, Village Voice, MAD* magazine, *Tikkun, Reform Judaism*, and other publications. Bush was the founding editor of *Reconstructionism Today*. His other books include *American Torah Toons: 54 Illustrated Commentaries*; *Jews, Money and Social Responsibility* (with Jeffrey Dekro); *BESSIE: A Novel of Love and Revolution*, and two fictions for adolescents, *Rooftop Secrets* and *Emma Ansky-Levine and Her Mitzvah Machine*.

Michael Gluzman is Chair of the Department of Literature at Tel Aviv University. His first book, *The Politics of Canonicity: Lines of Resistance in Modernist Hebrew Poetry* was published by Stanford UP (2003). His second book, *Ha-guf ha-tziyoni* (The Zionist Body), was published in Hebrew in 2007. He has written widely on Jewish/Israeli masculinity from feminist and queer perspectives.

Jackson Katz, PhD, is an educator, author, and filmmaker who is a pioneer in the field of gender violence prevention education with men and boys, particularly in the sports culture and the military. He is cofounder of the Mentors in Violence Prevention (MVP) program, the most widely utilized sexual and domestic violence prevention initiative in college and professional athletics. He is the creator of popular educational films, including *Tough Guise: Violence, Media and the Crisis in Masculinity*. He is the author of *The Macho Paradox: Why Some Men Hurt Women and How All Men Can Help*. He lectures in the United States and around the world on violence, media, and masculinities.

Rabbi Mordechai Liebling is the Director of the Social Justice Organizing Program at the Reconstructionist Rabbinical College. Previously he served as the executive vice-president of Jewish Funds for Justice. He is a graduate of the Reconstructionist Rabbinical College, has an MA from Brandeis University and a BA from Cornell University. Liebling served as the executive director of the Jewish Reconstructionist Federation for 12 years and was a member of the Conference of Presidents of Major Jewish Organizations for that period. He serves on the boards of the Faith and Politics Institute, Interfaith Center for Corporate Responsibility, Rabbis for Human Rights-North America, and The Shalom Center. He has taught at numerous institutes, conferences, and synagogues and has led workshops about Jewish male identity. He is a coauthor of the *Children of Abraham Haggadah* and has had articles published in many Jewish publications. Liebling is married to Lynne Iser, and they have five children.

Rabbi Kerry M. Olitzky holds a doctorate in Jewish education. He is Executive Director of the Jewish Outreach Institute, the only national independent organization dedicated to bringing Judaism to interfaith families and the unaffiliated. He was recently named as one of the 50 Leading Rabbis in North America by *Newsweek*. Formerly, he served as vice president of the Wexner Heritage Foundation, the premier adult Jewish learning and Jewish leadership program in North America. Previously, he was national dean of adult Jewish learning and living of Hebrew Union College-Jewish Institute of Religion, where he served on the faculty and administration for 15 years following his tenure at Congregation Beth Israel in West Hartford, Connecticut. A leader in the development of innovative Jewish education, particularly for adults, he has shaped training programs for clergy of all faiths, especially in the area of pastoral care and counseling in the Jewish community. He has done pioneering work in the areas of Jewish Twelve Step spirituality as well as Jewish gerontology. He is also the author of numerous books and articles that bring the Jewish wisdom tradition into everyday life, including *From Your Father's House ... Reflections for Modern Jewish Men* (Jewish Publication Society).

Sylvia Paskin is a writer, lecturer, and editor. She lectures on film and literature at several colleges, including the London Jewish Cultural Centre and the National Portrait Gallery. She has coedited various poetry anthologies: *Angels of Fire* (Chatto & Windus) *Dancing the Tightrope* (The Women's Press), and *The Dybbuk of Delight: Jewish Women's Poetry* (Five Leaves). She has edited a reader on Yiddish film: *When Joseph Met Molly* (Five Leaves). She writes for the *Jewish Quarterly* and *The Guardian*. Currently she is reading plays for the Young Writers' Programme at the Royal Court Theatre and is on the board of the Operating Theatre Company as literary consultant. Her first short film *L'Esprit de l'Escalier* has just been completed and she is working on a second short film as well as a longer one with her son Leo.

Simcha Paull Raphael, PhD, was ordained by Rabbi Zalman Schachter-Shalomi as a rabbinic pastor and studied transpersonal psychology at the California Institute of Integral Studies in San Francisco. He teaches in the Jewish Studies program of Temple University, serves as a spiritual director at Reconstructionist Rabbinical College, and works as a psychotherapist, specializing in bereavement. Author of *Jewish Views of the Afterlife*, Raphael has written and taught extensively on the spirituality of Jewish death traditions. He is completing a program of rabbinical ordination at the Academy for Jewish Religion. His web site is http://www.simcharaphael.com.

Sharon M. Ravitch, Ed.M., Ph.D. is a Senior Lecturer and Director of Executive Leadership Development at the University of Pennsylvania's Graduate School of Education where she is Founding Co-Director of the Penn Leadership Network across the Americas. Ravitch teaches master's and doctoral-level courses at the Graduate School of Education and at the Aresty Institute of Executive Education at The Wharton School of Business. Ravitch has published three books: *Metodología de la inves-*

tigación cualitativa (Ed.: Qualitative Research Methods: A Reader, Centro Integral de la Familia, 2009), *School Counseling Principles: Diversity and Multiculturalism* (American School Counselor Association Press, 2006) and, with Michael Nakkula, *Matters of Interpretation: Reciprocal Transformation in Therapeutic and Developmental Relationships with Youth* (Jossey-Bass, 1998). She is currently working on several books: *Reason and Rigor: The Role of Conceptual Frameworks in Research* and *Intercultural Understanding in an Age of Standards: An Interpretive Framework for Education and Professional Development*. Ravitch publishes, speaks and consults internationally in the areas of evidence-based practice, qualitative research, ethnography, practitioner and action research, applied research in developing countries, institutional ethnography and issues of gender, race, culture and equity in organizations.

Michael C. Reichert, PhD, presently serves as Executive Director of the Center for the Study of Boys' and Girls' Lives. He cofounded, and for 10 years directed, a youth violence prevention program in communities around Philadelphia. He also serves as a consulting psychologist associated with a number of schools and has maintained a clinical practice for the past 25 years. Current research interests include the impact of gender curricula on children's lives and in the life of schools, trajectories toward violence, and youth development programming. Recent publications include "The Primacy of Relationship in Teaching Boys" (with R. Hawley, forthcoming in *Thymos: Journal of Boyhood Studies*; "Defying Normative Male Identity: The Transgressive Possibilities of Jewish Boyhood" (with S.M. Hawley, in *Youth and Society*, 2009); and "Don't Love No Fight: Healing and Identity Among Urban Youth" (with colleagues, in *Urban Review*, 2006). A new book, *Reaching Boys, Teaching Boys*, is scheduled for publication by Jossey-Bass/Wiley in Summer, 2010.

Warren Rosenberg is a professor of English at Wabash College in Crawfordsville, Indiana. He has published articles on Jewish writers and filmmakers, such as David Mamet, Tony Kushner, and Barry Levinson. His book *Legacy of Rage: Jewish Masculinity, Violence, and Culture* was published in 2001 (University of Massachusetts Press).

Rabbi Rami Shapiro is an adjunct professor of religion at Middle Tennessee State University and director of One River, a not-for-profit foundation devoted to the art of contemplative conversation (www.one-river.com). An award-winning author, lecturer, and columnist, Shapiro's most recent books are *The Sacred Art of Lovingkindness* and *The Divine Feminine* (2006, Woodstock Paths Publishing).

Eric Silverman is a cultural anthropologist in the American Studies and Human Development departments at Wheelock College, who is also affiliated with the Women's Studies Research Center at Brandeis University. Silverman divides his research and writing between a community in Papua New Guinea and American Jews. He is completing a book for Berg Press on the history of Jewish clothing, focusing on gender, ethnicity, and assimilation, and starting a project on contemporary American Jewish fatherhood. His book *From Abraham to America: A History of Jewish Circumcision* was published in 2006 (Rowman & Littlefield). For more information, see Eric's website at www.eksilverman.com

Allen Spivack has been active in men's work for over 30 years. He has attended fourteen of the Jewish Men's Retreats (JMRs) and organized three of them. He has participated in a number of men's groups during his adult life and facilitated such a group for five years at a Boston-based synagogue. He has pursued a variety of careers, including professional fundraiser, stay-at-home father, building contractor, and clinical social worker (focusing on work with men), and he currently works on housing and client services issues for the Massachusetts Department of Public Health, Office of HIV/AIDS. He has two adult sons, Avi and Lev, and is married to Sherry Grossman. Over the years, Spivack has recruited scores of men from the Boston area and beyond to attend the JMR. Most are still his friends.

Rabbi Ed Stafman was ordained in the ALEPH Rabbinic program, part of the trans-denominational Jewish renewal movement. He serves as rabbi to Congregation Beth Shalom, in Bozeman, Montana. Prior to Rabbinic ordination, he spent 27 years as a trial lawyer in Tallahassee, Florida, specializing in defending death penalty cases. In addition to a law degree and rabbinic ordination, he holds a master's degree in religion and has completed the course work for a PhD in religion of western antiquity from Florida State University.

Jacob Staub, PhD, graduated as a rabbi from the Reconstructionist Rabbinical College (RRC). He has served on the RRC faculty since 1983, where he is chair of the Department of Medieval Jewish Civilization and professor of Jewish philosophy and spirituality. He served as RRC's academic dean and vice president for academic affairs from 1989 to 2004. Instrumental in developing RRC's groundbreaking Program in Spiritual Direction, he has taught Jewish spiritual direction across North America, including at the Institute for Jewish Spirituality. He completed certification in Mindfulness Leadership Training with Sylvia Boorstein and teaches meditation and contemplative practice at RRC. Staub's poetry has appeared in *Zeek*, *Kerem*, *Ashe*, *Jewish Currents*, and *White Crane*, among others. He is the author of *The Creation of the World According to Gersonides* (1982) and of numerous articles and essays. He is coeditor with Jeffrey L. Schein of *Creative Jewish Education: A Reconstructionist Perspective* (1985) and coauthor with Rebecca T. Alpert of *Exploring Judaism: A Reconstructionist Approach* (2000).

Billy Yalowitz, director, playwright and community-based artist, is an Associate Professor at Temple University's Tyler School of Art, where he founded and co-directs the Arts in Community Program. He has directed critically acclaimed community-based performance productions in several Philadelphia neighborhoods, dealing with issues including urban dispossession (profiled in *White Men Challenging Racism*, Duke University Press, 2003), educational civil rights, Black-Jewish Relations, and immigration. His *Six Actors in Search of a Plot*, co-written with Palestinian playwright Mohammad Zaher, was performed throughout Israel and off-Broadway in 2005-06. Yalowitz was named "Best Unclassifiable Theater Artist" by Philadelphia's City Paper in 1997 and Best Choreographer by the Philadelphia Inquirer in 1999. His work has been featured in the New York Times, Jerusalem Post, San Francisco Chronicle and Philadelphia Inquirer, on Public Radio, and profiled in *Body and Bible* (Trinity, 1992) and *Readings for Diversity and Social Justice* (Routledge, 2010). He holds an MFA in Dance and a doctorate in Intercultural Community Performance from Temple University. He has been working with men's groups since 1977, and has led workshops for Jewish men in Israel, California, Pennsylvania and New York.

Raz Yosef is a senior lecturer in the film and television department at Tel Aviv University, Israel. He is the author of *Beyond Flesh: Queer Masculinities and Nationalism in Israeli Cinema* (2004). His work on gender, sexuality and ethnicity in Israeli visual culture has appeared in *GLQ*, *Third Text*, *Framework* and *Camera Obscura*. He is currently completing a new book entitled *The Politics of Loss and Trauma in Contemporary Israeli Cinema*.

Rabbi Shawn Israel Zevit (www.rabbizevit.com) is a graduate of the Reconstructionist Rabbinical College, with *smichah* (ordination) from Rabbi Zalman Schachter-Shalomi. He has many years of experience in spiritual leadership and *hashpa'ah* (spiritual direction), human relations training, educational arts, teaching, and performing. He is a founding member of Shabbat Unplugged, codirector of the Davennen Leader's Training Institute, and core faculty for the ALEPH Hashpa'ah program on spiritual direction. He has served as a rabbi and consultant to numerous faith-based, nonprofit, and corporate organizations, and he performs traditional and new music from his many liturgical and musical recordings (http://www.cdbaby.com/Artist/ShawnZevit). He has been involved with gender and men's issues in Toronto and later as part of the annual Jewish Men's Retreat at Elat Chayyim/Isabella Freedman, The Federation of Temple Brotherhoods, Men's Clubs of Conservative Judaism, Kolot: The Center for Gender Studies at RRC, and Moving Traditions. Since 1998 he has served as a congregational consultant and the director of outreach & tikkun olam for the Jewish Reconstructionist Federation; he has written and developed resources in the areas of community building, leadership, prayer, interactive midrash, contemporary views of God, money and Jewish values, *tikkun olam* (social justice), and Jewish men's issues. He has published numerous articles, written the guide to the documentary *Praying with Lior*, and published a book, *Offerings of the Heart: Jewish Values-Based Approaches to Money in Community*, published by the Alban Institute in 2005.

Selected Listing of Web Resources for Jewish Men

Books for Jewish Men

Search for "Jewish" in this Men's Bibliography
http://mensbiblio.xyonline.net

Jewish Men's Retreat (JMR) (Elat Chayyim/CIF)
http://www.isabellafreedman.org/jmr

Jewish Reconstructionist Federation
http://www.jrf.org

Audio program on *Jewish Men Today*, Rabbi Shawn Zevit host, Harry Brod guest
http://jrf.org/showres&rid=131

Men in Transition: One Synagogue's Response by Rabbi George Dreisen
http://jrf.org/files/RT%2015.1.pdf

Kolot: Center for Jewish Women's and Gender Studies
http://www.kolot.org

Men of Reform Judaism

Men of Reform Judaism http://nftb.org/resources
Achim Magazine http://nftb.org/achim.shtml
URJ Press http://www.urjbooksandmusic.com/home.php

Men's Clubs of USCJ (Conservative)
http://www.fjmc.org

Moving Traditions: Campaign for Jewish Boys
http://www.movingtraditions.org

Rabbi Shawn Zevit (Jewish men's articles)
http://www.rabbizevit.com

Raising Jewish Boys, Paul Kivel
http://www.paulkivel.com/articles/raisingjewishboys.pdf

INDEX

LaVergne, TN USA
25 September 2010
198452LV00005B/3/P